Learning Together Online
Research on Asynchronous
Learning Networks

Edited by

Starr Roxanne Hiltz
and
Ricki Goldman

2005

LAWRENCE ERLBAUM ASSOCIATES, PUBLISHERS
Mahwah, New Jersey   London

Lawrence Erlbaum Associates, Inc., Publishers
10 Industrial Avenue
Mahwah, New Jersey 07430

Library of Congress Cataloging-in-Publication Data

Learning together online : research on asynchronous learning /
edited by Starr Roxanne
  p. cm.
Includes bibliographical references and index.
ISBN 0-8058-4866-5 (cloth : alk. paper)
ISBN 0-8058-5255-7 (pbk. : alk. Paper)
  1. Computer-assisted instruction. 2. Internet in education. 3. Distance education—Computer-assisted instruction. I. Hiltz, Starr Roxanne. II. Goldman, Ricki.

LB1028.5.L3885 2004
371.33'4—dc22   2004043634
                                                    CIP

Books published by Lawrence Erlbaum Associates are printed on acid-free paper, and their bindings are chosen for strength and durability.

Printed in the United States of America
10   9   8   7   6   5   4   3   2   1

Contents

Preface

Starr Roxanne Hiltz and Ricki Goldman

> *The public debate over the merits of Internet-based distance learning too of-*
> *ten consists of high-pitched vitriol and hyperbole. Proponents ooze with blind*
> *adoration, declaring that online learning can resolve all the problems con-*
> *fronting traditional education. Opponents insist that courses taught on the net*
> *are incapable of living up to the standards of the traditional bricks and mortar*
> *classroom.*
>
> *—The Institute for Higher Education Policy, 2000*

This book is about the past and future of research on the effectiveness of learning networks, a type of e-learning, online learning, Web-based learning, computer-supported collaborative learning, or virtual classroom (to use a number of common terms) in which students and teachers learn together online. The formal term is *Asynchronous Learning Networks,* or ALN for short. An ALN course is one in which students and faculty can have online discussions and work together from their homes or offices or on an airplane, anytime, anywhere, via the Internet. Computer-mediated communication software stores and orders these communications. A much more complete definition and decomposition of the term *asynchronous learning network* is provided in chapter 1, but learning together online in a structured environment is the essence of the concept.

In this book, leading researchers use an integrated theoretical framework to organize what past research has shown and where future research is going. We call this integrated theoretical model the *Online Interaction Learning Theory* (see chap. 2). It models the variables and processes that are important in determining the relative effectiveness of communities of online learners, who are working to reach a deep level of understanding by interacting with each other and with the materials under investigation. Rather than being based on unsupported vitriol and hyperbole, this book is a synthesis of what research shows to date about what we know and what we need to know about the effectiveness of online courses that use the learning networks approach.

The emphasis of this book is on text-based asynchronous (anytime, anyplace; e.g., e-mail and web pages) use of networks to support student-to-student as well as teacher-to-student communication and collaborative learning (which simply means students working together in groups of two or more). However, the scope of this book and of the studies reviewed also includes courses that use synchronous (same-time) media via the Internet—such as text or audio chat, or video conferencing—or that compare face-to-face, synchronous, and asynchronous learning processes. These courses might occur totally online, or be blended combinations of face-to-face meetings and online work.

We know that there are thousands of online courses and millions of faculty and students engaged in courses via asynchronous learning networks. For instance, according to Massachusetts-based International Data Corp., about 15% of all postsecondary students—or 2.2 million people—were enrolled in online courses in the academic year 2002 in the United States alone, compared with 5% in 1998. (http://www.galtglobalreview.com/education/virtual_classrooms.html). Another estimate based on a survey of chief academic officers at U.S. institutions of higher learning (Allen & Seaman, 2003) put the total number of students in completely on-line courses at 1.6 million in the fall 2002 semester projected to be at 1.9 million for fall 2003, with over one third of these students taking all of their courses online. Moreover, 81% of all U.S. institutions of higher learning offer at least one fully or partially online course, and 34% offer complete online degrees.

Institutions that offer online courses project continued growth in the higher education sector. For example, more than 50 U.S. online learning program directors who belong to a (foundation-supported, not-for-profit) consortium of colleges and universities that offer fully online university degree programs responded to a survey in October 2002 that showed the projections in the accompanying table (see http://www.aln.org/publications/view/v2n3/lms3.htm).

We can see from these projections that online courses are not a passing fad; not only are totally online courses projected to continue growing at a fast pace, but

Student Enrollment

Percent of students who:	Current	In 3 Years
Are enrolled in a distance education **course**?	20.2%	36.6%
Are enrolled in a **program** that is delivered entirely at a distance?	11.7%	22.1%
Are enrolled in a **"blended"** course?	7.6%	21.1%

Sloan-C Program Directors, 2002

many courses that are now offered as entirely face-to-face on-campus courses are projected to become blended courses that combine on-campus meetings with continued online interaction among the members of the class.

Anecdotal articles and books based on limited experiences with a few courses or a single program at a single school abound, but what does the empirical evidence show? This book summarizes this empirical research to date and also highlights the areas in which more future research is particularly needed.

WHO THIS BOOK IS FOR

This is both a textbook for graduate students and a professional reference book for scholars who need to know the state of the art of research in the area of online learning. This includes faculty teaching online, researchers conducting studies, administrators establishing new online programs, and graduate students taking courses about learning technologies. Particularly for use as a text, we have included questions for discussion and research at the end of each chapter.

WHY AND HOW THIS BOOK EVOLVED: ANSWERING A NEED FOR UNDERSTANDING ALNS

The WebCenter Project

Since the early 1990s, the field of asynchronous learning networks has been growing as a research community, with meetings, a journal, and informal networking among its practitioners. At the end of a decade of extraordinary growth, it is time to take stock and assess what we know and what we still need to know about the effectiveness of ALNs, and about appropriate research methods for studying it.

Almost daily, there are articles in the press about online courses that approach the subject from either a negative or positive angle. Most of these articles cite a few faculty members or students who have been interviewed, or cite a single study of a single course, with unknown quality of research methods. Many of them do not distinguish asynchronous learning networks, which emphasize extensive student–student and teacher–student interaction, from distance modes that simply post materials on the Web and use individual e-mail assignments, without any collaborative learning activities or formation of a class of interacting students.

Claims and counterclaims are likely to persist unless a comprehensive and authoritative knowledge base of information about evaluation research studies of ALN is created and made available to the public. Meanwhile, in colleges and universities and corporations all over the United States and the world, new online courses and programs are being designed and introduced. Faculty need to be able to learn what pedagogical techniques work best in this environment. Those assuming the role of researchers—either because it is necessary to evaluate the online programs in connection with accreditation activities, or because they are interested in pursuing research on this relatively new phenomenon—need to know what theories, methods, and previous findings are available to help them in designing their research.

There has previously been no place where faculty, researchers, potential students, or the press could go to find out what information exists about the following:

- What theoretical foundations are there for the field of ALN? What theories are most appropriate for framing research studies in this area?
- What empirical studies have been conducted about ALN? What were the methods used, variables studied, and findings discerned?
- What is the current overall picture of these research findings, in terms of comparisons of the effectiveness of ALN with other modes of delivery of college-level courses? What do we know about relatively effective and ineffective ways of teaching and learning asynchronously?
- What are the strengths and weaknesses of various research methods for studying ALN, and what methods are recommended by experts in the field as being especially appropriate for understanding this form of educational medium?
- What are the important but unresolved research issues and new methods that we most need to be aware of in designing research in the next decade?

This book, and the Learning Networks Effectiveness Research Project of which it is a part, aim to make this kind of information available. The goal of this research project, sponsored by the Alfred P. Sloan foundation and begun in January 2001, is to increase the quality, quantity, and dissemination of results of research on the effectiveness of ALNs. The project includes a WebCenter for Learning Networks Research (currently hosted at www.ALNResearch.org). The web site includes a series of online knowledge bases that are regularly updated. Readers of this book are invited to join the WebCenter virtual community and to contribute to these knowledge bases, as well as to use the information already there. In addition, the project includes a number of workshops for ALN researchers, one of which led to this book.

Workshop

In spring 2002, leading researchers on ALN were invited to take part in a 2-day workshop at NJIT (New Jersey Institute of Technology) to plan this book. Each of the participants has taught using ALN and thus has direct experience of the issues involved, and has published research on how computer-mediated communication, in the broadest sense, affects education. The first day of the workshop was primarily devoted to laying out the top research issues; reaching agreement on them and rank ordering them, through discussion and voting; and then translating this ranked list into an outline for the book. On the second day, subgroups of authors for each proposed chapter worked on the outline of the chapter contents, and then presented this to the entire workshop for discussion. These invited researchers included Maryam Alavi, Ben Arbaugh, Raquel Benbunan-Fich, John Bourne, Nancy Coppola, Martha Crosby, Donna Dufner, Charles Dziuban, Ricki Goldman, Linda Harasim, Starr Roxanne Hiltz, Peter Shea, Karen Swan, and Murray Turoff. In addition, several NJIT graduate students who are doing dissertation research related to this topic helped to facilitate the process, participated in the issue formation stage, and assisted with this book: Hyo Joo Han, Eunhee Kim, David Spencer, and Yi Zhang.

AN OVERVIEW OF THE SECTIONS

Part I of the book presents the foundations of research on learning networks: the history of ALN, an integrated theoretical framework, appropriate research methods, and the results of research so far on the relative effectiveness of traditional face-to-face versus ALN courses. Part II surveys what we know and what we need to know about each of the major factors delineated in the framework that strongly influence the effectiveness of online courses.

Part I: Foundations of Research on Learning Networks

Chapter 1: What Are Asynchronous Learning Networks?

In this introductory chapter, Starr Roxanne Hiltz and Ricki Goldman present definitions and illustrations and a brief history of what is meant by *learning networks* in general and *asynchronous learning networks* in particular. Core themes and issues are previewed with a discussion of the historical precedents and theories that lead to the use of technologies for online learning and teaching.

Chapter 2: The Online Interaction Learning Model: An Integrated Theoretical Framework for Learning Networks

Theory is central to good research, software design, and teaching practice. In this chapter, Raquel Benbunan-Fich, Starr Roxanne Hiltz, and Linda Harasim present a dynamic integrative theory of key factors to the effectiveness of learning networks is presented. The online interaction learning model can help to give direction and coherence to research and to support the generation of cumulative, generalizable knowledge that can inform future practice.

Chapter 3: Effectiveness for Students: Comparisons of "In-Seat" and ALN Courses

If students do not learn as effectively in an online course as in traditional "in-seat" courses, then other outcomes, such as student or faculty satisfaction, really do not matter very much. What does the empirical evidence tell us? Are online courses using learning networks effective? In what ways?

In chapter 3, Jerry Fjermestad, Starr Roxanne Hiltz, and Yi Zhang examine over 20 empirical studies published in peer-refereed journals or conference proceedings that both measure learning effectiveness for students, and compare ALN to traditional face-to-face courses on the same campus. The evidence is overwhelming that, at the university level, ALN tends to be as effective or more effective than traditional modes of course delivery.

Chapter 4: Improving Quantitative Research on ALN Effectiveness

In this chapter, J. B. Arbaugh and Starr Roxanne Hiltz address two main themes concerning quantitative studies of ALNs: issues related to measuring learning, and suggestions for improving the generalizability of findings in ALN studies. Historically, this stream of research has been highly reliant on single-course studies. Arbaugh and Hiltz identify several concerns with the methodology of previous quantitative ALN research and provide recommendations for addressing them in future studies.

Chapter 5: Qualitative and Quisitive Research Methods for Describing Online Learning

Ricki Goldman, Martha Crosby, Karen Swan, and Peter J. Shea move beyond the qualitative or quantitative research debate to develop the foundations of qualitative inquiry for understanding learning networks. Learning networks are social worlds that people create, and qualitative research allows us to tap into these worlds to hear, see, or feel what people actually do. This chapter provides a unique perspective for ALN research that expands on traditional paradigms and perspectives. It closely examines the role of ALN researchers, diverse forms of ALN methodologies, technologies for mixed-media data analysis, and what these authors believe to be the next frontier in ALN research methods, *quisitive research.*

Part II: Learning Networks: What We Know and What We Need to Know

A series of chapters covers the top ALN research areas and issues that we identified. Each of these chapters follows a common outline:

- What are the major issues? Why are these important? What are the major concepts, definitions, and theoretical frameworks in this area?
- What do we know based on current research results?
- Three to five specific research issues, and how they might best be studied in the future, are presented.
- What do we need to know?

Chapter 6: Contextual Factors That Influence ALN Effectiveness

As the theoretical framework presented in chapter 2 suggests, there are several factors related to the specific context in which a course occurs that influence ALN effectiveness, including characteristics of (a) the individual instructor and course, (b) the technology used, and (c) the organization through which the course is offered. In this chapter, J. B. Arbaugh and Raquel Benbunan-Fich review existing literature on contextual factors, identify significant characteristics that emerge from the findings, suggest some other potential factors, and describe ways in which these characteristics might be more thoroughly studied in future research.

Chapter 7: The Student in the Online Classroom

The asynchronous nature of the online classroom has caused a change in learner roles from the traditional face-to-face environment. Through years of research, we now have an idea of the benefits and challenges to this Web environment from the student's perspective. In this chapter, Starr Roxanne Hiltz and Peter J. Shea address research issues related to the online student and environment, including: What is the profile of students who choose this mode of instruction, and the profile of those who thrive and succeed in it? What characteristics of students (e.g., gender, learning style, etc.) are related to successful learning in the ALN environment?

Chapter 8: Faculty Roles and Satisfaction in Asynchronous Learning Networks

If online learning is going to be successful, then faculty must play a central role. However, there is much to learn about how the role of faculty changes in this new learning environment. In this chapter, Charles D. Dziuban, Peter J. Shea, and J. B. Arbaugh discuss what (if anything) has changed, and what new roles and new responsibilities ALN has engendered, required, or afforded.

Chapter 9: Technology-Mediated Collaborative Learning: A Research Perspective

Some learning theories emphasize the social genesis of learning and view it as a process involving interpersonal interactions in a cooperative (vs. a competitive) context. Over the past 2 decades, one such theory—collaborative (group or team-based) learning—has gained in popularity. Several studies have demonstrated the positive motivational and learning outcomes of collaborative learning in higher education. Maryam Alavi and Donna Dufner's objective in this chapter is to motivate future research and dialogue on technology-mediated collaborative learning by suggesting some potentially productive research venues in this area.

Chapter 10: Media Mixes and Learning Networks

In the beginning, there was—the word! Text dominated the first decade of asynchronous learning networks. Recently, however, the hardware and software have become available to allow the integration of many other forms of computer-mediated communication into an ALN. Chief among these are synchronous chats, digital audio via freely available software such as Real Audio, posting of digital photos, synchronous Internet meetings via video or audio, and interaction via virtual reality types of mechanisms such as avatars. In this chapter, Ronald E. Rice, Starr Roxanne Hiltz, and David H. Spencer discuss what we know about the effects of media in general, and what we know in specific about adding these new media to online courses. Do they enhance the teaching and learning experiences, or are they more trouble than they are worth? How do digital multimedia change the nature of collaboration among students and faculty? What are the major research issues that need to be explored?

Chapter 11: The Development of Virtual Learning Communities

In this chapter, Karen Swan and Peter J. Shea look at the considerable body of research in face-to-face teaching and learning that suggests that teacher immediacy/intimacy behaviors can significantly affect student learning. Teacher immediacy behaviors are behaviors that lessen the psychological distance between teachers and students. In an asynchronous online environment, nonverbal and vocal cues are lost, and thus there has been some question as to whether such environments can foster the development of intimacy and/or the larger issue of whether or not they can support what we know are important social aspects of learning and the development of learning communities. Happily, there is a growing body of research attesting that asynchronous online environments can and do support the development of learning communities.

Many questions, however, remain; for example: How are learning communities developed online? How is social context developed in the absence of the physical presence that is an important part of traditional learning? What factors contribute to the development of presence in online courses? What are the affordances and constraints of asynchronous online media?

Chapter 12: Asynchronous Learning Networks: Looking Back and Looking Forward

In this chapter, Ricki Goldman and Starr Roxanne Hiltz explore the notion of educational transformation by first *looking back* to the theories of Ivan Illich, a leading educational philosopher who recommended the creation of learning webs for deschooling society. The chapter then connects these theories to what actually has happened in ALN over the past decade by exploring some of the important themes of teaching and learning in ALN environments. In the second part of the chapter, Goldman and Hiltz move their lenses toward what could happen in the future. By looking forward, they raise many controversial issues that appear in both the press and academic publications about the nature of educational change. Is online education disruptive, transformative, innovative, or evolutionary? What will ALN be like in another 25 years? What will universities be like then, and will they still exist in a form that resembles the traditional university of today? Stakeholders hold many conflicting points of view about what online education means to the future of education. The authors raise these issues to guide readers to critically address them before education becomes a commercialized production.

REFERENCES

Allen, I. E., & Seaman, J. (2003). *Seizing the opportunity: The quality and extent of online education in the united states, 2002 and 2003.* Needham, MA: SCOLE (Sloan Center for Online Education at Olin and Babson Colleges).

Institute for Higher Education Policy. (2000). Quality on the line: Benchmarks for success in Internet-based distance education. Retrieved September 11, 2003, from http://www. ihep.com

Acknowledgments

Major funding for this project was provided by a grant from the Alfred P. Sloan Foundation. Funding for the laboratory where much of the work was accomplished was contributed by the National Science Foundation (CISE—ITO 9732354 and NSF 9818309), the UPS Foundation, and the state of New Jersey. The opinions expressed in this book are solely those of the authors and do not necessarily reflect those of the sponsors.

A preliminary version of chapter 4 appeared in the following publication; portions are reused by permission of the publisher: Arbaugh, B., & Hiltz, S. R. (2003). Studies of the effectiveness of ALN: Improving quantitative research methods. In J. Bourne & J. C. Moore (Eds.), *Quality studies: Online education practice and direction* (Vol. 4, pp. 59–74). Needham, MA: SCOLE (Sloan Center for Online Education).

We would like to thank David Spencer and Zhengh Li for editorial assistance; and our reviewers, Richard E. Mayer and John R. Bourne, for many helpful suggestions for improving this book. The editorial and production team at Lawrence Erlbaum Associates (Naomi Silverman, Lori Hawyer, Marianna Vertullo), and copyeditor Gale Miller did a fantastic job.

About the Authors

Dr. Maryam Alavi is the Senior Associate Dean of Faculty and Research and the John M. and Lucy Cook's Chair in Information Strategy at the Goizueta Business School of Emory University. She also serves as the Director of Knowledge @Emory, a Web-based knowledge management system.

Maryam was awarded the distinguished Marvin Bower Faculty Fellowship at the Harvard Business School. She also was a recipient of the University of Maryland Distinguished Scholar-Teacher Award, and was twice awarded the University of Maryland Robert H. Smith School of Business' Krowe Award in Teaching Innovation. She was elected as the recipient of the prestigious AIS (Association of Information Systems) Fellows Award in 2000.

Maryam has authored numerous scholarly papers in the areas of decision support systems, collaboration support, and technology-mediated learning and knowledge management. Her research in the areas of technology-mediated learning has been supported by funds and hardware grants from the AT&T Foundation, AT&T Corporation, and Lucent Technologies. She was the recipient of the IBM Faculty Partnership Award in 2001. She has served on the editorial boards of several scholarly IS journals, including *MIS Quarterly (MISQ), Information Systems Research (ISR),* and *Journal of Management Information Systems (JMIS).* She is also a member of the editorial board of *Encyclopedia of Computer and Information Systems.*

Maryam has done innovative work in the area of computer-mediated collaborative learning and distance learning by applying knowledge and expertise gained from her research directly to classroom teaching. She has developed and implemented pedagogical approaches, which optimally utilize computer and communication technology in support of teaching/learning processes, and has developed unique ways to improve these processes. Her teaching innovations have been featured in *U.S. News and World Report.*

Dr. J. B. (Ben) Arbaugh (BBA, Marshall University; MBA, Wright State University; MS, PhD, Ohio State University) is Curwood Inc. Endowed Professor in the College of Business Administration at the University of Wisconsin–Oshkosh. His current research interests include the delivery of education via the Internet, international entrepreneurship, project management, and the intersection of spirituality and strategic management research. His recent publications include articles in the *Journal of Management Education,* the *Journal of High Technology Management Research, Management Learning, Frontiers of Entrepreneurship Research,* the *Blackwell Handbook of Entrepreneurship, Business Communication Quarterly,* the *Academy of Management's Best Papers Proceedings,* and *Academy of Management Learning and Education.* Ben's recent research on characteristics of effective ALNs has allowed him to win the Academy of Management's Best Paper in Management Education in 2001 and 2002, the Academy of Management's Best Paper in Management Learning in 2003, and the 2001 Fritz Roethlisberger Award for the best article in the *Journal of Management Education.*

Dr. Raquel Benbunan-Fich is an Assistant Professor of Information Systems at the Zicklin School of Business, Baruch College, City University of New York (CUNY). She received her PhD in Management Information Systems from Rutgers University—Graduate School of Management in 1997. She got her MBA (1989) from IESA, the leading Venezuelan business school, and her BS in Computer Engineering (1986) from Universidad Simón Bolívar in Caracas, Venezuela. Her research interests include asynchronous learning networks, computer-mediated communication systems, evaluation of Web-based systems and e-commerce. She has published articles on related topics in *Communications of the ACM, Group Decision and Negotiation, Information & Management, Journal of Applied Management and Entrepreneurship, Journal of Computer Information Systems,* and *Journal of Computer-Mediated Communication,* and has forthcoming articles in the *Case Research Journal* and *Decision Support Systems.*

Dr. Martha E. Crosby is a Professor and Associate Chair in the Department of Information and Computer Sciences at the University of Hawaii. She received her BS in Mathematics at Colorado State University, her MS in Information and Computer Sciences, and her PhD in Educational Psychology at the University of Hawaii. The underlying theme of her research is to understand how to make computers more usable for the individual. Knowledge about how users search, perceive, and understand information presented via a computer can be applied generally to improving human–computer interfaces and specifically to distance learning applications. (The University of Hawaii has been developing distance learning environments for over 30 years.)

Dr. Crosby performs research that has implications for such applications as building user models that are employed in adaptive–user interfaces and intelligent tutoring systems; constructing hypermedia environments, particularly in language learning; and evaluation of multimedia systems in cross-cultural environments. Specific topics that she emphasizes in her research are the areas of visual search, user models, individual differences, problem solving, and evaluation of computer interfaces. Current research efforts (supported by grants from NSF, the Office of Naval Research, and DARPA) involve designing controlled experiments to determine several potential indicators of cognitive load. The best combination of these indicators will be used to adapt information filtering to the user's current cognitive state. These studies can lead to the development of cognitive design criteria for more effective distance learning environments.

Dr. Donna Dufner is an Associate Professor in the Department of Information Systems in the College of Information Science and Technology at the University of Nebraska at Omaha (UNO). She received her PhD from Rutgers University in Management (Computer and Information Science) in 1995; an MS, in Computer and Information Science from The New Jersey Institute of Technology; and an MBA from the University of Chicago. Dr. Dufner has over 12 years of industry experience in telecommunications, and information systems design, development and implementation for major corporations such as AT&T, Chemical Bank Corp., ARDIS (a joint venture of IBM and Motorola), and Bell Atlantic Nynex. Her research interests are Web-enabled technologies, asynchronous group support systems, and asynchronous learning networks. Dr. Dufner's research has been published a variety of journals, including *The Journal of Group Decision and Negotiation, The Journal of Organizational Computing, Communications of AIS (CAIS),* and *Public Productivity and Management Review.* Dr. Dufner appears in a video gallery of prominent researchers in the area of asynchronous learning networks funded by the Sloan Foundation, at www.ALNresearch.org. She is a senior referee for *IEEE Computer* and serves on the Editorial Board of *CAIS.* She is listed in *Who's Who in the World,* and in *Who's Who in America.* Before joining UNO in 2000, for 3 years Dr. Dufner taught at the University of Illinois, where she was named a University Scholar in 1998, the highest honor awarded by that University.

Dr. Charles Dziuban is Director of the Research Initiative for Teaching Effectiveness at the University of Central Florida (UCF), where he has been a faculty member since 1972, teaching research design and statistics. He received his PhD from the University of Wisconsin. Since 1998, he has directed the impact evaluation of UCF's distributed learning initiative, examining student and faculty outcomes as well as gauging the impact of online courses on the university. Chuck has published in numerous journals, including: *Multivariate Behavioral Research, the Psychological Bulletin, Educational and Psychological Measurement,* the *American Education Research Journal,* and *Phi Delta Kappan.* His methods for determining psychometric adequacy are featured in both the SPSS and the SAS packages. He has received funding from several government and industrial agencies, including the Ford Foundation and the Centers for Disease Control. In 2000, Chuck was named UCF's first-ever Pegasus Professor for the professor who exemplified extraordinary research, teaching, and service to the university.

Dr. Jerry Fjermestad is an Associate Professor in the School of Management at the New Jersey Institute of Technology (NJIT). He received his BA in chemistry from Pacific Lutheran University, an MS in operations research from Polytechnic University, an MBA in operations management from Iona College, and an MBA and PhD in management information systems from Rutgers University. Jerry has taught ALN courses on management information systems, decision support systems, systems analysis and design, and electronic commerce. His current research interests are in collaborative technology, decision support systems, data warehousing, electronic commerce, global information systems, customer relationship management, and enterprise information systems. Jerry has published in the *Journal of*

Management Information Systems, Group Decision and Negotiation, the *Journal of Organizational Computing and Electronic Commerce, Information and Management, Decision Support Systems, Logistics and Information Management, International Journal of Electronic Commerce,* the *Journal of Computer-Mediated Communication, Technology Analysis & Strategic Management,* and the *Proceedings of Hawaii International Conference on System Sciences.*

Dr. Ricki Goldman is author and designer of *Points of Viewing Children's Thinking: A Digital Ethnographer's Journey* and the accompanying interactive website with video cases at http://www.pointsofviewing.com. An expert in learning theory, she is most renowned as the founder of the subfield of ethnography called digital video ethnography and her work in digital media and ethnographic methods has been awarded with grants from prestigious agencies and foundations. In 2001, she accepted a position as Professor of Information Systems at the New Jersey Institute of Technology to set up a laboratory dedicated to understanding the role of learning systems, new media, and human interaction. After completing her doctorate at MIT's Media Lab in 1990, Ricki established the Multimedia Ethnographic Research Laboratory (MERLin) in the Faculty of Education at the University of British Columbia, where she and her team of graduate researchers conducted longitudinal video-based research and designed media-rich video tools and cases for over a decade.

Ricki is the recipient of Canada's National Center of Excellence in Telelearning Technology Award for an online digital video analysis tool, WebConstellations (aka ORION), which she created to organize and analyze digital video data. She is also winner of an MIT Arts Council award. Additionally, her book has been positively reviewed in seven journals, and was nominated for the American Educational Research Association's Best Book Award. In addition to her publications in journals, chapters, and online productions, she has presented papers in over 100 conferences, keynote scholarly gatherings, professional meetings, and academic communities in leading universities.

Dr. Linda Harasim is currently a professor in the School of Communication at Simon Fraser University. From the mid-1990s until 2001, Dr. Harasim was the Network Leader and CEO of the former TeleLearning Network of Centres of Excellence (TeleLearning.NCE). Recognized internationally as a pioneer in designing, testing, delivering, and demonstrating the effectiveness of online education, she also founded the Global Educators' Network, leads the Virtual-U Research Project, involving the largest field trials of postsecondary education in the world. She is also the director and chair of Virtual Learning Environments Inc. (VLEI) and eLearningSolutionsInc.com (ELSI).

Active in the design, delivery and study of online postsecondary education since the early 1980s, Dr. Harasim addresses the educational impacts and implications of the Internet past, present, and future.

Dr. Starr Roxanne Hiltz is Distinguished Professor, Information Systems Department, College of Computing Sciences, New Jersey Institute of Technology. She received her AB from Vassar and her MA and PhD from Columbia. She has spent most of the last 20 years engaged in research on applications and social impacts of computer technology. Her research interests include educational applications of computer-mediated communications, human–computer interaction, and computer support for group decision making. In particular, with major funding from the Corporation for Public Broadcasting and the Alfred P. Sloan Foundation, she created and experimented with a Virtual Classroom® for delivery of college-level courses. This is a teaching and learning environment that is constructed not of bricks and boards but instead of software structures within a computer-mediated communication system.

Her publications include six previous books and over 150 articles and professional papers. *The Network Nation: Human Communication via Computer* (with Murray Turoff; 1978, Addison-Wesley; 1993 revised ed., MIT Press) is probably the best known. She is the recipient of the Electronic Frontier Foundation's "Pioneer" award in 1994 for "significant and influential contributions to computer-based communications and to the empowerment of individuals in using computers." In 2000, she was named one of "New Jersey's Women of the Millennium" by the Easter Seals Foundation for "creating solutions and changing lives, in the field of educational technology." Among the editorial boards on which she serves are JALN, JCMC, and ACM Transactions on Computer–Human Interaction.

Dr. Ronald E. Rice was formerly Professor [II (Distinguished)] and Chair of the Department of Communication, School of Communication, Information and Library Studies, Rutgers University. As of 2004, he is Arthur N. Rupe Endowed Chair, Department of Communication, University of California, Santa Barbara. Dr. Rice received his BA in Literature from Columbia University and his MA and PhD in Communication Research from Stanford University. He also has corporate experience in systems and communication analysis, banking operations, data processing management, publishing, statistical consulting, and high school teaching.

Ron has co-authored or co-edited *Public Communication Campaigns* (1st ed:1981; 2nd ed: 1989; 3rd ed: 2001; Sage), *The New Media: Communication, Research and Technology* (1984; Sage), *Managing Organizational Innovation* (1987; Columbia University Press), *Research Methods and the New Media* (1988; Free Press), *The Internet and Health Communication* (2001; Sage), *Accessing and Browsing Information and Communication* (2001; MIT Press), and *Social Consequences of Internet Use: Access, Involvement and Interaction* (2002; MIT Press). His publications have won awards such as best dissertation from the American Society for Information Science; half a dozen times as best paper from International Communication Association divisions; and twice as best paper from Academy of Management divisions. Dr. Rice has been elected divisional officer in both the ICA and the Academy of Management, and served for 3 years on the ICA Publications Board. He has served as Associate Editor for *Human Communication Research,* as well as for *MIS Quarterly.*

Dr. Peter J. Shea is the Interim Director of the SUNY Learning Network, the multiple-award-winning online education system for the 64 colleges of the State University of New York. Dr. Shea is also manager of the SUNY Teaching, Learning, and Technology Program and Project Director for SUNY's participation in the Multimedia Educational Resource for Learning and Online Teaching (MERLOT), an international collaboration for peer review of discipline specific online learning resources. Formerly Lead Instructional Designer for the SUNY Learning Network (SLN), he has assisted in the design of more than 100 online courses. Dr. Shea has also served as a visiting assisting professor in the Department of Educational Theory and Practice at the University at Albany, where he has taught at the graduate level both online and in the classroom. He is the author of many articles and several book chapters on the topic of online learning, and co-author of *The Successful Distance Learning Student* (2003; Wadsworth/Thomson Learning).

Dr. David Spencer completed his PhD in Management in the joint Rutgers University/NJIT program in 2002. He holds an MBA from Rutgers, an MS in Management from NJIT, and a BS in Electrical Engineering from Carnegie Mellon. The title of his PhD dissertation is *A Field Study of the Use of Synchronous Computer-Mediated Communication in Asynchronous Learning Networks*. Dr. Spencer has presented papers on the ALN topic at AMCIS, HICSS, and ALN conferences. His work on compiling a database of published ALN research studies was the start of the alnresearch.org Web site database. His 25-year industrial career involved designing computer communication terminals for Unisys Corporation.

Dr. Karen Swan (BA, Philosophy, University of Connecticut; MEd, Curriculum and Instruction, Keene State College; EdM, EdD, Columbia University, Instructional Technology) is Research Professor at the Research Center for Educational Technology (RCET), Kent State University. Dr. Swan's research has been focused mainly in the general area of media and learning. She has published and presented both nationally and internationally in the specific areas of programming and problem solving, computer-assisted instruction, hypermedia design, technology and literacy, and asynchronous online learning. Her current research focuses on the latter, and on student learning in technology-rich environments. She has also co-edited a book on social learning from broadcast television. Dr. Swan has authored several hypermedia programs, including *Set On Freedom: The American Civil Rights Experience* for Glencoe and *The Multimedia Sampler* for IBM, as well as three online courses. She served as project director for the technology strands of three rounds of federally funded research on literacy learning as part of the National Research Center for English Learning and Achievement, and directed large-scale, multiyear investigations of integrated learning systems for the city of New York as principal investigator for the Computer Pilot Program and the Integrated Learning Systems Project. Dr. Swan serves on the program committees for several international education and educational technology conferences. She is an Effective Practices Editor for the Sloan Consortium, and is the Special Issues Editor for the *Journal of Educational Computing Research*.

Dr. Yi Zhang was a PhD student in the Information Systems Department at the New Jersey Institute of Technology (NJIT). For her dissertation, she experimented with and studied the acceptance of special features to improve the usefulness of the WebCenter for Learning Networks Research (http://ALNResearch.org). She is co-author of several research papers and book chapters, including those in the Proceedings of the Hawaii International Conference on Systems Sciences and the Association for Information Systems. In fall 2004 she will join the faculty of California State University, Fullerton.

I

FOUNDATIONS OF RESEARCH ON LEARNING NETWORKS

1

What Are Asynchronous Learning Networks?

Starr Roxanne Hiltz and Ricki Goldman
New Jersey Institute of Technology

How the Term ALN Originated

http://www.aln.org
By Frank Mayadas (retrieved May 15, 2003)

The origin of the ALN idea stems from a meeting in 1994 of a small number of Sloan grantees at the Omni Hotel in New York. ... I recall making the point to the assemblage that we had to develop some terminology for what were doing, since we couldn't just keep referring to "it." Our basic ideas involved cohort-style on-line classes that were actually taught by a professor and encouraged peer-to-peer collaboration. We wanted to make a distinction with alternative models providing expensive multi-media or knowledge-based software with no cohort-base or professor, or the synchronous interactive TV model, or the broadcast TV/videotape model.

Roxanne Hiltz and Murray Turoff mentioned that they had used the term Learning Networks (in fact that is the title of one of their books). I had previously been using the term asynchronous learning networks, and suggested we all adopt the terminology Asynchronous Learning Networks. The group agreed and I subsequently posted an ALN definition on the http://www. sloan.org website. ... Asynchronous distinguished between synchronous models—e.g., interactive TV—while Learning Networks is intended to capture the idea that networks of people are essential to the process, and that collaboration is achieved through computer networks.

Survey Finds College Administrators Optimistic About the Future of Online Education

http://chronicle.com/prm/daily/2003/09/2003090401t.htm
By Brock Read (retrieved September 4, 2003)

Many college administrators say the quality of their institutions' online courses may soon eclipse that of their brick-and-mortar offerings, according to a report released yesterday.

The report collects the results of a survey conducted by Babson College and the Sloan Consortium, an organization that promotes standards for online learning. The college and the consortium e-mailed questionnaires to about 3,000 chief academic officers and university presidents last spring, and received responses from representatives of almost 1,000 public and private institutions.

One-third of the survey's respondents said that online education would be superior to in-class instruction at their institutions within three years; 57 percent said that Internet-based courses at their institutions were already at least equivalent to lecture-hall ones in educational quality.

The survey also identifies significant pockets of resistance to online education: One in three university officials said that Internet courses would not play a major role in the future of their institutions. Most of the skeptical responses came from private baccalaureate institutions ... where many faculty members distrust teaching outside the lecture hall.

INTRODUCTION

This chapter lays the foundation for the theories and research reviews that follow in this volume. It begins with a detailed definition of Asynchronous Learning Network (ALN) and its components, including examples and participants' accounts of what it means to teach and learn together online. A brief history shows the extremely fast growth rate in online courses and students, not only in the United States but around the world. Mini-case studies and scenarios illustrate some of the human stories that lie behind this growth. The end of the chapter introduces some of the controversies surrounding this new form of learning, and the issue of ALNs as a disruptive or transformative force, depending on one's point of view; this is a theme to which we return in the volume's final chapter.

Not all online courses use learning networks; some simply post materials (e.g., lectures and quizzes) on web pages, and then collect tests and homework from individual students. This can be thought of as a computerized version of the "correspondence" course—there is no interaction among students, no "class." We exclude this category of courses from the definition of ALN because such courses do not use learning networks as an important part of their composition. However, any instructor who has begun to use the Internet for any aspect of course delivery has made the first step toward teaching a course that makes full use of the potentials of computer and networking technologies to improve access and/or to improve its effectiveness.

DEFINING ALN

What are Asynchronous Learning Networks, one might ask? What distinguishes ALN courses from regular distance education, synchronous learning networks, or e-learning? For that matter, why are ALN courses different from other web-based virtual learning environments (VLEs) or computer-supported collaborative learning environments (CSCLs)? This section provides a complete definition and decomposes the term.

According to the official definition (http://www.aln.org):

> ALNs are people networks for anytime and anywhere learning. ALN combines self-study with substantial, rapid, asynchronous interactivity with others. In ALN learners use computer and communications technologies to work with remote learning resources, including coaches and other learners, but without the requirement to be online at the same time. The most common ALN communication tool is the World Wide Web.

By this definition, a web-based workshop that requires frequent online conferencing and collaboration with others is ALN. So is a text- or computer-based training course that requires learners to use e-mail to discuss assignments with each other and with the coach. ALN also encompasses a proctored examination at a specified time and place, occasional synchronous chat or lab sessions for near-campus learners, or an in-person kick-off meeting.

Also, by this definition, distance education based primarily on a synchronous audio or video presentation or conference is not ALN, because these require learners and instructors to be available at the same time. A videotaped course, mail-based correspondence course, or computer-based training is not ALN, because these do not include substantial and rapid interactivity with others, even though the learner might mail in a paper or test and receive a reply days later.

In this book, the definition of the scope of ALN courses includes "blended" or mixed-mode courses, in which online interaction is combined with a substantial amount of face-to-face meeting time. Examples of the blended mode include a Master's program at the University of Illinois that requires an intensive summer residential "boot camp" before the online courses begin, and the University of Central Florida, where many courses meet for half of the "normal" classroom time each week, which is supplemented with continuous ALN course activities.

Asynchronous Means Anytime, Anywhere

Several key features characterize an ALN. The most important is that each person can work at his or her own pace and preferred times. This means that the members of the class typically are not present at the same time or at the same place. They may be together by chance or by plan, but typically they are spread out in both space and time. ALN courses exist as a rolling present or continuously unfolding conversation that goes on around the clock, 7 days a week. Each student sends and receives communications at the pace and time that is most convenient. Typically, students won't get a response to questions right away, but usually by the next time they sign online someone will have responded. After the course is "over," the materials may be archived, and other students or faculty, months or years later, may be given permission to look in and see what happened in that particular virtual classroom.

This different rhythm of interaction takes some time to get used to. However, asynchronicity, which may at first seem to be a disadvantage, is the single most important factor in creating a collaborative teaching and learning environment. It means that every participant may contribute at the times, places, and pace that is most convenient for him or her. That one of the group members can only take part after putting the children to bed at night, for instance, or that some of the members take two to three times longer than others to be able to read and respond to material, does not determine the ability of others to work at the time and pace that best suits them (Hiltz, 1994).

Asynchronous communication, as contrasted to real-time chat or face-to-face meetings, has both advantages (illustrated in scenarios later in this chapter) and disadvantages (e.g., decreased "immediacy" of communication, to be explored in detail in chap. 10). An advantage is that every person can think about and compose and revise their contributions at their own optimal speed, before posting them. Because more time is spent on refining contributions to a discussion before sharing them, online discussions are generally considered to be "deeper" than are in-classroom discussions.

Learning and Learning Networks or Communities

The second key characteristic of ALN as a form of teaching and learning is that it involves students "learning together" in a cooperative or collaborative manner that ideally leads to the development of a learning community or "learning network." The following quotes help to make the term *learning networks* come to life, by showing the feelings of experienced faculty about their perceptions of facilitating learning and building a community or network of learners. Twenty New Jersey Institute of Technology (NJIT) faculty were interviewed about how their teaching and the learning process changes when they move from the traditional to a "virtual" classroom, an ALN (Coppola, Hiltz, & Rotter, 2002). These excerpts from their responses illustrate that their perceptions of learning in the ALN environment tend to be "deeper":

"I do think that in terms of [comparisons to] face-to-face, it's a better learning experience. They have time to think about the materials, digest it and internalize it."

"With ALN, with text, you have a lot more time to think about what they are really asking."

"What was interesting is the comments you get—in many ways they are more thoughtful. They [students] have more time to reflect."

Students and faculty in other programs echo these statements that "real, deep" learning can (but not always does) take place in ALN courses. For instance, the University of Liverpool (http://www.kitcampus.com, retrieved September 2003) quoted one of its students as saying: "Online learning is exciting, challenging and tough—really tough—but it is also, oddly enough, extremely supportive almost as though students are competing on the same team rather than against each other."

In the following excerpts, faculty from a variety of disciplines at NJIT described the learning network or community that emerges in a successful online class (Coppola et al., 2002):

"There is a possibility for more intimacy online than in the regular classroom. That's definitely a plus."

"I have more of a direct relationship with the students.... The discussion part is much more developed. Shy students have to get into it. It draws everybody out."

"I am in closer contact with the students online than in the classroom. Probably because I am more frequently in contact with them."

Building a learning community, a social and mutually supportive network of learners, is perhaps the greatest challenge and the greatest opportunity offered by ALN. How this occurs is discussed in chapter 11.

ALN'S BEGINNINGS AND GROWTH

At the beginning of the 1990s only a handful of educators and educational researchers were seriously involved with creating and teaching ALN courses, yet a decade later millions of students are online, not only in the United States but also around the world. Growth figures were cited in the Preface to this volume, and similar estimates are given by the marketing research firm Edventures (Barker, 2003): Roughly 915,000 U.S. students were taking online courses in 2003–2004. This number swells to 2 million online if one counts students in blended (partially online) courses. Online learning is not just a North American phenomenon, although it began there. The British Open University has experimented for some time with the use of ALN in its courses, under the leadership of Robin Mason (1989, 1998). The largest field trials in the 20th century occurred in Canada, through the TeleLearning Network of Centres of Excellence and the Virtual-U project, headed by Linda Harasim. The University of Liverpool has online MBA and Master of Science in Information Technology (IT) programs that are taught by an international faculty and taken by students from many nations (see http://www.kitcampus.com). Among the many other nations in which studies of ALN have been conducted are Australia (Klobas & Gaby, 2000), Finland (Marttunen, 1998), Germany (Stahl & The_BSCW_Development_Group, 2003), and Taiwan (Jehng, 1997).

More recently, many international consortia have been attempting to put together virtual universities, but these are more difficult to bring about than are single-university programs. For instance, the European Union has created an initiative to promote online education among European citizens. Information about the project is available from its web site at: http://prometeus.org (which stands for PROmoting Multimedia access to Education and Training in European Society). Universitas21 is an international consortium of 21 universities that planned to offer its first product, a master's degree, throughout Asia and the South Pacific early in 2003. However, fearing for the academic reputations of the member universities, faculty unions in five countries protested their institutions' participation in U21 Global, the company that the consortium co-owns with Thomson Learning, a major academic publisher. The faculty unions assert that professors from the partner institutions have been given too limited a role in creating and teaching the courses (Arnone, 2002).

Much of the growth of ALNs over the last decade can be traced to grants to universities to develop and study ALN-based degree programs. The Alfred P. Sloan Foundation, through the ALN program initiated and led by Frank Mayadas, has been the major contributor. Since 1994, an annual international meeting is held for both ALN practitioners (teachers and administrators) and researchers. The *Journal of Asynchronous Learning Networks* (JALN) at http://www.jaln.org has been published for years, and there is an active ALN e-mail listserv.

Besides offerings by individual traditional colleges and universities, there are also for-profit online programs, of which the largest is the University of Phoenix Online, which in 2002 had over 37,000 students. There are many statewide systems to organize and integrate online offerings throughout many different institutions; one example is the SUNY Learning Network, part of the State University of New York. In its first academic year in 1995–1996, the SUNY Learning Network enrolled 119 students in eight courses on two campuses. By 2000–2001, over 20,000 students were taking online courses (Shea, Swan, Fredericksen, & Pickett, 2002). By the 2002–2003 year, SLN's online enrollments had swollen to over 50,000 students in 3,200 courses, with 60 online degree programs and courses offered through 56 different SUNY campuses.

Another of the largest online programs is offered by the University of Maryland University College, which in 2002 had over 30,000 students enrolled in online courses worldwide. It is interesting that these courses are a typical 15 weeks in length, but there are five start dates during the year, compared to the usual three or four for campus-based courses (Stover, 2003). The Illinois Virtual University reported offering 2,156 courses via the Internet that generated 23,254 student course enrollments during fall term 2001, a 71% increase in online enrollments from the 13,582 online enrollments reported in fall term 2000 (Oakley, 2002). By the winter/spring term of 2003, this was up to over 50,000 students in almost 4,000 online courses.

Illinois Virtual Campus Is a Hit with Students— One Million Times Over

From the "Technology Forum" section of the Chronicle of Higher Education, December 6, 2002 (http://chronicle.com)

In a world of competing attention, when life and work and higher education become a precarious balancing act, where does the put-upon prospective stu-

dent turn for that much-needed academic program, those continuing education credits that career-advancing degree? … Today's students are finding
their educational needs in a single visit—to the virtual campus, those veritable
cyber-malls of academe where dozens of institutions of higher learning gather
into one tidy, Internet-accessible space…. From the Connecticut Distance
Learning Consortium (www.ctdlc.org) to the California Virtual Campus
(www.cvc.edu), more and more statewide collectives of higher education institutions involved in distance learning are banding together … to create such
vibrant, feature-rich "academic shopping malls"….

One of the first and most frequently visited cybermalls in academia is the Illinois Virtual Campus or IVC (http://www.ivc.uillinois.edu/)…. From the original 15 participating institutions, the site over the past three years has grown to
encompass nearly 70 different colleges and universities throughout Illinois,
presenting students with a searchable database of more than 3,500 distance
learning courses and 115 certificate and degree programs…. This past August, as the site celebrated its third anniversary, it reached an impressive visi-
tation milestone: logging more than one million hits in a one-month span.

Although ALN began at the university level, it is percolating down to the high
school and Grade 1–8 levels. One of the K–12 applications is to aid networks of parents and children involved in home schooling. Another is statewide "virtual high
schools." According to Tracy Dell'Angela of the *Chicago Tribune* (http://www.
chicagtotribune.com):

As it begins its second full year of operation, the Illinois Virtual High School, which
offers online classes to highly motivated students, is tripling in size…. With few ex-
ceptions, the first batch of students were top achievers who wanted to take an advanced class online because it was not available at their home school or because the
online version could fit better into their busy schedules.

Now Chicago is jumping into the online venture with all of its high schools…. The expansion could reach almost 8,000 students by 2006…. Illinois is one of 14 states with
government-sponsored virtual high Schools…. "This is where high school instruction
is going in a larger sense," said Edward Klunk, the Chicago district's deputy chief of
high school development…. (Copyright © 2002 Chicago Tribune, September 8, 2002)

E-merging Applications

Beyond individual courses and programs of study is the idea of the virtual university
that can be a worldwide learning entity. One of the most striking of the virtual universities is E-ArmyU, a consortium of providers managed by Pricewaterhouse-
Coopers, the largest military education initiative since the GI Bill. EArmyU, which
is officially called Army University Access Online (AUAO), first started offering
online asynchronous courses in January 2001, and had 15,834 soldier-students by
the middle of its second year of operation. Soldiers were standing in line all night in
the rain in order to be among those who signed up before the initial quotas were

reached. Funding was then allocated to accept another 17,166 students by October 1, 2002, for an estimated grand total of 33,000 students. The eArmyU program has anticipated enrolling 80,000 students by the end of 2005 (Lorenzo, 2002).

Besides offering individual courses, online or "virtual" universities increasingly also try to offer a full range of services and activities for their students, such as online registration, advising, and grade reporting. For instance, Kentucky Virtual University has a fantasy, virtual football team, the @vengers. Innovations abound; this is an exciting and also perilous time in higher education, with online courses raising many issues about what the future of the university will be.

Virtual universities have attracted venture capitalists as well as academicians interested in harnessing technology to improve what they already do. For example, after initial successes by a small number of pioneers, the allure of getting in on e-learning wafted up to Ivy League schools such as Columbia University's Business School, which signed on as the first academic institution to provide educational materials to a start-up company called UNEXT.com that was founded to deliver postgraduate-level training electronically to corporations around the world. In exchange, Columbia Business School would receive royalties that it could convert into stock in the company. With the dot-com "bust" also came the demise of many of these early for-profit schemes, but it is likely that more will be seen when the economy heats up again.

Increasingly, regional or worldwide consortia are being formed to pool online programs and resources, with the aim of creating a much stronger virtual university than any one "bricks and boards" campus could create and support. One example of this is Illinois Online, profiled in the *Chronicle of Higher Education* (see inset, p. 8–9).

For-Profit Online Learning

The lines between for-profit and not-for-profit are increasingly fuzzy in the world of online learning, and the roles of faculty and the very nature of the university are being challenged. Not all such efforts to cash in on the potentially huge worldwide market meet with success of course. For instance, the British Open University, the largest distance-learning institution in the world, announced around the turn of the 21st century that it was establishing partnerships with American universities and intending to dominate the American market for online learning; by 2002, they were losing millions of dollars and withdrew from the market. Likewise, after investing over $25 million, NYUOnline, which focused on corporate education and training rather than on degree programs, closed and consolidated its operations into its continuing professional education division; it never exceeded 500 students (Hafner, 2002).

BEHIND THE NUMBERS: THE NEED FOR ALN

People unfamiliar with ALN often ask why it has become an important form of learning in the last decade. What is the need for this anytime and anywhere form of educational collaborative practice? The following two cases are based on actual situations experienced by students enrolled at the New Jersey Institute of Technology.

Scenario #1

"This is the highlight of my day," the young soldier wrote, "I am back from two runs near Kosovo today.... My assignment for this week is attached." A few weeks earlier, the air force reserve pilot had been a husband, father, employee, and student in New Jersey. Then his unit was called up. The rest of the online class read the daily news about the Kosovo war with some trepidation, knowing that "one of their own" was there. They were relieved to see him "rejoining" the class, so far away but still safe and still able to complete the course.

Scenario #2

A young American was living in China with her family. Her busy day job prevented her from advancing in her career. She started searching the web to find a course in her subject of interest—information systems. She found the perfect match for her career advancement at a technology university in Newark, New Jersey. The New Jersey Institute of Technology offered several distance education courses that enabled her to work anytime, anyplace. Late into the night, after her day job, she sat at her desk in Beijing completing her course assignments, informally and formally chatting with the other students and the professors, and becoming so involved in the virtual community that she decided to return to the United States to complete her degree at NJIT. Within days of her arrival in New Jersey, she was busy planning a course she was teaching as a graduate teaching assistant, totally and obviously comfortable and immersed in the culture of the community. Her success as an asynchronous learner not only enabled her to participate from a distance; it also created the conditions for her success in the on-campus community.

STRENGTHS AND WEAKNESSES

Both face-to-face classes and ALNs have strengths and shortcomings. The relative effectiveness of an ALN is contingent not only on access to the necessary hardware and software facilities, but also on the teacher conducting the course in a manner that fits the characteristics of the medium, the nature of the course materials, and the characteristics of the students; also, on students being motivated and able to participate actively and regularly. It is the instructor who must take the primary responsibility for building a sense of connectedness and community in an online course. Woods and Ebersole (2003) noted, "Affective and cognitive learning are inextricably intertwined in the online learning process."

Common Critiques and Responses

Those who have not experienced a well-taught online course tend to feel that it will not be as good a forum of learning as the traditional classroom. Some argue that online interaction may seem less rich in social cues than does face-to-face interaction. ALN teachers point out that a computer-mediated collaborative learning environment can support some types of activities that are difficult or impossible to conduct in face-to-face environments, particularly if the class size is large. Discussion and communication about the course becomes a continuous activity, rather than being limited to a short scheduled time once or twice a week. Whenever a student has an idea or question, it can be communicated immediately, while it is "fresh."

However, there are many people who seriously doubt the efficacy of moving from the traditional classroom to the virtual classroom, and for good reasons. The field is still young and not everyone will benefit from this form of learning.

An example of common critiques arose after a presentation by Burks Oakley, one of the founders of the Illinois Virtual University, at the Midwestern Higher Education Commission (MHEC) in 2002. Each of the ten states in MHEC has five commissioners: a representative of the governor, someone from the state senate, someone from the state house, and two at-large members (one is typically the SHEEO—state higher education executive officer). These are people with an interest in higher education in their state. Burks summarized their doubts in an e-mail listserve message to members of the Sloan Consortium:

- How can you teach all of a course online? Don't students need the "spark" of being in a classroom with an instructor? Don't students need to see a person to get motivated? I can see that you could do some things this way, but certainly you couldn't do case studies and group projects.
- Are you saving a lot of money with this? Do you charge a lot less for this (obviously inferior) type of instruction? I can't believe that students are willing to pay regular tuition for this type of instruction. Are these degrees accepted in the workplace? I can't imagine hiring someone who earned a degree in this way.
- I talk with the business leaders in my state. They want to see higher education become more productive—just as they have been forced to do. Since you are using computers and technology, why aren't the costs coming way down?

To summarize how ALN researchers address these concerns in this volume, we would like to acknowledge that a healthy community is one in which there is room for serious critique and even discordant views. Experienced ALN teachers and researchers of ALN have some common responses that they make to these important questions. For example, they point out that there are lots of *sparks* and a great deal of interaction in (most) ALN courses. In fact, students tend to participate more online than they do in the traditional classroom (Heckman & Annabi, 2003). Moreover, collaborative learning and group projects are much easier for student teams who can work together anytime, rather than having to find common times to meet.

With digital multimedia, almost any course can be designed and delivered primarily online. The greatest challenges are perhaps laboratories for science courses, but these can be handled with online simulations, home experimental kits, or intensive summertime laboratory weeks on campus. For example, Brigham Young University (2003) reported on its Virtual ChemLab, designed to demonstrate the feasibility of simulating a complete instructional laboratory environment sufficiently to accomplish effective instruction. Comparative results on exams between winter 2001 (the semester before first use of the organic lab simulation) and spring

2001 suggested that students have gained more organic chemistry knowledge from their practice on Virtual ChemLab™ than they did in traditional laboratories. The average on the final exam increased from 77.6% to 80.8%, and the percentage of students who received a 97% or higher increased from 0.5% to 10% (7/71) students (http://www.sloan-c.org/effective/details2).

The main cost of teaching is the compensation (salary and benefits) of the instructor. Instructors report that they spend as much or more time on their online courses as they do on their face-to-face courses, because they interact with students on a daily basis. Therefore, it is unlikely that one is going to save a great deal of money on educational costs for "course delivery." In fact, the costs of initial development of the digital materials and of providing "24-7" support to students often mean that there is a surcharge for online courses, rather than a smaller charge. However, in the long run, there is room for savings, because online degree programs do not have to bear the expense of the "four P's" of residential programs—parking, pillows, pizza, and pools—not to mention campus security concerns and costs. Perhaps most importantly for the future of education, avoiding the cost of building and maintaining additional physical campus facilities as demand for higher education increases can result in significant savings.

We have noted that ALN is not without its disadvantages, and it is not the preferred mode for all students (let alone all faculty). Students (and faculty) report that they spend more time on a course taught in this mode than they do on traditional courses. Students also find it more demanding in general, because they are asked to play an active part in the work of the class on a daily basis, rather than just passively taking notes once or twice a week. For students who want to do as little work as possible for a course, this mode of learning may be considered a burden rather than an opportunity. ALN is also not appropriate for students who are deficient in basic reading, writing, and computational skills (e.g., they don't know what a "mouse" is, and have never used a word processing program), or for those who do not have access to the necessary equipment and an Internet service provider (ISP) at home or at work.

The recent survey of chief academic officers by Allen and Seaman (2003) suggests that faculty are more resistant to ALN than are either students or administrators. At a majority of institutions (59.6%), faculty are perceived to accept the value and legitimacy of online education; but this leaves a substantial 40% of institutions where faculty are neutral or do not feel that ALN is "as good or better" than face-to-face courses.

Discussion on these and many other issues can be found in this book, which presents an organized summary of what we know from past research on ALN, as well as key questions for future research. We hope that you, the readers, will be involved in helping to provide more answers. In concluding our introduction of the book, we would like to explore one final topic that ripples throughout the book and is more fully addressed in the conclusion: Why is it that educational changes, such as ALN, are met with a preservationist response?

CONCLUSION: MAKING CHANGES

Changes to the educational system are often met with marked resistance, regardless of the recommended alterations that are proposed or the advanced technologies that offer new opportunities. It is no surprise that ALN has been enthusiastically accepted by those who adapt easily to change, and resisted by educators who, once they have developed a method that works for them, are reluctant to divert from their course of action. And yet, ironically, members of educational communities make changes every moment of the learning event. One could say that flexibility is the cornerstone of good teaching and learning.

The current state of most of our learning systems is that most students gather at the same place to learn the same curriculum at the same time. However, in ALN, this core tenet is contradicted. In spite of the remarkable growth of ALN and the obvious need for many students to be able to participate in a learning community anywhere and anytime, academia is still reluctant to embrace ALN as an equally effective learning environment for some students, some of the time. Why?

Why Educational Change Is Difficult

The topic of implementing educational change has been addressed since long before Dewey (1938) introduced the idea of an educational system emphasizing project-based learning. Socrates, for example, felt that the use of written text would ruin education (see chap. 12, this volume).

Fullan (1991), a leading educational reform scholar, stated that teachers need to change themselves or they will be subjected to external changes being forced on them by educational systems. In other words, teachers need to operate from within the system. He noted that the current educational system leads to teacher isolation rather than collaboration and community. What is needed, he added, is more interactivity and reflection on the practice of teaching. Kozol (1991) critiqued educational practice, convincingly arguing that the current educational system both excludes nonmainstream students from becoming full members of the society and stifles educational change.

Focusing on technological changes, Cuban and Tyack (1995) pondered how economic priorities often force changes on an educational system that was, according to them, designed to create a democratic society. They reinforced Kozol's recommendation to "tinker" with reforms in order to correct the current injustices within the system rather than implementing changes for the sake of making changes.

Shulman's (1987) discussion on educational reform issues focused more on what he termed *pedagogical content knowledge*, the combination of content and curriculum expertise. The cornerstones of his theory are student comprehension, transformation, instruction, evaluation, and reflection—qualities that many of the chapters in this book discuss in relation to ALN.

In fact, ALN is a form of education that dramatically changes the teaching and learning environment. It creates changes throughout the educational system, not only affecting teachers and learners as with other educational reforms, but also altering the very tenets we hold as sacred, such as what it means to be a learner, how teachers teach, how universities organize learning programs of study, and, most important, how the society as a whole understands the importance of life-long knowledge construction. As we discuss in more depth in the final chapter of this book, many of these changes can be viewed as deeply disturbing or troubling, and some might well be in actuality. We do not know how the university or the school of the future will carry on its role as the guardian of knowledge or even if that should define the role of the university.

In light of continually emerging online technologies for collaboration and community building, we do not know if these ALN educational practices will enhance what Salomon (1993) referred to as *distributed cognitions* and what Salomon, Perkins, and Globerson (1991) called *partnerships with technologies*. For example, Goldman-Segall (1998) predicted that online communities will create a distributed *platform for multiloguing* in which all participants, learners, teachers, even researchers, engage in layering their viewpoints to negotiate meaning with each other to better comprehend the subject they are investigating and to create new knowledge in the process. Will this prediction be realized in the ALN learning environment? In Goldman-Segall's *Points of Viewing Theory* (Goldman-Segall & Maxwell, 2002), the various perspectives of the learner, the teacher, and the research are integrated with the course content, context, and the culture of the learning environment. These complex interwoven perspectives are not only integrated, they are continually affecting each other, changing the conversation. Will these ideas be realized or will online technologies, with their power to thread our responses into sequential categorizations, lead us further down the path of conformity and mediocrity? Will we know domains of knowledge better, worse, or in a new interdisciplinary way? And most important, how will we know what we have achieved? What methods will we use to determine what we know to be good or bad use of ALNs?

Although many faculty are resistant to the idea of ALNs, those who have taught this way, at least in institutions that provide good support, are very satisfied with their experiences. For example, a survey of 255 SUNY faculty from 31 colleges who had taught online found that 96% of these faculty expressed general satisfaction. Perhaps more interestingly, faculty reported that they were nine times more likely to have systematically redesigned their instruction for ALN than for their classroom courses, and 85% believed that having taught online would improve their subsequent teaching in the classroom (Shea, Pelz, Fredericksen, & Pickett, 2002). In other words, ALN is a transformational force that reaches beyond changes in teaching style within an online course.

In the process of reading the chapters that follow, we hope that the theme of transformation is developed by engaging you, the reader, in understanding what we know about ALN and what we still need to know.

QUESTIONS FOR DISCUSSION AND FURTHER RESEARCH

This introductory chapter includes scenarios and quotes that illustrate some of the controversies about asynchronous learning networks (ALN).

1. Initially, educators thought that online courses were a kind of "niche" medium for nontraditional students who could not travel to a campus for classes. Can you add examples to the case-based scenarios in this chapter on "nontraditional" ALN students who might otherwise be unable to complete university courses?

2. In fact, most students enrolled in ALN courses could take on-campus courses, but choose to take some or all of their courses online. Some universities

have put strict limits on this option. For example, NJIT does no allow its full-time freshmen to take online courses. The federal government restricts foreign students in the United States on student visas to only one distance course a semester. What do you think are the reasons for such policies, and are they justified? Can you think of a way to design a study which would test the assumptions underlying such restrictions?

3. In addition to resistance from some legislators and educational administrators, many faculty members are opposed to or fearful of the trend toward online courses. The extent of and reasons for such resistance have not been carefully researched. If you wanted to gain a better understanding of faculty resistance, what questions would you ask, and how would you design a study to answer these questions?

FOR FURTHER READING

Barker, D. (2003). Course management systems: The next generation. *Tools for Teaching Technology*, 8–11.

Bourne, J., & Moore, J. C. (Eds.). (2003). *Quality studies: Online education practice and direction* (Vol. 4). Fourth in a series of case studies drawn from ALN projects funded on various campuses by the Alfred P. Sloan Foundation. Needham, MA: Alfred P. Sloan Foundation.

Goldman-Segall, R. (1998). *Points of viewing children's thinking: A digital ethnographer's journey*. Mahwah, NJ: Lawrence Erlbaum Associates. Interactive video cases available at: http://www.pointsofviewing.com/

Harasim, L. (Ed.). (1990). *Online education: Perspectives on a new environment*. New York: Praeger.

Harasim, L., Hiltz, S. R., Teles, L., & Turoff, M. (1995). *Learning networks: A field guide to teaching and learning online*. Cambridge, MA: MIT Press. Based on the authors' personal experiences with teaching many online courses, this book emphasizes "how to" create and facilitate successful learning networks-based courses.

Hiltz, S. R. (1994). *The virtual classroom: Learning without limits via computer networks*. Norwood, NJ: Ablex. (Currently available from Intellect at: http://www.intellect-net.com) The first extensive, multicourse, and multiinstitutional empirical study of the comparative process and outcome of traditional versus "virtual" classrooms. *Virtual Classroom* is a registered trademark of New Jersey Institute of Technology.

Mason, R., & Kaye, A. (Eds.). (1989). *Mindweave: Communication, computers and distance education*. Oxford, UK: Pergamon. This and Harasim's (1990) book are collections of chapters summarizing the experiences and perspectives of many of the early "pioneers" of online learning.

REFERENCES

Allen, I. E., & Seaman, J. (2003). *Seizing the opportunity: The quality and extent of online education in the United States, 2002 and 2003*. Needham, MA: SCOLE (Sloan Center for Online Education).

Arnone, M. (2002). International consortium readies ambitious distance education effort. *The Chronicle of Higher Education* (online), *48*(42), A28–30. Retrieved June 28, 2002, from http://www.chronicle.com

Barker, D. (2003). Course management systems: The next generation. *Tools for Teaching Technology*, 8–11.

Brigham Young University. (2003). *"Virtual ChemLab" and "Effective Practice."* Retrieved March 17, 2004, from: http://vchemlab.chem.byu.edu/home/index.htm

Coppola, N. W., Hiltz, S. R., & Rotter, N. (2002). Becoming a virtual professor: Pedagogical roles and Asynchronous Learning Networks. *Journal of Management Information Systems, 18*(4), 169–190.

Cuban, L., & Tyack, D. B. (1995). *Tinkering toward Utopia: A century of public school reform.* Cambridge, MA: Harvard University Press.

Dewey, J. (1938). *Experience and education.* New York: Collier.

Fullan, M. G. (1991). *The new meaning of educational change.* New York: Teachers College Press.

Goldman-Segall, R. (1998). *Points of viewing children's thinking: A digital ethnographer's journey.* Mahwah, NJ: Lawrence Erlbaum Associates.

Goldman-Segall, R., & Maxwell, J. W. (2002). Computers, the Internet, and new media for learning. In W. M. Reynolds & G. E. Miller (Eds.), *Handbook of psychology* (Vol. 7, pp. 393–427). New York: Wiley.

Hafner, K. (2002, May 2). Lessons learned at dot-comU. *The New York Times.*

Heckman, R., & Annabi, H. (2003). A content-analytic comparison of FtF and ALN case study discussions. In *Proceedings of the 36th Hawaii International Conference on Systems Sciences* (CD-Rom). Washington, DC: IEEE Press.

Hiltz, S. R. (1994). *The virtual classroom: Learning without limits via computer networks.* Norwood, NJ: Ablex.

Jehng, J. C. (1997). The psycho-social processes and cognitive effects of peer-based collaborative interaction with computers. *Journal of Educational Computing Research, 17*(1), 19–46.

Klobas, J., & Gaby, H. (2000). International computer-supported collaborative teamwork in business education: A case study and evaluation. *International Journal of Education Technology,* 2, 1. Retrieved March 19, 2004, from http://www.ao.vivc.edu/ijet/v2nlarticles.html

Kozol, J. (1991). *Savage inequalities.* New York: Crown.

Lorenzo, G. (2002, May/June). eArmyU and the future of distance education. *The Technology Source.*

Marttunen, M. (1998). Electronic mail as a forum for argumentative interaction in higher education Studies. *Journal of Educational Computing Research, 18*(4), 387–405.

Mason, R. (1989). An evaluation of CoSy on an open university course. In R. Mason & A. Kaye (Eds.), *Mindweave: Communication, computers and distance education* (pp. 115–145). Oxford, UK: Pergamon.

Mason, R. (1998). *Globalising education: Trends and applications.* London: Routledge.

Oakley, B. (2002, May 2, December 10). *List-serve Messages to Sloan Consortium.*

Salomon, G. (1993). No distribution without individuals' cognition: A dynamic interactional view. In G. Salomon (Ed.), *Distributed cognitions: Psychological and educational considerations.* Cambridge, UK: Cambridge University Press.

Salomon, G., Perkins, D. N., & Globerson, T. (1991). Partners in cognition: Extending human intelligence with intelligent technologies. *Educational Researcher, 20*(3), 2–9.

Shea, P. J., Pelz, W., Fredericksen, E. E., & Pickett, A. M. (2002). Online teaching as a catalyst for classroom-based instructional transformation. In J. Bourne & J. C. Moore (Eds.), *Elements of quality online learning* (Vol. III, pp. 103–123). Needham MA: SCOLE (Sloan Center for Online Education).

Shea, P. J., Swan, K., Fredericksen, E. E., & Pickett, A. M. (2002). Student satisfaction and reported learning in the SUNY Learning Network. In J. Bourne & J. C. Moore (Eds.), *Elements of quality online learning* (Vol. III, pp. 145–155). Needham MA: SCOLE (Sloan Center for Online Education).

Shulman, L. (1987). Knowledge and teaching: Foundations of the new reform. *Harvard Educational Review, 57,* 1–22.

Stahl, G., & The_BSCW_Development_Group. (2003). Knowledge negotiation in asynchronous learning networks. In *Proceedings of the 36th Hawaii International Conference on System Sciences* (CD-Rom ed.). Washington, DC: IEEE Computer Society Press.

Stover, M. (2003). Access issues and the current state of practice at the University of Maryland University College. In J. Bourne & J. C. Moore (Eds.), *Elements of Quality Online Learning* (Vol. IV, pp. 139–158). Needham, MA: SCOLE (Sloan Center for Online Education).

Woods, R., & Ebersole, S. (2003). Becoming a "communal architect" in the online classroom—integrating cognitive and affective learning for maximum effect in Web-based learning. *Online Journal of Distance Learning Administration, 6*(1). Retrieved March 6, 2004, from www.westga.edu/~distance/ojdla/spring61.htm

2

The Online Interaction Learning Model: An Integrated Theoretical Framework for Learning Networks

Raquel Benbunan-Fich
Baruch University

Starr Roxanne Hiltz
New Jersey Institute of Technology

Linda Harasim
Simon Fraser University

Theories are productions ... that attempt to analyze and to generalize about the interaction of human beings, using a set of concepts and/or variables.... (Mullins, 1973, p. 5)

There has been much written about eLearning practice, however little attention has been given to eLearning theory.... A lack of established theory will hinder further development in eLearning.... Practice based research can be likened to the branches of a tree.... Theoretical principles can be likened to the roots; it is the root system that determines the health of the tree and also the extent to which it can grow. (Nichols, 2003, p. 5)

INTRODUCTION

A theoretical framework is the first step in generating a comprehensive theory for a field. It models the key concepts, and the relationships among these concepts, that can be used to organize the knowledge and to generate hypotheses for empirical testing. Aspects of the learning process itself occupy the central place in the online interaction learning model. In particular, the role of collaborative learning (learning together with one's peers) is given a prominent place in the model, and chapter 10 is devoted to theories and research on it.

At the core of any educational course, online or face to face (F2F), is the process of learning and the *pedagogy* that supports effective learning; that is, the processes structured and facilitated by the instructor in order to engage the student in understanding and applying the key analytical (and practical) concepts appropriately in relation to the topic of study and the field. The instructor also provides assessment and feedback to students, especially because their use and understanding of key concepts relates to the "knowledge communities" that represent the field. In a chapter entitled "Education as Conversation," Bruffee (1999) wrote that "Education initiates us into conversation, and by virtue of that conversation initiates us into thought" (p. 133). Nonetheless, professors and students initially come together (into conversations) speaking different "languages" that reflect the different communities of which they are members.

The importance of collaborative learning is that it acknowledges these differences and creates conditions in which students can negotiate the boundaries between the knowledge communities to which they belong and the one to which the professor belongs. The professor's goal is to help students learn fluency in that discourse (of the knowledge community)—to make it become normal discourse for them too. That is, the professor's goal is to reacculturate students into membership in the knowledge community they aspire to join (Bruffee, 1999).

This chapter thus begins with a brief summary of the leading theories of the learning processes that occupy the central causal place in the online interaction learning model, with special focus on constructivist/collaborative learning, which has increasingly defined the learning sciences and practice since the early to mid-20th century. We then move on to introduce the full integrative theoretical model for understanding the determinants of the success of online learning. The online interaction learning model builds on earlier frameworks for understanding the effectiveness of computer-mediated communication and group support systems in general (e.g., DeSanctis & Gallupe, 1986; Hiltz, 1988) and of online learning in particular (Hiltz, 1994). It is based on an input >process>output model with feedback loops. In deconstructing the process of collaborative learning online, it adapts Harasim's theory of collaborative knowledge building (CKB) that explains the relative effectiveness of communities of online learners working to reach a deeper level of understanding by interacting with each other, with the faculty (and indirectly the knowledge community), and with the texts under investigation. Harasim's CKB is process oriented, identifying three key phases of conceptual change and knowledge work as learners engage collaboratively to advance from divergent to convergent thinking and understanding.

THEORETICAL FOUNDATIONS OF LEARNING PROCESSES

The *constructivist* concept of education views learning as resulting from complex interactions, beyond what has been termed as the *objectivist* or *knowledge transmission* model in which "knowledge" is viewed as a product that can be transmitted one way from the professor (or the textbook) to the students. Basically, constructivism means that as people experience something new they compare this experience to internalized knowledge constructs based on past experiences, and then modify their constructs accordingly. Watzawick (1984) explained, "Constructivism can be defined as that philosophical position which holds that any so-called reality is, in the most immediate and concrete sense, the mental construction of those who believe they have discovered and investigated it" (p. 136). The constructivist theory holds that knowledge has to be discovered, constructed, practiced, and validated by each learner; learning involves "active struggling by the learner" (Duffy & Cunningham, 1996, p. 174). Pedagogical methods using this approach, including collaborative learning, create learning situations that enable learners to engage in active exploration and/or social collaboration, such as laboratories, field studies, simulations, and case studies with group discussion.

Foreshadowed in the work of John Dewey at the beginning of the 20th century and by Jean Piaget's work in the middle of the 20th century on how children learn, collaborative and constructivist learning became very popular during the last two decades of the 20th century. Constructivism is typically presented as opposite to but sometimes complementary with the *objectivist* model of learning (also referred to as the *behaviorist* or *instructivist* model). The objectivist model assumes that there is a single objective reality that exists independently of learners. The goal of learning is to understand that objective reality, and this knowledge is received exclusively through the senses. By contrast, the *constructivist* perspective assumes that knowledge is actively created or constructed by every learner (Leidner & Jarvenpaa, 1995).

As Goldman-Segall and Maxwell pointed out (2003), the objectivist approach was the subject of much research at the beginning of the 20th century. Among its most famous theorists were Pavlov and Skinner. Ivan Pavlov, renowned for his experiments with dogs, discovered they could be taught to salivate at the sound of a bell; Pavlov called his theory *conditioning*. The dogs were initially fed while a bell rang; later on they would salivate at the sound of the bell that had previously accompanied their eating, even when they received no food. This was expanded to a theory called *operant conditioning* by Burrhus Frederic (B. F.) Skinner, who detailed how positive and negative reinforcement (reward and punishment) can be used as stimuli to shape how humans respond. Skinner asserted that educators could shape, reinforce, and modify human behavior through repeated drills (Goldman-Segall & Maxwell, 2003). During the second half of the 20th century, these objectivist or behaviorist theories were instantiated in computer-supported learning with drill-and-practice methods to improve memorization tasks (e.g., Suppes, 1966).

The objectivist approach is based on the notion that students learn passively by receiving and assimilating knowledge individually, independent from others (Bouton & Garth, 1983). This is based on a one-way or professor-centered model of knowledge transmission, in which each student learns individually. The professor is someone who has attained a high degree of understanding and knowledge in a particular subject by virtue of years of experience, research, and study in the field. The student is someone who is interested in extending (or is *required* to extend) his or her knowledge in that particular area. To learn, students read texts or online tutorials, watch video lectures, take quizzes, or do homework problems that are graded by either computer or by the teacher, and then receive this feedback to condition or correct their mistakes. Many ALN courses include at least some components of objectivist pedagogy and individual learning.

By contrast, collaborative learning is based on a model that treats the student as active participants in individual or group activities. The learner becomes actively involved in constructing knowledge by applying concepts to problems and/or formulating ideas into words, and these ideas are elaborated on through reactions and responses of others (Alavi, 1994; Bouton & Garth, 1983). In other words, learning is not only active but also interactive. Active involvement can take place through communication with the instructor or with peers. For this reason, collaborative (or group) learning is one of the most important implementations of the constructivist approach.

Collaborative learning refers to instructional methods that encourage students to work together on academic tasks. It involves interpersonal processes as a small group of students work together to complete an academic problem-solving task that promotes learning. Collaborative learning is essentially different from the traditional "direct-transfer" or "one-way knowledge transmission" model (objectivist approach) in which the instructor is the only source of knowledge or skills (Harasim, 1990). The pedagogical assumption that students learn by constructing knowledge through group interaction is the theoretical foundation of ALN (Harasim, Hiltz, Teles, & Turoff, 1995; Roblyer, Edwards, & Havriluk, 1997). An online class using asynchronous computer-mediated communication is able to engage each participant at length and in detail on the construction of common understanding. Within the online learning context, collaboration with the class using a discussion forum allows students to construct meaning from exploration of ideas put forth by classmates as well as by the instructor (Spencer, 2002). Students create knowledge by interacting their existing knowledge and beliefs with the ideas put forth in the class discussion (Airasian & Walsh, 1997). The teacher uses facilitative techniques to foster that discussion among all members of the class.

Two major types of explanations for how participating in a group endeavor helps members to learn have been given (Webb 1982); socioemotional explanations and cognitive explanations.

1. Group members learn by virtue of mediating *socioemotional* variables (e.g., motivation, reduced anxiety, or satisfaction) that create an emotional or intellectual climate favorable to learning. When working with peers instead of alone (or with the instructor), anxiety and uncertainty are reduced as learners find their ways through complex or new tasks (Harasim, 1990). These effects tend to increase motivation and satisfaction with the learning process in general.
2. As reviewed by Dillenbourg and Schneider (1994), several collaborative learning mechanisms directly affect *cognitive* processes, including:
    *   *Conflict or disagreement:* When disagreement occurs between peers, social factors prevent learners from ignoring conflict and force them to seek additional information and find a solution.
    *   *Internalization:* The concepts conveyed by the interactions with more knowledgeable peers are progressively integrated into the learner's

knowledge structures. When integrated, they can be used in the learner's own reasoning.

- *Self-explanation:* Less knowledgeable members learn from the explanations of more advanced peers. But, surprisingly, the more able peers also benefit because providing an explanation improves the explainer's own knowledge (self-explanation effect). Explaining to others may be more beneficial to the explainer when the material is complex than when the material is simple (Webb, 1982). In collaborative learning, explanation occurs naturally or spontaneously.

THE ONLINE INTERACTION LEARNING MODEL: AN OVERVIEW

Several research frameworks (e.g., Alavi & Leidner, 2001; Hiltz, 1988, 1994) have been proposed to guide research in the area of online learning. Most frameworks organize research variables in terms of an input-process-output model, which has been adopted for our model. In this model (see Fig. 2.1), input factors, also called "moderator variables," are those that are expected to influence how the technology is actually used to influence the individual and collaborative learning processes. And these processes, in turn, will determine the outcomes.

Any use of ALN technology is located within a particular social context. The characteristics of the user and of the hardware/software system shape the dynamics of human–computer interaction during a session in which a teacher or student uses a system.

In the model, the "inputs" or moderators include the characteristics of:

1. The technology (in particular, the media mix).
2. The individual student.
3. The instructor.
4. The group (course or class) and the organizational setting (college or university), which define the context in which the technology is used.

These four sets of factors are expected to act as moderator variables (Barron & Kenny, 1986) that influence how the technology is adapted for a particular course (Dennis, Wixom, & Vandenberg, 2001). The model is a contingency theory, because unless minimal levels of these "input" or moderator variables are reached, then it is not expected that a course will be conducted in such a way as to lead to the online interaction and communication that are necessary for the outcomes to be favorable. For example, if the technology used is unreliable, or difficult to learn and use, or requires hardware or software that many of the students do not have access to, then the barriers to a successful online course are almost insurmountable. A second example is the experience and effort of the instructor. If the instructor has no experience and no training on how to design and teach a course online, then he or she is not likely to be able to use ALN effectively. Likewise, if the instructor in essence "misses class" by failing to evidence a daily and active guiding presence, then most students will stop participating, too, just as they will leave an empty classroom if the instructor does not show up within a certain time of the scheduled start of class. Finally, unless the student has at least the minimal required level of motivation and ability to do the required activities in a course, he or she will fail to reach a satisfac-

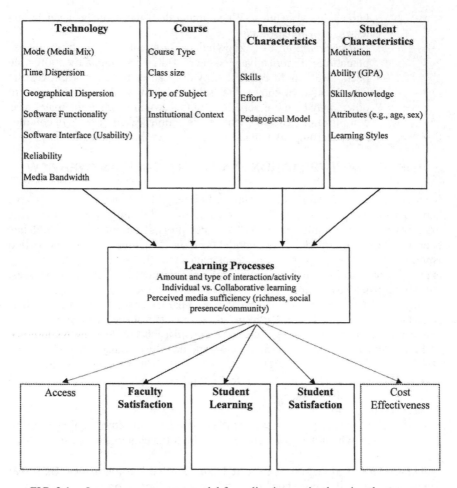

FIG. 2.1.   Input-process-output model for online interaction learning theory.

tory level of learning. As an extreme example, if the student is unable to read or write in the English language at even an eighth-grade level, he or she will not do well in an ALN course, which (in the United States) is based almost totally on reading and writing in English.

Each of the contextual factors listed can be logically assumed to be related to the probability that the interaction within an ALN will be lively and produce desirable learning outcomes. However, the relative importance of the variables, individually and as they may interact, is a question for research. Various chapters in this book examine the results of past research in terms of the findings and the unknowns about the effects of each of these classes of variables. For example, the contextual factors related to technology, the course, and the instructor are reviewed in detail in chapter 6.

The contextual or "input" factors lead to the communication and social and learning processes within the online classroom: the amount and type of communication, the nature of the activities conducted there (individual and/or collaborative learning), and perceptions of the environment by the participants (e.g., perceived social presence and media richness/sufficiency, perceived sense of community). Favorable outcomes of the ALN educational process are contingent on the nature of the actual process that occurs within a specific "virtual classroom." How many people are actively participating, how often, and with what kinds of activities and communications patterns? To what extent does a learning community actually emerge from the collection of people, resources, and media that were assembled for the course?

The dependent variables are measures of the quality of the learning experience. They include measures of student learning, measures of subjective satisfaction (for students and instructors), and measures of access and cost effectiveness. In this chapter and throughout this book, we focus on learning and student satisfaction outcomes.

Inputs: The Contextual or "Moderating" Factors

These sets of variables are shown at the top of the model depicted in Fig. 2.1. In statistical terms, they are often called "moderator" variables because they modify or influence the effect that ALN will have on learning.

Technology. Many attributes define the characteristics of the technology. From the technical point of view, functionality, usability, reliability, and media bandwidth determine the capabilities of the system. From a communications perspective, the system can be classified in terms of its ability to be used from different times and places. Different modes of interaction along the time and place dimensions can be described in terms of the framework proposed by Johansen (1992). Interaction can occur at the same time (synchronous) or at different times (asynchronous). Members can meet in the same place (proximate) or in different places (distributed). (See Fig. 2.2.)

Same time/same place refers to teams that meet in the same room or labs in which each student has access to a personal computer. *Same time/different place* situations occur when team members are located in (at least two) different places, and communicate via computers using chat rooms or desktop-video conferences. The

Time

		Same	Different
Place	Same	Synchronous/Proximate	Anytime/Same (virtual) Place
	Different	Synchronous/Dispersed	Asynchronous/Dispersed

Source: Johansen (1992)

FIG. 2.2.   Time and place dispersion. Source: Adapted from Johansen (1992).

different time/same place category normally refers to people who work in shifts but share a common meeting room (project room) where they leave messages for each other and share materials. This category can be expanded to include the notion of dedicated *virtual workplaces* whose use is restricted to a particular class or group of students. A course homepage on the Web as a shared *virtual* space to store class materials can be placed in this category. Finally, *different time/different place* refers to asynchronous/dispersed teams that rarely meet face to face and carry on all their work using the e-mail and computer-conferencing facilities of ALNs (Hiltz & Wellman, 1997). This latter condition might be called "pure ALN," but many primarily ALN courses in fact are "blended" or "mixed" mode.

Perhaps the most important of the technological characteristics is the "media mix" employed in a particular instantiation of a learning network. Theories about the characteristics of various media and evidence about effects of different media mixes (e.g., trying to include synchronous chats in a primarily asynchronous course) are examined in detail in chapter 10.

Course.   The subject matter (more technical vs. less technical) and the level and type of the course (undergraduate vs. graduate, credit vs. noncredit) will influence the amount and type of technology used and the type of educational processes employed. In general, "more technical" courses include substantial mathematical analysis (algorithms, programming, etc.), whereas the "less technical" courses are more oriented toward qualitative analysis and discussion.

Effective educational applications of IT are those that match the disciplinary nature of the course. Many disciplines are characterized by two broad categories of knowledge: conceptual and pragmatic. Conceptual knowledge is based on the fundamental concepts or methods, whereas pragmatic knowledge represents the processes that transform concepts into practical solutions (Benbunan-Fich, 2002).

Another characteristic of a specific course is the number of students enrolled. If it is too few, then "critical mass" will not be reached; the online learning space may seem empty. If too many, then the amount of postings online may lead to information overload and confusion, particularly if no technological features or pedagogical interventions are made to structure and organize the interactions of a large number of students.

Course characteristics are among the contextual or "input" factors that are described in more detail in chapter 6.

Instructor Characteristics.   The mode of adaptation of technology in different courses by different instructors, in particular their actions in terms of pedagogical design (objectivist vs. constructionist/collaborative), the degree and nature of structuring or scaffolding of the course, and the instructor's style are key factors in determining the nature of the educational processes and outcomes. For example, what is the balance between individual and collaborative assignments and activities, and how does the instructor grade or reward students for class discussion participation and for group projects? Another example is the clarity of the course requirements. From the beginning of the course, can the student see a syllabus or calendar, in order to know what is expected and when? In terms of an online persona or teaching style, does the instructor act so as to establish swift trust during the first week of the course (Coppola, Hiltz, & Rotter, 2002) by establishing a lively and responsive environment and working to create an online learning community from the start?

Besides course design, other attributes of the instructor's behavior also crucially affect the process and outcomes of online learning. How much skill and experience does the instructor have with online learning? Does he or she even know how to use the technologies without fumbling? Does he or she have any training, if not experience, in the role changes that must be made in moving toward becoming a virtual professor? And very important, how present is the instructor in the virtual classroom? A good rule of thumb is that the instructor should sign in at least once a day and respond to questions and comments, so that no student has to wait more than 24 hours for a reply. If the instructor is not "there," then very shortly, the students will not participate either, just as students leave a physical classroom if the instructor does not show up within 10–20 minutes of the supposed start of the class.

Student Characteristics.   Individual characteristics of the students—such as learning style, cultural values, cognitive ability, and motivation—will also influence the processes and will determine outcomes. Especially important is motivation of the student. Note that this is not a static entity; the amount and nature of feedback received during a course will continuously affect motivation. The influence of student characteristics on ALN learning is explored in chapter 7.

Learning Processes: Mediator or Intervening Variables

This section introduces the mediator (intervening or process) variables (Barron & Kenney, 1986), which include the extent to which the experiences in an ALN are or are not perceived as motivating, actively involving, socially rich (conveying social presence), and collaborative rather than individual in nature. The middle portion of the framework thus characterizes the mode of adaptation or use of the technology. For example, students may passively browse or listen, rather than be actively involved in discussions and other class activities. The instructor may or may not provide a daily presence online. The students may or may not engage in collaborative assignments with other students, depending on the way the way the instructor has structured the course and their own regularity in interacting with their peers. Depending on the extent to which these processes take place, the members of class may or may not form a "learning network" or "learning community."

In looking at the learning processes (in the middle of the model shown in Fig. 2.1), the first questions might be: What is the amount and type of interaction evidenced? How many contributions of what type and length are made by the instructor and the students? Three major kinds of interactivity may occur in online courses: interaction with content (cognitive presence), interaction with instructors (teaching presence), and interaction with classmates (social presence) (Moore, 1989). All of these types of interaction are likely to be affected by and related to whether the learners experience the medium as a rich or as a sufficient one. These types of interaction are also related to the extent to which collaborative learning pedagogy, rather than an individual learning model, is used.

Among the theoretical frameworks developed to explain the extent to which on-line courses become online learning communities is one presented by Garrison, Anderson, and Archer (2000). This theoretical model for the emergence of a "community of inquiry" (another term similar to a learning network or a learning community) states that it occurs through the interaction of the three kinds of interactivity: cognitive presence, social presence, and teaching presence. *Cognitive presence* is the extent to which the participants are able to construct meaning through sustained communication. *Social presence* is defined as the ability of participants to project personal characteristics and appear to others as "real people." Not only does social presence support cognitive presence, but it also makes online interaction more enjoyable, and thus contributes to motivation and enjoyability. Research has demonstrated that social presence affects not only learning, but also student, and possibly instructor, satisfaction with a course (Moore, Masterson, Christophel, & Shea, 1996; Richardson & Swan, 2003). *Teaching presence* is broken into two functions: the design of the educational experience, usually by the instructor (including the selection, organization, and presentation of course content, and the design and use of learning activities and assessment); and facilitation of discussion and collaboration, which may be shared among all participants, not just the designated instructor. This theoretical framework is further discussed and illustrated in chapter 11.

New theories have been developed over the past two decades to help understand how collaboration and discourse contribute to learning and under what circumstances this has occurred in face-to-face environments and increasingly as related to online environments. Researchers have come to focus on how collaborative learning contributes to educational effectiveness at the cognitive and social levels. Findings indicate that collaboration facilitates higher developmental levels in learners than those accomplished by the same individuals working alone (Johnson, 1981; Stodolsky, 1984; Webb, 1983). Conversation, argument, and multiple perspectives that arise in groups contribute to such cognitive processes as verbalization, cognitive restructuring, and conflict resolution.

There are also critical social or motivational factors involved in collaborative learning. These include the reduction of uncertainty as learners find their way through complex activities (Webb, 1983), and increased engagement with the learning process as a result of peer interaction and collaboration (Cohen, 1984).

Bruffee (1999) argued that learning is a social, negotiated, consensual process for which discourse is key. He suggested a process in which students collaborate first in small groups, and then in larger or plenary groups, to increasingly come to intellectual convergence (even if that means agreeing to disagree). He identified a process of five steps as standing between "successful knowledge work and what might be called 'mere group work': composing small consensus groups, designing tasks, unpacking small group consensus in plenary discussions, and representing larger knowledge communities" (p. 44). Thomas Kuhn (1970) similarly argued that scientific knowledge changes as scientists revise the conversation among themselves and reorganize their relations.

Roschelle (1996) posited that the "crux of learning by collaboration is convergence," a process of mutual construction of knowledge. He elaborated, "Democratic participation, intellectual progress, and gradual convergence are base attributes of social inquiry practices that enable scientists to undergo conceptual change. A convergent account alone suggests the attractive possibility that students develop their concepts in the course of learning to participate in the practices of inquiry that scientists themselves use to develop scientific concepts" (p. 245).

Harasim's (1990) model of conceptual change focused on collaborative learning in the online (Web-based) discourse environment, identifying three processes/phases describing the path from divergent to convergent thinking. The three processes are theoretically complimentary with those of Roschelle (1996), focusing on collaboration as a key process in conceptual change. Although identified and developed in different contexts from one another, both resonate with Bruffee's theoretical position that intellectual convergence through collaborative discourse is key, and in combination suggest a framework for understanding discourse in online seminars. Following is a new framework that builds on previous formulations and incorporates the communication process into conceptualization of online learning processes that use discussion-based collaborative learning.

1. *Idea generating.* The first process, idea generating, implies divergent thinking, brainstorming, verbalization, and thus sharing of ideas and positions. Participants engage and contribute. Indicators include verbalization, divergent thinking activities such as brainstorming, generating input, generating information, and general democratic participation.

2. *Idea linking.* The second process, idea linking, provides evidence of conceptual change, intellectual progress, and the beginning of convergence as new or different ideas become clarified, identified, and clustered into various positions (agreement/disagreement; questioning/elaboration). This is an early form of convergence, a mutual contribution to and construction of shared knowledge and understanding. This phase involves organizing and elaborating various ideas into intellectual positions or clusters, demonstrating intellectual progress through recognizing multiple perspectives and how these relate (or not) to one another.

3. *Intellectual convergence.* The third phase, intellectual convergence, is typically reflected in shared understanding (including agreeing to disagree) and is especially evident in coproduction, whether a theory, a publication, an assignment, a work of art, or a similar output authored by the group or subgroup. Idea structuring, through gradual convergence, reaches a level of intellectual synthesis, understanding and consensus, agreeing to disagree, and/or coproduction.

The three stages of collaborative discourse, from idea generating to intellectual convergence, are illustrated in Fig. 2.3. At the idea generating stage, individual participants (represented by squares) contribute their ideas and opinions (represented by small circles) on the topics to the shared space (represented by larger circles). Through the process of brainstorming, the participants begin to relate to each other's ideas. This leads to the second stage of the discourse—idea organizing. At this stage, the participants begin to agree or to disagree, clarify and elaborate, and reflect and organize their own and others' ideas and positions. As a result, discrete ideas start to come together; many smaller ideas become a few big ones, and individual understandings grow into group shared understanding. At this point, the discourse is ready to advance to the next higher level—intellectual convergence. At

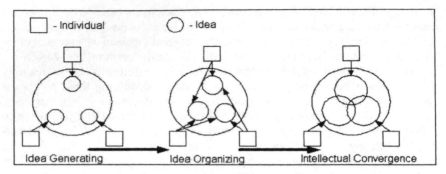

Idea Generating → Idea Organizing → Intellectual Convergence

FIG. 2.3.   Stages of learning and collaborative knowledge work.

this third stage, the group actively engages the co-construction of the knowledge based on shared understanding. The group members synthesize their ideas and knowledge into explicit points of view or products (e.g., theories, positions, works of art, manifestos, scientific theories/hypotheses). They may also extend their ideas and understanding to new territories. The outcomes of this stage are consolidated shared understanding and group convergence as evidenced by coproduction.

Outcomes (the Dependent Variables)

Learning processes, in turn, lead to the degree of attainment of the desired outcomes, particularly learning and satisfaction. These are referred to by the ALN research community as the "five pillars of quality" or effectiveness of online learning (Mayadas, Bourne, & Moore, 2002): learning effectiveness, cost effectiveness, access, student satisfaction, and faculty satisfaction. One can find a description of the five pillars at the URL http://www.sloan-c.org/effectivepractices. The following descriptions draw on these definitions, which have shaped the measurement of outcomes for much ALN research.

Learning effectiveness refers to mastery of the course materials. It also means that learners who complete an online program receive an education that is representative of the distinctive quality of the institution. The goal is that online learning is equivalent to or better than learning through the institution's other delivery modes, in particular in its traditional face-to-face, classroom-based instruction. For this book, learning effectiveness outcomes are the main focus. Objective measures of effectiveness—such as exam grades, project quality, or course grades—have been used about equally with students' or faculty's subjective impressions of quality of learning in order to measure student learning (Hiltz, Zhang, & Turoff, 2002). The results for research so far on relative learning effectiveness of the ALN and classroom environments are reviewed in chapter 3.

Student satisfaction is the second pillar of desired quality outcomes to which we pay considerable attention in this book. It:

reflects the effectiveness of all aspects of the educational experience. The goal is that all students who complete a course express satisfaction with course rigor and fairness, with professor and peer interaction, and with support services. Online students put a primary value on appropriate, constructive, and substantive interaction with faculty and other students. Effective professors help students achieve learning outcomes that match course and learner objectives by using current information and communications technologies to support active, individualized, engaged, and constructive learning. As consumers, students are satisfied when provider services—learning resources, academic and administrative services, technology and infrastructure support—are responsive, timely, and personalized. (Sloan Consortium, http://www.sloan-c.org/effectivepractices)

It is important to note that quality of learning does not always vary directly with student satisfaction. For instance, more students may express high satisfaction with a course if everybody in the course receives an A, but objective measures of their learning may show that if grades are not used as a motivator, the students do not work very hard or learn very much. Or, to take another extreme, a physics class that gets sidetracked with jokes and friendly discussions of current events may result in students who say they enjoyed the class very much, but they may not have learned a lot of physics.

Even if students are learning effectively and are satisfied, an online program cannot grow and prosper unless faculty are satisfied with their teaching experiences and find them rewarding. Most faculty find the face-to-face classroom experience very enjoyable and satisfying. If they do not like ALN teaching as well, then, in the long run, ALN will not remain a valid means of conducting a course. This outcome, which is treated in depth in chapter 8, has been described as follows:

Faculty satisfaction means that instructors find the online teaching experience personally rewarding and professionally beneficial. Personal factors contributing to faculty satisfaction with the online experience include opportunities to extend interactive learning communities to new populations of students and to conduct and publish research related to online teaching and learning. Institutional factors related to faculty satisfaction include three categories: support, rewards, and institutional study/research. Faculty satisfaction is enhanced when the institution supports faculty members with a robust and well-maintained technical infrastructure, training in online instructional skills, and ongoing technical and administrative assistance. Faculty members also expect to be included in the governance and quality assurance of online programs, especially as these relate to curricular decisions and development of policies of particular importance to the online environment (such as intellectual property, copyright, royalties, collaborative design and delivery). Faculty satisfaction is closely related to an institutional reward system that recognizes the rigor and value of online teaching. Satisfaction increases when workload assignments/assessments reflect the greater time commitment in developing and teaching online courses and when online teaching is valued on par with face-to-face teaching in promotion and tenure decisions. (http://www.sloan-c.org/effectivepractices)

Improving access to educational opportunities is one of the important goals and hoped-for outcomes of programs of online learning. It has been described as follows:

Access provides the means for all qualified, motivated students to complete courses, degrees, or programs in their disciplines of choice. The goal is to provide meaningful and effective access throughout the entire student "life cycle." Access starts with enabling prospective learners to become aware of available opportunities through effective marketing, branding, and basic program information. It continues with providing program access (for example, quantity and variety of available program options, clear program information), seamless access to courses (for example, readiness assessment, intuitive navigability), and appropriate learning resources. Access includes three areas of support: academic (such as tutoring, advising, and library); administrative (such as financial aid, and disability support); and technical (such as hardware reliability and uptime, and help desk). (Sloan Consortium, http://www.sloan-c.org/effectivepractices)

As summarized by Sener (2003), three frames of reference are useful in defining access to online learning:

- Target scope and domain.
- Strategies for improving access.
- Areas of effective practice.

In terms of target scope and domain, most ALN programs thus far have focused on enabling qualified and motivated learners to succeed and complete a course, degree, or program through online access to mainly higher learning in their chosen discipline, at a place and time of their choosing, and at affordable cost. However, in the future, we are likely to see expansions of the target scope for online programs to include many more examples of students with less than college-ready levels of skill or motivation (e.g., single mothers who are high school dropouts), precollege and lifelong learning educational levels, programs outside the United States, and programs that might be very costly, or on the other hand, free. Strategies for improving access include removing barriers, such as removing place, time, cost, or technology obstacles. Specific situations in which access barriers or issues may arise include online access to academic services (registration, counseling, academic advising) and learning resources needed (textbooks, library; Sener, 2003).

Measuring Access.   It is possible to get some subjective measures of access by asking students. For example, when students in NJIT's Virtual Classroom® project were asked about the relative convenience of online versus traditional classrooms, the vast majority of students (71%) felt that online courses provide better access to their professor, and more than two thirds felt that online learning networks are "more convenient" overall (Hiltz & Wellman, 1997). Another way to measure access opportunities is to compare the demographic profile of online students to that of face-to-face students.

Finally, cost effectiveness is an admittedly important outcome, but the accounting bottom line is generally proprietary information and has not been published in very many empirical studies. However, one noted that:

Cost-effective practices enable institutions to offer their best educational value to learners. Online programs are regionally accredited (and otherwise as applicable) in the same way as on-campus courses and, generally, online courses are part of a complete degree or certificate program. Institutional commitment to quality and finite resources require continuous improvement policies for developing and assessing cost-effectiveness measures and practices. The goal is to control costs so that tuition is affordable yet sufficient to meet development and maintenance costs—and to provide a return on investment in startup and infrastructure. (http://www.sloan-c.org/effectivepractices)

In future studies, more attention should be paid to issues of relative costs, including the amount of time required for both students and faculty. However, this book is about empirical studies of effectiveness, and because this criterion is seldom included in existing empirical studies of programs, it also plays a minor role in this text.

Dynamic Framework

The contextual factors described in the input-process-outcomes model interact with each other to define particular technology-mediated contexts in which educational processes take place. The learning and satisfaction outcomes produce feedback loops over time that result in changes to the technology, the pedagogy used by instructors, the expectations and skills of students, and the nature of the higher educational organizations themselves. Therefore, our research model is dynamic one. (See Fig. 2.4 for an attempt to illustrate dynamic change without the benefit of animation.)

For example, although student motivation is shown as an input variable, collaborative learning can in and of itself increase the motivation of learners. In a field study of the Virtual Classroom®, for instance, 55% of the students felt more motivated to work hard on their assignments because other students would be reading them (Hiltz & Wellman, 1997). A study of the effects of a computer-mediated networked learning environment on the writing of fifth-grade students compared an experimental group who sent their work via e-mail to an audience of readers who read and responded to their writing with the control group who sent their work only to the teacher. Findings suggest that when students knew they would be sending their writing to an outside reader and when they received a prompt response, there was a positive effect on the quality of writing (Allen & Thompson, 1995).

This is just one example of a feedback loop, one that occurs during the conduct of a course. Other feedback loops tend to take a longer time, such as an entire course offering or perhaps a year or two of experience. For example, if data show that online students like their courses better than they like traditional courses, this may change the institutional context by leading universities to increase faculty training, support, and rewards for online training.

SUMMARY

The online interaction learning model serves as the framework for organizing the chapters and materials in this book. In the chapter that follows, we used it as the basis for organizing and coding the results of all empirical studies that have compared face-to-face (traditional "in-seat" courses) with online learning. In part II of this text, the various chapters focus on specific portions of the model. The relationship between the model and the chapter organization is shown in Fig. 2.5.

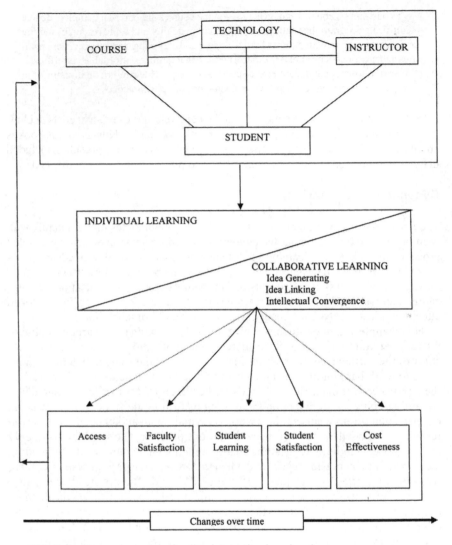

FIG. 2.4.   Dynamic model of online interaction learning theory.

QUESTIONS FOR DISCUSSION AND RESEARCH

1.   Based on the model, formulate a specific hypothesis about a variable or pro-
     cess that will increase learning effectiveness in ALNs.
2.   What are the methodological implications of the model? That is, how can
     one actually test such a complex model with feedback loops over time?
3.   Do you think that there are any important variables that are omitted from this
     model? What are they? (Cite one or more sources that include this variable.)

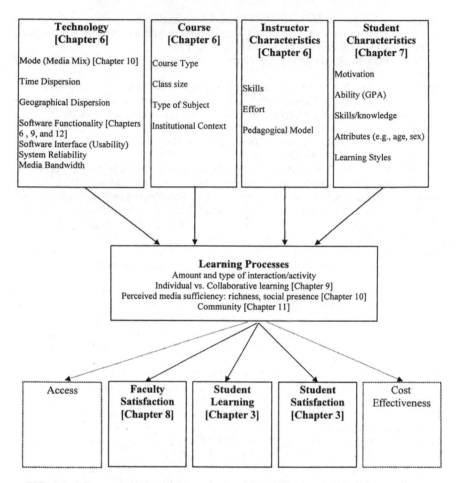

FIG. 2.5. Correspondence between the model and chapters in this volume.

REFERENCES

Airasian, P. W., & Walsh, M. E. (1997). Cautions for classroom constructivists. *Phi Delta Kappan, 78*(6), 444–449.

Alavi, M. (1994). Computer-mediated collaborative learning: An empirical evaluation. *MIS Quarterly, 18*(2), 150–174.

Alavi, M., & Leidner, D. E. (2001). Research commentary: Technology-mediated learning—a call for greater depth and breadth of research. *Information Systems Research, 12*(1), 1–10.

Allen, G., & Thompson, A. (1995). Analysis of the effect of networking on computer-assisted collaborative writing in a fifth grade classroom. *Journal of Educational Computing Research, 12*(1), 65–75.

Barron, R. M., & Kenny, D. A. (1986). The moderator-mediator variables distinction in social psychology research: Conceptual, strategic and statistical considerations. *Journal of Personality and Social Psychology, 51*(6), 1173–1182.

Benbunan-Fich, R. (2002). Improving education and training with IT. *Communications of the ACM, 45*(6), 94–99.

Bouton, C., & Garth, R. Y. (1983). *Learning in groups.* San Francisco: Jossey-Bass.

Bruffee, K. A. (1999). *Collaborative learning: Higher education, interdependence, and the Authority of Knowledge* (2nd ed.). Baltimore: Johns Hopkins University Press.

Cohen, E. G. (1984). Talking and working together: Status, interaction, and learning. In P. L. Peterson, L. C. Wilkinson, & M. Hallinan (Eds.), *The social context of education* (pp. 171–187). New York: Academic Press.

Coppola, N. W., Hiltz, S. R., & Rotter, N. (2002). Becoming a virtual professor: Pedagogical roles and asynchronous learning networks. *JMIS, 18*(4), 169–190.

Dennis, A. R., Wixom, B. H., & Vandenberg, R. J. (2001). Understanding fit and appropriation effects in group support systems via meta analysis. *MIS Quarterly, 25*(2), 167–193.

DeSanctis, G., & Gallupe, B. (1986). A foundation for the study of group decision support systems. *Management Science, 33*(5), 589–609.

Dillenbourg, P., & Schneider, D. (1994). *Collaborative learning in the Internet.* Paper presented at the Fourth International Conference on Computer Assisted Instruction, Taiwan, March.

Duffy, T. M., & Cunningham, D. J. (1996). Constructivism: Implications for the design and delivery of instruction. In D. H. Johansson (Ed.), *Handbook of research for educational communications and technology* (pp. 170–198). New York: Macmillan.

Garrison, D. R., Anderson, T., & Archer, W. (2000). Critical inquiry in a text-based environment: Computer conferencing in higher education. *The Internet and Higher Education, 2*(3), 87–105.

Goldman-Segall, R., & Maxwell, J. W. (2003). Computers, the Internet, and new media for learning. In W. M. Reynolds & G. E. Miller (Eds.), *Handbook of psychology. Volume 7: Educational psychology* (pp. 393–427). New York: Wiley.

Harasim, L. (Ed.). (1990). *On-line education: Perspectives on a new medium.* New York: Praeger/Greenwood.

Harasim, L., Hiltz, S. R., Teles, L., & Turoff, M. (1995). *Learning networks: A field guide to teaching and learning online.* Cambridge, MA: MIT Press.

Hiltz, S. R. (1988). Productivity enhancement from computer-mediated communication: A systems contingency approach. *Communications of the ACM, 31*(12), 1438–1454.

Hiltz, S. R. (1994). *The virtual classroom: Learning without limits via computer networks.* Norwood, NJ: Ablex.

Hiltz, S. R., & Wellman, B. (1997). Asynchronous learning networks as a virtual classroom. *Communications of the ACM, 40*(9), 44–49.

Hiltz, S. R., Zhang, Y., & Turoff, M. (2002). Studies of effectiveness of learning networks. In J. Bourne & J. C. Moore (Eds.), *Elements of quality of online education* (pp. 15–41). Needham, MA: SCOLE (Sloan Center for Online Education).

Johansen, R. (1992). An introduction to computer augmented teamwork. In Bostrom, Watson, & Kinney (Eds.), *Computer augmented teamwork: A guided tour* (pp. 5–15). New York: Van Nostrand Reinhold.

Johnson, D. W. (1981). Student-student interaction: The neglected variable in education. *Educational Research, 10*(1), 5–10.

Kuhn, T. S. (1970). *The structure of scientific disciplines* (Rev. ed.). Chicago: University of Chicago Press.

Leidner, D., & Jarvenpaa, S. (1995). The use of information technology to enhance management school education: A theoretical view. *MIS Quarterly,* 265–291.

Mayadas, F., Bourne, J. & Moore, J. C. (2002). Introduction. In J. Bourne & J. C. Moore (Eds.), *Elements of quality of online education* (pp. 7–11). Needham, MA: SCOLE (Sloan Center for Online Education).

Moore, M. G. (1989). Three types of interaction. *American Journal of Distance Education, 3*(2), 1–6.

Moore, A., Masterson, J. T., Christophel, D. M., & Shea, K. A. (1996). College teacher immediacy and student ratings of instruction. *Communication Education, 45*, 29–39.

Mullins, N. (1973). *Theory and theory groups in contemporary American sociology.* New York: Harper & Row.

Nichols, M. (2003). A theory for e-learning. *Educational Technology & Society, 6*(2), 1–10. Retrieved June 21, 2003, from http://ifets.ieee.org/periodical/6-2/1.html

Richardson, J. C., & Swan, K. (2003). Examining social presence in online courses in relation to students' perceived learning and satisfaction. *Journal of Asynchronous Learning, 7*(1). Retrieved March 6, 2004, from http://www.aln.org/publications/jaln/v7nl_richardson.asp

Roblyer, M. D., Edwards, J., & Havriluk, M. A. (1997). Learning theories and integration models. In M. D. Roblyer & J. Edwards (Eds.), *Integrating educational technology into teaching* (pp. 54–79). Englewood, NJ: Prentice-Hall.

Roschelle, J. (1996). Learning by collaborating: Convergent conceptual change. In T. Koschmann (Ed.), *CSCL: Theory and practice of an emerging paradigm* (pp. 209–248). Mahwah, NJ: Lawrence Erlbaum Associates.

Sener, J. (2003). *Improving access to online learning: Current issues, practices & directions.* In J. Bourne & J. C. Moore (Eds.), *Elements of quality online education* (Vol. 4, pp. 119–158). Needham, MA: Sloan Center for Online Education.

Sloan Consortium (2004). Retrieved March 6, 2004, from http://www.sloan-c.org/effective/framework.asp

Spencer, D. H. (2002). *A field study of use of synchronous computer-mediated communication in asynchronous learning networks.* Unpublished doctoral dissertation, NJIT/ Rutgers University, Newark, NJ.

Stodolsky, S. S. (1984). Frameworks for studying instructional processes in peer-workgroups. In P. L. Peterson, L. C. Wilkinson, & M. Hallinan (Eds.), *The social context of education* (pp. 107–124). New York: Academic Press.

Suppes, P. (1966). The uses of computers in education. *Scientific American, 215*(3), 206–220.

Watzawick, P. (1984). *The invented reality.* New York: Norton.

Webb, N. (1983). Predicting learning from student interactions. *Educational Psychologist, 18*(1), 33–41.

Webb, N. M. (1982). Student interaction and learning in small groups. *Review of Educational Research, 52*(3), 421–445.

3

Effectiveness for Students: Comparisons of "In-Seat" and ALN Courses

Jerry Fjermestad and Starr Roxanne Hiltz
New Jersey Institute of Technology

Yi Zhang
California State University, Fullerton

Can online courses match traditional face-to-face (F2F) courses in academic quality and rigor? Can online courses achieve the same elearning objectives as F2F courses? Can students learn as much and as well online as they do in F2F courses? Not only is the answer to these questions a resounding "yes," but there are many ways that online courses may actually surpass traditional F2F courses in quality and rigor. (Kassop, 2003)

INTRODUCTION

If students cannot learn at least as effectively in ALN as in traditional face-to-face courses, then exploring the factors that make online learning work best would not be important. Thus, the first question asked by those who are new to online learning is: Does it "work"? This chapter reviews all of the studies that have empirically compared the two modes of course delivery, and comes to an unequivocal conclusion: Yes, the evidence overwhelmingly shows that ALN is at least as effective as classroom-based learning.

One of the main components of the WebCenter for ALN Effectiveness Research (http://ALNResearch.org) is a knowledge base of empirical studies (compiled primarily by the second and third authors of this chapter). Each qualifying research article has been gleaned for key aspects of its methods and findings, which are placed into a database template, including details of the variables and hypotheses or research questions; the research methods used, including how the variables were measured; and the findings. Studies in this collection that compare measures of student outcomes for ALN versus traditional modes of delivery were analyzed in order to describe the methods that are being used, and the findings of such studies to date. This chapter describes how the analysis was conducted, and reviews the findings about comparisons of the effectiveness of ALN versus traditional face-to-face courses. It updates earlier summaries based on fewer studies and a less systematic and comprehensive review of such comparative studies (Hiltz, Zhang, & Turoff, 2002; Spencer & Hiltz, 2001). It answers the following key questions:

- What empirical studies have been conducted that compare the effectiveness of ALN and traditional courses? What were the methods, variables studied, and findings? (This information is gathered in the Appendix to this chapter.)
- What is the current overall picture of these research findings, in terms of comparisons of the effectiveness of ALN with other modes of delivery of college-level courses?

CRITERIA FOR INCLUSION IN THE PUBLISHED RESEARCH DATABASE

Papers included in the ALNResearch database must be empirical studies of the effectiveness of learning networks, and must have been published in a scientific refereed (peer-reviewed) journal or conference proceedings in the English language. The definitions and details of the criteria include:

- They are full papers (not just extended abstracts) at least five pages in length.
- *Learning networks* technology and pedagogy refers to the use of computer-mediated communication among students, as well as between instructor and students, for a substantial part of the course work. Learning networks may be used asynchronously and/or synchronously, although we are mainly concerned with courses that include substantial use of asynchronous (anytime) media. They may be used alone or in combination with other media (also known as *blended learning*), such as face-to-face lectures, videotapes, Web postings of lecture or reading or tutorial material, and so on. Not all Web-based courses use learning networks; some just post lecture-type materials or exams for downloading, do not involve extensive interaction among students in a class, and therefore do not qualify as learning networks courses.
- *Effectiveness,* as used in this chapter, is primarily concerned with learning outcomes for students, but also includes effectiveness from the instructor's point of view. It thus incorporates studies that look at student perceptions, student performance, or faculty perceptions, satisfaction, or performance in this mode of course delivery.
- To be considered as an empirical research study, a paper must include research questions or hypotheses (at least implicitly), describe some data col-

lection methods, and report some empirical results. In order to be considered an adequate empirical study, a study must have a reasonable number of subjects on which conclusions are based, defined as a minimum of at least 20 subjects included in quantitative studies. (Qualitative studies may use fewer subjects.)

CODING OF THE STUDIES FOR THIS CHAPTER

Only those studies that compare the process and outcomes of traditional face-to-face courses with courses using ALN were selected; as of November 2002, this comprised 30 studies from the database of over 100 empirical studies of ALN. The third author extracted the key aspects of research methods and findings from the database and created the Appendix table. Then, the first two authors categorized and coded the types of methods and measures used—and the findings—using the online interaction learning model (See Fig. 3.1). Thus, the dependent variable codes are aspects of the learning process (individual vs. collaborative learning, perceived media richness or sufficiency, amount and type of interaction), and outcomes (access, faculty satisfaction, student learning—broken down into objective and subjective measures—student satisfaction, and cost). The independent variable, in all cases reported in this chapter, is mode of course delivery (ALN, traditional face to face, or blended). Note that the unit of coding for this analysis is the "hypothesis"; some studies compared ALN and traditional courses on only one variable, but most included comparisons on several variables. Finally, "supercategories" were created for the dependent variables, and each finding was coded in terms of whether it showed ALN to be better (positive for ALN) than traditional courses, no different (no significant differences), or worse (negative for ALN).

HOW HAS LEARNING EFFECTIVENESS
IN ALNS BEEN MEASURED?

As shown in Table 3.1, the field study is the most frequently used method to date for comparing ALN and traditional classes. This means that students and faculty self-select the mode of course delivery, but then two or more classes are compared using measures that are as identical as possible. There were only five truly experimental studies conducted, in which students were randomly assigned to conditions. In the majority of studies that reported experimental design, almost all were a simple comparison of two conditions—face to face and ALN.

The most popular course level reported was undergraduate college courses, but nine studies did not report the course level. The number of students studied ranges up to 8,000, but the modal number is in the 50 to 100 range, which is fairly small to test for statistically significant differences. For studies that reported the type of subject matter, computer and information science (CIS) is the most frequent, followed by management. Because the use of computers is prevalent in these disciplines, this might be expected for the earliest studies.

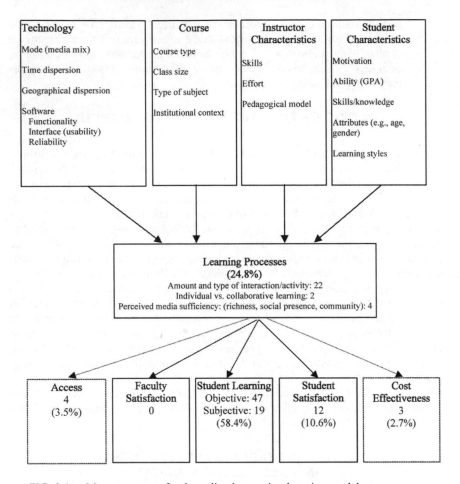

FIG. 3.1.   Measure counts for the online interaction learning model.

RESULTS: ALN VERSUS TRADITIONAL DELIVERY

In Tables 3.2 and 3.3, the results of tests of hypotheses were examined and classified. The results show that ALN is significantly "better" than traditional course sections, not significantly different, or worse. There were a total of 112 tests of various hypotheses across the seven outcome segments of the model for online interaction (Fig. 3.1); 44% of the instances were positive for ALN, 42% suggested no differences between ALN and traditional methods, whereas only 14% were not favorable to ALN. Thus, in 86% of the instances, ALN was found to be either better or equal to traditional classroom methods.

TABLE 3.1
Methods Used to Compare ALN and Traditional Courses

Study Type	Design Type	Number of Subjects	Course Level	Course Type
Case (3)	2 x 1 (14)	Up to 25 (4)	Undergrads (14)	CIS (9)
Experiments (5)	3 x 1 (2)	26 to 50 (3)	Grads (4)	Management (3)
Field (20)	2 x 2 (1)	51 to 100 (8)	Grads/under (2)	Social Science (2)
Quasi-experiment (1)	3 x 2 (1)	101 to 150 (3)	K-12 (1)	English (2)
Survey (1)		200 to 300 (5)	Not reported (9)	Education (1)
		300 to 400 (2)		Nursing (1)
		500 + 5		Other (5)
				Not reported (8)

Learning Process Measures

The learning process measures (collaborative learning, perceived media suffi-ciency, and amount and type of interaction) account for 25% (28/112) of the hy-potheses tested. Looking first at the collaborative process variables, we find that, surprisingly, only two comparative studies measured differences related to col-laborative learning. Allen and Thompson (1995) noted that fifth graders who e-mailed their work to an audience that gave feedback had significantly better writing scores than did those students who simply wrote for their teacher. Ocker and Yaverbaum (1999) discerned no significant difference in process satisfac-tion for groups of MBA students working collaboratively face to face or asynchronously.

For the few studies of media sufficiency there is a suggestion that there may be less social presence and more interaction difficulty in ALN, no difference in sense of community, and greater ease of use for ALN only. However, there is only one comparative study for each of these media sufficiency variables, so no conclusions are warranted.

By contrast, there are 21 instances (20% of all hypotheses) in which the amount and type of interaction has been compared. The results are very mixed; nine positive instances in which ALN was significantly better, five instances for no differences, and seven studies negative for ALN. What is interesting here is that the majority of the positive effects for ALN deal with communication. ALN methods clearly in-crease the communication among students (Heckman & Annabi, 2003) whether in small groups or the whole course. Furthermore, Heckman and Annabi (2003) sug-gested that instructor presence (dominance) is more pervasive in traditional face-to-face discussions than in the online discussions. This leads to communica-tion inhibition in the classroom and increased student participation in ALN.

TABLE 3.2
Summary of Measures of Learning Process

Measures	Positive for ALN	No Differences	Negative for ALN
Learning process: Collaboration			
Ideas useful	1		
Process satisfaction		1	
Total: 2	**1**	**1**	
Learning process: Media sufficiency			
Social presence			1
Interaction difficulty			1
Sense of community		1	
Ease of use	1		
Total: 4	**1**	**1**	**2**
Learning process: Interaction			
Comment length	1		
Comments—humanizing		1	
Comments—organizing	1		
Comments—student driven	2		
Comments—teacher driven			2
Comments—social process			1
Comments—number	1		
Coordination approach		1	
Critical thinking	1		
Critical thinking—lower order			1
Critical thinking—higher order	1		
Discussion quality & breadth	1		3
Information transfer		1	
Interaction dynamics & quality		2	
Student participation	1		
Total: 21	**9**	**5**	**7**

TABLE 3.3
Summary of Measures

Measures	Positive for ALN	No Differences	Negative for ALN
Access			
Access to instructor	2		
Access to course materials	1		
Perceived access		1	
Total: 4	**3**	**1**	
Student satisfaction			
Boring	1		
Extent of communications	1		
Class evaluations			1
Overall Web experience	1		
Participation in learning		1	
Recommend a friend			1
Satisfaction	1	3	1
Take another class	1		
Total: 12	**5**	**4**	**3**
Learning: Objective measures			
Conceptual understanding	1		
Content		1	
Course completion		1	
Course grade	2	7	
	1 (ALN + FtF)		
Creativity		1	
Documentation		1	
Final exam grade	3	8	
Midterm/quiz grades		4	
Quality	2		
	1 (ALN + FtF)	1	1
Leaning effectiveness	1 (ALN + FtF)		
Postwriting score	1		

(continued on next page)

TABLE 3.3 (continued)

Measures	Positive for ALN	No Differences	Negative for ALN
Report completeness	1		
Report length	2		
Software specification	1	1	
Task completion		1	
Teamwork		1	
Technical ability			1
Timeliness		1	
Tool use		1	
Total: 47	**16**	**29**	**2**
Student learning: Subjective measures			
Class evaluation	1		
Deep learning	1		
Learning interest	1		
Overall learning		1	1
Expected grade		1	
Group case evaluation	1		
Perceived learning	3	3	
Perceived skill development	1		
Quality learning	2		
Self-reported learning	1		
Solution satisfaction	2		
Total: 19	**13**	**5**	**1**
Cost			
Development cost	1		
Operational cost		1	1
Total: 3	**1**	**1**	**1**
Grand Totals: 112	**49**	**47**	**16**

Access

In the four instances in which relative access was studied, three showed better access for ALN, whereas one showed no difference. For instance, in Sandercock and Shaw's (1999) study of first-year sports science students, 94% of students agreed that ALN made it easier to access course materials.

Faculty Satisfaction

Although there are some studies of sources of satisfaction and dissatisfaction among ALN faculty, surprisingly there are no comparative empirical studies of faculty satisfaction. This creates an opportunity for research. From the authors' point of view, ALN methods require more work than the traditional classroom situation. The trade-off comes from not having to be in a scheduled classroom versus being online several times a day, every day, for the duration of the course.

Student Satisfaction

Student satisfaction represents 11% (12 instances) of all of the measures that were contrasted; five were positive for ALN, four showed no difference, and three were negative for ALN. For example, Andriole's (1997) study at Drexel found that 80% of the students felt that conventional courses are more boring than ALN courses. In an experiment on team learning in a laboratory exercise by Wagner and Tuttas (2001), students in a distributed online lab were more satisfied than were those in a traditional laboratory room. In another study by Arvan, Ory, Bullock, Burnaska, and Hanson (1998) that included 8,000 undergraduates at the University of Illinois, the subjects rated the overall Web experiences as very satisfying, and most would take another class in this format.

Student Learning: Objective Measures

Student learning has been the most frequently measured variable for comparative studies. In 47 instances, objective measures of learning have been used, including course grade (10 instances), midterm examination grade (4 instances), or final exam grade (11). For 16 comparisons of objective measures, ALN was found to be significantly better. This includes Alavi's 1994 study, which noted significantly higher final exam scores for online students. The majority of studies (29 instances) discerned no significant difference in objective outcomes, including Arbaugh's (2000) study of MBA students, in which those in the traditional classroom outperformed the Internet students on a precourse test, but there was no significant difference in postcourse scores. Piccoli, Ahmad, and Ives (2001) also reported that there were no significant differences in performance on midterm and final exams between students enrolled in a virtual course versus those in a traditional classroom environment. Among the minority of two cases of significantly worse objective results for ALN, Parker and Gemino (2001) found that ALN students scored significantly lower on a technical ability test, but higher on a test of conceptual understanding.

Student Learning: Subjective Measures

There are 19 findings related to subjective measures of student learning (in which the students themselves assess the results, usually on a postcourse questionnaire). Thirteen of these 19 show better results for ALN. For example, Hiltz (1993) found that the majority of ALN students reported that the technology improved the quality of their learning; this was replicated in a 2000 study in which ALN students self-reported higher levels of learning than did face-to-face students. There were four examples of no difference in subjectively reported learning, including a study of almost 2,000 students conducted by Benbunan-Fich and Hiltz (2002), which determined that although students in ALN sections obtained significantly higher grades than did those in traditional sections, there was no difference in perception of learning.

Perceived learning was used in six instances. Three were positive and three were neutral for ALN. Piccoli et al. (2001) reported that self-efficacy was higher in the virtual environment than in the traditional one. They went on to further suggest that the undergraduates in the virtual environments attributed learning outcomes to their own effort and ability. This supports some observations by Simon, Grover, Teng, and Whitcomb (1996) that many students are unfamiliar with the new learning environments (i.e., ALN) and that they have not developed the strategies that allow them to take advantage of the high levels of learner control and flexibility available to them. This may account for the large number of "no differences" in the objective learning measures as well as the counts for perceived learning. There was only one instance in which subjective assessments of learning were poorer for ALN.

Cost Effectiveness

The only study of comparative costs was conducted by Arvan et al. (1998) for the University of Illinois. For both development cost and operational cost, there were so many variations related to the specific measure, course, experience of the instructor, and so on that there are no significant differences overall. This is a very important area for further study.

SUMMARY

As we stated at the beginning of this chapter, the most important question about the effectiveness of ALN is: How well can students learn, relative to traditional courses? The results for this variable are quite positive. Of 47 comparisons of objective measures of learning, 16 showed ALN to be significantly better, 29 showed no significant difference, and in only 2 did face-to-face sections score higher. For student self-assessments of learning, results are similar: 11 significantly better for ALN, 4 "no difference," and 2 higher for traditional sections. Thus, there is a great deal of empirical evidence to support the finding that students can learn at least as well online as they do in traditional sections.

On measures of the amount of interaction and of student satisfaction, the results for comparisons are mixed, with "no significant differences" being the overall conclusion. However, when these fairly global concepts are decomposed into more specific components, there may be more consistent differences (e.g., students are satisfied with ALN in specific ways, and dissatisfied in other specific ways).

There are relatively few studies of other aspects of the comparative process and outcome of learning. In particular, there are no comparative studies of faculty satisfaction, only one of relative costs, and only four dealing with access.

Details of the methods and findings of each of the comparative studies of ALN versus traditional course effectiveness are shown in the Appendix to this chapter. The reader is encouraged to look through these studies to obtain a concrete feel for the state of the art of existing ALN research. In addition, many of these studies are mentioned in subsequent chapters, and thus the familiarity with the studies that can be gained by reading through the detailed descriptions here will be helpful in understanding those discussions.

We have presented the results of these comparative studies at the beginning of the book, because doubts about the efficacy of online learning need to be dispelled. However, we agree with many critics that these comparative field studies that simply ask the question "Which is better?" are not very fruitful and tend not to be very methodologically rigorous. In the next two chapters, we suggest how both quantitative and qualitative methods for studying ALN can be optimized to obtain deeper understanding of its dynamics. ALN is different from but not "better" or "worse" than traditional classrooms. Part II of the book discusses what we do know and do not know, and what we need to know, about specific aspects of learning online.

QUESTIONS FOR DISCUSSION AND RESEARCH

1. In an earlier paper that compared a subset of the studies included in the analysis for this chapter, Hiltz, Zhang, and Turoff (2002) concluded: "The evidence is overwhelming that ALN tends to be as effective or more effective than traditional modes of course delivery, at the university level. There really is no need for more studies to explore this question. What we need is more research that will enable us to make it even more effective, especially as new technologies proliferate" (p. 25). At a meeting of ALN researchers, this proved to be a very controversial statement. Many felt that because there are a substantial number of "doubters" who have not been convinced that ALN is at least as effective as traditional courses by the 30 or so empirical studies that have already been published, there should be more such studies whose main objective is to compare the outcomes of the two modes. What do you feel about whether there should be more studies that try to compare the outcomes of the two modes, and why?

2. How might you design a study of relative faculty effort and satisfaction with teaching the same courses in both face-to-face and online modes? What dependent variables would be important to include, and how would your study design take into account changes in reactions with experience teaching online?

3. The issue of relative "access" opportunities for students provided by on-campus versus online courses has not been studied much at all. Why do you think that this is so? How would you design a study of this for your university, taking into account prospective students as well as current students?

APPENDIX: SUMMARY OF INDIVIDUAL COMPARATIVE STUDIES

Paper Reference	Method	Hypotheses	Measures of Effectiveness	Findings
Alavi (1994)	Field Experiment • Comparative analysis of treatment groups (treatment: teaching theater with group decision support systems, or GDSS two groups; non-GDSS traditional classroom, 1 group). • 127 MBA students, with 79 in GDSS condition and 48 in non-GDSS condition.	(Implicit) Individuals in GDSS groups have higher collaborative learning effectiveness than do individuals in non-GDSS groups.	Dependent variable: Collaborative learning effectiveness. Measures of the dependent variable: Perceived skill development, self-reported learning, learning interest, class evaluation, group case evaluation, expected grade, exam scores. *Note:* The first five measures emanate as factors from the principal component analysis of 28 self-reported learning and class evaluation variables. The last measure is an objective measure of effectiveness.	• Higher perceived skill developed by participants in GDSS groups ($p < 0.001$). • Higher collaborative learning effectiveness for participants in GDSS groups, in terms of self-reported learning, learning interest, class evaluation, and group case evaluation ($p < 0.05$) • No significant difference in mean expected grades. • Midterm exam scores were not significantly different, but GDSS groups achieved significantly higher final exam scores ($p < 0.01$).

| Alavi, Yoo, and Vogel (1997) | 46 MBA students, with 21 students at University of Maryland and 25 at the University of Arizona.

• Case study.

• Comparative analysis of groups (in-class learning experience of local/distance students).

• Implicit longitudinal analysis (in-class learning experience: time of measurement is a main effect).

• Cross-sectional analysis (out-of-class learning experience). | *(Implicit)*

H1: Information-technology-enabled partnership in management education is less effective than the traditional classroom pedagogy.

H1a: In-class experiences of students in remote locations are different from the experiences of local students, when classes are linked in virtual space.

H1b: In-class experiences of students vary with the time of sampling/measurement (times of measurement: Weeks 4, 9, 13 of the semester). | Dependent variable: pedagogical effectiveness.

Measures of the dependent variable: In-class learning experience (perceived learning, participation in learning, social presence, classroom evaluation). All four measures are factors emanating from the principal component analysis with varimax rotation; the first two factors emanated from the learning variables, the last two from the classroom assessment variables.

Exam scores | In-class learning experience: No significant main or interaction effects of time or location were found on students' perceived learning or participation in the learning process. Distant students rated both social presence and classroom dynamics significantly lower than did the local students.

Out-of-class learning experience: Student scores for satisfaction with learning experience and with participation were significantly higher than for the information technology-enabled partnership. Individual students' self-reported learning scores were not significantly different. |

(continued on next page)

Paper Reference	Method	Hypotheses	Measures of Effectiveness	Findings
Allen and Thompson (1995)	• Field experiment compared collaborative writing in traditional classroom and ALN. • In the experimental group, the four writing assignments were sent by e-mail to the college student readers. In the control group, the teachers wrote comments on the paper. • Subjects were 93 fifth-grade students (45 males and 48 females) in a K–12 public school in a rural Midwestern state.	*(Implicit)* Students with the computer network-linked audience will: • Write longer and higher-quality texts. • Have an improved attitude toward writing and computers.	• A pre- and postquestionnaire was given to each student to obtain demographic data and to ascertain the attitude of the student toward writing with computers and writing to an audience. • A pre- and postwriting assignment was rated using a holistic scoring instrument. • Data from the writing samples were analyzed using ANCOVA to factor out initial differences and determine if there was a statistically significant difference in the final writing sample. • Text length.	• For the holistic score of the post-writing assignment, the experimental ALN group had a significantly higher mean score. • Posttest writing length was longer for the experimental (ALN) group. • Overall, females scored significantly better on the holistic quality of the posttest writing sample. • Males in the experimental group scored significantly higher on the holistic quality of the posttest writing sample. • There was no significant difference in the means of the composite attitude items of writing with a computer, writing with a partner, or writing to an audience.

| Andriole (1997) | • Students from three face-to-face (FTF) and three ALN courses taught by the same instructor (number not available), for comparative evaluation of student performance.
• 207 students from 17 courses, for student survey (course evaluation).
• Case study.
• Concurrent design and evaluation of an ALN course.
• Comparative evaluation of FTF and ALN courses. | (Unstated but tested, albeit informally)
• Student performance (in "systems analysis & design" courses) is consistently superior in the ALN mode relative to the FTF mode.
• Student evaluations of ALN courses are more positive relative to their evaluation of FTF courses. | Student performance (comparative measures): Quality of requirements models, prototypes, prototype evaluation, software specifications, documentation, teamwork; overall creativity; ability to use design tools; timeliness. Student evaluation measures: Perceived learning, extent of communication, access to instructor, and overall attitude. | Student performance: ALN students always performed at least as well and often better than did their conventional counterparts on all measures. Prototype quality was consistently higher in the ALN courses than for the conventional courses. Student Evaluation:
• 97% of students felt they had more access to the instructor in ALN courses.
• 80% felt that conventional courses were more boring than ALN courses
• 67% felt they had more communication with peer students in ALN courses.
• 66% felt they had learned more in the ALN course.
• 99% of the ALN students felt that seeing the ideas and assignments of others was useful. |

(continued on next page)

Paper Reference	Method	Hypotheses	Measures of Effectiveness	Findings
Arvan, Ory, Bullock, Burnaska, and Hanson (1998)	8,000 undergraduate students, with subjects in individual case studies ranging from 110 to 200. • Case study. • Comparative analysis of groups (ALN/non-ALN, ALN/ALN). • Implicit longitudinal analysis (performance through the term). • Cost-benefit analysis.	*(Implicit)* H1 (not formally tested): ALN achieves lower operational cost per student relative to traditional classroom. H2 (formally tested in some cases): ALN results in lower instructional quality relative to traditional classrooms.	• Operational cost per student measured by: class size; student–faculty ratio; total instructional hours; distribution of instructional hours over full-time faculty, graduate TAS, and undergraduate TAS. • Instructional quality measured by: Exam scores, student assessments (difficulty of the material, perceived learning, overall experience, recommendation to self/peers, ease of use of the Web, overall Web experience).	Overall, mixed results on differences between ALN and traditional, which can be summed up as "no significant differences." This depends on the specific measure, course, experience of the instructor, etc.

| Benbunan-Fich and Hiltz (1999) | 140 undergraduate students in CIS350 (computers and society).

• Field experiment.

• Two-by-two factorial design, crossing two modes of communication (manual offline vs. Asynchronous computer conference) and two types of teamwork (individuals working alone vs. Individuals working in groups). | H1a: Groups will produce higher-quality solutions to ethical dilemmas.
H1b: Participants working through an ALN will produce higher-quality solutions.

H2a: Groups will submit longer reports.
H2b: Participants working through an ALN will submit longer reports.
H2c: Interaction:
ALN-supported groups will produce the longest reports. | Task performance:

• Solution quality (expert panel evaluation of reports based on clarity, organization of ideas, concept application, correctness and effectiveness of recommendations).

• Length of reports.
Learning: Perceived (self-reported) learning, perceived collaborative learning, final exam grades.
Satisfaction: Solution satisfaction (self-reported), perception of discussion quality. | • ALN-supported participants had significantly better solution quality than did their manual counterparts ($p = 0.05$; H1b supported).

• Group reports were significantly longer than were individual reports; online conditions submitted longer reports; average length of reports produced by computer-supported groups was significantly greater than individual manual reports (H2 fully supported). |

(continued on next page)

APPENDIX (continued)

Paper Reference	Method	Hypotheses	Measures of Effectiveness	Findings
		H3a: Group participants will perceive higher levels of self-reported learning. H3b: ALN-supported participants will perceive higher levels of learning. H3c: ALN-supported groups will perceive the highest levels of self-reported learning. H3d: ALN-supported and face-to-face groups will report about the same levels of perception of collaborative learning. H4a: Solution satisfaction will be greater for those participants working in groups. H4b: Solution satisfaction will be lower for ALN-supported participants. H4c (interaction): Individuals working through an ALN will be the least satisfied. H5: ALN-supported groups will report lower levels of discussion quality.		• Perceived learning, no significant main effects; no significant differences among conditions were found for perceptions of collaborative learning (H3d) and final exam scores; but there was a significant interaction effect between teamwork and technology (H3c supported). Groups/online reported better perceived learning than did other conditions. • Groups reported significantly higher levels of solution satisfaction than individual participants (H4a supported); individuals online reported the lowest levels of solution satisfaction (H4c), but this interaction effect was not statistically significant. • Manual groups reported significantly better perceptions of discussion quality than did ALN-supported groups (H5 supported).

Benbunan-Fich and Hiltz (2002)	1,974 students who completed postcourse questionnaires, in undergraduate and graduate courses in CIS, computer engineering, management, and the humanities, between 1997 and 2000: • Field study with postcourse questionnaires. • Independent variable is three modes of course delivery: completely distance courses using ALN for class discussions and assignments plus other recorded media for lectures; mixed-mode courses using FTF lectures plus ALN; and traditional FTF courses with no use of ALN.	H1a: Grades earned by students using the virtual classroom ALN system will be equal to or better than those earned by students in traditional FTF courses. H1b: Perceptions of learning outcomes by students using the ALN system will be equal to or better than those earned by students in traditional FTF courses. H2a: Female students will achieve better grades than male students in ALN courses. H2b: Female students will be more likely than male students to perceive favorable learning outcomes from ALN.	Learning perception measured through a student survey and learning performance as evidenced by the final grades obtained by the students in each course. The unidimensionality of the learning perception construct was validated using factor analysis. *Index Items:* • Perceived learning (Cronbach's Alpha = .90). • Gained more interest in the subject. • Learned a lot of factual material. • Gained understanding of basic concepts. • Improved ability to communicate clearly.	• H1a: Students in ALN sections obtained higher grades than did those in FTF sections. • H1b: The perception of learning is about the same across modes. • H2a: Female students obtained higher grades than did their male counterparts, but this achievement is not affected by mode. • H2b: In terms of learning perceptions, all conditions reported similar levels; these perceptions were not affected by gender. • H3a: Final grades were higher for graduate courses than for undergraduate courses, regardless of the delivery mode; no significant interaction.

(continued on next page)

Paper Reference	Method	Hypotheses	Measures of Effectiveness	Findings
	• Course type: "More technical" courses conveyed a higher degree of technical knowledge (e.g., calculus, programming languages, operating systems), whereas the "less technical" courses focused more on social or managerial subject matter.	H3a: Final grades in ALN courses will be higher for graduate students than for undergraduate students. H3b: Graduate students will be more likely than undergraduate students to perceive course outcomes in ALN to be positive. H4a: The use of ALN in less technical courses will result in higher student grades. H4b: Students taking less technical courses and using an ALN will report better learning perceptions than students in other conditions.	• Increased critical thinking skills. • Improved ability to integrate facts. • Became more confident in expressing ideas.	• H3b: Significant interaction: graduate students in mixed mode courses reported the highest perceptions of learning, whereas undergraduates in the same mode reported the lowest. • H4a: Students in less technical courses received higher grades than did those in technical courses, and students in ALN conditions also earned higher grades. However, there was no interaction between mode and course type. • H4b: No significant differences in learning perceptions could be attributed to the mode, the course type, or their interaction.

Benbunan-Fich, Hiltz, and Turoff (2001)	50 CIS350 students, with 28 in the FTF (control) condition, and 22 in the ALN (experimental) condition. The 28 subjects in the FTF condition were (randomly) grouped into five teams, and the 22 subjects in the ALN condition were also organized into five teams. • Field experiment. • Comparative analysis of groups: experimental (ALN)/control (FTF) • Level of analysis: group. • Pilot tests to determine the appropriate allocation of time for task completion, for each condition.	H1: ALN-supported groups will have broader discussions than will their manual counterparts. H2: When transferring the contents of their discussion to the final report, FTF groups will incur a greater loss of information than will ALN-supported groups. H3: ALN-supported groups will submit more complete reports than will their manual counterparts. H4: ALN-supported groups will produce longer solutions to the case than will their manual counterparts. H5: ALN-supported groups will report lower levels of discussion quality than will FTF groups.	Dependent variables and measures: • Discussion breadth (% of issues discussed, with reference to a master list). • Efficiency in information transfer (% of the issues discussed that were represented in the final report). • Completeness of reports (and % of the issues in the master list, represented in the final report). • Report length (word count). • Discussion quality (perceived discussion quality—overall quality, process effectiveness, outcome satisfaction, quality of execution of discussion, adequacy of exploration of issues, development of content). • Coordination approach (based on discussion transcripts).	• H1: Asynchronous groups had broader discussions than did their manual counterparts. On average, ALN groups mentioned about 72% of the issues whereas FTF covered about 52% of them. • H2 was not supported; both conditions revealed 15% loss of items. • H3: More complete reports were generated by ALN groups. • H4: The ALN-supported groups were able to produce longer reports (682 words on average) than did their manual counterparts (405 words on average). • H5: Manual groups reported significantly better perceptions of discussion quality than did ALN groups ($p = .0001$).

(continued on next page)

APPENDIX (continued)

Paper Reference	Method	Hypotheses	Measures of Effectiveness	Findings
		H6: ALN-supported groups will tend to follow parallel or pooled coordination approaches, while FTF groups will adopt a more tightly coupled mode.		• H6: ALN groups adopted (parallel/pooled) coordination approaches, whereas FTF groups adopted approaches with medium degree of interdependence (concurrent/sequential; $p < 0.01$).
Carr-Chellman, Dyer, and Breman (2000)	• Field study. • First group of 28 learners enrolled in traditional university's graduate program and met as a group once a week for 3-hour sessions. Second group of 23 learners were enrolled in the distance university's program. It employed FTF meetings at its campus along with telephone, IRC Internet relay (chat), Web discussion boards, and e-mails.	Research question: Will there be collaborative, authentic problem-based learning and solving at a distance?	• Interviews with volunteers from each group. • Both groups were observed through focused participant observations. Field notes were collected as well as a variety of documents such as class projects and problem solutions. All documents were analyzed (along with interview transcripts, student journals, surveys, audio conference transcripts, and observed field notes) using content analysis and thematic analysis.	The distance university students were able to complete a complex instructional project with equal success to that of the traditional residential students.

Dutton, Dutton, and Perry (2002; see also Dutton, Dutton, & Perry, 2001)

- A field experiment with two class sections on Programming in C++ at North Carolina State University in fall 1999.

- 104 students in the on-campus lecture sections of CSC114 met in two 50-minute lectures sessions with a once-per-week 3-hour structured lab. 89 students in the online section, which consisted of online lectures and materials, took the lab online or on campus and exams online or on campus.

Research questions:

- Who is likely to take online classes?

- What factors influence performance among online students, and are those factors different for online and lecture students?

- Factor that relates to the difference between online and lecture students. Measures: survey data.

- Students' performance (four explanatory variables are homework completion, undergraduate status, working, and prior computer experience). Measures: the final exam scores, a modified course grade, and the course completion rate. The comparisons between online and lecture students were carried out using ordinary least squares (OLS) regression.

Factors that relate to the difference between online and lecture students:

- Online students were, on average, more than five years older than were lecture students.

- Degree program: Only 48% of the online students were enrolled in an undergraduate program, as opposed to nearly 85% of the lecture students ($p < .01$)

- Number of credit hours: 82% of the lecture students carried 12 or more semester hours, whereas only 38% of the online students were full time.

- Responsibilities outside class: Online students expected to work more during the semester (84% vs. 55%). Child-care responsibilities were 14.6% for online as opposed to 6.7% for lecture students (significant).

(continued on next page)

APPENDIX (continued)

Paper Reference	Method	Hypotheses	Measures of Effectiveness	Findings
Dutton, Dutton, & Perry, 2002, (con't.)				• Commuting: The 48% online students with a long commute is double the percentage of comparable lecture students (23%; significant). • Preparation for online class: More than half of the online students had some previous programming experience vs. 36.5% of the lecture students (significant). • Perceived needs: Opportunity for FTF contact with the instructor and other students, motivation from regular class meetings, better learning from hearing a lecture, and advice from advisor or other official were more important for lecture students; time commuting to class and flexibility in setting pace and time for studying were more important for online students (significant).

Student Performance:

• Online students made significantly higher exam grades than did lecture students. Course grades for online students were higher (but not significant).

• Working lowered grade performance, and prior computer experience improved grade performance.

• Probability of completion was no longer significant when enrolled semester hours were controlled. Homework grade showed significant positive effects for both online and lecture students; semester hours was a significant predictor of course completion for online students but not for lecture students.

(continued on next page)

APPENDIX (continued)

Paper Reference	Method	Hypotheses	Measures of Effectiveness	Findings
Fallah, How, and Ubell (2000)	• Field experiment: 19 graduate students in telecommunication management (7 in Web-campus condition, and 12 in the on-campus condition). • Blind study procedure: Grading of (identical) midterm exams of students in both conditions by the instructor, who was ignorant of the identities of students or condition.	*(Implicit)* Student performance in the Web-campus condition is different from student performance in the on-campus condition.	Dependent variable: student performance. Measure: Midterm exam scores.	The average score for the online class was slightly higher than that of the conventional class; the dispersion was much lower for the online class than for the conventional class; however, a comparison of means (standard *t*- test) could not reject the null hypothesis of equal means.
Hadidi and Sung (2000)	66 graduate MIS students: • Comparative. • Survey.	*(Implicit)* There will be no difference in quality of education between the online and FTF sections.	Grades and six questions on evaluation of the course and instructor.	No significant differences between the FTF and online classes in any of the subjective satisfaction measures, self-reported motivation, or in grades.

Heckman and Annabi (2003)	120 undergraduate students at University of Syracuse.	*(Implicit)*	Content coding of all utterances into major categories, each with 3–4 subcategories.	• FTF had more individual utterances (mean = 287) than did ALN (mean = 74).
	• Repeated measures field experiment with four groups of students, each of whom completed two case study discussions, one FTF and one via ALN (counterbalanced for order).	Discourse processes will differ between FTF and ALN discussions. ALN discussions will evidence more complex and critical thinking by students.		• FTF was much more "back and forth," with the teacher asking questions and the students responding.
	• Content analysis scheme was based on Garrison and Aviv's methods (interaction coded into four main categories: social, teaching, cognitive, and discourse). The observation period was one week for each condition (90 minutes FTF; 7 days asynchronous, using WebCT). Coding by two judges; interrater reliability = 86%.			• Presence of the teacher much more pervasive in FTF (141) vs. ALN (11 utterances). (Ratio of student to teacher utterances was 5:1 in ALN, compared to 1:1 in FTF.)
				• Student utterances were longer in ALN (100 words vs. 30 words), whereas teacher utterances were shorter in ALN (50 words vs. 80 words).
				• ALN discussions were much more formal and employed passive voice more.
				• There were a greater number of social processes utterances in FTF (154 vs. 124), but the proportions of the three major categories (affective response, cohesive response, interactive response) were very similar.

(continued on next page)

65

APPENDIX (continued)

Paper Reference	Method	Hypotheses	Measures of Effectiveness	Findings
Heckman & Anabi, 2003 (con't.)				• The FTF discussions were much more driven by questions from the teacher. • There were nearly twice as many instances of cognitive process in the FTF discussion than in ALN, but they were predominantly in the lower-order "exploration" category (e.g., rote factual response). In contrast, the ALN discussion contained more high-level cognitive process instances, both in absolute and relative terms. There were almost twice as many instances of "analysis" in ALN discussions.

| Hillman (1999) | • Field experiment: Four FTF courses and two comparable courses taught by CMC were analyzed.

• Content analysis of discourse. | *(Implicit)*
• Teachers will utter at least two thirds of the sentences in the class.

• FTF teachers will use the highest amount of organizing.

• FTF teachers will use lecturing more than any other group.

• Computer-mediated communication (CMC) participants will have higher levels of humanizing and opining than will FTF participants. | • The coding system used was an adaptation of Bellack et al.'s (1966) model of pedagogical moves.

• Each sentence is coded on three levels: the purpose of the sentence, the mechanism of the sentence (how the subject of the sentence was discussed), and the subject (what was being discussed).

• Intercoder agreement (Cohen's kappa) was > .90. | • 73% of the sentences in the FTF classroom were uttered by the instructor, as opposed to 49% in the CMC course.

• The percentage of sentences used for organizing was highest for CMC teachers (25%), then CMC students (18%), then FTF teachers (2%), then FTF students (0%).

• CMC students used lecturing the most (59% of their sentences), then CMC teachers (40%), then FTF teachers (37%), then FTF students (7%).

• CMC participants used humanizing sentences only slightly more than did FTF participants.

• CMC students had a greater percentage of opining (11%) than did other groups (4%, 4%, 3%). |

(continued on next page)

Paper Reference	Method	Hypotheses	Measures of Effectiveness	Findings
Hiltz (1993; see also Hiltz, 1994)	• Longitudinal, comparative, and quasi-experimental study of 315 undergraduates in ALN (virtual classroom, or VC) and traditional courses in a variety of disciplines on three campuses, mid-1980s.	H1: There will be no significant differences in scores measuring mastery of material.	Pre- and postquestionnaires, grade distributions in matched sections of courses.	H1: Supported—in one of five courses (computer science), VC final grades were significantly better.
		H2: Students will report that the VC improves the overall quality of the learning experience.		H2: Supported.
		H3: Those students who experience "group" or "collaborative" learning in the VC are most likely to judge the outcomes of online courses to be superior to the outcomes of traditional courses.		H3: Supported.
		H4: High-ability students will experience more positive outcomes in the VC.		H4: Supported. Although students with the highest SAT scores (500 and above) received higher grades and gave the highest subjective ratings to the VC, even students at the lowest levels were, on average, able to perform at a satisfactory level in the VC.
		H5: Students with more positive precourse attitudes will be more likely to participate actively online and to perceive greater benefits from the VC mode.		H5: Supported.

| Hiltz, Benbunan-Fich, Coppola, Rotter, and Turoff (2000). | A 3-year longitudinal field study of 26 courses that are part of an undergraduate degree in information systems compared the process and outcomes of learning using an online anytime/anywhere environment to sections taught in the traditional classroom. | H6: Students with a greater "sphere of control" will be more likely to regularly and actively participate online and to perceive greater benefits from the VC mode.

H7: There will be significant differences in process and outcome among courses when mode of delivery is controlled (an interaction effect between mode and course).

H1: ALNs can improve access to education, as compared to traditional FTF classrooms.

H2: ALNs can improve the quality of learning as self-reported by students.

H3: ALNs can improve quality of learning as measured by grades. | • Access to education was measured by student self-reports of convenience and access to professors.
• Quality of learning (via student self-reporting) was measured by questionnaire.
• Quality of learning as measured by grades or similar assessments of quality of student mastery of course material. | H6: Not supported.

H7: There are significant differences among courses in grade distributions; no consistent differences between modes of course delivery; and some interaction between course and mode.

• H1: ALNs improve access to education (supported).
• H2: ALNs improve the quality of learning as self-reported by students (supported).
• H3: ALN = FTF (no significant differences in grades). |

(continued on next page)

APPENDIX (continued)

Paper Reference	Method	Hypotheses	Measures of Effectiveness	Findings
Hsu, Hiltz, and Turoff (1992)	Third- and fourth-year engineering students taking an introduction to management course. Over a 2-year period, five introductory management courses were divided into competitive teams and participated in their virtual companies for a semester-long period.	*(Implicit)* H1: Students in a virtual classroom will perform better than those in only an FTF classroom. H2: Availability of shared database and spreadsheet tools will further enhance performance.	Effectiveness of learning management, quality of business decisions. Measures: • A group summary report. • A composite index derived from the final performance scoreboard built into the game model.	For the group summary report, the differences in grade between the control groups and the experimental groups were statistically significant. The performance index of the experimental groups is double that of the control groups, on the average.
Kwok and Ma (1999)	83 second-year undergraduate students enrolled in a distributed information systems course, average age 21.5. • 1×2 experiment on the use of an Internet-based group support system (GSS) for the assessment of student projects (compared to FTF).	H1: Subjects in a GSS-supported collaborative assessment environment will score higher on deep approach to learning than will subjects in a collaborative assessment environment that is not supported by GSS. H2: Subjects in a GSS-supported assessment environment will achieve a higher level of project grades than will subjects not supported by GSS.	• Questionnaires. • A bilingual version of the study process questionnaire (SPQ) was chosen to assess students' approaches to learning, in which students are asked to rate themselves on a 5-point scale for 42 items addressing learning motives and strategies. • Students' project grades.	• The mean score of deep approach to learning of the GSS-supported groups achieved after the treatment (47.69) was significantly higher than the mean score before the experiment (43.63; $p < .01$). • The mean score (79.27) for students' projects in the GSS-supported group was significantly higher than that of the control group (77.13; $p = .04$).

Leasure, Davis, and Thievon (2000)	• Comparative field experiment, 48 in a traditional section vs. 18 in a Web-based section.	Research questions: • What are the differences in outcomes between students who completed the course via Web-based course delivery as compared to students who completed the course via traditional classroom methods? • What reasons do students use in choosing to enroll in either a Web-based course or a traditionally delivered educational course? • Examination grades and course grade. • Pre- and postcourse surveys.	Course outcome: There was no significant difference in examination scores on the three multiple-choice examinations or the course grade. Reasons for enrolling in different sections: • Traditional section: the perception of increased interaction, decreased opportunity to procrastinate, immediate feedback, and more meaningful learning activities. • Web sections: cost, convenience, and flexibility. These students also perceived themselves as more knowledgeable in the use of computers. • At the end of the semester, both groups indicated satisfaction with their choice.
Navarro and Shoemaker (2000)	Field study compared "cyberlearners" ($N = 49$) to traditional learners ($N = 151$).	Research question: Can "cyberlearners" perform as well as traditional learners? H1: Cyberlearners will be as satisfied as traditional learners. Two evaluation instruments used in the study: • Final exams with 15 identical questions were graded using blind scoring. • Attitudinal survey.	• Cyberlearners performed significantly better on the final exam than did the traditional learners. • No significant difference in perceived course quality and student satisfaction with the course. *(continued on next page)*

APPENDIX (continued)

Paper Reference	Method	Hypotheses	Measures of Effectiveness	Findings
Ocker and Yaverbaum (1999)	43 graduate MBA students participated in an experiment using a single-factor, counterbalanced, repeated measures design. Experimental groups completed two back-to-back collaborative assignments. For the other assignments, groups met FTF for the initial meeting.	H1: There will be no difference in learning between asynchronous and FTF groups.	Dependent variable: learning performance.	H1: Learning measure—no significant differences in quizzes.
		H2: There will be no difference in the quality of written case analyses.	Measures:	H2: Quality measure—no significant difference. ($p = 0.235$).
		H3: There will be no difference in content of the written case analyses.	• Postexperiment questionnaire for satisfaction with both the case study solution and the process.	H3: Content measure—not significant.
		H4: FTF groups will be more satisfied with the group interaction process.	• Quality of the written case analysis was evaluated by two judges.	H4. Process satisfaction measure—not significant. ($p = 0.023$)
		H5: FTF groups will be more satisfied with the discussion quality.	• A multiple-choice quiz was administered to subjects at the end of each 2-week experimental period.	H5: Discussion quality measure—subjects collaborating FTF were more satisfied ($p = 0.004$).
		H6: There will be no difference in solution satisfaction.		H6: Solution satisfaction measure—no significant difference.

Study	Description	Hypotheses	Measures	Findings
Parker and Gemino (2001)	107 students in place-based sections and 128 students in ALN sections of an undergraduate system analysis and design class using "FirstClass."	H1: There is no difference in overall results of a comprehensive final examination between a course offered in an ALN format or a place-based format. H2: Students taking a course in an ALN format will have significantly higher scores on conceptual understanding. H3: Students taking a course in an ALN format will have significantly lower scores on technical ability.	The score of two sections (conceptual and technique) in the test were measures of the performance of students.	An ALN format facilitated significantly greater opportunities for student participation and communication. H1: There was no difference in overall results of a comprehensive final examination. H2: Students taking a course in an ALN format had significantly higher scores on conceptual understanding than did those taking the same place-based course. H3: The students taking a course in an ALN format had significantly lower scores on technical ability.

(continued on next page)

APPENDIX (continued)

Paper Reference	Method	Hypotheses	Measures of Effectiveness	Findings
Piccoli, Ahmad, and Ives (2001)	Case & experimental. Synchronous same room vs. asynchronous conferencing ("virtual learning environment," or VLE).	H1: Students in the VLE will achieve higher test scores than will their counterparts in the traditional learning environment. H2: Students in the VLE will report higher levels of computer self-efficacy than will their counterparts in the traditional learning environment. H3: Students in the VLE will report different levels of satisfaction than will their counterparts in the traditional learning environment.	H1: Midterm and final exam grades by a pool of six graders, blind to condition. H2 and H3: Questionnaires.	H1: Although in the aggregate, the students in the VLE consistently outperformed their counterparts, the results were not statistically significant. H2: Students in the VLE reported significantly higher computer self-efficacy. H3: Students in the VLE were significantly less satisfied. Subjects reported being dissatisfied with the shell application (inefficient interface, slow system, not user friendly).
Rovai (2002)	Adult learners who were enrolled in 14 undergraduate and graduate courses (52 were enrolled in 7 Blackboard.com courses and 274 in 7 traditional FTF courses).	Research question: How does sense of community differ between students enrolled in traditional FTF and ALN courses?	Descriptive statistics were calculated for classroom community, as operationalized by the SCCI (sense of classroom community index), and for the number of messages posted by subjects to the Blackboard.com discussion boards.	• Overall, subjects enrolled in ALN courses manifested somewhat higher levels of classroom community than did subjects enrolled in traditional courses, but these differences were not significant.

| Sandercock and Shaw (1999) | 80 first-year sports science /sports therapy students. A control group took the module in semester A (FTF) whereas the experimental group took the module in Semester B (supplemented with Web CT). | Research question: What are the effects of mode of delivery? | • Attitudes toward the module were assessed in both using a standard end-of-module questionnaire.

• Attitudes of the control group compared to the Web CT experimental group were assessed using an online questionnaire constructed by the author. | • A moderate positive relationship was found between classroom community and number of messages posted by subjects ($r = .42$, $p = .003$).

• The items in which the traditional courses scored higher were learner feelings of: similarity of learner needs, connectedness, friendship, group identity, and absence of confusion.

• No significant ($p > 0.05$) difference in A-level points between the two groups.

• No significant difference in either the course work or examination marks for each group.

• 94% agreed that Web CT made it easier to access course materials. |

(continued on next page)

APPENDIX (continued)

Paper Reference	Method	Hypotheses	Measures of Effectiveness	Findings
Sener and Stover (2000)	Sample: 950 students in eight ALN undergraduate and graduate courses at Northern Virginia Community College, in different majors. Class sizes varied from 4 to 88 students.	Research question: What factors explain ALN success?	Focus groups, faculty and student questionnaires, grade distributions.	• Students' perception of learning effectiveness: A large majority (84%) of students felt that they had equal (74%) or greater (10%) access to learning resources in ALN. Two thirds felt that ALN courses were equal to or more effective than were on-campus experience. • Course grades: Overall, grades were the same with ALN and on-campus courses. ALN courses had a higher student withdrawal rate than did on-campus courses.
Swigger, Brazile, and Shin (1995)	72 computer science majors enrolled in an undergraduate software engineering course at the University of North Texas were randomly assigned to 24 three-member teams. Half of the groups performed the requirements elicitation task using only FTF methods, whereas the other half interacted with a computer-supported cooperative training (CSCT) environment.	Research questions: • Did groups interacting with the CSCT environment do as well as the groups who used FTF technique? • In terms of specific performance indicators, what are the characteristics of those groups who were more successful in the CSCT environment?	• Scores designed to measure the effectiveness of the requirements elicitation task (the number of relevant requirements specified). • Detailed computer history lists of all group actions.	• Groups using the CSCT demonstrated more effective skills than did groups who performed the same task FTF ($p < .001$).] • The competencies relating to group problem description and generation of alternative solutions were the most predictive of successful cooperation.

Reference	Description	Hypothesis	Variables/Methods	Results
Thoennessen, Tsai, and Davis (1999)	In 1997, at Michigan State University, ALN was added to CAPA (computer-assisted personalized approach) for an introductory physics class for engineers with over 500 students. A comparison of learning performance between using ALN and not using ALN was conducted.	Students who use ALN and CAPA are more motivated to learn and will earn better grades.	Dependent variable: Learning performance. Measures: Grades, drop rate.	• Students taking the ALN/CAPA available class received 20% higher midexam grades than did students in previous traditional classes. • In classes with ALN/CAPA, students using the ALN received approximately 10% higher grades and missed 12% fewer classes.
Wagner and Tuttas (2001)	20 students in electronic engineering. 1×3 experiment: • 1: Tutors, learners, and the test object in one room. • 2: Learners are in different rooms, receive video transmission, and use software tools. • 3: The experiment and the tutorial supervision are spread out over different rooms.	Evaluation questions: E1: What result do experts arrive at on evaluating the program? E2: How do learners react to the program? E3: What learning successes were achieved? E4: Could the learning content be transferred? E5: What effect did the learning unit have?	The performance was judged from the observation of teams doing their task. Other variables were judged from the online questionnaire.	• All teams from both groups finished successfully. No difference in the achieved results was observed. • Subjective satisfaction: The remote teams rated the whole lab experiment much better than did the local group.

(continued on next page)

REFERENCES

Alavi, M., Yoo, Y, & Vogel, D. (1997). Using technology to add value to management education. *Academy of Management Journal, 40*(6), 1310–1333.

Allen, G., & Thompson, A. (1996). Analysis of the effect of networking on computer-assisted collaborative writing in a fifth grade classroom. *Journal of Educational Computing Research, 12*(1), 65–75.

Andriole, S. J. (1997). Requirement-driven ALN course design, development, delivery, and evaluation. *Journal of Asynchronous Learning Networks, 1*(2). Retrieved March 7, 2004, from http://www.sloan-c.org/publications/JALN

Arbaugh, J. B. (2000). Virtual classroom versus physical classroom: An exploratory study of class discussion patterns and student learning in an asynchronous Internet-based MBA course. *Journal of Management Education, 24*(2), 213–233.

Arvan, L., Ory, J., Bullock, C. D., Burnaska, K. K., & Hanson, M. (1998). The SCALE efficiency projects. *Journal of Asynchronous Learning Networks, 2*(2). Retrieved March 7, 2004, from http://www.sloan-c.org/publications/JALN

Benbunan-Fich, R., & Hiltz, S. R. (1999). Impacts of asynchronous learning networks on individual and group problem solving: A field experiment. *Group Decision and Negotiation, 8,* 409–426.

Benuban-Fich, R., & Hiltz, S. R. (2002). Correlates of the effectiveness of learning networks: The effects of course level, course type and gender on outcome. In *Proceedings of the 35th Hawaii International Conference on System Sciences* (pp. 1–8). Washington, DC: IEEE Computer Society, CD-Rom.

Benbunan-Fich, R., Hiltz, S. R., & Turoff, M. (2001). A comparative content analysis of face-to-face vs. ALN mediated teamwork. In *Proceedings of the 34th Hawaii International Conference on System Sciences*. Washington, DC: IEEE Computer Society, CD-Rom.

Carr-Chellman, A. A., Dyer, D., & Breman, J. (2000). Burrowing through the network wires: Does distance detract from collaborative authentic learning? *Journal of Distance Education, 15,* 1. Retrieved March 7, 2004, from http://cade.athabascau.CA/vol15.1/carr.html

Dutton, J., Dutton, M., & Perry, J. (2001). Do online students perform as well as lecture students? *Journal of Engineering Education, 90*(1), 131–136.

Dutton, J., Dutton, M., & Perry, J. (2002). How do online students differ from lecture students? *Journal of Asynchronous Learning Networks, 6,* 1. Retrieved March 7, 2004, from http://www.sloan-c.org/publications/JALN/vgn/vgn-dutton.asp

Fallah, M. H., How, W. J., & Ubell, R. (2000). Blind scores in a graduate test: Conventional compared with Web-based outcomes. *ALN Magazine, 4*(2). Retrieved March 7, 2004, from http://www.sloan-c.org/publications/magazine/v4n2/fallah.asp

Hadidi, R., & Sung, C. (2000). Pedagogy of online instruction—can it be as good as face-to-face? In *Proceedings of the Americas Conference on Information Systems (AIS)* (pp. 2061–2065). Atlanta, GA: AIS.

Heckman, R., & Annabi, H. (2003). A content analytic comparison of FTF and ALN case-study discussions. In *Proceedings of the 37th Hawaii International Conference on Systems Science*. Washington, DC: IEEE Computer Society, CD-Rom.

Hillman, D. C. A. (1999). A new method for analyzing patterns of interaction. *American Journal of Distance Education, 13*(2), 37–47.

Hiltz, S. R. (1993). Correlates of learning in a virtual classroom. *International Journal of Man–Machine Studies, 39,* 71–98.

Hiltz, S. R. (1994). *The virtual classroom*. Norwood, NJ: Ablex.

Hiltz, S. R., Benbunan-Fich, R., Coppola, N., Rotter, N., & Turoff, M. (2000). Measuring the importance of collaborative learning for the effectiveness of ALN: A multi-measure, multi-method approach. *Journal of Asynchronous Learning Networks, 4*(2). Retrieved March 7, 2004, from http://www.sloan-c.org/publications/jaln/v4n2_hiltz.asp

Hiltz, S. R., Turoff, M., & Zhang, Y. (2001, September). *Studies of effectiveness of learning networks*. Paper presented at the Sloan ALN Workshop, Lake George, NY.

Hiltz, S. R., Zhang, Y., & Turoff, M. (2002). Studies of effectiveness of learning networks. In J. Bourne & J. C. Moore (Eds.), *Elements of quality of online education* (pp. 15–41). Needham, MA: SCOLE (Sloan Center for Online Education).

Hsu, E. Y. P., Hiltz, S. R., & Turoff, M. (1992). Computer mediated conferencing system as applied to a business curriculum: A research update. In *Proceedings of the 20th Annual North American Conference of the International Business School Computer Users Group* (pp. 214–227). Retrieved March 8, 2004, from http://www.alnresearch.org/jsp/empirical_research

Kassop, M. (2003). *Ten ways online education matches, or surpasses, face-to-face learning. The Technology Source,* May/June. Retrieved March 7, 2004, from http://ts.mivu.org

Kwok, R. C. W., & Ma, H. (1999). Use of a group support system for collaborative assessment. *Computers and Education, 32,* 109–125.

Leasure, A. R., Davis, L., & Thievon, S. L. (2000). Comparison of student outcomes and preferences in a traditional vs. World Wide Web-based baccalaureate nursing research course. *Journal of Nursing Education, 34*(4), 149–154.

Navarro, P., & Shoemaker, J. (2000). Performance and the perception of distance learners in cyberspace. *American Journal of Distance Education, 14*(2), 15–35.

Ocker, R. J., & Yaverbaum, G. J. (1999). Asynchronous computer-mediated communication versus face-to-face collaboration: Results on student learning, quality and satisfaction. *Group Decision and Negotiation, 8,* 427–440.

Parker, D., & Gemino, A. (2001). Inside online learning: Comparing conceptual and technique learning and performance in place-based ALN formats. *Journal of Asynchronous Learning Networks, 5*(2). Retrieved March 7, 2004, from http://www.sloan-c.org/publications/jaln/v5n2/pdf/v5n2_parkergemino.pdf

Piccoli, G. B., Ahmad, R., & Ives, B. (2001). Web-based virtual learning environments: A research framework and a preliminary assessment of effectiveness in basic IT skills training. *MIS Quarterly, 25*(4), 401–426.

Rovai, A. P. (2002). A preliminary look at the structural differences of higher education classroom communities in traditional and ALN courses. *Journal of Asynchronous Learning Networks, 6*(1), 41–56.

Sandercock, G. R. H., & Shaw, G. (1999). Learners' performance and evaluation of attitudes towards Web course tools in the delivery of an applied sports science module. *ALN Magazine, 3*(2). Retrieved March 7, 2004, from http://www.sloan-c.org/publications/magazine/v3n2/sandercock.asp

Sener, J., & Stover, M. (2000). Integrating ALN into an independent study distance education program: NVCC case studies. *Journal of Asynchronous Learning Networks, 4*(2). Retrieved March 7, 2004, from http://www.sloan-c.org/publications/jaln/v4n2/pdf/v4n2_sener.pdf

Simon, S. J., Grover, V., Teng, J. T., & Whitcomb, K. (1996). The relationship of information systems training methods and cognitive ability to end-user satisfaction, comprehension, and skill transfer: A longitudinal field study. *Information Systems Research, 7*(4), 466–490.

Spencer, D., & Hiltz, S. R. (2001). Studies of ALN: An empirical assessment. In *Proceedings of the 34th Hawaii International Conference on Systems Sciences* (CD-Rom ed.). Los Alamitos, CA: IEEE Computer Society Press.

Swigger, K. M., Brazile, R., & Shin, D. (1995). Teaching cooperation and requirements via a computer-supported problem solving environment. *Proceedings of the 31st ASEE/IEEE Frontiers in Education Conference* (CD-Rom ed.). Reno, NV: IEEE Computer Society.

Thoennessen, M., Kashy, E., Tsai, Y., & Davis, N. E. (1999). Impacts of asynchronous learning networks in large lecture classes. *Group Decision and Negotiation, 8,* 371–384.

Wagner, B., & Tuttas, J. (2001). Team learning in an online lab. In *Proceedings of the 21st ASEE/IEEE Frontiers in Education Conference* (Session T1F, 18–22). Washington, DC: IEEE Computer Society.

4

Improving Quantitative Research on ALN Effectiveness

J. B. Arbaugh
University of Wisconsin–Oshkosh

Starr Roxanne Hiltz
New Jersey Institute of Technology

> *Further research, more rigorous research, and more creative research are definitely needed. In particular, research should explore the unique characteristics of asynchronous online environments that matter or that can be made to matter in learning and instruction. (Swan, 2003, p. 37)*

INTRODUCTION

This chapter addresses two main themes concerning quantitative studies of ALNs. The first theme is issues related to measuring learning. We have seen that most of the existing studies comparing online and face-to-face courses suggest either that there is no significant difference or that ALNs result in significantly higher learning than do traditional classroom settings. Although such findings might be encouraging, these studies typically contain a variety of methodological problems that make it difficult to reach definitive conclusions concerning ALN learning effectiveness.

A second theme of this chapter concerns suggestions for improving the generalizability of findings in ALN studies. Historically, this stream of research has been highly reliant on single-course studies. Although these studies have provided some insights, the idiosyncratic characteristics of the single course setting make it difficult to generalize these findings to other learning environments. In this chapter, we identify several concerns with the methodology of previous quantitative ALN research and provide recommendations for addressing them in future studies.

(QUANTITATIVE) WAYS OF MEASURING LEARNING EFFECTIVENESS

The first and most basic measure of learning effectiveness is to ask, "How much did the students learn? How much of the skills and knowledge in a course did they master?" If we cannot validly measure learning, then we cannot compare the relative effectiveness of learning. Thus, we begin here with a review of the major ways in which learning can be assessed "objectively" or quantitatively within a course, including some problems and limitations with each of the possible measures.

Besides the assessment of learning within a course and the assignment of a grade, there are also other criteria of effectiveness of a course, including students' own evaluations of the course and of their satisfaction with it, and measures of resource expenditures (e.g., how much time the students and faculty spent to achieve their learning objectives). If students in Mode A learn the same as those in Mode B but they spend twice as much time to do so or it takes twice as much faculty time to achieve this result, then this cannot really be called effective. We thus look briefly at the use of attitudinal surveys and at time logs and other alternatives to measuring expenditures of effort in a course.

Methods of Assessing Student Learning[1]

Although we begin with the traditional examination process as a means of assessing student learning, we emphasize some of the alternatives that are currently used or could be used in the ALN environment. This includes collaborative examination processes, portfolios, and direct measurement of online participation.

Grades (On Exams or in the Course)

The most typical way of assessing student learning is to give an examination. This may include objective questions such as true/false or multiple choice, or essay questions that are open ended and require the student to compose the answer. The questions are either obtained from a test bank that comes with the instructor's manual for many textbooks, or composed by the instructor. In the traditional exam, there is a fixed amount of time allowed, and the students are proctored to make sure that they do not cheat by copying from notes or other students.

There have been many volumes written about the proper techniques for and the limitations of the examination for assessing student learning (see, e.g., Clark, 1979). Ebel and Frisbie (1986) pointed out that the main purposes of a test are to measure student achievement and to motivate and direct student learning; also, the process of taking an exam and discussing its scoring should be a richly rewarding

---

[1]Portions of this section are adapted from the online tutorial that Constance Steinkeuler and Sharon Derry (2001) created for the WebCenter for Learning Networks Effectiveness Research (www.alnresearch.org).

learning experience in itself. In addition, the process of constructing tests should cause instructors to think carefully about the goals of instruction in a course.

Among the limitations of the exam are that test taking is in and of itself a skill; many students suffer from test anxiety and do not do well under time pressure. Other students are good at guessing the correct answer when they see a list, even if they do not really know the answer. Second, in a limited time, such as an hour or two, only fairly simple skills can be tested. Meyers and Jones (1993) noted that traditional instruction and examination methods do not promote deep learning and long-term retention in physics teaching; this is probably true of other subjects as well. Third, the items may have poor content validity; students often feel that the questions are unfair or tricky and do not adequately cover what are supposed to be the main learning objectives of the course. Fourth, for a course conducted as a learning network in which one of the methods and objectives is to have students working as collaborative teams, the individual examination is not in keeping with all of the rest of the course. Finally, despite proctoring, there may be cheating, on objective exams in particular.

Perhaps most important, critics of objective exams and standardized tests assert that they measure only surface learning at the level of unrelated bits of memorized information (Entwistle, 2001). There are many ways of to define a higher level of deep learning. These include Bloom's (1956) well-known taxonomy of cognitive process levels, which begins with knowledge and comprehension and moves up to higher levels such as application analysis, synthesis, and evaluation (Wright, 2003). Resnick's (1987) list of the characteristics of higher-order thinking and learning includes the application of multiple and possibly conflicting criteria, "meaning-making" (discerning patterns), and that it is "effortful"—it takes considerable time and mental effort. Short multiple choice exams cannot tap this kind of thinking and learning—thus, the emergence of alternatives such as projects, portfolios, and collaborative essay exams, which are described later in this chapter.

Despite the limitations of the objective examination, it will probably always remain one of the means of assessing student learning, because the instructor effort needed for grading this sort of exam is relatively low; in fact, if the exam is objective, the task can be offloaded to a teaching assistant or a computer program (e.g., Scantron® sheets). However, in terms of comparing the effectiveness of different teachers or different modes of course delivery, the main problem with test scores, or even course grades, is that instructors tend to curve grades within a section. That is, they tend to add points or make other adjustments so that each section of each course has a grade distribution that looks something like a normal curve, with a sufficient number of As (although, with grade inflation, these curves tend to be skewed toward A and away from F). In addition, different instructors have different grading patterns; some are considered easy graders and seldom flunk students or give lower than a B, whereas others are considered hard graders and tend to reserve A grades to designate outstanding work. Thus, even "objective" grades tend to have a strong element of subjective evaluation and grading preferences that differ among instructors.

Collaborative Examinations

In a collaborative exam, students work together in all phases of the exam process (although in the version to be described later, the actual exam questions are answered by individuals). Experimentation with collaborative examinations at NJIT was described in Shen, Hiltz, Cheng, Cho, and Bieber (2001), in which the process over a two-semester study of a graduate information systems course was:

> First, each student composed essay questions; next, each student selected one question and answered it; third, the student who created the question graded the answer and provided a justification of the grading. Subsequently, Ph.D. students enrolled in the course did an intermediate review of the grading, and lastly, the instructor provided a final grade. If the scores of the grader and intermediate reviewer were within a few points of each other, the instructor assigned the higher score. If the two disagreed, then the instructor graded the question himself. (The instructor ended up regrading between 20–30% of the questions.) (pp. 2–3)

Although the instructor initially thought that a collaborative exam would be less work, it turned out to need quite a bit of facilitation. Besides regrading, in subsequent trials the instructor edited questions to make them clearer and at an appropriate level of difficulty, and also assigned questions for students to answer rather than allowing the students to choose. Although saving work is not an objective that was supported, other possible advantages of the collaborative exam were reported by students, in postcourse surveys ($N = 138$ responses). Results show the majority of students felt they learned throughout the process (including making up questions, and grading others' answers), the exams were successful in demonstrating what the students learned, and it was an enjoyable process. Students found the collaborative online exam to be a less stressful experience than traditional exams, and a majority recommended that it be used for other courses. In follow-up studies over subsequent semesters (Wu, Bieber, & Hiltz, 2003), the process was refined, and most students reported that they enjoyed this learning process and found that it promotes students' "deep learning." The students also reported better perceived learning compared with traditional exams.

Projects and Portfolios

A project is an artifact, prepared by an individual student or a collaborative group of students, that is assigned by the instructor to provide an opportunity to apply the knowledge and skills covered by texts and lectures. For instance, in a programming course, the student may have to write a program. In a course on computer ethics, the student may have to analyze a case scenario and apply ethical principles to arrive at a suggested resolution of the problem situation. In an architecture course, the student may construct a paper or computerized model of a building. The project has the dual aim of improving the students' skills though practice, and of demonstrating whether the student can actually use the knowledge supposedly gained in a course.

Portfolios are student-prepared collections of documents that demonstrate understanding of important concepts or mastery of key skills, requiring students to organize, synthesize, and communicate their achievements throughout the semester. Several different types of portfolios can be used, but most are variations of students' personalized collections of their work over the entire duration of the course. For online courses, these portfolios are often created on a web page so they can be seen by other students as well as the instructor. A strong motivational factor is that the work done during the course can later be shown to prospective employers or people, even after the course is over.

For a project or portfolio approach to assessment to work well, the instructor must communicate his or her expectations to students at the beginning of the course, outlining: the kinds of mastery students are to demonstrate, given the goals of the course; the types of materials that are considered evidence that those goals have been met; and the criteria by which the portfolios will be evaluated. Because procrastination is more likely in online courses, a series of assignments with specific due dates, for the items that will appear in the portfolio, is usually presented. Appropriate scoring rubrics should be used for each type of document contained in the portfolios, and these rubrics should be described as part of the assignment. (A *rubric* is a systematic guideline as to what is being looked for in an answer, and how much each criterion is to be counted in the overall grade.) Some or all of the assignments may be collaborative, in which case the scoring rubric needs to describe how the individual contribution to the group project will be assessed.

A study by Slater (1997) examined the effectiveness of different types of portfolios in three separate courses: a college physics course at an urban community college, a course in physical science for elementary education majors at a medium-sized university, and a large introductory environmental science course for nonscience majors at a major university. For each course, two grading treatments were compared (one assessed by portfolio, the other assessed by more traditional means such as tests and quizzes) on the following measures: a common final examination, a pretest/posttest self-report survey, open-ended surveys, and focus group interviews.

The findings were that students assessed by portfolios scored just as well on a traditional multiple-choice final examination as did students who were assessed by more traditional means. Student surveys and focus-group transcripts revealed that portfolios reduced test anxiety and students' preoccupation with note taking rather than participation during class discussions. Students assessed by portfolios also reported spending considerable time on desirable types of learning activities—they spent substantial time reviewing the textbook to make sure they understood the content deeply, thought about course content outside of class, and felt they would remember the course material better than the material from other courses given the time and energy they invested in creating their final products. Thus, the process of building projects or portfolios seems to be more educationally valuable than the process of studying for a traditional examination. Slater's study was of traditional sections; common sense says that the findings should replicate for online courses, but such research has not yet been reported.

Among the major limitations are that portfolios can be time consuming to assess and often require multiple grading rubrics, one for each type of artifact they may contain. As such, they are best suited for courses with smaller enrollments; however, they can be modified for larger courses by reducing their scope and tightly structuring their format to ensure some level of uniformity. If there are group projects, then there are fewer total items to assess, and larger classes become more viable for a project/portfolio grading approach. It has been found that assessing on an assignment-by-assignment basis is more reliable than assessing on a portfolio-by-portfolio basis (Nystrand, Cohen, & Dowling, 1993).

Participation (Number, Frequency, Length of Comments)

Because the process of learning networks involves students making regular contributions to class discussions and activities, it is possible to try to directly assess this constant participation, rather than have a separate assessment activity. One can simply count things like the number, regularity, and length of contributions. The problem with such an approach is that if students know this is the basis of grading, they will simply load the class discussion with items that are not very thoughtful or original, or perhaps not even on the subject. For a small class, the instructor can grade the quality and relevance of every contribution as if it were an essay. For larger classes, with hundreds of comments every week, this becomes an impossible burden.

We are not aware of any studies of the efficacy and methodology for directly assessing online learning from the transcript of the class discussions. Perhaps some software could be developed to aid in this process. For example, in the original Virtual Classroom® software, there was a program that could count and display the number and percentage of contributions by each student during any specified time period, including numbers of lines or words and their percentage distribution. This made it easy for the instructor to at least use weekly data to see at a glance if any students seemed to be acting like lurkers instead of active participants, and to encourage more regular or active contributions. Conceivably, a program could be written to automate the feedback each week, based on such an analysis, showing students what their contributions compared to the average for the rest of the class.

Methods for Evaluating Course Outcomes

Whatever the method used to assess student learning, there are other aspects of the course process and outcomes that need to be measured in order to have a complete picture of course effectiveness. These include subjective assessment of instructor and course quality by students, of course satisfaction by both students and faculty, and measures of resource expenditures, particularly time.

Attitudinal Surveys: Perceived Learning/Satisfaction

Attitudinal surveys, which are most often administered as postcourse student evaluations, can provide valuable information on students' perceptions of the course, the discipline, the instructor, the materials and tools used, and their individual progress and knowledge gains. This strategy is highly useful for teasing apart which elements of the pedagogy and/or technology students feel are most easily mastered, most comfortable, and/or most personally rewarding (as well as which elements are perceived as most difficult, most frustrating, and/or most futile). In general, such surveys can be administered quickly and conveniently. The use of Scantron® forms, or of computer-administered surveys that are automatically transferred into a statistical database for analysis, can simplify the analysis process. However, there are a number of problems with surveys that must be kept in mind.

Often, the surveys administered do not seem to match the range of criteria on which online course quality should be evaluated. As Achtemeier, Morris, and Finnegan (2003) concluded after examining a number of such instruments, they "seem to include what[ever)] someone decides to ask the students at a given time" (p. 10). These authors suggested that designers of postcourse surveys should review the "principles for good practice in undergraduate education" compiled by the American Association of Higher Education in 1983, and use these as the basis for designing questions:

- Encourage student–faculty contact,
- Encourage cooperation among students,
- Encourage active learning,
- Give prompt feedback,
- Emphasize time on task,
- Communicate higher expectations, and
- Respect diverse talents and ways of learning.

In addition, Achtemeier and colleagues (2003) suggested that items should be included that measure some of the principles for effective teaching specifically in the online classroom, including the following from Weiss, Knowlton, and Speck (2000):

- Did students have the necessary technological equipment and skills required for the course?
- Was there adequate technical support if they encountered difficulties?
- Were there sufficient instructions given to complete all assignments?
- Did students participate in online conversations with their classmates?
- After being sure to include an appropriate range of items in course surveys, another guideline is that in order to obtain valid data, students' responses should be *anonymous or confidential*, and this fact should be clearly communicated to those who participate. The survey should be administered and collected and analyzed by someone other than the instructor. If students believe their grade may be affected by their responses, they may give answers they think the instructor will want to hear instead of what they really think, feel, and believe. (emphasis added)

One serious source of invalidity in survey data is that respondents may be different than nonrespondents; thus, it is important to take steps to try to get all students to complete a questionnaire. This issue is further discussed in the last part of this chapter.

Limitations.   Data collected through student surveys can be both valid and reliable, but the development of adequate instruments is a nontrivial task. Luckily, many valid scales to measure various constructs have already been developed and tested to ensure that they measure what was intended (i.e., they are valid), and that they are reliable across students and across groups. Such instruments can be adopted or carefully adapted to meet most instructors' needs. When adopting a measure for use in a particular course context, be wary—if you change features of the original instrument, you may compromise its validity and/or reliability and end up with data that has little meaning. Whenever previously validated scales are modified, they should be pretested before widespread application, and the pretest data should be assessed for reliability and validity.

Also, keep in mind that the data generated through such surveys is *self-report* rather than direct observation. One problem is the tendency toward a *halo effect*; if the student is generally happy with the course, including the instructor and the grade, then all questions on a survey tend to be answered positively, and vice versa. Attitudinal surveys can provide a summative overview of how and/or what students do, think, or feel about a given course, but a more detailed understanding of students' attitudes requires the use of supplementary research methods such as individual or group interviews (see the next chapter on incorporating qualitative methods).

Measuring Time and Effort

In addition to reported outcomes, an evaluation of the effectiveness of a learning medium ought to also include measures of the costs of the course delivery. This includes both money expended to produce course materials and get them to the students (e.g., on-campus courses include the costs of constructing and maintaining the physical plant) and the amount of time spent by the instructor and the students during the delivery of a particular section of the course. Both of these measures are difficult to obtain, although reasonable approximations of the monetary cost of producing and offering a course ought to be available from university accounting records.

Getting an accurate measure of how much time is spent by both the instructor and the students is more difficult. Reported perceptions are generally not very accurate. Also, although some software packages like Blackboard may do some tracking of participants' engagement in the course, these tracking mechanisms tend to focus on the number of times a student visits the course site rather than time spent, quality of time spent, or student engagement, therefore making these mechanisms subject to the concerns about counting number of comments mentioned previously. Some sort of time-logging procedure needs to be instituted, but in order to motivate someone to actually keep a log of all of the time spent on a course, and what they were doing while online, strong incentives are needed. One way to provide these incentives for students could be to make the log a percentage of their course grade, but then this would need to be taken into account if course grades were going to be used as a measure of student learning. Faculty might be encouraged to keep logs by making them a requirement for obtaining ALN course development grants. However, each of these suggestions could produce an enormous amount of data that may limit the number of courses and students examined without a fairly sizable team of researchers.

Lazarus (2003) reported a self-study of the time required to teach special education courses via ALN. The method involved logging the number and duration of each of the following: reading and responding to e-mails; reading, participating in, and grading online discussions; and grading assignments. A stopwatch was used to time each of these daily activities. For the author's course with 25 students, which had been developed and taught online previously, these activities took only 3–7 hours a week, which is not more than traditional courses could take. However, this study did not directly log teaching time for comparable face-to-face sections of the course.

Experimental Studies

In order to reach valid conclusions about cause and effect in terms of the impact of a medium of course delivery or of any of the moderating and mediating variables shown in the causal model of ALN effectiveness in chapter 2, or posited by other theoretical models, an experimental design is required. However, it is generally very difficult to achieve the standards of a controlled laboratory experiment, which requires random assignment of students to conditions. For example, one cannot randomly assign a student to take a section of a course that meets at a time and place that conflicts with other obligations of the student. Without random assignment, there is no assurance that the treatment groups are comparable and that the observed differences in learning are the result of the intervention. On the other hand, it is possible to experiment with various treatments within the sections of a course. For instance, students could be randomly assigned to be graded by an exam constructed and graded by the instructor, or constructed and assessed by the students themselves as a collaborative exam. Also, a quasi-experimental design that doesn't use random assignment could be used to measure items such as knowledge gain through the use of precourse and postcourse exams (Arbaugh, 2000a; 2000b).

The guidelines for designing and carrying out experiments are beyond the scope of this book. However, some of the limitations should be noted. A course is not a "laboratory"; many other things are happening to the student while he or she is taking a particular course. In other words, it is impossible to control all of the sources of variance during a semester-long course. In order to realize the best chance of finding relationships between variables in field experiments, it is especially important to have a large sample of students, so that the laws of probability can have an opportunity to allow the effects of the independent variable(s) of interest to become apparent. It is also important that "instructor" be one of the controlled variables; that is, the same instructor should be offering all of the conditions being studied, rather than, say, one instructor offering a face-to-face version of a course and another instructor offering an online version. In past studies, variations among instructors were much larger than variations associated with mode of course delivery (e.g., Hiltz, 1993).

EXPANDING THE SCOPE AND VALIDITY OF ALN STUDIES

A general historical progression of quantitative ALN research is presented in Fig. 4.1. As the figure shows, ALN research has generally progressed from anecdotal experiences with single courses to comparisons with classroom learning in single-course settings to multicourse and multidiscipline ALN studies. This pattern first emerged via the efforts of researchers at the New Jersey Institute of Technology (NJIT) beginning in the mid-1980s and progressing through their Virtual Classroom® project during the 1990s (Benbunan-Fich & Hiltz, 2002; Coppola, Hiltz, & Rotter, 2002; Hiltz, 1993, 1994; Hiltz, Johnson, & Turoff, 1986; Hiltz & Wellman, 1997). This was followed by a similar pattern in other institutional settings beginning in the early to mid-1990s (Andriole, 1997; Arbaugh, 2000b; Arvan, Ory, Bullock, Burnaska, & Hanson, 1998; Bailey & Cotlar, 1994; Boston, 1992; Dumont, 1996; Sorg et al., 1999; Swan et al., 2000).

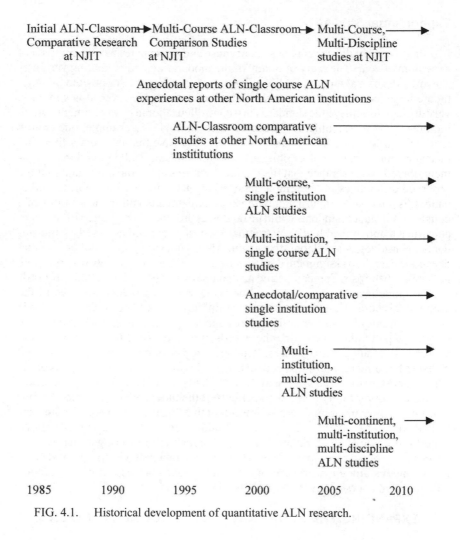

FIG. 4.1.   Historical development of quantitative ALN research.

Based on this progression of research, we would like to help encourage future researchers to build on this emerging body of knowledge. Part of understanding how to expand on this research requires identifying areas in which the value added of additional future research would be rather limited. Obviously, the novelty of ALNs is now essentially gone. As a result, we are now familiar enough with them to know that anecdotal reports of single-course experiences by a single instructor no longer help to substantially increase our knowledge about ALNs.

Although they do allow for some more definitive conclusions, much the same also can be said for single-course empirical studies. Besides suffering from a lack of external validity, single-course empirical studies have tended to possess sample sizes that are too small to generate the necessary statistical power to adequately assess the potential significance of all variables typically included in these studies.

These concerns also can often be leveled against one of the recent bastions of ALN research, the single-course comparison study of ALNs and classrooms (Alavi, Yoo, & Vogel, 1997; Arbaugh, 2000b; Card, 2000; Freeman & Capper, 1999; Piccoli, Ahmad, & Ives, 2001; Redding & Rotzien, 2001; Sandercock & Shaw, 1999; Warkentin, Sayeed, & Hightower, 1997). Based on the results of some recent reviews of the ALN–classroom comparative literature (Arbaugh & Stelzer, 2003; chap. 6, this volume), it appears that there is more than enough research comparing student performance in ALN and face-to-face courses to conclude that the ALN medium at worst has a neutral impact on student performance. There may yet be some useful additional insights gained from comparing aspects of web-based delivery, such as timing of communication, the performance of various course delivery software packages, student performance in ALNs versus that of ALN/classroom hybrid courses (Hartman, Dziuban, & Moskal, 2000), or further study of disciplines not yet examined by comparative research (Helmi, Haynes, & Maun, 2000). However, the research published to date suggests that we should generally move away from merely comparing ALNs and classrooms and toward research that helps determine which characteristics best predict ALN effectiveness. This line of inquiry suggests the need for increased research using multicourse, multi-discipline, and/or multi-institution samples. Therefore, the remainder of this section of the chapter focuses on research in those settings to date and identifying issues that should be addressed in future studies.

Research Needs

Clear Causal Models

Often, the mode of delivery of a course (e.g., ALN vs. face-to-face) is confounded with the pedagogy or instructional technology used (e.g., objectivist vs. constructivist/collaborative learning; see chap. 2). At the extreme, a large face-to-face lecture course might be compared to a much smaller, discussion-based ALN course. As Clark (2000) pointed out, delivery (mode) and pedagogy or instructional technology are typically confused in distance education evaluations; it is important to isolate or control for all of the other variables that might influence the process and outcome of a course besides the delivery mode, before attributing differences observed to delivery mode.

Multicourse Studies

Multicourse studies would provide several methodological benefits for ALN research. Two direct benefits would be increased external validity and statistical power. Because ALN research has historically been reliant on many studies based on individual courses (Arbaugh, 2000c; Berger, 1999; Ellram & Easton, 1999; Taylor, 1996), many of their findings may reflect idiosyncrasies of the instructor rather than provide accurate prescriptions for best practice in web-based course delivery. Multicourse studies increase the likelihood that these instructor-unique characteristics can be controlled for, thereby allowing for increased generalizability of findings.

Although multicourse studies would control for individual faculty effects, an additional benefit would be the opportunity to examine faculty characteristics and attitudes more thoroughly. Relative to concerns over student course experiences, faculty have traditionally been ignored in research on distance education in general (Dillon & Walsh, 1992), and the same has been true in ALN research until relatively recently. However, recent multicourse studies of faculty have yielded some useful insights. Coppola et al. (2002) found that faculty changed their teaching persona toward more precision in their presentation of materials and instructions, combined with a shift to a more Socratic pedagogy, emphasizing multilogues with students. Smith, Ferguson, and Caris (2001) found that although instructors had more difficulty getting their point across and were more constrained in managing on-the-spot behavioral issues and educational opportunities, they could also integrate online materials seamlessly into the course, draw from a broader pool of potential online guests, and often saw stronger one-to-one relationships formed in online courses than in face-to-face courses. Hartman et al. (2000) also found that instructors reported increased course interaction and that in spite of the fact that they thought ALN courses required greater amounts of work, they were excited about doing more of them in the future. Certainly future multicourse studies of faculty will provide more specific insights into faculty characteristics and attitudes and the relationship of these variables to effective performance in ALNs.

Multi-Institution Studies

Although the recent trend toward multicourse studies is welcome, other factors must also be addressed to advance the state of ALN research. In addition to providing increased external validity, multi-institution studies also provide an opportunity to increase statistical power in studies of ALN courses. Because the concept of online delivery of education in some disciplines is still relatively new, it is somewhat rare that an individual institution would offer a large number of class sections in a web-based format. As a result, most ALN studies have tended to use relatively small sample sizes. These small samples result in low statistical power (Cohen, 1988). Therefore, there may be some variables that have a significant but relatively small statistical effect that have not been detected in earlier studies (Ferguson & Ketchen, 1999). Using multiple-institution samples is one way to efficiently increase sample sizes. These larger sample sizes, in turn, would allow us to see a more complete picture of web-based courses, thereby allowing us to gain a better understanding of them and better address the concerns of their critics.

In addition to providing statistical benefits, multi-institution studies would provide the opportunity to further generalize research findings. Presently, nearly all multicourse studies have been conducted with a single college or university as the research setting. Although the findings of these studies have certainly been fruitful, there are often some institution-unique characteristics that may limit the generalizability of these findings to other settings. For instance, consider two of the primary sources of multicourse studies, the Virtual Classroom® project at NJIT and the Research Initiative for Teaching Effectiveness at the University of Central Florida (UCF). The majority of published research conducted at NJIT suggests that ALNs have a positive impact on participant satisfaction and student learning (Benbunan-Fich & Hiltz, 2002; Hiltz, 1994; Hiltz &

Wellman, 1997). Although this is encouraging news for ALN supporters, isn't this what one would expect to find at what Yahoo has labeled the "perennially most wired campus" in America? NJIT is ranked among the 25 "most wired" universities in the United States (Dukcevich, 2003).

Recent research conducted by UCF's Research Initiative for Teaching Effectiveness suggests that ALNs compare favorably to classroom courses on student evaluations (Moskal & Dziuban, 2001). However, UCF also happens to be one of the fastest-growing universities in the United States, and their move to adopt ALNs was driven at least in part by the fact that they do not have enough classroom capacity to house all the courses they offer (Sorg et al., 1999). This situation presents a rather unique question for students: Would you rather take a course that would probably be offered at an inconvenient time in a classroom that is likely to be quite overcrowded, or take the course when it meets your schedule via ALN? In addition, UCF has a nationally recognized "best practices" program of training and support for ALN faculty. Almost certainly, at least some context-specific characteristics also help explain findings from other large-scale multicourse ALN offerings such as those offered as part of the SCALE project at the University of Illinois (Arvan et al., 1998) and the SUNY Learning Network (Swan, 2001).

Therefore, collaborative efforts of researchers at different institutions should be particularly encouraged. Historically, there has been a paucity of multi-institution ALN research, and most of that has been conducted on a rather small scale, usually between two institutions and a limited number of courses. In spite of these limitations, cross-institutional ALN research has yielded valuable insights, such as the usefulness of ALN in cross-cultural settings (Yoo, Kanawattanachai, & Citurs, 2002), the role of interaction in ALN courses (Hiltz, 1993), the importance of instructor experience, and the perceived flexibility of the medium in predicting ALN effectiveness (Arbaugh & Duray, 2001, 2002; Sullivan, 2001).

Another benefit of multi-institutional studies would be the opportunity for comparison of delivery approaches of online degree programs. There is presently nearly as much variation in approaches to delivery as there are schools offering these courses. Delivery platforms range from a combination of e-mail and electronic bulletin boards (Bailey & Cotlar; 1994; Dumont, 1996; Partee, 1996) to web-based proprietary software that allows for transmission of multimedia, threaded discussions, and chatroom capability (Arbaugh & Duray, 2002; Greco, 1999; Hiltz, 1994; Phillips, 1998). Another continuum on which schools vary is the extent to which the online environment is supplemented with other teaching pedagogies, such as the use of streaming audio and/or video, videotapes, video conferencing, or conducting a portion of a course or program on campus (Alavi & Leidner, 2001; Greco, 1999; Phillips, 1998). To date, studies comparing these differing delivery platforms or supplemental tools of multiple schools are extremely limited. Therefore, this body of knowledge would be greatly enhanced by multiplatform, multi-institution studies.

Multinational Studies

If comparisons of institutional practices merit additional research, then certainly an emerging area of future research would be the study of ALN practices in different national or cultural contexts. Presently, much of this research is rather small in scope, often focusing on multinational collaboration between schools in the context of a single course or activity within a course (Jarvenpaa & Leidner, 1999; Yoo et al., 2002). However, as more schools seek to deliver education via the Internet to a global audience and create collaborative ventures with schools in other countries, opportunities for multinational ALN studies will certainly increase in the future. In addition to the comparative, statistical, and validity enhancements to ALN research previously mentioned, multinational studies would allow additional research in topics such as cross-cultural learning network selection and development (Jarvenpaa & Leidner; 1999; Nulden, 1999), teaching and learning styles of international audiences (Carswell, Thomas, Petre, Price, & Richards, 2000; Hanningan & Browne, 2000), and technological impacts on learning (Yoo et al., 2002).

Longitudinal Studies

One consequence of the relative newness of delivery of education via the Internet is that opportunities for the study of ALN-related changes in student, instructor, program, and institutional behavior over time have been extremely limited. Again, researchers associated with the Virtual Classroom® project have been among the leaders in this research (Hiltz, Coppola, Rotter, Turoff, & Benbunan-Fich, 2000). Otherwise, longitudinal studies have tended to be limited to designs such as repeated measurement of subjects over a semester (Alavi et al., 1997; Piccoli et al., 2001; Yoo et al., 2002) or following a small cadre of students through their ALN experiences over a 1- or 2-year period of time (Kazmer, 2001; Levin, Levin, & Waddoups 2001).

In addition to seeing changes in student behavior, longitudinal research examining program and institutional changes over time can be very useful for schools still developing their online programs. For instance, Arbaugh (2002a) found that the flexibility and convenience of ALN courses were significant predictors of student learning and satisfaction in the first 2 years of his study, but ceased to be significant predictors after that. This finding suggests that the days in which schools can compete on the basis of the convenience of their ALN offerings may be numbered. Also, initial work by Coppola et al. (2002) on changes in instructor behavior suggested that transitions in teaching styles and personas are very much works in progress. Additional research in these areas will greatly enhance our understanding of how ALNs evolve, and will provide us with insights on how they may further change in the future.

Future Performance of ALN Participants

This would be a natural extension from increased longitudinal work. Studies tracking students' subsequent performance after their ALN experiences are essentially nonexistent. Multiyear studies would measure the long-term retention of course materials. For instance, students who take an introductory computer science course in various modes could be followed through the second and third courses in the typical course sequence, to see if their performance in these subsequent courses is any different.

Beyond the academic career, are there effects of different modes of learning that carry over to the job, or to subsequent loyalty to the alma mater? For example, online courses that use collaborative learning give students a lot of practice of working in teams. This is a skill that employers say they want. Employers could be surveyed about the performance of different alumni who had different numbers of online courses, and asked to rate their teamwork skills. Very large numbers would be required in order to overcome the variations introduced by many other factors, but there are now large numbers of alumni who have gone through extensive numbers of ALN courses.

The universities are interested in loyal alumnae who will contribute time and money to the schools after graduation. Do students who had most of their courses online versus on campus differ in these respects? A relatively easy to accomplish study might look, for instance, at the rate at which graduates join the alumni association within the first year.

Key Issues in Quantitative ALN Studies

Survey Response Rates

When ALN research was still in its infancy, highly dependent on single-course studies, student participation rates of well over 50% were typically guaranteed (Althaus, 1997; Arbaugh, 2000a; 2000b; Hislop, 1999). However, participant response rates are going to become an increasingly important issue as students become more geographically dispersed and less likely to meet face to face. Student response rates below 50% in studies of multiple courses in purely asynchronous environments are becoming more common (Arbaugh & Duray, 2001; Fredericksen, Pickett, Shea, & Pelz, 2000). This concern is likely to become even more magnified for multicourse and multi-institutional studies. Nonresponse bias is important because nonrespondents to surveys may very well have differing perceptions of the ALN experience, thereby making the conclusions drawn from studies with low response rates rather misleading (Fowler, 1988; Fraenkel & Wallen, 1990).

There are at least three ways that researchers can address the nonresponse issue. First, they can increase the level of their own hands-on involvement in the data collection process by means such as personalizing the appeal-for-participation letters and initiating additional mailings to boost response rates (Fowler, 1988; Tomaskovic-Devey, Leiter, & Thompson, 1994). Arbaugh (2001, 2002a, 2002b) has used an approach in which electronic surveys are followed up with a personalized appeal and a paper version of the survey sent through the mail. As a result, he has seen response rates of 65% to 80% in his ALN research. However, unless multiple researchers are involved in the project, this approach is limited to collecting data on a few courses at any particular time. An additional benefit of multiple mailings is that they allow for comparisons between early and late responders. Because late respondents often closely resemble nonrespondents, these comparisons can be used to test for the likelihood of nonresponse bias.

Second, researchers can decrease the inconvenience of completing and returning surveys, or increase the rewards to students for completing them. Online surveys that can be submitted with a click instead of an envelope and a trip to the mailbox seem to help response rate somewhat, especially if automatic reminders are built into software to notify nonrespondents. Another strategy that has worked at NJIT is to have instructors distribute and collect postcourse questionnaires at proctored final examinations.

A $25.00/person incentive would be sure to increase response rates for course evaluation questionnaires, but this is likely to be beyond the budget of most projects. However, at NJIT, "thank you" presents of boxes of cookies distributed at final exams did seem to increase the number of students who filled in questionnaires before leaving the room. And in some studies, such as the collaborative examination studies at NJIT, completing a questionnaire was credited as part of a class participation grade, with a certain number of points. Because there are many other opportunities to get points credited for class participation, these bonus points should be considered acceptable by human subjects committees. Response rates of over 80% were achieved when students felt that they might get the point or two that they would need to raise their averages to the next threshold.

Another way researchers can control for nonresponse is through comparing respondents and nonrespondents based on some other data source, such as GPA, part-time versus full-time status, number of credits completed, or course grades. In order to conduct such an analysis, however, the responses must be confidential rather than anonymous.

Quality of Measures

In a recent research commentary, Alavi and Leidner (2001) criticized research on technology-mediated learning for its general lack of theoretical grounding and rigor. Certainly, ALN research is not immune from this criticism. Historically, construct validity has not usually been considered unless researchers use validated measures from previous research. Also, although the reliability of measures is being reported with more regularity in ALN studies, there are still many studies that do not address the topic. There are at least two ways in which ALN researchers can mitigate these concerns in the future. Pilot testing instruments before using them in official studies can help refine measures. Also, researchers could increase their usage of previously validated measures, modifying them for use in the ALN context where necessary. In time, the use of expert panels for developing instruments could become common.

Control Variables

Along with the need for better-defined, more reliable constructs, another aspect of rigor that would benefit future ALN research is the more consistent consideration of appropriate control variables. Control variables have infrequently been considered in previous research. Appropriate control variables enhance the internal validity of studies by eliminating potential alternative explanations for research findings (Keppel, 1982). Therefore, as research moves beyond the mere establishment of the viability of the delivery medium toward the determination of how well different variables predict ALN effectiveness, the use of control variables becomes increasingly important.

Historically, the use of control variables in ALN research has tended to focus on the more basic variables such as student age, student gender, previous grade point average, and time on task. Other control variables that may be important to consider in future studies are suggested by the theoretical model in chapter 2. They include the amount of students' or instructors' prior ALN experience, course enrollment, the types of media used in a course (as ALNs move from merely text based to digital multimedia), and course characteristics such as whether the course is required or elective, course duration, course level (undergraduate vs. graduate), the types of assignments, or institutional learning effects.

Making Better Use of Archival Data

Archival data related to the study of ALN may be gathered from a number of sources. Some of these include course syllabi, examination scores, and student records. Such data have already been collected for other purposes, and their use is "nonintrusive" as long as strict confidentiality processes are followed. Course syllabi are usually available publicly on websites. The use of archival data on individual students will probably require a signed consent form, which can be combined with the consent form used with a postcourse questionnaire or the informed consent procedure if a field experiment is being conducted.

A benefit of using archival data is that it reduces the likelihood that relationships between variables may be biased by common methods variance (Williams, Cole, & Buckley, 1989). Common methods variance may occur when the data for a study is collected using a single tool, such as a survey in which all data is self-reported. It has been estimated that as much as one fourth of the variance in findings reported in organizational research can be attributed to common method variance (Doty & Glick, 1998). Using archival data can provide multiple measures of constructs, thereby diminishing those concerns. As discussed earlier in this chapter, collecting data from multiple sources is quite useful when measuring student learning.

SUMMARY

In this chapter, we examined two significant criteria that must be addressed if quantitative ALN research is to be useful for informing future educational research and practice: more attention to valid and pedagogically sound measurement of ALN learning effectiveness, and increased rigor in studies of ALNs. Although the quality of ALN research on these criteria has improved dramatically within the last half-decade or so, clearly there is much more that can be done. In terms of measuring ALN effectiveness, a clear implication from this review is that multiple measures of effectiveness should be used, preferably collected from different data sources. These should include qualitative data collection methods in order to gain greater depth of understanding, such as direct observation (electronic ethnography), content analysis of actual interaction patterns, and interviews (which are covered in the next chapter).

Recent advances in multicourse, multidiscipline ALN research are encouraging. Extending this research to study ALNs beyond institutional, state, and even national boundaries is vital for us to gain understanding about the contextual factors that most significantly influence ALN effectiveness.

Many of the challenges to ALN effectiveness research can begin to be addressed as researchers in the field become more aware of each other and begin to move beyond merely researching their own institutions, toward more collaborative, multi-institutional research. Perhaps one of the most encouraging developments for quantitative ALN research in recent years has been the increasing numbers of venues in which ALN researchers can meet one another to share their research and discuss future collaborative opportunities, such as the Sloan Foundation's annual ALN conference, the Hawaii International Conference on System Sciences, and workshops such as the one from which this book was developed, as well as in the WebCenter for the research community (www.alnresearch.org). The mutual stimulation and inspiration that will come from these interactives can only help to improve the quality of ALN research. We look forward to seeing the results of those endeavors.

QUESTIONS FOR DISCUSSION AND RESEARCH

1. The purpose of educational research should be to provide feedback so that improvements to courses will occur in the future. How can educational evaluations make more productive use of all of the results obtained from student surveys and other evaluation methods?

2. Quasi-experimental studies have been suggested as a good way to obtain valid conclusions about cause and effect in ALN courses and programs. Select a course you are currently teaching or taking. Suggest the design of a longitudinal quasi-experimental study that would compare different methods for assessing student learning. (Specify the treatments, the hypotheses, the measures of the dependent variables, and how you would assign students to condition.) What problems or limitations do you see in carrying out such a quasi-experimental study?

3. What can be done to encourage more multi-institutional and multinational studies?

ACKNOWLEDGMENT

A preliminary version of this chapter was published as S. R. Hiltz and J. B. Arbaugh (2003), Improving quantitative research methods in studies of asynchronous learning networks, in J. Bourne and J. Moore (Eds), Elements of Quality Online Education: Practice and Direction (Needham MA: SCOLE), pages 59-74. Adapted by permission.

REFERENCES

Achtemeier, S. D., Morris, L. V., & Finnegan, C. L. (2003). Considerations for developing evaluations of online courses. *Journal of Asynchronous Learning Networks, 7*(1). Retrieved June 1, 2003, from http://www.aln.org/publications/jaln/index.asp

Alavi, M., & Leidner, D. E. (2001). Research commentary: Technology-mediated learning—A call for greater depth and breadth of research. *Information Systems Research, 12*(1), 1–10.

Alavi, M., Yoo, Y., & Vogel, D. R. (1997). Using information technology to add value to management education. *Academy of Management Journal, 40*(6), 1310–1333.

Althaus, S. L. (1997). Computer-mediated communication in the university classroom: An experiment with online discussions. *Communication Education, 46,* 158–174.

Andriole, S. J. (1997). Requirement-driven ALN course design, development, delivery, & evaluation. *Journal of Asynchronous Learning Networks, 1*(2). Retrieved June 1, 2002 from http://www.aln.org/publications/jaln/index.asp

Arbaugh, J. B. (2000a). Virtual classroom characteristics and student satisfaction in Internet-based MBA courses. *Journal of Management Education, 24*(1), 32–54.

Arbaugh, J. B. (2000b). Virtual classrooms versus physical classrooms: An exploratory study of class discussion patterns and student learning in an asynchronous Internet-based MBA course. *Journal of Management Education, 24*(2), 207–227.

Arbaugh, J. B. (2000c). An exploratory study of the effects of gender on student learning and class participation in an internet-based MBA course. *Management Learning, 31,* 533–549.

Arbaugh, J. B. (2001). How instructor immediacy behaviors affect student satisfaction and learning in web-based courses. *Business Communication Quarterly, 64*(4), 42–54.

Arbaugh, J. B. (2002a). A longitudinal study of technological and pedagogical characteristics of web-based MBA courses. *Proceedings of the Sixty-Second Annual Meeting of the Academy of Management* (CD), MED A1–A6. ISSN 1543-8643.

Arbaugh, J. B. (2002b). Managing the on-line classroom: A study of technological and behavioral characteristics of web-based MBA courses. *Journal of High Technology Management Research,13,* 203–223.

Arbaugh, J. B., & Duray, R. (2001). Class section size, perceived classroom characteristics, instructor experience, and student learning and satisfaction with web-based courses: A study and comparison of two on-line MBA programs. In D. Nagao (Ed.), *Proceedings of the Sixty-First Annual Meeting of the Academy of Management* (CD), MED A1–A6. ISSN 1543-8643.

Arbaugh, J. B., & Duray, R. (2002). Technological and structural characteristics, student learning and satisfaction with web-based courses: An exploratory study of two MBA programs. *Management Learning, 33,* 331–347.

Arbaugh, J. B., & Stelzer, L. (2003). Learning and teaching management education on the web: What do we know? In C. Wankel R. DeFillipi (Eds.), *Educating managers with tomorrow's technologies* (pp. 17–51). Greenwich, CT: Information Age Publishing.

Arvan, L., Ory, J., Bullock, C. D., Burnaska, K. K., & Hanson, M. (1998). The SCALE efficiency project. *Journal of Asynchronous Learning Networks.* Retrieved March 18, 2004, from http://www.sloan-c.org/publications/jaln/v4n3/pdf/v4n3_arvan.pdf

Bailey, E. K., & Cotlar, M. (1994). Teaching via the Internet. *Communication Education, 43*(2), 184–193.

Benbunan-Fich, R., & Hiltz, S. R. (2002, January). *Correlates of effectiveness of learning networks: The effects of course level, course type, and gender on outcomes. Proceedings of the 35th Hawaii International Conference on System Sciences HICSS-35* (CD-Rom). Abstracts proceedings, 7–10 January 2002, Big Island, HI, USA. IEEE Computer Society, 2002-Track 1.

Berger, N. S. (1999). Pioneering experiences in distance learning: Lessons learned. *Journal of Management Education, 23,* 684–690.

Bloom, B. (1956). *A taxonomy of educational objectives.* New York: D. McKay.

Boston, R. L. (1992). Remote delivery of instruction via the PC and modem: What have we learned? *The American Journal of Distance Education, 6*(3), 45–57.

Card, K. A. (2000). Providing access to graduate education using computer-mediated communication. *International Journal of Instructional Media, 27,* 235–245.

Carswell, L., Thomas, P., Petre, M., Price, B., & Richards, M. (2000). Distance education via the Internet: The student experience. *British Journal of Educational Technology, 31*(1), 29–46.

Clark, J. L. D. (1979). Measures of student learning. In J. A. Centra (Ed.), *Determining faculty effectiveness* (pp. 93–119). San Francisco: Jossey-Bass.

Clark, R. E. (2000). Evaluating distance education: Strategies and cautions. *The Quarterly Review of Distance Education, 1*(1), 3–16.

Cohen, J. (1988). *Statistical power for the behavioral sciences* (2nd ed.). Hillsdale, NJ: Lawrence Erlbaum Associates.

Coppola, N. W., Hiltz, S. R., & Rotter, N. G. (2002). Becoming a virtual professor: Pedagogical roles and asynchronous learning networks. *Journal of Management Information Systems, 18*(4), 169–189.

Dillon, C. L., & Walsh, S. M. (1992). The neglected resource in distance education. *The American Journal of Distance Education, 6*(3), 5–21.

Doty, D. H., & Glick, W. H. (1998). Common methods bias: Does common methods variance really bias results? *Organizational Research Methods, 1*(4), 374–406.

Dukcevich, D. (2003). America's most connected campuses. Forbes.com, 10-02-03. Retrieved March 19, 2004, from http://www.forbes.com/2003/10/02/cx_dd_1002campus.html

Dumont, R. A. (1996). Teaching and learning in cyberspace. *IEEE Transactions on Professional Communication, 39*(4), 192–204.

Ebel, R. L., & Frisbie, D. A. (1986). *Essentials of educational measurement* (4th ed.). Englewood Cliffs, NJ: Prentice-Hall.

Ellram, L. M., & Easton, L. (1999). Purchasing education on the Internet. *Journal of Supply Chain Management, 35*(1), 11–19.

Entwhistle, N. (2001). Promoting deep learning through teaching and assessment. *Assessment to promote deep learning: Insight from AAHF's 2000 and 1999 assessment conferences* (pp. 9–20). Washington, DC: American Association of Higher Education.

Ferguson, T. D., & Ketchen, D. J., Jr. (1999). Organizational configurations and performance: The role of statistical power in extant research. *Strategic Management Journal, 20*, 385–395.

Fowler, F. J., Jr. (1988). *Survey research methods* (Rev. ed.). Newbury Park, CA: Sage.

Fraenkel, J. R., & Wallen, N. E. (1990). *How to design and evaluate research in education.* New York: McGraw-Hill.

Fredericksen, E., Pickett, A., Shea, P., & Pelz, W. (2000). Student satisfaction and perceived learning with on-line courses: Principles and examples from the SUNY Learning Network. *Journal of Asynchronous Learning Networks, 4*(2). Retrieved March 4, 2004, from http://www.sloan-c.org/publications/jaln/v4n2/v4n2_fredericksen.asp

Freeman, M. A., & Capper, J. M. (1999). Exploiting the web for education: An anonymous asynchronous role simulation. *Australian Journal of Educational Technology, 15*(1), 95–116.

Greco, J. (1999). Going the distance for MBA candidates. *Journal of Business Strategy, 20*(3), 30–34.

Hannigan, C., & Browne, M. (2000). Project management: Going the distance. *International Journal of Instructional Media, 27*, 343–356.

Hartman, J., Dziuban, C., & Moskal, P. (2000). Faculty satisfaction in ALNs: A dependent or independent variable. *Journal of Asynchronous Learning Networks, 4*(3). Retrieved March 4, 2004, from http://www.sloan-c.org/publications/jaln/v4n3/v4n3_hartman.asp

Helmi, D. G., Haynes, G., & Maun, C. (2000). Internet teaching methods across the discipline. *Journal of Applied Business Research, 16*(4), 1–13.

Hiltz, S. R. (1993). Correlates of learning in a virtual classroom. *International Journal of Man–Machine Studies, 39*, 71–98.

Hiltz, S. R. (1994). *The virtual classroom: Learning without limits via computer networks.* Norwood, NJ: Ablex.

Hiltz, S. R., Coppola, N., Rotter, N., Turoff, M., & Benbunan-Fich, R. (2000). Measuring the importance of collaborative learning for the effectiveness of ALN: A multi-measure, multi-method approach. *Journal of Asynchronous Learning Networks, 4*(2). Retrieved March 4, 2004, from http://www.sloan-c.org/publications/jaln/v4n2/v4n2_hiltz.asp

Hiltz, S. R., & Wellman, B. (1997). Asynchronous learning networks as a virtual classroom. *Communications of the ACM, 40*(9), 44–52.

Hiltz, S. R., Johnson, K. D., & Turoff, M. (1986). Experiments in group decision making: Communication process and outcome in face-to-face versus computerized conferences. *Human Communication Research, 13*(2), 225–252.

Hislop, G. W. (1999). Anytime, anyplace learning in an online graduate professional degree program. *Group Decision and Negotiation, 8,* 385–390.

Jarvenpaa, S. L., & Leidner, D. E. (1999). Communication and trust in global virtual teams. *Organization Science, 10,* 791–815.

Kazmer, M. M. (2001). Juggling multiple worlds: Distance students online and offline. *American Behavioral Scientist, 45,* 510–529.

Keppel, G. (1982). *Design and analysis: A researcher's handbook* (2nd ed.). Englewood Cliffs, NJ: Prentice-Hall.

Lazarus, B. D. (2003). Teaching courses online: How much time does it take? *Journal of Asynchronous Learning Networks, 7*(3). Retrieved March 18, 2004, from http://www.sloan-c.org/publications/jaln/v7n3/v7n3_lazarus.asp

Levin, S. R., Levin, J. A., & Waddoups, G. L. (2001, January). CTER Online: Evaluation of an online Master of Education focusing on curriculum, technology and education reform. *Proceedings of the 34th Hawaii International Conference on System Sciences* (CD-Rom). Proceedings, January 2001, Maui, HI, USA. IEEE.

Meyers, D., & Jones, T. B. (1993). *Promoting active learning: Strategies for the college classroom.* San Francisco: Jossey-Bass.

Moskal, P., & Dziuban, C. (2001). Present and future directions for assessing cybereducation: The changing research paradigm. In L. R. Vandervert, L. V. Shavanina, & R. A. Cornell (Eds.), *Cybereducation: The future of long-distance learning* (pp. 151–184). New York: Liebert.

Nulden, U. (1999). Thematic modules in an asynchronous learning network: A Scandinavian perspective on the design of introductory courses. *Decision and Negotiation, 8,* 391–408.

Nystrand, M., Cohen, A. S., & Dowling, N. M. (1993). Addressing reliability problems in the portfolio assessment of college writing. *Educational Assessment, 1*(1), 53–70.

Partee, M. H. (1996). Using e-mail, web sites and newsgroups to enhance traditional classroom instruction. *T.H.E. Journal, 24,* 79–82.

Phillips, V. (1998). On-line universities teach knowledge beyond the books. *HR Magazine, 43,* 120–128.

Piccoli, G., Ahmad, R., & Ives, B. (2001). Web-based virtual learning environments: A research framework and a preliminary assessment of effectiveness in basic IT skills training. *MIS Quarterly, 25,* 401–426.

Redding, T. R., & Rotzien, J. (2001). Comparative analysis of online learning vs. classroom learning. *Journal of Interactive Instruction Development, 13*(4), 3–12.

Resnick, L. (1987). *Education and learning to think.* Washington, DC: National Academy Press.

Sandercock, G. R. H., & Shaw, G. (1999). Learners' performance and evaluation of attitudes towards web course tools in the delivery of an applied sports medicine module. *ALN Magazine, 3*(2). Retrieved March 4, 2004, from http://www.sloan-c.org/publications/magazine/v3n2/v3n2/sandercock.asp

Shen, J., Hiltz, S. R., Cheng, K. E., Cho, Y., & Bieber, M. (2001). Collaborative examinations for asynchronous learning networks: Evaluation results. In *Proceedings of the 34th Hawaii International Conference on Systems Science* [CD Rom]. Los Alamitos, CA: IEEE Computer Society Press.

Slater, T. F. (1997). The effectiveness of portfolio assessments in science. *Journal of College Science Teaching, 26*(5), 315–318.

Smith, G. G., Ferguson, D. L., & Caris, M. (2001). Teaching college courses: Online vs. face-to-face. *T.H.E. Journal, 28*(9), 18–24.

Sorg, S., Truman-Davis, B., Dzubian, C., Moskal, P., Hartman, J., & Juge, F. (1999). Faculty development, learner support and evaluation in web-based programs. *Interactive Learning Environments, 7*(2–3), 137–153.

Steinkeuler, C. A., & Derry, S. J. (2001). Strategies for assessing learning effectiveness. Retrieved March 19, 2004, from http://www.alnresearch.org/jsp/tutorials/assessmenttutorial/index.jsp

Sullivan, P. (2001). Gender differences and the online classroom: Male and female college students evaluate their experiences. *Community College Journal of Research and Practice, 25*, 805–818.

Swan, K. (2001). Building learning communities in online courses: The importance of interaction. *Distance Education, 22*(2), 306–331.

Swan, K. (2003). Learning effectiveness: What the research tells us. In J. Bourne & J. Moore (Eds.), *Elements of quality online education: Practice and direction* (pp. 13–45). Needham MA: Sloan Consortium.

Swan, K., Shea, P., Fredericksen, E., Picket, A., Pelz, W., & Maher, G. (2000). Building knowledge building communities: Consistency, contact, and communication in the virtual classroom. *Journal of Educational Computing Research, 23*, 389–413.

Taylor, J. (1996). The continental classroom: Teaching labor studies on-line. *Labor Studies Journal, 21*, 19–38.

Tomaskovic-Devey, D., Leiter, J., & Thompson, S. (1994). Organizational survey nonresponse. *Administrative Science Quarterly, 39*, 439–457.

Warkentin, M. E., Sayeed, L., & Hightower, R. (1997). Virtual teams versus face-to-face teams: An exploratory study of a web-based conference system. *Decision Sciences, 28*, 975–996.

Weiss, R. E., Knowlton, D. S., & Speck, B. W. (Eds.). (2000). *Principles of effective teaching in the online classroom. New directions for teaching and learning* (Vol. 84). San Francisco: Jossey-Bass.

Williams, L. J., Cole, J. A., & Buckley, M. R. (1989). Lack of method variance in self-reported affect and perceptions at work: Reality or artifact? *Journal of Applied Psychology, 74*, 462–468.

Wright B. (2003, September). *More art than desire: The post secondary assessment movement today.* Paper presented at the Sloan C. Summer Research Workshop, Needham, MA.

Wu, D., Bieber, M., & Hiltz, S. R. (2003). *Improving perceived learning by participatory examination.* Unpublished manuscript.

Yoo, Y., Kanawattanachai, P., & Citurs, A. (2002). Forging into the wired wilderness: A case study of a technology-mediated distributed discussion-based class. *Journal of Management Education, 26*, 139–163.

5

Qualitative and Quisitive Research Methods for Describing Online Learning

Ricki Goldman
New Jersey Institute of Technology

Martha Crosby
University of Hawaii, Manoa

Karen Swan
Kent State University

Peter Shea
State University of New York

ALN researchers at the University of Hawaii were confronted with data that was so contextually rich that they had to move away from numerical coding to explore the more semantic aspects of collaborative work. Rita Vick and her colleagues (2000), teaching human–computer interaction (HCI) courses, were interested in observing how students worked collaboratively online to share and build knowledge. To do so, Vick et al. watched activities in as naturalistic a setting as a virtual classroom can be. They designed a unique cross-institutional and cross-cultural version of the HCI course and then they observed the chats generated by project-based team learning. Researchers analyzed the chats by negotiating meaning as a community of inquiry. Their conclusions were based on emergent themes that arose from a deep description of complex interactions among a group of learners, teachers, and researchers. Is this qualitative research?

INTRODUCTION

This chapter discusses the use of qualitative research methodologies to describe the meaning of learning and teaching within asynchronous learning networks (ALNs). Asynchronous learning networks are distributed online social learning communities in which people advance their shared understanding of a subject under investigation, often becoming epistemologists as they create new learning cultures in the process. First, we explore why qualitative research has, to date, not been a method more fully employed when conducting research about ALN. We argue that the reason is rooted in the dualistic mindset that separates empiricism from rationalism, creating boundaries that may no longer be necessary given computer environments that offer new bridges between the traditional qualitative and quantitative divide. After describing the role of qualitative researchers and diverse methods and examples of conducting this kind of research, we explain why researchers may want to consider combining qualitative and quantitative measures, methods, and tools by using a mixed method called quisitive research (Goldman-Segall, 1998). Quisitive research combines both the quality of inquisitiveness underlying research practices and the notion of a quiz, which supports finding answers to questions. In ALN, which takes advantage of the capabilities and affordances of new media technologies, quisitive research may become a particularly important paradigm for studying learning and teaching practices.

The questions woven throughout this chapter are: Why has qualitative methodology, with all its potential for deeply and richly describing the mindsets of learners and teachers, not played a more key role in the asynchronous learning network research community? Is there a reason for the focus on numeric coding rather than engaging the research audience with the experiences of learners as they participate in the online community? Is there some comfort in numbers for educational social scientists who give their account of learning events? Are the numerical results that quantitative researchers derive more convincing to an audience when effectiveness is the goal? We also ask: Whose interpretation of effectiveness do we value? It is clear that as more students are engaged in this form of learning now than a decade ago—and these numbers will continue to grow, learners and teachers will participate more as research collaborators, thus increasing the need for more interactive research methods.

We propose that to understand the range of human experience in ALNs, a full range of methods also needs to be employed. Researchers must strive for a variety of points of viewing (Goldman-Segall 1998) the data. The *points of viewing theory*, also defined in Goldman-Segall and Maxwell (2002), states that to fully understand teaching and learning in technology-based environments, researchers need to explore how learners and teachers design emerging learning cultures by layering a variety of perspectives to reach conclusions. Geertz (1973) would say that layering the *thick description* improves the validity of conclusions. However, Geertz was not addressing what happens with research in a collaborative online interactive environment using emerging communication and research technologies. Perhaps it is time to address a more integrative picture of what happens to all stakeholders in the asynchronous learning environment. Expanding on the online interaction learning theory (see chap. 2), we put forward a complementary methodological framework for conducting ALN research. This theory, the online interaction research theory, enables researchers to understand the basic premise underlying online research: We study *with* others, not only *about* others, as a community of practice. We use the full array of methods and tools to better understand what we know about learning and teaching as we learn together.

THE CLASSICAL QUANTITATIVE VERSUS QUALITATIVE DIVIDE

Dualistic thinking has been with us since long before biblical times. Day and night; good and evil; man and woman; mind and body. What we know today is that these diverse points serve us best when they remain reference points, not ultimate truths. As simple as it is to have a bifurcated sense of the world, reality is more often about range than polarity. However, philosophers over the centuries have neatly divided the world into two poles: empiricism—the mind as an empty slate (*tabula rasa*), evolving with experience; and rationalism—the mind as an innate structure, open to change through reflection on one's actions. In other words, the empiricist maintains that we can only know what we observe and what we experience in the world, whereas the rationalist argues that we have the capacity to know things that are both a priori and naturalistic. Positivism—the belief that there can be no knowledge of the world that does not directly emerge from observable phenomena—is a direct descendant of empirical thinking, and became the basis of modern sociology. The goal of the positivist is to describe human learning as a science that can be easily replicated given the same conditions. A critique of positivism—postpositivism—states that learning is a more complex, multidimensional, and contextual range of realities and perspectives. Postpositivism assumes that social reality is constructed, and that it is constructed differently by different people. This assumption has some interesting consequences for the role of the qualitative researcher, which we discuss later in this chapter.

Empiricism and rationalism have set the rules of what we describe as (and more important, what we do *not* describe as) science and knowledge. When employing empirical methods, great effort is taken to eradicate personal perspective (or what is commonly referred to as *noise*) in a given study, in order to be as objective as possible. Quantitative researchers claim that to be accurate in one's results, one must eradicate the bias of the human filter. This approach is evident in the language style of most of educational research reports based in the quantitative tradition, which is influenced by common guidelines for reporting educational research, such as the *Publication Manual of the American Psychological Association*. An analysis of the manuals reporting recommendations by Madigan, Johnson, and Linton (1995) concluded:

> In APA style, language use is not allowed to call attention to itself. Dillion (1991) described this as the "rhetoric of objectivity" that has evolved to create the impression of neutrality or impersonal detachment and that is generally characteristic of the empirical studies. This effect is enhanced by giving the persona of the writer a low profile....
>
> APA style leads toward practices that make language appear as a transparent medium for conveying objective information about a fixed external reality. (p. 431)

The standard format for writing reports of quantitative research reflects the epistemology of scientific inquiry—that of objectivity. For the qualitative investigator, research is not so tidy.

THE ROLE OF QUALITATIVE RESEARCHERS

Qualitative researchers do not think that research must be purely objective to be valid. Many qualitative researchers observe people engaged in an act, a process, or an event. The differences are how they observe, how they gather data, and what they do with these data. The range—not only in method but also in the presentation of results—is extremely varied, because authors do not erase themselves from their texts. Qualitative researchers pay attention to personal filters. They do not think that research must be objective to be valid. In contrast with the purportedly objectivist stance of the quantitative researcher, qualitative researchers often describe their personal experiences and reactions in the field, including their interpretation of the effects of data collection on results reported. The attention that researchers place on their roles as co-constructors of the social reality under investigation is called *reflexivity,* and is often evident in the research report. Indeed, many qualitative investigators argue that research is always conducted by a person with a perspective, a filter, and a way of thinking about what she or he is observing coding, interpreting, and writing. Describing their *points of viewing* does not detract from the "story" being told; instead, it validates that the author was "there," meaning that the researcher participated as a member of the culture being studied, even if only as a stranger or outsider. Altheide and Johnson (1994) suggested that good ethnographies— a form of qualitative research that includes participant observation—"show the hand of the ethnographer" (p. 493).

The informants who share their stories with the researcher are the qualitative equivalent of quantitative "research subjects," but because the focus is different in qualitative research, equivalency is not being sought. Meredith Gall, Walter Borg, and Joyce Gall (1996) provided an interesting example. Whereas a quantitative researcher may analyze instances of A grades—represented, for example, by gold stars—to determine whether an intervention had a significant effect on an experimental group of students, the role of the qualitative researcher is quite different. In this instance, the qualitative researcher would interview the students to discover that for some the gold star indicates that they have outperformed their classmates, whereas others might feel that the same gold star indicates that the instructor was too occupied to provide more helpful written feedback. The researcher might find still another interpretation from the teacher, indicating that the gold star was meant to indicate to students that they had written a better paper than previous papers they had submitted (Gall, Borg, & Gall, 1996). Thus, for the quantitative researcher the gold star may have an independent meaning (a fixed measure of high performance), whereas for the qualitative researcher the gold star represents differently constructed social realities, and his or her role as researcher is to uncover and help others learn from these different social constructions of reality.

DEFINITIONS OF QUALITATIVE RESEARCH

Qualitative research is primarily viewed as an inquiry process based on building a holistic, complex understanding of a social problem. It is characterized by data collection in which the researcher acts as a key instrument. Furthermore, the research contains deep rich description and is more concerned with process. Campbell (1997) noted, "[They] assume reality is socially constructed and that variables are complex, interwoven, and difficult to measure. *The researcher seeks the insider's point of view and is personally involved in the process* (p. 125, emphasis added).

Qualitative research methods are used to explore the meanings that people attribute to given circumstances from diverse *points of viewing*. Some qualitative researchers study naturalistic settings and some claim they study *in* settings (Geertz, 1973; Hammersley & Atkinson, 1983). Others consider their impact on the setting the moment they become a member of the culture (Heisenberg, 1958). Some are engaged in postmodern debates on the nature of validity (Goldman-Segall, 1995; Lather, 1986; Maxwell, 1992; Peshkin, 1993). Others are more focused on the story and the method of storytelling, exploring how the text becomes a fiction in and of itself (Barone, 1992; Carter, 1993; Clifford & Marcus,1986; Eisner, 1991; Tyler, 1986; Wolcott, 1990). But, for all the differences of focus, most qualitative researchers conduct hermeneutical (or interpretive) description and analyses.

Qualitative research also includes many methods of inquiry, including ethnographic, case study, phenomenological, hermeneutical, psychoanalytic, feminist, cultural studies, and deconstructionist (Denzin & Lincoln, 1994). Many qualitative researchers use observations and/or interviews to gather data, employing a variety of tools such as pen and paper, audio tape recorders, or video camcorders. They transcribe the gathered data and then perform detailed analyses using tools and interpretation strategies. The key issue in qualitative research is reaching valid conclusions (not generalizations) by convincing description, triangulation, member check, construct validity, and configurational validity, to name but a few.

Ethnography, an important branch of qualitative research, describes the culture of the community being studied. As Hammersley and Atkinson (1983) so aptly described in their definition, ethnography (a branch of qualitative research) "is part of the social world it studies" (p. x) They added:

> We act in the social world and yet are able to reflect upon ourselves and our actions as objects in that world. By including our own role within the research focus and systematically exploiting our participation in the world under study as researchers, we can develop and test theory *without placing reliance on the futile appeals to empiricism,* of either positivist or naturalistic varieties. (p. 25, emphasis added)

Ethnographers are, for the most part, postpositivists who bring their diverse points of viewing to the forefront of the description. They write texts (or make videos) to convince the reader (or viewer) that a particular account of the description is valid. Once collected, research data can be put through a semiotic analysis consisting of assigning signs or attributes to the topic being studied. Alternatively, smaller groupings of data chunks can be clustered so that patterns emerge and conclusions are reached. Generalizations are not the goal of this form of research; *local knowl-*

edge attempts to reach a platform of *commensurability* (Geertz, 1973)—the ability of communities to communicate with each other.

Many ethnographers now work collaboratively, building conclusions as a community of inquiry. Investigators often revisit a field site to ask participants if their experience of the intervention or innovation under investigation was captured in the description and interpretation. Often, during the course of a research study, participants become members of the research community, partaking in the design, implementation, and analysis of the data. This method of reaching conclusions on the data collected about the learner offers interesting possibilities for ALN students who, by reflecting on their role as participants within a study, could become more thoughtful of their learning processes, thereby thinking about the nature of their thinking and becoming an epistemologist. This process of *reflection* (Schön, 1991) on one's learning becomes *reflexion,* what Hammersley and Atkinson (1983) called an interaction among the members of a given culture.

DIVERSE FORMS OF ALN METHODOLOGIES

Surveys

In the previous section, we suggested that most forms of research on ALN have been conducted in the quantitative tradition. Some researchers have mixed quantitative and qualitative approaches. For example, the most commonly used source of information to study ALNs is survey data. However, some ALN surveys have been designed to elicit qualitative data with open-ended questions, which, in turn, have been used by researchers to create quantitative datasets. Surveys in ALN have been used to explore students' and sometimes teachers' perceptions of communication effectiveness (Benbunan-Fich & Hiltz, 1999; Witt, Wheeless, Reyna, & Swigger, 2000), social support (Haythornthwaite, 2002; Walther & Boyd, 2002), interaction (Arbaugh, 2000; Hiltz, Coppola, Rotter, Turoff, & Benbunan-Fich, 2000; Picciano, 2002), collaboration (Curtis & Lawson, 2001), social presence (Gunawardena & Zittle, 1997; Perse, Burton, Kovner, Lears, & Sen, 1992; Picciano, 2002; Richardson & Swan, 2001), teaching presence (Coppola, Hiltz, & Rotter, 2002; Shea, Fredericksen, Pickett, & Pelz, 2002; Shea, Swan, Fredericksen, & Picket, 2002), community (Rovai, 2002), satisfaction (Benbunan-Fich & Hiltz, 1999; Gunawardena & Zittle, 1997), and learning (Arbaugh, 2000; Hiltz et al., 2000; Picciano, 2002; Richardson & Swan, 2001). Surveys are particularly useful for exploring hypothesized relationships among variables, and sometimes, as in the case of open-ended questions, for generating them.

An interesting example of survey-based ALN is the sense of classroom community index (SCCI) developed by Alfred Rovai (2002) to explore the development of learning communities in both traditional and online environments. Rovai used this survey to explore students' sense of community in seven online and seven face-to-face classes. He found that although overall sense of community was the same in both formats, it varied on components contributing to that sense. Moreover, the variability in overall SCCI scores among the online courses was much greater than among face-to-face classes, indicating that the development of community in online courses is more sensitive to course design and pedagogical factors than it is in traditional classrooms.

Transcripts and Grounded Theory

Most qualitative researchers use some form of grounded theory in which conceptual structures are built up from the observations in an inductive matter. In ALN qualitative research, conclusions are continually being refined as layers are constructed in the analyses and new interpretations emerge while analyzing the data transcripts of online discussions. For example, these transcripts of online discussions are digitally stored, and thus they provide readily accessible records of the evolution of social relationships in online classes. Researchers have used transcripts of online chats (Orvis, Wisher, Bonk, & Olson, 2002) and threaded discussions (Hawkes & Romiszowski, 2001; Poole, 2000) to study the social aspects of online learning (Bullen, 1998; Curtis & Lawson, 2001; Gunawardena, Lowe, & Anderson, 1997; Levin, Kim, & Riel, 1990; Rafaeli & Sudweeks, 1997) and the development of social presence itself (Rourke, Anderson, Garrison & Archer, 2001; Swan, 2003).

Transcripts of online discussion provide very rich sources of data about a variety of communicative issues and thus can support, among other things, the development of grounded theories of social learning and the development of community online. For example, Swan (2002) used content analysis of asynchronous course discussions to provide support for an equilibrium theory of social presence in online learning (Danchak, Walther, & Swan, 2001), which argues that students used *verbal immediacy behaviors* in online discussions to replace the nonverbal and vocal clues present in face-to-face discussions. Verbal immediacy behavior lessens the psychological distance between people by providing personal information about oneself and acting friendly (also see chap. 2). Swan's research also gives some indication that different kinds of verbal immediacy behaviors serve different social functions and thus change in importance over time. However, it should be noted that researchers report that coding discussion transcripts is very time consuming, as compared to the time necessary to use a statistical analysis package to tabulate the results of a survey with fixed response categories.

Vicarious Interaction and Witness Learning

In addition, some researchers have noted that students participate in online discussion not just by posting to it but also by reading it. Sutton (2001), for example, suggested that direct participation in online discussion is not necessary for all students all of the time, but that those who actively observe and process both sides of direct interactions among others will benefit from that process, which she called "vicarious interaction." Similarly, Fritsch (1997) noted that what he termed "witness learning" is an integral part of learning from face-to-face discussions. Fritsch was interested in how witness learning is enacted in online environments. Virtual interaction/witness learning may play an important part in legitimate peripheral participation (Lave & Wenger, 1990) and in drawing students into full participation in virtual communities. It cannot be observed in transcripts of online discussions. Some indication of vicarious interaction can be determined through reviewing logs of user access of course pages. Indeed, Fritsch found that users access many times more discussion messages than the number to which they reply. Future research might use something like ratios of message reading to message postings to get some sense of vicarious interaction on the part of individual discussion participants.

Protocols, Message Mapping, and Protocol Analysis

Protocols (step-by-step procedures) have also been developed for content coding of discussions for interaction (Gunawardena et al., 1997; Wang & Tucker, 2001), critical thinking (Bullen, 1998), collaboration (Curtis & Lawson, 2001), verbal immediacy (Witt et al., 2000), and social presence (Rourke et al., 2001; Swan, 2003). Other promising qualitative approaches include message mapping (Bullen, 1998; Levin, et al., 1990) and sociograms (Haythornthwaite, 2002), which create visual maps of communication patterns in online discussion. Caroline Haythornthwaite, for example, suggested studying online learning communities by mapping the social and task support relationships within them. Using interview data to elicit communication patterns among discussion participants, she has mapped task and social support relationships among them to produce sociograms that graphically identify such things as central and peripheral "players" and cliques among students.

Another way of getting this sort of data involves having students "think aloud" as they participate in online discussion, and videotaping this activity. This method is called *protocol analysis*. Using this technique, Polhemus and Swan (2002) found ample evidence of vicarious interaction as well as interesting patterns of student responses. For example, many students identified individuals they regarded as "smart" whose messages they read but to which they did not respond. The very act of thinking aloud, however, changes the way students interact. Interviews with students can help alleviate this problem by including questions about how they normally participate in discussion.

Interviews

Indeed, interviews that are audiotaped or videotaped are another rich source of information in ALN. Interestingly, interviews have been used almost exclusively to gather longitudinal data about the development of virtual communities (Brown, 2001; Haythornthwaite, Kazmer, Robins, & Shoemaker, 2000; Renninger & Shumar, 2002; Stacey, 1999; Wegerif, 1998), perhaps because they can provide detailed and unique information about individuals' perceptions and their changes over time that cannot be obtained otherwise. Ruth Brown (2001), for example, used extensive interviews with selected students and faculty in three graduate-level online education classes, as well as content analysis of course discussion, to develop a grounded theory about the process through which community forms in asynchronous classes.

Mixed and Blended Methods: Quisitive Research

To avoid the problems with various measures noted previously, many researchers use multimeasure, multimethod approaches to data analysis (Hiltz et al., 2000).

These are frequently combined in case studies of individual courses or programs (Gunawardena et. al., 1997; Nolan & Weiss, 2002; Picciano, 2002; Poole, 2000; Russell & Daugherty, 2001; Ryder & Wilson, 1995; Stacey, 1999; Wegerif, 1998) or in comparisons of online and face-to-face courses (Hawkes & Romiszowski, 2001; Hiltz et al., 2000; Rovai, 2002), employing both quantitative and qualitative methodologies. Anthony Picciano (2002), for example, used a mixed method design to relate student perceptions of social presence to actual and perceived interactions and learning in an online graduate course in education. Although he found no overall correlations between perceptions and actual performance in the course, qualitative categorization of students into high, medium, and low groupings showed that students who had the highest perceptions of social presence in the course both interacted more and scored higher on a written assignment than did students in either the medium or low groupings.

Blending of research methodologies has been used to study ALNs due to their focus on complex social phenomenon and their development over time. Researchers tend to employ naturalistic designs: case studies of particular online classes (Coppola et. al., 2002; Gunawardena et al., 1997; Picciano, 2002) or programs (Haythorn-thwaite et al., 2000; Hunter, 2002 Russell & Daugherty, 2001); comparative studies examining particular concepts across multiple course contexts (Rourke et. al., 2001; Swan et al., 2000) or as instantiated in online and traditional environments (Benbunan-Fich & Hiltz, 1999; Hawkes & Romiszowski, 2001; Rovai, 2002); and field studies employing sampling techniques to investigate social supports in participant groups (Brown, 2001; Rafaeli & Sudweeks, 1997; Walther & Boyd, 2002). Because of the nature of their focus, most are likewise at least partially qualitative. They make use of a variety of data collection strategies, often within studies, aimed at eliciting participant perceptions and/or recording participant behaviors.

EMERGING QUISITIVE METHODS

Quisitive research recognizes the continuum between qualitative and quantitative methodologies, thus avoiding the need for a dualistic qualitative/quantitative choice. It examines how both sides of the continuum can be used to inform the research audience about what happened in a given research field study. As mentioned earlier, quisitive research (Goldman-Segall, 1998) combines both the quality of inquisitiveness and inquiry and the notion of the quantitative numerical quiz to understand the learning event. In ALN, which takes advantage of the capabilities of emerging media technologies, quisitive research bridges the qualitative versus quantitative divide by providing new methodological tools and techniques.

Without quantitatively measuring participation in a medium that has been defined by participation, it would difficult if not impossible to study the effectiveness of ALN. However, one can also make a case for examining the actual discourse of the interactions—the nature of the culture of the online learning network. Is it supportive? Does it enable learners to become more fluent in their understanding of the content? To use a more obvious example, let us say that we are gathering data about drivers in traffic paying tolls electronically. We might learn, as quantitative researchers, quite a lot about the patterns of their journeys. Yes, we might even learn, as Resnick and Wilensky (1998) pointed out, how traffic patterns form complex yet understandable patterns. But we will not know what it means to be a person in a car caught in traffic. This person is in the process of interacting with many conditions simultaneously—the surrounding cars, the weather conditions, and the discussion with family members, just to name a few. We will not know what such travelers are thinking about without observing and interviewing them in situ or after their travels are completed. Similarly, if one is studying learning, one needs not only to measure outcomes; one also needs to engage learners in reflecting on their thinking to find how they make meaning of what they are learning.

Researchers who use qualitative methods collect data from various sources such as observation, interviews, and videotape. Yet, in reality, some data are quantified but analyzed qualitatively whereas other data begin qualitatively and are quantified for analysis. Qualitative and quantitative data can be blended to increase validity. Regardless of the primary methodology chosen, researchers should be encouraged to combine methodologies.

One of the characteristics of the use of qualitative methods in ALN research is the role of the observer in the process. Because ALN by definition refers to any-time/anyplace instruction, the researcher must rely heavily on technology to provide most of the information about the students' assumptions and their interactions with other students and their teacher. Much of this information can be gained from the way the students interact with the computer as they complete their assignments. These artifacts can vary widely depending on the type of pedagogy employed, the software environment used, and the type of analysis desired. The amount of information we create and exchange in ALN environments is an essential source of information for the researchers. Observations can also be acquired from the users' actions or their physiological data. These "bottom-up" techniques lead to grounded theory building.

Using mixed methods (an example of quisitive research), Barker and his colleagues (2002) designed, implemented, and evaluated a multimedia learning application. They used a grounded theory based on Strauss and Corbin's model (1994) to understand the many and complex interactions that took place among learners, the course materials, and the learning environment. By blending a variety of research techniques, they developed insights into why the quality of learning was improved.

Traditional quantitative researchers are beginning to recognize the necessity of employing more qualitative methods to interpret their data. For example, Kantor (2000) suggested that qualitative measures such as observation, context, and knowledge of the user should be included in the analysis of physiological measures to provide clues about students' states of mind. In describing eye movements for example, she noted, "[W]e are finding that searchers tend to follow their eyes with the mouse (presumably in order to facilitate the necessary clicking when their eyes fall on an interesting option). Thus, information gleaned by recording and analyzing mouse activity might be of real value *in trying to infer what the user is thinking*" (Kantor, 2000, p. 114, emphasis added).

Computer scientist Rosalind Picard (1997) and members of her research team at the MIT Media Lab have focused on understanding the use of affective technologies for understanding emotions. Technologies can detect a person's physiological states and actions. Researchers now assess mental effort using technologies that can provide feedback using measures such as eye tracking, heart rate, skin temperature, electrodermal activity, and the pressures applied to a computer mouse during task performance. Although at first consideration we tend to categorize these researchers as quantitative, what they are measuring is affective response, a physiological subjective response to both their internal and external worlds. For example, Howard and Crosby (1993) used contextual measures to understand how students in an ALN course examined reference material online. In other words, quantitative measures such as eye movements were used to make sense of students' viewing strategies on bibliographic citations. In related studies, Crosby, Iding, and Speitel (2001), Crosby and Iding (1997), Vick, Crosby, and Ashworth (2000) watched captured representations of simple physiological measurements such as eye movements, galvanic skin response (GSR), heart rate, temperature, and pressure applied to a computer mouse within the overall context of the learning events. Because they were analyzing data at a distance, the researchers had to rely heavily on the descriptive information of the class context to continually negotiate the meaning of the measurements.

SUMMARY

The Research Frontier

The first research frontier we described in this chapter is the need *for quisitive research*—a blend of qualitative and quantitative research practices. ALN researchers will need to gain more understanding of both quantitative and qualitative methods and become well versed in the connections among the two practices. For example, issues of robustness, validity, and reliability will take a subtle shift in meaning; a valid quisitive study will undoubtedly show more triangulation as different tools and perspectives will be used to substantiate a given set of claims.

We predict that the second research frontier will be the inclusion of visual technologies once they become accessible both as a medium of communication in the virtual classroom and as a research tool. Over the coming decade, visual technologies will strongly affect how research on ALN is conducted and researched. With broadband video streaming, it will not be long before video is used routinely in asynchronous learning networks. Although, at first glance, video may not seem to be a viable ALN tool, the medium is certain to become used as soon as the technological infrastructure of online learning can facilitate the additional bandwidth needed to use video and photographs. Teachers may demonstrate a moving event; students may use webcams to personalize their discussions; and researchers may use these images as part of their analysis. Emerging video research tools can address a new set of questions for asynchronous online video learning environments, such as: How will researchers address and resolve issues of diverse cultural contexts? How will researchers understand the creation of gestural meaning once the visual component of ALN is distributed within a culturally diverse world? How will they agree on the meanings of gestures, for example? And, more simply, how will they make meaning of streams of personalized visual artifacts (not only threaded conversations) hanging together like parts of an unfinished symphony? Or, should one argue that *partial knowledge* (Clifford & Marcus, 1986) has always been at the root of every electronic tree structure in the online learning community? One can only wonder, ask, and make predictions about the future knowing that whatever we believe to be true will be affected by future technological and societal advances.

We envision that the third research frontier will be the use of rich media cases in the analysis of the data and in presenting our research results to the consumers of our research, as first described in the use of web constellations, a collaborative online digital data analysis tool, a creative narrative case in organizational knowledge systems (Goldman-Segall & Rao, 1998) Although cases have been extensively used in teaching practices as a way to engage the students in better understanding underlying theoretical principles, case-based research is still used more for a "teaser" than an artifact representing the situation that is being researched. On the research frontier, ALN researchers may use models for designing cases that have already been developed by medical, legal, and some educational research communities, such as the International Society of the Learning Sciences. In these communities, text and video cases are being used extensively to both understand and present findings (Derry, 2003; Goldman-Segall, 1993, 1998; Hmelo, 2001; Tobin & Davidson, 1990).

Most tools have been designed for the analysis of text-based qualitative analysis. However, one research tool has been specifically designed for online digital video ethnographic research—ORION (http://orion.njit.edu; Goldman, 2000). ORION is a digital video ethnographic research tool designed for use by a community of researchers, teachers, and learners in distributed locations to make meaning of rich video data. The metaphor is stellar. Each video data chunk is a star. Stars can be linked together into constellations. Galaxies are datasets, originated by the user. Previous functioning iterations of ORION were Learning Constellations (1989), Constellations (1993), and WebConstellations (1998). Each of these tools enabled groups of users to link video with annotation tools. WebConstellations was a server-based application that enabled users in dispersed locations to upload any data type for analysis.

ORION has returned to the original conception of using only video data and then text for commentary and description. It is based on the multiple perspectives concept that each participant becomes a member of the research community, adding layers of meaning as data are tagged, commented on, linked to related websites, and clustered to build groupings that show patterns of meaning. The most advanced aspect of the tool is the feature that enables users to contribute to the layering of descriptors and to rate them according to their perspective. The rating scheme is a numerical, quantitative aspect of the tool, blending the construction of storymaking with numerical coding—an example of the kind of quisitive tools we expect will be developed over the coming years in many research sites for analysis of complex video-based datasets.

Some of the current features of ORION include:

- Galaxy assignment for each video database, with assignment of users and descriptors.
- Community discussion board.
- An administrator/researcher controls permissions to each function (e.g., add or delete star chunks; add or delete descriptors, create or delete constellation video clusters, etc.).
- Privacy protection of database for assigned users.

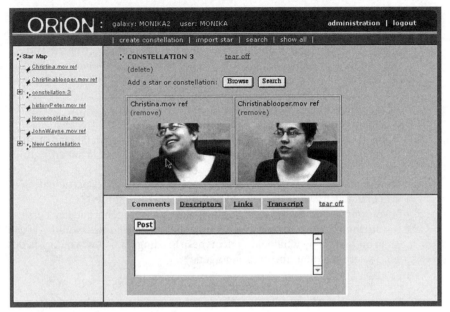

FIG. 5.1.   ORION, an online collaborative research tool for analyzing digital video data, designed by Ricki Goldman.

- Immediate video upload, into ORION, from computer to server.
- Collaborative treelike descriptor attributes assignment while the user is viewing it.
- Annotations, transcripts, links to external websites.
- Numerical video data coding and tables.
- Tear-off pages for additional desktop real estate.
- Deep search (as many levels down as needed).
- Clustering into constellations with comments, transcripts, and external links.

The fourth frontier we have addressed throughout this chapter is how researchers, learners, and teachers can become a community of epistemologists—a group of collaborators considering their own thinking processes as they learn the subject under investigation. Researchers who study learning and teaching will become active members of the diverse communities of inquiry they study. They will be more than the traditional *observer* or *participant observer*, and even more than what has been previously referred to as *participant recorders* (Goldman-Segall, 1998). Researchers on the coming educational frontier will participate fully as community members (Riel, 1993, 1996), facilitators (Collison, Elbaum, Haavind, & Tinker, 2000), and cultural creators making meaning not *about* others, but *with* others.

QUESTIONS FOR DISCUSSION AND RESEARCH

1. If you were writing a literature review, how would you describe the current dichotomy between quantitative and qualitative research and its effect on ALNs?
2. How would you conduct a qualitative or a quisitive research study as new ALN students and teachers form a learning community? How would the two studies be different?
3. What visual technologies would you want to incorporate in either a qualitative or quisitive study? What benefits would you envision? What difficulties could occur?
4. How could you ensure the privacy of students and teachers participating in ALN studies in which visual technologies were being used?
5. If you were to write a proposal to study a group of students and teachers using streaming video in an ALN setting, what main headings would you use as an outline? Why would you select these headings and how would you defend your method to the granting agency?

REFERENCES

Altheide, D. L., & Johnson, J. M. (1994). Criteria for assessing interpretive validity in qualitative research. In N. K. Denzin & Y. S. Lincoln (Eds.), *Handbook of qualitative research* (pp. 485–499). Thousand Oaks, CA: Sage.

Arbaugh, J. B. (2000). How classroom environment and student engagement affect learning in Internet-based MBA courses. *Business Communication Quarterly, 63*(4), 9–26.

Barker, T., Jones, S., Britton, C., & Messer, D. J. (2002). The use of a co-operative student model of learner characteristics to configure a multimedia application. *User Modelling and User Adapted Interaction, 12*(3), 207–241.

Barone, T. E. (1992). Beyond theory and method: A case of critical storytelling. *Theory into Practice, 31*(2), 142–146.

Benbunan-Fich, R., & Hiltz, S. R. (1999). Impacts of asynchronous learning networks on individual and group problem solving: A field experiment. *Group Decision and Negotiation, 8*, 409–426.

Brown, R. E. (2001). The process of community-building in distance learning classes. *Journal of Asynchronous Learning Networks, 5*(2), 18–35.

Bullen, J. (1998). Participation and critical thinking in online university distance education. *Journal of Distance Education, 13(2).* Retrieved March 10, 2003, from http://cade.icaap.org/vol12.2/billen.html

Campbell, T. (1997). Technology, multimedia, and qualitative research in education. *Journal of Research in Computing Education, International Society for Technology in Education, 30*(2), 122–132.

Carter, K. (1993). The place of story in the study of teaching and teacher education. *Educational Researcher, 22*(1), 5–12.

Clifford J., & Marcus, G. E. (Eds.). (1986). *Writing culture: The poetics and politics of ethnography.* Berkeley: University of California Press.

Collison, G., Elbaum, E., Haavind, S., & Tinker, R. (2000). *Facilitating online learning: Effective strategies for moderators.* Madison, WI: Artwood Publishing.

Coppola, N. W., Hiltz, S. R., & Rotter, N. (2002). Building trust in virtual teams. *Communications of the ACM, 45*(4), 56–59.

Crosby, M., & Iding, M. (1997). The influence of cognitive styles on the effectiveness of a multimedia tutor. *Computer Assisted Language Learning, 10*(4), 375–386.

Crosby, M., Iding, M., & Speitel, T. (2001). Capturing students' note-taking strategy with audio recording techniques. In M. J. Smith, G. Salvendy, D. Harris, & R. J. Koubek (Eds.), *Usability evaluation and interface design: Cognitive engineering, intelligent agents and virtual reality* (pp. 327–331). Mahwah, NJ: Lawrence Erlbaum Associates.

Curtis, D. D., & Lawson, M. J. (2001). Exploring collaborative online learning. *Journal of Asynchronous Learning Networks, 5*(1), 21–34.

Danchak, M. M., Walther, J. B., & Swan, K. (2001, November). *Presence in mediated instruction: Bandwidth, behavior, and expectancy violations.* Paper presented at the Seventh Annual Sloan-C International Conference on Online Learning, Orlando, FL.

Denzin, N. K., & Lincoln, Y. S. (Eds.). (1994). *Handbook of qualitative research.* Thousand Oaks, CA: Sage.

Derry, S. (2003, April). *Cognitive art, cognitive science: A video case of teacher cognition.* Paper presented at the American Educational Research Association Annual Meeting, Chicago.

Eisner, E. W. (1991). *The enlightened eye: Qualitative inquiry and the enhancement of educational practice.* New York: Macmillan.

Fritsch, H. (1997). *Witness learning.* Hagen, Germany: Fern Universitat Central Institute for Distance Education Research.

Gall, M., Borg, W., & Gall, J. (1996). *Educational research: An introduction.* White Plains, NY: Longman.

Geertz, C. (1973). *The interpretation of cultures.* New York: Basic Books.

Goldman, R. (2000). ORION video data analysis software. Retrieved from http://orion.njit.edu

Goldman-Segall, R. (1993). Interpreting video data: Introducing a "significance measure" to layer descriptions. *Journal for Educational Multimedia and Hypermedia, 2*(3), 261–282.

Goldman-Segall, R. (1995). Configurational validity: A proposal for analyzing ethnographic multimedia narratives. *Journal of Educational Multimedia and Hypermedia, 4*(2/3), 163–182.

Goldman-Segall, R. (1998). *Points of viewing children's thinking: A digital ethnographer's journey.* Mahwah, NJ: Lawrence Erlbaum Associates. (Interactive video cases available at: http:www.pointsofviewing.com/)

Goldman-Segall, R., & Maxwell, J. W. (2002). Computers, the Internet, and new media for learning. In W. M. Reynolds & G. E. Miller (Eds.), *Handbook of psychology. Vol. 7: Educational psychology* (pp. 393–427). New York: Wiley.

Goldman-Segall, R., & Rao, C. (1998). WebConstellations: A collaborative online digital data tool for creating living narratives in organizational knowledge systems. In *Proceedings for the 31st Hawaii International Conference for Systems Sciences, IEEE* (pp. 194–200).

Gunawardena, C. N., Lowe, C. A., & Anderson, T. (1997). Analysis of a global online debate and the development of an interaction analysis model for examining social construction of knowledge in computer conferencing. *Journal of Educational Computing Research, 17*(4), 397–431.

Gunawardena, C., & Zittle, F. (1997). Social presence as a predictor of satisfaction within a computer mediated conferencing environment. *American Journal of Distance Education, 11*(3), 8–26.

Hammersley, M., & Atkinson, P. (1983). *Ethnography: Principles in practice.* London: Tavistock.

Hawkes, M., & Romiszowski, A. (2001). Examining the reflective outcomes of asynchronous computer-mediated communication on inservice teacher development. *Journal of Technology and Teacher Education, 9*(2), 285–308.

Haythornthwaite, C. (2002). Building social networks via computer networks: Creating and sustaining distributed learning communities. In K. A. Renninger & W. Shumar (Eds.), *Building virtual communities: Learning and change in cyberspace* (pp. 252–259). Cambridge, UK: Cambridge University Press.

Haythornthwaite, C., Kazmer, M. M., Robins, G., & Shoemaker, S. (2000). Community development among distance learners: Temporal and technological dimensions. *Journal of Computer-Mediated Communications, 6*(1). Retrieved March 10, 2003, from http://www.ascusc.org/jcmc/vol6/issue1/haythornthwaite.html

Heisenberg, W. (1958). The role of modern physics in the present development of human thinking. In R. Nanda (Ed.), *Physics and philosophy* (pp. 194–206). New York: Harper and Row.

Hiltz, S. R., Coppola, N., Rotter, N., Turoff, M., & Benbuanan-Fich, R. (2000). Measuring the importance of collaborative learning for the effectiveness of ALN: A multi-measure, multi-method approach. *Journal of Asynchronous Learning Networks, 4*(2). Retrieved March 10, 2003, from http://www.sloan-c.org/publications/jaln/index.asp

Hmelo, C. (2001, April). *Using video-cases to support problem-based learning.* Paper presented at the 2001 American Educational Research Association Annual Meeting, Seattle, WA.

Howard, D., & Crosby, M. (1993). Snapshots from the eye: Towards strategies for viewing bibliographic citations. In G. Salvendy & M. Smith (Eds.), *Advances in human factors/ergonomics: Human–computer interaction: Software and hardware interfaces* (pp. 488–493). Amsterdam: Elsevier Science.

Hunter, B. (2002). Learning in the virtual community depends upon changes in local communities. In K. A. Renninger & W. Shumar (Eds.), *Building Virtual communities: Learning and change in cyberspace* (pp. 96–126). Cambridge, UK: Cambridge University Press.

Kantor, P. B., Boros, E., Melamed, B., Mekov, V., Shapira, B., & Neu, D. J. (2000). Capturing human intelligence in the net. *Communications of the ACM, 43*(8), 112–115.

Lather, P. (1986). Issues of validity in openly ideological research: Between a rock and a soft place. *Interchange, 17*(4), 63–84.

Lave, J., & Wenger, E. (1990). *Situated learning: Legitimate peripheral participation.* Cambridge, UK: Cambridge University Press.

Levin, J. A., Kim, H., & Riel, M. M. (1990). Analyzing instructional interactions on electronic message networks. In L. Harasim (Ed.), *On-line education: Perspectives on a new environment* (pp. 185–214). New York: Praeger.

Madigan, R., Johnson, S., & Linton, P. (1995). The language of style: APA style as epistemology. *American Psychologist, 50*, 428–436.

Maxwell, J. A. (1992). Understanding and validity in qualitative research. *Educational Review, 62*(3), 279–300.

Nolan, D. J., & Weiss, J. (2002). Learning in cyberspace: An educational view of the virtual community. In K. A. Renninger & W. Shumar (Eds.), *Building virtual communities: Learning and change in cyberspace* (pp. 156–172). Cambridge, UK: Cambridge University Press.

Orvis, K. L., Wisher, R. A., Bonk, C. J., & Olson, T. M. (2002). Communication patterns during synchronous web-based military training in problem solving. *Computers in Human Behavior, 18*(6), 783–795. (Special journal issue on computer-based assessment of problem solving.)

Perse, E. M., Burton, P. I., Kovner, E. S., Lears, M. E., & Sen, R. J. (1992). Predicting computer-mediated communication in a college class. *Communication Research Reports, 9*(2), 161–170.

Peshkin, A. (1993). The goodness of qualitative research. *Educational Researcher, 22*(2), 23–29.

Picard, R. (1997). *Affective computing*. Cambridge, MA: MIT Press.

Picciano, A. G. (2002). Beyond student perceptions: Issues of interaction, presence, and performance in an online course. *Journal of Asynchronous Learning Networks, 6*(1), 21–40.

Polhemus, L., & Swan, K. (2002, June). *Student roles in online learning communities: Navigating threaded discussions*. Paper presented at ED MEDIA 2002, Denver, CO.

Poole, D. M. (2000). Student participation in a discussion-oriented online course: A case study. *Journal of Research on Computing in Education, 33*(2), 162–177.

Rafaeli, S., & Sudweeks, F. (1997). Networked interactivity. *Journal of Computer-Mediated Communication, 2*(4). Retrieved February 9, 2003, from http://www.ascusc.org/jcmc/vol2/issue4/rafaeli.sudweeks.html

Renninger, K. A., & Shumar, W. (2002). Community building with and for teachers at the Math Forum. In K. A. Renninger & W. Shumar (Eds.), *Building virtual communities: Learning and change in cyberspace* (pp. 60–95). Cambridge, UK: Cambridge University Press.

Resnick, M., & Wilensky, U. (1998). Diving into complexity: Developing probabilistic decentralized thinking through role-playing activities. *Journal of Learning Sciences, 7*(2). Retrieved March 9, 2003, from http://ccl.sesp.northwestern.edu/cm/papers/starpeople/

Richardson, J., & Swan, K. (2001, April). *An examination of social presence in online learning: Students' perceived learning and satisfaction*. Paper presented at the Annual Meeting of the American Educational Research Association, Seattle, WA.

Riel, M. (1993). Global education through learning circles. In L. M. Harasim (Ed.), *Global networks: Computers and international communication* (pp. 187–207). Cambridge, MA: MIT Press.

Riel, M. (1996). Cross-classroom collaboration: Communication and education. In T. Koschmann (Ed.), *CSCL: Theory and practice of an emerging paradigm* (pp. 221–236). Mahwah, NJ: Lawrence Erlbaum Associates.

Rourke, L., Anderson, T., Garrison, D. R., & Archer, W. (2001). Assessing social presence in asynchronous text-based computer conferencing. *Journal of Distance Education, 14*(2). Retrieved February 25, 2003, from http://www.sloan-c.org.publications/jaln/v4n2/index.asp

Rovai, A. P. (2002). A preliminary look at the structural differences of higher education classroom communities in traditional and ALN courses. *Journal of Asynchronous Learning Networks, 6*(1), 41–56.

Russell, D., & Daugherty, M. (2001). Web crossing: A context for mentoring. *Journal of Technology and Teacher Education, 9*(3), 433–446.

Ryder, M., & Wilson, B. (1995, April). *From local to virtual learning environments: Making the connection*. Paper presented at the annual meeting of the American Educational Research Association, San Francisco.

Schön, D. A. (1991). *The reflective turn: Case studies in and on educational practice*. New York: Teachers Press, Columbia University.

Shea, P. J., Fredericksen, E. E., Pickett, A. M., & Pelz, W. E. (2002, February). *A preliminary investigation of "teaching presence" in the SUNY Learning Network*. Paper presented at the Fourth Annual Sloan ALN Workshop, Boltons Landing, NY.

Shea, P. J., Swan, K., Fredericksen, E. E., & Pickett, A. M. (2002). Student satisfaction and reported learning in the SUNY Learning Network. In J. Bourne & J. C. Moore (Eds.), *Elements of quality online education* (Vol. 3). Olin and Babson Colleges, Sloan Center for Online Education.

Stacey, E. (1999). Collaborative learning in an online environment. *Journal of Distance Education, 14*(2). Retrieved February 25, 2003, from http://cade.iccap.org/vol14.2/stacey.html

Strauss, A., & Corbin, J. (1994). Grounded theory methodology: An overview. In N. K. Denzin & Y. S. Lincoln (Eds.), *Handbook of qualitative research* (pp. 1–18). London: Sage.

Sutton, L. A. (2001). The principle of vicarious interaction in computer-mediated communications. *International Journal of Educational Telecommunications, 7*(3), 223–242.

Swan, K. (2003). Developing social presence in online discussions. In S. Naidu (Ed.), *Learning and teaching with technology: Principles and practices* (pp. 147–164). London: Kogan.

Swan, K., Shea, P., Fredericksen, E., Pickett, A, Pelz, W., & Maher, G. (2000). Building knowledge building communities: Consistency, contact and communication in the virtual classroom. *Journal of Educational Computing Research, 23*(4), 389–413.

Tobin, J., & Davidson, D. (1990). Ethics of polyvocal ethnography. *International Journal of Qualitative Studies in Education, 3*(3), 271–283.

Tyler, S. (1986). Post-modern ethnography: From document of the occult to occult document. In J. Clifford & G. E. Marcus (Eds.), *Writing culture: The poetics and politics of ethnography* (pp. 122–140). Berkeley: University of California Press.

Vick, R., Crosby, M., & Ashworth, D. (2000). Japanese and American Students meet on the Web: Collaborative languagelearning through everyday dialogue with peers. *Computer Assisted Language Learning, 13*(3), 199–219.

Vick, R. M., & Ikehara, C. S. (2003). Methodological issues of real time data acquisition from multiple sources of physiological data. *Proceedings of the 36th Annual Hawaii International Conference on System Sciences (HICSS36), 1–7*, 0-7695-1874-5 2003 IEEE.

Walther, J. B., & Boyd, S. (2002). Attraction to computer-mediated social support. In C. A. Lin & D. Atkin (Eds.), *Communication technology and society: Audience adoption and uses of the new media* (pp. 153–188). Cresskill, NJ: Hampton.

Wang, A. Y., & Tucker, T. L. (2001). A discourse analysis of online classroom chats: Predictors of cyber-student performance. *Teaching of Psychology, 28*(3), 222–226.

Wegerif, R. (1998). The social dimension of asynchronous learning. *Journal of Asynchronous Learning Networks, 2*(1), 34–49.

Witt, P. L., Wheeless, L. R., Reyna, J., & Swigger, K. (2000, November). *An initial examination of observed verbal immediacy and participants' opinions of communication effectiveness in on-line group interaction.* Paper presented at the annual meeting of the National Communication Association, Seattle, WA.

Wolcott, H. (1990). *Writing up qualitative research.* Newbury Park, CA: Sage.

II

LEARNING NETWORKS:
WHAT WE KNOW
AND WHAT WE NEED TO KNOW

6

Contextual Factors That Influence ALN Effectiveness

J. B. Arbaugh
University of Wisconsin–Oshkosh

Raquel Benbunan-Fich
City University of New York

There seems to be little question that our present understanding of the use of CMC and computer conferencing for purposes of online learning is seriously limited. Progress will necessitate a concerted and multipronged approach to studying the technology, pedagogy, and organization of online learning. Moreover, scholars in the field of distance education must take a leading role in this work or risk being marginalized in an area where we have previously provided innovative leadership. The importance to the field of distance education of further research on the use of computer-mediated communication (CMC) for purposes of online learning should not be underestimated. Perhaps no other area of study will have a greater impact on the future of distance education. (Garrison, Anderson, & Archer, 2003, p. 127)

INTRODUCTION

As the theoretical framework presented in chapter 2 suggests, there are several contextual or environmental factors that influence ALN effectiveness. These include characteristics of the technology used (e.g., the software platform and the media mix), the instructor and his or her pedagogical style, the course, and especially the type of support provided by the institution through which the course is offered.

Although characteristics of individual instructors and/or students certainly impact the learning environment, institutions seeking to develop online courses and programs need to consider additional factors in developing their virtual instructional capability. These factors are important because student expectations for overall quality of online instruction are rising both quickly and dramatically. Identifying a set of noninstructor-specific characteristics that positively influence online learning could help build a more level playing field for all instructors, and raise the overall quality of the online educational experience they provide. This chapter examines some of those "nonperson-specific" characteristics that may be the most influential for ALN effectiveness. We review existing literature on contextual factors, identify significant characteristics that emerge from the findings, suggest some other potential factors, and describe ways in which these characteristics might be more thoroughly studied in future research.

TECHNOLOGICAL CHARACTERISTICS

From their humble beginnings as extensions of proprietary computer-mediated communication systems or combinations of electronic tools such as e-mail, web pages, and newsgroups (Dumont, 1996), delivery platforms for ALNs have evolved in a relatively short time period into fairly sophisticated, increasingly interactive software packages. Although a substantial body of research has been conducted on institution-specific platforms such as NJIT's Virtual Classroom® (Benbunan-Fich & Hiltz, 1999; Coppola, Hiltz, & Rotter, 2002; Hiltz, 1994; Hiltz & Turoff, 2002; Hiltz & Wellman, 1997) and the SUNY Learning Network's Course Management System (Fredericksen, Pickett, Shea, & Pelz, 2000; Swan, 2002; Swan et al. 2000), many institutions are adopting platforms produced by outside software companies. Research on these commercial platforms is growing rapidly.

Software Platforms

The predominant courseware packages are Blackboard®, an online course management system that traces its technology roots to Cornell University, and WebCT®, another popular asynchronous course management system developed at the University of British Columbia, Vancouver. Other systems include First Class®, TopClass®, and Lotus LearningSpace®. The latter is an add-on application written in Lotus Notes, which requires setup and configuration, because it is a client-based software platform.

WebCT®, developed by Dr. Murray Goldberg and a group of researchers at the University of British Columbia (Wernet, Olliges, & Delicath, 2000), was intended to make the development and maintenance of ALNs a relatively simple exercise for faculty. Studies of WebCT® to date have generally been favorable, particularly in situations in which it is used to supplement classroom courses (Hartman, Dziuban, & Moskal, 2000; Sandercock & Shaw, 1999; Wernet et al., 2000) or synchronous online course offerings (Borthick & Jones, 2000).

Another commonly used software platform that has received research attention is Lotus Notes®, and its learning software derivative, LearningSpace®. Unfortunately, results of research on ALN courses using LearningSpace® have been mixed. Although LearningSpace® has performed favorably in comparisons of student performance in ALNs and classroom courses (Alavi, Yoo, & Vogel, 1997;

Arbaugh, 2000a; Piccoli, Ahmad, & Ives, 2001), it also has been associated with increased interaction difficulty (Arbaugh, 2000b; Yoo, Kanawattanachai, & Citurs, 2002), scored significantly lower in user friendliness compared to other software packages (Arbaugh, 2002a; Arbaugh & Duray, 2001), and has required the installation of Lotus Notes® on student machines to ensure that the students did not lose their work (Smith, 2001). These difficulties may be part of the reason that Lotus Development has been seeking to use LearningSpace® as more of a synchronous learning tool in the future.

Despite its increasing popularity, research on the Blackboard®/CourseInfo software package is rather limited. However, a recent study shows it as having higher scores of perceived usefulness and ease of use along with significantly higher student satisfaction scores when compared with LearningSpace® (Arbaugh, 2002a). Other software platforms on which research has been conducted include FirstClass® (McIssac et al. 1998), TopClass® (Freeman & Capper, 1999); and MeetingWeb® (Warkentin, Sayeed, & Hightower, 1997). Although each of these software platforms has received varying degrees of research attention, comparative research on the effectiveness of these software packages is rather limited (Palloff & Pratt, 2001).

Functionality

ALN functionality as implemented in these commercial software applications includes a variety of features in three main areas:

- Content delivery: includes document posting (e.g., course syllabus, lecture notes, assignments, etc.) and file sharing for homework submission.
- Communication: in two modes, synchronous and asynchronous. Synchronous communication refers to real-time chats, whereas asynchronous refers to e-mail, bulletin boards, and threaded discussions.
- Assessment: tools for the evaluation of student performance. They include online quizzes with time monitoring, exams, and surveys.

In addition, these software platforms typically include capabilities for secure student log-in, centralized database-centered syllabus with links to internal or external web pages, and integrated e-mail. As in the early ALN implementations, the objective of this new generation of commercial applications is to provide a central location for delivery of course content and additional information or links, and communication between instructors and students or among students.

Quality and Reliability

The quality and reliability of any ALN environment is critical, especially when it is used as the only instructional delivery medium. Technology-mediated distance courses in which the technology is reliable and of high quality tend to be more successful (Webster & Hackley, 1997). However, the effects of system quality and/or reliability typically have not been measured in the design of most ALN research. This is likely because intentionally varying system quality and reliability would be inappropriate in actual educational environments. However, if researchers considered and designed their studies for the possibility that systems may not work as planned, they could produce useful research on the management of technological crises in the delivery of education via ALNs.

Media Bandwidth

Historically, courses delivered using ALNs have relied extensively on text-based transmission of course content and discussion. This is true for a number of reasons, such as limited bandwidth, concerns over minimum hardware/software requirements for students, and the learning curve required for both students and instructors to effectively manage the ALN environment. As a result, research that examines the effects of various types of media on ALN course outcomes is rather limited, and the body of research available on the use of media in ALNs has produced mixed results. (See chap. 10 in this volume for a more extensive review of media research.)

For instance, Webster and Hackley (1997) studied 29 technology-mediated distance courses with full-motion video and compressed video. Findings suggest that in order to be successful, technology-mediated distance learning courses should use rich media, few student locations, and instructors who project positive attitudes, employ interactive teaching styles, and help students become comfortable with having their images displayed on the screen.

LaRose, Gregg, and Eastin (1998) compared traditional classroom instruction with a web telecourse based on prerecorded audio class interactions and a course web site. Findings show that students in the telecourse had test scores and perceptions (student attitude and teacher immediacy ratings) equal to those of students in the traditional classroom. Conversely, Arbaugh (2002b) found that the use of varying numbers of audio and/or video clips in a study of 13 ALN courses was not a significant predictor of student learning or course satisfaction. Some possible research questions in this area include: How much media variety is most effective within ALN settings? What are some of the contextual factors most likely to influence the optimal course media mix? In what ways can the various media types be used most effectively in ALNs? (These issues are explored further in chap. 10.)

THE INSTRUCTOR'S PEDAGOGY AND BEHAVIOR

Different pedagogical approaches and learning strategies suggest different ALN uses and may require different software capabilities. In fact, effective applications of ALN are those that match the pedagogical model driving the course (Benbunan-Fich, 2002). As previously described in chapter 2, there are two broad categories of pedagogies: instructivist and constructivist. The instructivist model is based on lecturing using a one-way transmission of knowledge from the professor (or recorded lectures or books) to the students. In this approach, each student learns individually. The constructivist perspective assumes that knowledge is created or constructed by every learner interacting with others (Leidner & Jarvenpaa, 1995). In this model, teaching is a communal experience in which knowledge is created through constructive dialogue and group discussion, and the professor's role is to *facilitate* the process. These different approaches make different demands on technology (Benbunan-Fich, 2002).

Teaching/Learning Models

Pedagogy emphasizing the one-way transmission of concepts (instructivist approach) calls for the use of a system that improves the efficiency of this transfer in the lecturing process. In contrast, constructivist models call for learner-centered applications in which students can construct their own knowledge by formulating ideas into words and building on these ideas through discussions, reactions, and responses of their peers. For constructivist methods based on collaborative group assignments, the technological platform should support communications among students (Benbunan-Fich, 2002).

A significant question meriting future research attention is whether either of these approaches or a combination of them best predicts student learning and/or satisfaction in the ALN environment. Evidence to date is somewhat mixed. Initial research on learning in computer-mediated communication environments suggests that ALNs support collaborative constructivist approaches better than classrooms do (Alavi, Wheeler, & Valacich, 1995; Chidambaram, 1996), but some subsequent studies have found that classroom settings are associated with greater student satisfaction with collaborative learning approaches (Card, 2000; Warkentin et al., 1997). However, these studies typically compared learning settings on their applicability for collaborative approaches rather than studying the viability of the approach itself. Also, many of these earlier studies were based on individual courses or a limited number of courses.

More recent research has examined collaborative learning in larger course samples, but results are inconsistent. Hiltz, Coppola, Rotter, Turoff, and Benbunan-Fich (2000) studied 26 information systems courses over a 3-year period and found strong evidence for the effectiveness of collaborative learning in ALN environments. However, a study conducted by Swan (2002) of 73 courses offered by the SUNY Learning Network found that collaborative learning was negatively associated with student learning in ALNs. She pointed out that it was difficult to determine whether this relationship could be attributed to the concept of collaborative learning being faulty or whether the concept is fine but was poorly practiced. The inconclusive nature of this research to date suggests that determining which pedagogical approaches are most appropriate or the contextual factors that make one more appropriate than another will be a topic meriting extensive research throughout the first decade of the 21st century (it is explored further in chap. 9).

One variable related to the instructor's behavior that has been well established is the extent to which quality interaction takes place among course participants (Fredericksen et al., 2000; Hiltz & Turoff, 2002; Nulden, 1999; Palloff & Pratt, 1999). Some studies suggest that it is the instructor's role in course interaction that is most critical (Arbaugh, 2000b, 2000a; Brower, 2003; Fredericksen et al., 2000), whereas others suggest that the students' role in interaction most significantly predicts student learning and/or satisfaction (Arbaugh, 2002b; Borthick & Jones, 2000; Nulden, 1999; Smith, Ferguson, & Caris, 2001), and still others suggest that both roles are equally important (Coppola et al., 2002; Hiltz, 1993; Jiang

& Ting; 2000; Palloff & Pratt, 2001). However, it is not certain whether this interaction should be primarily between the instructor and the students, or among the students themselves.

Although the prominence of the instructor's role in course interaction remains unclear, the nature of their interaction is becoming well established. The extent to which an instructor engages in immediacy behaviors appears to be strongly associated with student outcomes. Originally conceptualized by Mehrabian (1971), *immediacy* refers to communication behaviors that reduce social and psychological distance between people (Myers, Zhong, & Guan, 1998). In the ALN context, immediacy describes behaviors such as including personal examples, using humor, providing and inviting feedback, and addressing students by name (Gorham, 1988). There is increasing evidence that these behaviors are positively associated with student learning and satisfaction with the course format (Arbaugh, 2001, 2002b; Frietas, Myers, & Avtgis, 1998).

Pedagogical Techniques

ALNs allow instructors to increase the efficiency of knowledge transmission in regular courses by posting lecture materials, audio, and videos on the Web. In distance learning courses, these recordable lectures, delivered via computer, replace the traditional face-to-face lectures. In addition to supporting content transmission by posting materials electronically, ALNs can also support communication exchanges among students, and between professors and students. By using these communication capabilities, professors can effectively implement collaborative group assignments (e.g., case study discussions) without forcing the students to meet face to face after class (Benbunan-Fich, 2002).

In large lectures, where class discussions are not feasible, ALNs can be used to establish a virtual communication forum that allows students to asynchronously discuss topics covered in class. As a pedagogical technique, the availability of this virtual communication environment reduces the impersonal feelings traditionally associated with this mode of delivery (Althaus, 1997; Thoennessen, Kashy, Tsai, & Davis, 1999).

Another pedagogical technique that has been found to be very successful in ALNs is the use of the medium to provide peer evaluation and feedback. In this approach, students post their assignments or essays online and other students criticize and offer feedback. This allows students to learn from each other and to develop their critical thinking skills (Hiltz, 1994). ALNs are also suitable to support the discussion and debriefing of case studies, papers, projects, and exams. The success of any technique and pedagogical approach implemented in a technology-mediated environment is contingent on other factors that determine the dynamics of the course and the particular characteristics of the technological implementation.

COURSE CHARACTERISTICS

In addition to the pedagogical model, course characteristics also place different demands on ALNs. At this level, four characteristics have been identified as relevant for successful implementation of ALNs: demographics (class size, level, participant dispersion, etc.), mode of delivery, and discipline.

Course Demographics

Demographic characteristics such as the number of students enrolled in a course, the level (undergraduate or graduate) of the students, and the dispersion of the participants introduce different interaction dynamics that may determine the success (or failure) of an ALN implementation.

Class Size.   The number of students enrolled in a course produces different group dynamics. Large classes tend to be more impersonal and less individualized than smaller ones are. Hiltz and Wellman (1997) found that an ALN course of 96 students was a difficult setting for helping students get a personal feeling for each other, and noted that student rebellions were not uncommon. Using a sample of courses with enrollments of up to 50 students, Arbaugh and Duray (2001, 2002) found that class section size was negatively associated with student learning. Other studies with class sizes of 30 or fewer students have found that class size was not a significant predictor of student learning or satisfaction (Arbaugh, 2001, 2002a, 2002b).

These findings prompt at least two possible explanations or solutions to the class size issue. One possibility is that the class size–outcome relationship is curvilinear in nature (Piccoli et al., 2001); that is, increasing class size improves student learning to a point, but adding students beyond that point reduces the quality of the course experience. A possible solution for this issue may be through adding additional instructional support personnel as class sizes increase. Andriole (1997) proposed maximum instructor/course quality ratios: 1 instructor for every 30 students, 1 instructor + 1 ALN assistant for every 50 students, 1 instructor + 2 ALN assistants for every 75 students, and so on. Additional research is needed to identify optimal student–instructor ratios in ALN settings.

Level.   The level of the students enrolled in a course (undergraduate vs. graduate) also may dictate different approaches to the use of ALNs. Unfortunately, our present ability to make inferences about this factor is inhibited by the fact that most ALN studies have examined either undergraduate or graduate samples without combining the student populations. In one of the few comprehensive studies using both student groups in their sample, Benbunan-Fich and Hiltz (2002) studied 1,974 undergraduate and graduate students in several traditional, pure ALN, and mixed-mode courses. They found that graduate students in hybrid courses had the highest levels of perceived learning, whereas undergraduates in hybrid courses had the lowest scores in perceived learning. However, other studies using both groups suggest that undergraduates may be more excited about the use of technology for learning (Wernet et al., 2000) and more playful in their use of the Internet, therefore possibly better able to use it as a learning tool (Atkinson & Kydd, 1997). Clearly, this limited pool of research suggests that the relationship between student educational level and course outcomes is an area in which additional study is needed.

Participant Dispersion.   In ALNs, course participants can either be in the same geographic location (proximate) or in different places (dispersed). Initial research suggests that this dispersion may have limited impact on course effectiveness. Alavi et al. (1995) conducted a longitudinal field study (three work sessions) to investigate collaborative learning among nonproximate team members interacting at the same time by using Desktop Video Conferencing. The study compared the efficacy of this environment to that of a synchronous/proximate environment and a traditional unsupported face-to-face environment. Research findings indicate that the three environments are equally effective in terms of student knowledge acquisition and satisfaction with their learning process and outcomes. Distant teams showed higher critical skills and more commitment to their groups than did the students in the other conditions.

These initial findings have been supported by subsequent studies of participant dispersion in ALNs. Studies by Alavi et al. (1997), Jarvenpaa and Leidner (1999), and Yoo et al. (2002) of ALN applications within multilocation classroom-based courses suggested similar learning benefits from the use of ALNs. Therefore, future research on geographical dispersion should address the topic in combination with other variables such as learner/instructor cultural characteristics (Jarvenpaa & Leidner, 1999; Nulden, 1999), system and user hardware capability (Gallini, 2001; Liaw, 2001), or the variety of media used in the courses (Arbaugh, 2002b) to help determine whether contextual factors moderate the effects that participant dispersion might have on ALN effectiveness.

Online/Classroom Hybrid Courses

A course format increasing in popularity is the hybrid "mixed-mode" or "blended" course model (Cookson, 2002). In this model, a course combines traditional face-to-face class meetings with asynchronous electronic communication. Initial results from studies of these courses are encouraging. Althaus (1997) studied 115 of 142 undergraduate sociology students in three classroom-based courses supplemented with asynchronous communication from 1992 to 1993. (Only one fourth of the students had ever used e-mail prior to the study). He found that the students who participated in the asynchronous course communication tended to earn higher grades than did those who took part in face-to-face conversations only. Thoennessen et al. (1999) discerned that undergraduate physics students in a large lecture section supplemented by ALN had 20% higher midterm grades and 10% higher course grades, and missed 12% fewer classes, than did previous traditional classes.

In a collaborative project between two universities, Alavi et al. (1997) used a mixed-mode model of classroom, compressed video, and asynchronous communication. They found no significant differences in student performance between the synchronous and asynchronous activities within the course. Yoo et al. (2002) studied a similar mixed-mode approach in an international collaborative education project. They also reported no significant difference in student performance between the various communication modes, but found that group learning scores were significantly higher than were individual scores. They suggested that both the synchronous and asynchronous communication technologies seemed to enhance both group and individual thinking and learning as the course progressed.

Initial larger-scale studies comparing classroom, ALN, and mixed-mode courses have also yielded encouraging results. Hartman et al. (2000) surveyed faculty who evaluated 36 undergraduate ALN and mixed-mode courses offered by five colleges at the University of Central Florida in the spring of 1998. The faculty felt that the online and hybrid courses took more work, but also that these courses had increased interaction frequency and interaction quality for both web and hybrid compared to classroom. The authors compared student outcomes of those with the classroom courses conducted during that semester and found that students in hybrid courses significantly outperformed students in classroom settings. This finding is consistent to the one reported by Benbunan-Fich and Hiltz (2002), in which graduate students in mixed-mode courses exhibited the highest levels of learning perception.

Very few studies have included systematic comparisons among the three modes of course delivery: traditional, mixed mode, and pure ALN. Most of them present two-way comparisons (traditional vs. mixed or distance vs. mixed). The empirical evidence suggests that due to their hybrid nature, mixed-mode courses may combine the best of both worlds. Due in part to these encouraging initial findings, some researchers have called for the mixed-mode model to play an increasingly prominent role in the development of future courses and degree programs (Alavi & Leidner, 2001).

Discipline-Specific Characteristics

The majority of discipline-based research on ALNs resides in the information systems area. Some of the reasons for this are the pioneering work on ALNs in information systems courses done by Roxanne Hiltz, Murray Turoff, and colleagues at the New Jersey Institute of Technology (Benbunan-Fich & Hiltz, 1999; Hiltz, 1994; Hiltz & Turoff, 2002; Turoff & Hiltz, 2001), and this discipline's interest in topics such as technology adoption (Davis, 1989), computer-mediated communication (Chidambaram, 1996; Hiltz, Johnson, & Turoff, 1986; Jarvenpaa & Leidner, 1999), and decision support systems (Alavi et al., 1997).

Research on ALNs in information systems courses suggest that students perform as well or better via an ALN than in a classroom setting (Alavi et al., 1997; Andriole, 1997; Hiltz et al., 2000; Turoff & Hiltz, 2001). ALN promotes the acquisition of technical procedural knowledge (Piccoli et al., 2001), encourages collaborative learning (Borthick & Jones, 2000), and increases student access to instructors and student–instructor interaction (Hislop, 1999).

Recent research in ALNs has broadened to include studies in other disciplines, particularly in business, education, and the sciences. ALN research in business education to date has focused primarily on single course experiences (Eastman & Swift, 2001; Smith, 2001) and comparisons with face-to-face course activities (Arbaugh, 2000b; Hanningan & Browne, 2000; Yoo et al., 2002), but is beginning to move toward identifying characteristics such as perceived flexibility (Arbaugh, 2000b; 2000a; Arbaugh & Duray, 2002), interaction among course participants (Arbaugh, 2002b; Borthick & Jones, 2000; Salmon, 2000), and instructor behaviors and experience (Arbaugh, 2001, 2002b; Arbaugh & Duray, 2001; Coppola et al., 2002) that predict learning and/or satisfaction with ALNs.

Studies directly comparing business disciplines such as management, accounting, marketing, and finance are rather limited, but initial work in this area suggests that factors such as technology, course structure, and instructor-specific behaviors may be more significant predictors of differences in courses than characteristics of any particular subdiscipline (Arbaugh, 2000b; Arbaugh & Duray, 2002).

Like research in business courses, ALN research in science courses to date appears to have focused primarily on comparisons with classroom courses of student performance. For the most part, these studies suggest that students in science courses using ALNs perform as well or better than students in classroom settings (Ricketts, Wolfe, Norvelle, & Carpenter, 2000; Sandercock & Shaw, 1999; Thoennessen et al., 1999). In a variation within the online versus face-to-face course comparison research stream, DiBiase (2000) examined faculty workloads for a geography course. He discovered that although the online course required more focused attention, the total teaching and maintenance time per student was less than that needed for the classroom course (DiBiase, 2000).

ALN research in education courses has investigated primarily student and faculty behaviors. Swan (2002) and Gunawardena and Zittle (1997) found that increased student practice of immediacy behaviors is positively associated with their perceptions of their course experience. Other educational researchers have studied collaborative behaviors among students. Foley and Schuck (1998) noted that mathematics education students reported increased opportunity for collaboration, but this was constrained by difficulties with the technology and relatively large group sizes that inhibited collaborative activities.

When comparing asynchronous and face-to-face sections of a doctoral seminar in educational leadership, Card (2000) found that students in the face-to-face section had interactions based more on experiences, whereas the online students tended to cite literature and link their beliefs to the authors. Although class participation was more uniform across the online participants, the face-to-face students had higher perceptions that their cooperative learning environment promoted interaction. However, no significant differences were found in learning or satisfaction between the two class sections.

Still other researchers have investigated how student behaviors and attitudes change over time. Levin, Levin, and Waddoups (2001) surveyed 26 master's of education students at the University of Illinois at multiple points as they progressed through an online degree program. The students were mostly satisfied with their program and maintained positive attitude about technology throughout the program. They did report significantly less positive attitudes toward learning in lecture format, decreases in learning ability through online projects, and significant improvement in time management skills as they progressed through their online program.

An area that merits future research is cross-disciplinary studies of ALNs. Although there have been relatively few studies of this nature to date, initial results are encouraging. In a study of information systems, engineering, management, and humanities courses 1997–2000, Benbunan-Fich and Hiltz (2002) discerned that students in ALN courses tended to get higher grades than students in face-to-face courses did, with no significant differences between the more technical and less technical courses. Other cross-disciplinary studies have focused more on instructor perceptions. These studies suggest that instructors must be more organized in the preparation and presentation of their material, and that interaction within the course shifts toward evenly distributed participation between and among instructor and students (Coppola et al., 2002; Smith et al., 2001).

Studies directly comparing disciplines are even scarcer. A study of directors of ALN projects for courses in Spanish, microbiology, economics, mathematics, chemistry, and physics posited that all of the directors were satisfied with their experiences with ALNs (Arvan & Musumeci, 2000). However, because this was a study of relatively early adopters, the authors recommended that these findings should be taken with a note of caution.

Overall, it appears that, to date, ALN research has been conducted to a widely varying extent within disciplines. Whereas some disciplines such as information systems have been the subject of extensive ALN research, others such as the humanities have received little or no research attention. Therefore, although ALNs appear to be effective in a number of educational settings, making generalizations as to the applicability of ALNs across disciplines may be premature. These generalizations can only be made if previous results can be replicated in subsequent multicourse, multidiscipline studies. Certainly, research aimed at increasing the generalizability of these findings should be a high priority in the next decade.

INSTITUTIONAL CHARACTERISTICS

The broader contextual factor influencing ALN effectiveness is the institution. Unfortunately, most of the literature on asynchronous learning networks deals with the pedagogical and technological advantages of this environment while ignoring the institutional obstacles that may prevent the widespread implementation of ALNs (Alavi & Gallupe, 2003; Jaffee, 1998). The existing research regarding institutional characteristics is mostly prescriptive. Different authors advise institutions on how to embrace the promises of the technology and improve teaching and learning productivity without sacrificing the quality of instruction. However, some authors argue that in order to reap the benefits of the new technology, a total institutional restructuring must occur (Graves, 1997; Moore, 1999).

Although the more than 3,000 traditional institutions in the United States are different in terms of mission, size, location, degree programs, faculty, curriculum, and selectivity, they share a number of characteristics, such as a residential student body; a recognized geographic service area; full-time faculty members who engage in teaching, research, and service; a central library and physical plant; public or private status; and indicators of organizational effectiveness (Hanna, 1998).

Based on these characteristics, some studies (e.g., Hanna, 1998; Moore, 1999) present different organizational models of higher education that offer an alternative to the traditional residential model and, at the same time, meet the new challenges of the digital era. Other institutional studies are mainly focused on identifying the potential obstacles that may impede the successful implementation of ALNs (Hawkins, 1999; Jaffee, 1998). Although these obstacles may be different depending on each organizational context, typical institutional challenges can be classified in three critical areas: technological support, administrative support for faculty engaged in ALN course development and teaching, and policy issues.

Technological Support

A recent multi-institutional study of technology-mediated learning suggests that colleges and universities tend to underestimate the cost of providing the additional technical support for implementing ALN initiatives (Alavi & Gallupe, 2003). Increased demand to access the ALN system and other campus computing facilities may cause slowdowns or service outages that inconvenience students and faculty (Hiltz, 1994). Likewise, attacks on central servers that host ALN platforms may slow or completely halt their operation; the speed of recovery depends on the size and competence of the technical support staff. If the technological infrastructure is not adequate, it may be necessary to invest in new servers, more or better technical support staff, security measures, support and help desks, and high-speed and high-capacity networks (Hawkins, 1999). Hardware, software, and telecommunication upgrades must be constantly evaluated, not only because of increasing demand but also due to the rate of technical change.

Technical tools and services tend to change faster than does the institutional capacity to process and incorporate such changes. Traditionally slow organizational processes of universities cannot keep up with these changes. To compound this problem, institutions are increasingly unable to keep staff with cutting-edge technology skills. Despite the difficulties of managing technological change, institutions must develop strategies to deal with the issues around the infrastructure and technical support of information technology if they wish to achieve a successful ALN implementation.

Administrative Support

Another key element for the success of an ALN environment is administrative support. Institutions must examine if the current infrastructure is adequate to deal with the new demands of ALN courses and degrees. For example, will special marketing efforts be needed to enroll students in ALN courses? How can the institution project the demand for this new type of course? Hiltz (1994) suggested the development of new marketing strategies for this new mode of delivery. Another administrative issue deals with the proper training and supervision of adjuncts or teaching aides assigned to online sections.

To be competitive and successful, a campuswide ALN initiative will require more flexible and dynamic administrative structures (Kang, 2001), different from the typical ones found at many academic institutions.

Faculty Development and Support for Online Teaching

Faculty new to online teaching need training and support as they develop and deliver online courses. This should include short courses in use of the technologies (e.g., the ALN platform), how to create and update course web pages, and multimedia online lectures or simulations via the variety of software packages licensed by the institution. In addition, both new and more experienced faculty need to learn about, develop, and share experiences with appropriate pedagogical principles, such as how to develop, facilitate, and grade collaborative assignments, and how to facilitate high-quality online discussions (Alavi & Gallupe, 2003; Brower, 2003).

A leading source for descriptions of best practices in faculty development and support to improve faculty effectiveness and faculty satisfaction is the Sloan Consortium web site's "Effective Practices" section (http://www.aln.org/effective/SortByFacultySat.asp). Among the programs described there is the award-winning SUNY (State University of New York) Learning Network's programs and practices. This comprehensive approach now includes:

- An online faculty resource and information gateway.
- An asynchronous conference for all developers, which includes links (by permission) to ongoing ALN courses being offered by experienced ALN faculty.
- An asynchronous faculty orientation.
- A series of workshops for new faculty.
- Instructional design sessions for returning faculty.
- A comprehensive step-by-step course developer's handbook.
- A course template.
- A faculty help desk.
- Online mechanisms for faculty evaluation of SLN services.
- An assigned instructional design partner to support faculty development and course design.

It is essential that faculty are trained well before they develop and deliver their first online course. At SUNY, for instance, faculty are trained in cohorts, beginning in March for the following fall and in September for the spring term.

Policy Issues

As a new teaching/learning environment, ALNs challenge some of the existing practices and policies on campuses (Hiltz, 1994). In particular, issues such as faculty workload and compensation, intellectual property, and degree policies must be reexamined and adapted to the new context.

The amount of time that faculty is expected to allocate to teaching, research, and service must be clearly defined and understood when offering electronic education (Hawkins, 1999). The additional time commitments required from faculty to design and deliver ALN courses should be counted in the workload. If they aren't, are the intrinsic rewards associated with online teaching incentive enough for most faculty members to spend extra time and energy to develop ALN courses (Rockwell, Schauer, Fritz, & Marx, 1999)? What are the direct rewards for the faculty to embrace the ALN environment? If "release time" is the reward, what is the impact on courses traditionally offered in the residential curriculum?

How is faculty time devoted to developing, updating, and teaching online weighed in promotion and tenure decisions? If it is not given a positive weight, and the primary basis for promotion and tenure is publishing, then untenured faculty members will tend to make the rational decision of avoiding the time-consuming activities required of new ALN faculty.

Another complex policy issue deals with the intellectual property rights associated with the development of online learning materials. Who is the owner of the content of ALN courses—the institution, the faculty member, or both? What type of ownership is the most appropriate to deal with ALN materials—copyright or patent? Historically, universities have granted copyrights to faculty, who in turn transferred away the copyrights to their articles to the journals that printed those articles. However, the development of a new invention or process fell under the patent policy, on the grounds that the institution had committed significant resources and was thus entitled to share any of the benefits derived from this intellectual property. Thompson (1999) argued that neither copyright nor patent policy is well suited to dealing with electronic learning materials. Universities should focus instead on conflict-of-interest issues that define the role of the faculty member within the institution.

Another policy issue is whether to apply ALN course credits toward an academic degree, or whether a degree can be obtained entirely by ALN (forgoing any residency requirements), and, in this case, which degrees will be offered via ALNs (Turoff, 1997). In universities offering both traditional and ALN degrees, the issue is to what extent the ALN degree will be identical to or different from the traditional degree obtained by on-campus students. Because degrees can be considered the main university "product," degree policy is a crucial matter (Harris & DiPaolo, 1999).

CONCLUSIONS AND FUTURE RESEARCH DIRECTIONS

This chapter has examined the most influential contextual factors for developing effective ALN environments. We have reviewed and presented the results of current research related to technological, pedagogical, course, and institutional characteristics and their relationship to ALN effectiveness. Based on this review, we can now identify some areas in which future research pertaining to these characteristics is most needed.

There are several aspects of the technological characteristics of ALNs that merit additional research attention. Over the past several years, numerous commercial software platforms have been increasingly used to implement ALN courses (Palloff & Pratt, 2001). Although these platforms have received different degrees of research attention, empirical research that compares these packages is notably absent. To date, system quality and reliability usually have only been mentioned in ALN research if the system fails during the time period of the study. To fully assess the impact of system quality and reliability on ALN effectiveness, measures should be developed so that these characteristics can be controlled for at the beginning of a research study. Finally, with increasing bandwidth capability, the opportunity to easily incorporate a wider variety of media into ALNs should only increase. However, as is reviewed in more detail in chapter 10, at the present time there isn't enough research to help us determine whether additional media produce enough student learning and course satisfaction benefits to merit the additional time and expense required to develop and incorporate them into courses.

There are also a number of pedagogical and course content issues that need additional research. Although there have been some conceptual models that provide insights as to contextual factors that may influence the use of particular pedagogical approaches (Benbunan-Fich, 2002; Leidner & Jarvenpaa, 1995), these models have received limited empirical attention to date. Along with pedagogical approaches, the role of course content in determining ALN effectiveness needs to become more of a research focus. Some disciplines—such as information systems and management—have been the subject of extensive studies, whereas others have received little or no research attention. In order to make meaningful generalizations from the available empirical literature, replication studies and multicourse and multidiscipline comparative studies are required. Due in part to the newness of the application of the technology and perceptions of the need for shifts in participant roles in ALNs relative to traditional classrooms (Dede, 1990; Harasim, 1990), much of the ALN research to date has focused on instructor and student behaviors (i.e., Arbaugh, 2002b; Palloff & Pratt, 2001) while giving limited attention to content or disciplinary factors. However, we now have enough of an understanding of technological and behavioral issues in ALNs to begin to look more closely at the relationship between course content and ALN effectiveness. In other words, how much does "subject matter" matter?

Course structural issues are another area in which additional research is needed. Although there has been some initial research on the relationship between class size and ALN effectiveness, more research is needed to help us determine whether there is an optimal class size in ALN settings and what that number might be. More important, this is an example of how current findings also point to challenges for both research and practice. For many institutions, there are insufficient resources to permit an average class size of 25 to 30 students per full-time faculty member. We need research on how to scale up the size of ALN courses and still teach them effectively. We need more case studies of effective "large" ALN classes. (See Turoff & Hiltz, 2001, for one example.)

We presently have a limited number of studies that include both undergraduates and graduates as part of their sample. As a result, much of our ALN research has limited generalizability for how an entire institution might develop its ALN capability. Finally, we are beginning to see increasing numbers of blended face-to-face and ALN courses being developed (Cookson, 2002; Sorg et al., 1999). This trend generates a number of interesting questions such as: How do mixed-mode courses compare to other delivery modes? Is there an optimal arrangement of face-to-face and ALN activities within a course? What other factors may moderate or mediate the effectiveness of mixed-mode courses?

Although research in each of the previously mentioned areas would provide beneficial insights, perhaps the most glaring gap in the ALN literature is the lack of studies conducted at the institutional level. Comparisons across institutions with similar ALN environments may highlight specific institutional factors that contribute to the success of ALNs. An example of how institutions might be studied in an ALN context is the extent to which their structures, behaviors, and decision-making processes encourage ALN research. For instance, some longitudinal studies have attempted to measure student characteristics and preferences for ALNs only to find that the institution's decision to delegate the decision to offer online courses to the individual departments resulted in too few online courses being offered to generate statistically significant results for the study (Fornaciari, 2002; Fornaciari & Matthews, 2000).

Finally, ALN research would be greatly strengthened if researchers would simultaneously consider some of the topics we have mentioned in this chapter to help increase our understanding of how contextual factors may moderate relationships between particular variables and ALN effectiveness. Research of this nature will likely require the increased use of multicourse and multi-institutional research samples (see chap. 4 of this book).

For example, we have stated that the studies thus far suggest a curvilinear relationship between online class size and effectiveness, with classes in the range of 25 to 30 students being most successful. However, this "average," in turn, depends on the other contextual factors, such as:

- What is the subject matter? Perhaps science classes with a great deal of objective knowledge to impart can use "objectivist" delivery techniques such as tutorials, simulations, and self-testing via quizzes, and be very successful as large online courses. An account of an introductory physics class for 500 students (Thoennessen et al., 1999) gave an example of this.
- What level of skills and motivation and experience with online learning do the students bring to the course? What kind of training and support does the institution offer? If students are skilled in online interaction and/or have extensive technical or content tutoring available from sources other than the instructor, class sizes can be larger.
- What is the pedagogical model used by the instructor, and how experienced is the instructor with teaching online? For example, fully collaborative learning—in which students explicitly share responsibility for facilitating discussion and activities in the course—can help the faculty to accommodate more students (Picciano, 2003).
- What functions are available in the software to help the instructor with his or her job? For example, is there a built-in gradebook and/or quiz function? Can the instructor easily obtain a weekly summary of participation by student rather than having to search and count by hand?
- What training and support are provided by the institution? For instance, are there teaching assistants who can help with leading breakout discussion groups and with grading? This would make it much easier to handle classes of 50 or more online.

In conclusion, we feel that although great strides have been made in the last decade or so, research into the factors that influence ALN effectiveness is very much in its infancy. We look forward to seeing how our understanding of this phenomenon will be enhanced through the research efforts of the next decade.

QUESTIONS FOR DISCUSSION AND RESEARCH

1. Might the optimal media mix (in terms of all face to face, all ALN, or mixed) interact with the level of the student (K–12, undergraduate, graduate, continuing professional education) and the pedagogical techniques emphasized (objectivist vs. constructivist)? How could this question best be studied?

2. If online learning is offered at your institution, how do policies and procedures for training, supporting, and rewarding faculty for teaching in this mode compare to "best practices"? What would be necessary to change institutional policies and priorities to improve faculty support?

3. Why have some disciplines—such as the humanities, engineering, and architecture—been much slower than others to develop online courses and degree programs?

4. How would you design a study to assess institutional effects on ALN effectiveness? What are some variables you would include? How would you measure them?

SUMMARY

This chapter reviewed the contextual factors placed at the top of the theoretical model presented in chapter 2. In particular, we looked at the nonperson-specific characteristics of instructors and students, as well as issues related to technology and courses in general. One of the main contributions of this chapter is to introduce the many relations among the contextual factors. For example, the institution is in charge of developing policies to provide administrative, technical, and faculty development support. The technology defines the environment and the types of course delivery that are possible given the infrastructure. The course is the vehicle in which the student–instructor relationship is created. Because there is a hierarchy of contextual factors, we are representing them in a sequence of nested boxes (see Fig. 6.1); for each factor examined in this chapter, we highlight in italics the issues for which more research is needed.

REFERENCES

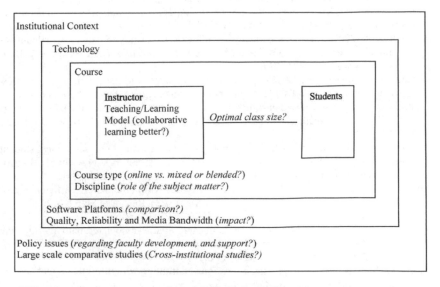

FIG. 6.1.   Revised conceptual model of contextual factors.

Alavi, M., & Gallupe, R. B. (2003). Using information technology in learning: Case studies in business and management education programs. *Academy of Management Learning and Education, 2,* 139–153.

Alavi, M., & Leidner, D. E. (2001). Research commentary: Technology-mediated learn-ing—a call for greater depth and breadth of research. *Information Systems Research, 12*(1), 1–10.

Alavi, M., Wheeler, B., & Valacich, J. (1995). Using IT to reengineer business education: An exploratory investigation to collaborative telelearning. *MIS Quarterly, 19,* 294–312.

Alavi, M., Yoo, Y., & Vogel, D. R. (1997). Using information technology to add value to management education. *Academy of Management Journal, 40*(6), 1310–1333.

Althaus, S. L. (1997). Computer-mediated communication in the university classroom: An experiment with on-line discussions. *Communication Education, 46,* 158–174.

Andriole, S. J. (1997). Requirement-driven ALN course design, development, delivery, & evaluation. *Journal of Asynchronous Learning Networks, 1*(2). Retrieved June 1, 2002, from http://www.aln.org/publications/jaln/index.asp

Arbaugh, J. B. (2000a). How classroom environment and student engagement affect learning in Internet-based MBA courses. *Business Communication Quarterly, 63*(4), 9–26.

Arbaugh, J. B. (2000b). Virtual classroom characteristics and student satisfaction in Internet-based MBA courses. *Journal of Management Education, 24*(1), 32–54.

Arbaugh, J. B. (2000c). Virtual classrooms versus physical classrooms: An exploratory study of class discussion patterns and student learning in an asynchronous Internet-based MBA course. *Journal of Management Education, 24*(2), 207–227.

Arbaugh, J. B. (2001). How instructor immediacy behaviors affect student satisfaction and learning in web-based courses. *Business Communication Quarterly, 64*(4), 42–54.

Arbaugh, J. B. (2002a). A longitudinal study of technological and pedagogical characteris-tics of web-based MBA courses. *Proceedings of the Sixtieth Annual Meeting of the Acad-emy of Management* (CD), MED A1–A6. ISSN 1543-8643.

Arbaugh, J. B. (2002b). Managing the on-line classroom: A study of technological and be-havioral characteristics of web-based MBA courses. *Journal of High Technology Man-agement Research, 13,* 203–223.

Arbaugh, J. B., & Duray, R. (2001). Class section size, perceived classroom characteristics, instructor experience, and student learning and satisfaction with web-based courses: A study and comparison of two on-line MBA programs. In D. H. Nagao (Ed.), *Proceedings of the Sixty-First Annual Meeting of the Academy of Management* (CD), MED A1–A6. ISSN 1543-8643.

Arbaugh, J. B., & Duray, R. (2002). Technological and structural characteristics, student learning and satisfaction with web-based courses: An exploratory study of two MBA pro-grams. *Management Learning, 33,* 331–347.

Arvan, L., & Musumeci, D. (2000). Instructor attitudes within the SCALE efficiency pro-jects. *Journal of Asynchronous Learning Networks, 4*(3). Retrieved March 4, 2004, from http://www.sloan-c.org/publications/jaln/v4n3/pdf/v4n3_arvan.pdf

Atkinson, M., & Kydd, C. (1997). Individual characteristics associated with World Wide Web use: An empirical study of playfulness and motivation. *The DATA BASE for Ad-vances in Information Systems, 28*(2), 53–62.

Benbunan-Fich, R. (2002). Improving education and training with information technology. *Communications of the ACM, 45*(6), 94–99.

Benbunan-Fich, R., & Hiltz, S. R. (1999). Effects of asynchronous learning networks: A field experiment. *Group Decision and Negotiation, 8,* 409–426.

Benbunan-Fich, R., & Hiltz, S. R. (2002). Correlates of effectiveness of learning networks: The effects of course level, course type and gender on outcomes. In *Proceedings of the*

35th Hawaii International Conference on System Sciences HICSS-35. Hawaii, January CD-Rom/Abstracts Proceedings 7–10 January 2002, Big Island, HI, USA. IEEE Computer Society, 2002—Track 1.

Borthick, A. F., & Jones, D. R. (2000). The motivation for collaborative discovery learning online and its application in an information systems assurance course. *Issues in Accounting Education, 15*(2), 181–210.

Brower, H. H. (2003). On emulating classroom discussion in a distance-delivered OBHR course: Creating an on-line community. *Academy of Management Learning and Education, 2*(1), 22–36.

Card, K. A. (2000). Providing access to graduate education using computer-mediated communication. *International Journal of Instructional Media, 27,* 235–245.

Chidambaram, L. (1996). Relational development in computer-supported groups. *MIS Quarterly, 20*(2), 143–163.

Cookson, P. (2002). The hybridization of higher education: Cross-national perspectives. *International Review of Research in Open and Distance Learning, 2*(2). Retrieved June 1, 2003, from http://www.irrodl.org/content/v2.2/editorial.html

Coppola, N. W., Hiltz, S. R., & Rotter, N. G. (2002). Becoming a virtual professor: Pedagogical roles and asynchronous learning networks. *Journal of Management Information Systems, 18*(4), 169–189.

Davis, F. (1989). Perceived usefulness, perceived ease of use and user acceptance of information technology. *MIS Quarterly, 13*(3), 319–340.

Dede, C. J. (1990). The evolution of distance learning: Technology-mediated interactive learning. *Journal of Research on Computing in Education, 22*(1), 247–264.

DiBiase, D. (2000). Is distance teaching more work or less work? *American Journal of Distance Education, 14*(3), 6–20.

Dumont, R. A. (1996). Teaching and learning in cyberspace. *IEEE Transactions on Professional Communication, 39*(4), 192–204.

Eastman, J. K., & Swift, C. O. (2001). New horizons in distance education: The online learner-centered marketing class. *Journal of Marketing Education, 23*(1), 25–34.

Foley, G., & Schuck, S. (1998). Web-based conferencing: Pedagogical asset or constraint? *Australian Journal of Education and Technology, 14*(2), 122–140.

Fornaciari, C. J. (2002, August). *Student personality types and enrollments in distance education: A longitudinal study.* Paper presented at the Academy of Management, Denver.

Fornaciari, C. J., & Matthews, C. S. (2000). Student personality types and predispositions toward distance education. In S. J. Havlovic (Ed.), *Proceedings of the Fifty-Ninth Annual Meeting of the Academy of Management* (CD), MED: B1–B6.

Fredericksen, E., Pickett, A., Shea, P., & Pelz, W. (2000). Student satisfaction and perceived learning with on-line courses: Principles and examples from the SUNY Learning Network. *Journal of Asynchronous Learning Networks, 4*(2). Retrieved March 4, 2004, from http://www.sloan-c.org/publications/jaln/v4n2/v4n2_fredericksen.asp

Freeman, M. A., & Capper, J. M. (1999). Exploiting the web for education: An anonymous asynchronous role simulation. *Australian Journal of Educational Technology, 15*(1), 95–115.

Freitas, F. A., Myers, S. A., & Avtgis, T. A. (1998). Student perceptions of instructor immediacy in conventional and disturbed learning classrooms. *Communication Education, 42*(4), 366–372.

Gallini, J. K. (2001). A framework for the design of research in technology-mediated learning environments: A sociocultural perspective. *Educational Technology, 41*(2), 15–21.

Garrison, D. R., Anderson, T., & Archer, W. (2003). A theory of critical inquiry in online distance education. In Michael Grahame Moore & William G. Anderson (Eds.), *Handbook of distance education* (pp. 113–127). Mahwah, NJ: Lawrence Erlbaum Associates.

Gorham, J. (1988). The relationship between verbal teacher immediacy behaviors and student learning. *Communication Education, 37*(1), 40–53.

Graves, W. H. (1997). "Free Trade" in higher education: The meta university. *Journal of Asynchronous Learning Networks, 1*(1). Retrieved March 4, 2004, from http://www.sloan-c.org/publications/jaln/v1n1/v1n1_graves.asp

Gunawardena, C. N., & Zittle, F. J. (1997). Social presence as a predictor of satisfaction within a computer-mediated conferencing environment. *American Journal of Distance Education, 11*(3), 8–26.

Hanna, D. E. (1998). Higher education in an era of digital competition: Emerging organizational models. *Journal of Asynchronous Learning Networks, 2*(1). Retrieved March 4, 2004, from http://www.sloan-c.org/publications/jaln/v2n1/v2n1_hanna.asp

Hannigan, C., & Browne, M. (2000). Project management: Going the distance. *Internatioanl Journal of Instructional Media, 27*, 343–356.

Harasim, L. (1990). *On-line education: Perspectives on a new medium.* New York: Praeger/Greenwood.

Harris, D. A., & Dipaolo, H. (1999). Institutional policy for ALN. *Journal of Asynchronous Learning Networks, 3*(1). Retrieved March 4, 2004, from http://www.sloan-c.org/publications/jaln/v3n1/v3n1_harris.asp

Hartman, J., Dziuban, C., & Moskal, P. (2000). Faculty satisfaction in ALNs: A dependent or independent variable. *Journal of Asynchronous Learning Networks, 4*(3). Retrieved March 4, 2004, from http://www.sloan-c.org/publications/jaln/v4n3/v4n3_hartman.asp

Hawkins, B. L. (1999, July/August). Distributed learning and institutional restructuring. *Educom Review, 34*(4). Retrieved July 1, 2002, from http://www.educause.edu/ir/library/html/erm9943.html

Hiltz, S. R. (1993). Correlates of learning in a virtual classroom. *International Journal of Man Machine Systems, 39*, 71–98.

Hiltz, S. R. (1994). *The virtual classroom: Learning without limits via computer networks.* Norwood, NJ: Ablex.

Hiltz, S. R., Coppola, N., Rotter, N., Turoff, M., & Benbunan-Fich, R. (2000). Measuring the importance of collaborative learning for the effectiveness of ALN: A multi-measure, multi-method approach. *Journal of Asynchronous Learning Networks, 4*(2). Retrieved March 4, 2004, from http://www.sloan-c.org/publications/jaln/v4n2/v4n2_hiltz.asp

Hiltz, S. R., Johnson, K. D., & Turoff, M. (1986). Experiments in group decision making: Communication process and outcome in face-to-face versus computerized conferences. *Human Communication Research, 13*(2), 225–252.

Hiltz, S. R., & Turoff, M. (2002). What makes learning networks effective? *Communications of the ACM, 45*(4), 56–59.

Hiltz, S. R., & Wellman, B. (1997). Asynchronous learning networks as a virtual classroom. *Communications of the ACM, 40*(9), 44–52.

Hislop, G. W. (1999). Anytime, anyplace learning in an online graduate professional degree program. *Group Decision and Negotiation, 8*, 385–390.

Jaffee, D. (1998). Institutionalized resistance to asynchronous learning networks. *Journal of Asynchronous Learning Networks, 2*(2). Retrieved March 4, 2004, from http://www.sloan-c.org/publications/jaln/v2n2/v2n2_jaffee.asp

Jarvenpaa, S. L., & Leidner, D. E. (1999). Communication and trust in global virtual teams. *Organization Science, 10*, 791–815.

Jiang, M., & Ting, E. (2000). A study of factors influencing students' perceived learning in a web-based course environment. *International Journal of Educational Telecommunications, 6*(4), 317–338.

Kang, S. (2001). Toward a collaborative model for the design of web-based courses. *Educational Technology, 41*(2), 22–30.

LaRose, R., Gregg, J., & Eastin, M. (1998). Audiographic telecourses for the Web: An experiment. *Journal of Computer-Mediated Communication, 4*(2). Retrieved July 8, 2003, from http://www.ascusc.org/jcmc/vol4/issue2/larose.htm

Leidner, D., & Jarvenpaa, S. (1995). The use of information technology to enhance management school education: A theoretical view. *MIS Quarterly*, 265–291.

Levin, S. R., Levin, J. A., & Waddoups, G. L. (2001). CTER online: Evaluation of an online Master of Education focusing on curriculum, technology and education reform. In *Proceedings of the 34th Hawaii International Conference on System Sciences*. CD-Rom Proceedings, January 2001, Maui, HI, USA. IEEE.

Liaw, S.-S. (2001). Designing the hypermedia-based learning environment. *International Journal of Instructional Media, 28*, 43–56.

McIsaac, M. S., Blocher, J. M., Mahes, V., & Vrasidas, C. (1998). Student and teacher perceptions of interaction in online computer-mediated communication. *Educational Media International, 36*(2), 121–131.

Mehrabian, A. (1971). *Silent messages*. Belmont, CA: Wadsworth.

Moore, M. G. (1999). Institutional restructuring: Is distance education like retailing? *American Journal of Distance Education, 13*(1), 1–5.

Myers, S. A., Zhong, M., & Guan, S. (1998). Instructor immediacy in the Chinese college classroom. *Communication Studies, 49*, 240–253.

Nulden, U. (1999). Thematic modules in an asynchronous learning network: A Scandinavian perspective on the design of introductory courses. *Journal of Group Decision and Negotiation, 8*, 391–408.

Palloff, R., & Pratt, K. (1999). *Building learning communities in cyberspace*. San Francisco: Jossey-Bass.

Palloff, R., & Pratt, K. (2001). *Lessons from the cyberspace classroom: The realities of online teaching*. San Francisco: Jossey-Bass.

Picciano, A. G. (2003, September). *Online learning and a faculty perspective: A course case study*. Presentation at the Sloan-C Summer Research Workshop, Wellesley, MA.

Piccoli, G., Ahmad, R., & Ives, B. (2001). Web-based virtual learning environments: A research framework and a preliminary assessment of effectiveness in basic IT skills training. *MIS Quarterly, 25*, 401–426.

Ricketts, J., Wolfe, F. H., Norvelle, E., & Carpenter, E. H. (2000). Asynchronous distributed education: A review and case study. *Social Science Computer Review, 18*(2), 132–146.

Rockwell, S. K., Schauer, J., Fritz, S., & Marx, D. (1999). Incentives and obstacles influencing higher education faculty and administrators to teach via distance. *Online Journal of Distance Learning Administration, 2*(4). Retrieved June 1, 2003, from http://westga.edu/jdistance/rockwell24.html

Salmon, G. (2000). Computer-mediated conferencing for management learning at the Open University. *Management Learning, 31*, 491–502.

Sandercock, G. R. H., & Shaw, G. (1999). Learners' performance and evaluation of attitudes towards web course tools in the delivery of an applied sports medicine module. *ALN Magazine, 3*. Retrieved March 4, 2004 from http://www.sloan-c.org/publications/magazine/v3n2/sandercock.asp

Smith, G. G., Ferguson, D. L., & Caris, M. (2001). Teaching college courses: Online vs. face-to-face. *T.H.E. Journal, 28*(9), 18–24.

Smith, L. J. (2001). Content and delivery: A comparison and contrast of electronic and traditional MBA marketing planning courses. *Journal of Marketing Education, 23*(1), 35–44.

Sorg, S., Truman-Davis, B., Dziuban, C., Moskal, P., Hartman, J., & Juge, F. (1999). Faculty development, learner support and evaluation in web-based programs. *Interactive Learning Environments, 7*(2–3), 137–153.

Swan, K. (2002). Building learning communities in online courses: The importance of interaction. *Education Communication and Information, 2*(1), 23–49.

Swan, K., Shea, P., Fredericksen, E., Picket, A., Pelz, W., & Maher, G. (2000). Building knowledge building communities: Consistency, contact, and communication in the virtual classroom. *Journal of Educational Computing Research, 23*, 389–413.

Thoennessen, M., Kashy, E., Tsai, Y., & Davis, N. E. (1999). Impacts of asynchronous learning networks in large lecture classes. *Group Decision and Negotiation, 8*, 371–384.

Thompson, D. F. (1999). Intellectual property meets information technology. *Educom Review, 34*(2), 14–24.

Turoff, M. (1997). Costs for the development of a virtual university. *Journal of Asynchronous Learning Networks, 1*(1). Retrieved March 4, 2004, from http://www.sloan-c.org/publications/jaln/v1n1/v1n1_turoff.asp

Turoff, M., & Hiltz, S. R. (2001). Effectively managing large enrollment courses: A case study. In J. Bourne & J. C. Moore (Eds.), *Online education, vol. 2: Learning effectiveness, faculty satisfaction, and cost effectiveness. Proceedings of the 2000 Summer Workshop on Asynchronous Learning Networks* (pp. 55–80). Needham, MA: SCOLE.

Warkentin, M. E., Sayeed, L., & Hightower, R. (1997). Virtual teams versus face-to-face teams: An exploratory study of a web-based conference system. *Decision Sciences, 28*, 975–996.

Webster, J., & Hackley, P. (1997). Teaching effectiveness in technology-mediated distance learning. *Academy of Management Journal, 40*(6), 1282–1309.

Wernet, S. P., Olliges, R. H., & Delicath, T. A. (2000). Postcourse evaluations of WebCT classes by social work students. *Research on Social Work Practice, 10*, 487–514.

Yoo, Y., Kanawattanachai, P., & Citurs, A. (2002). Forging into the wired wilderness: A case study of a technology-mediated distributed discussion-based class. *Journal of Management Education, 26*, 139–163.

7

The Student in the Online Classroom

Starr Roxanne Hiltz
New Jersey Institute of Technology

Peter Shea
State University of New York

I believe that virtual classrooms are a great resource for learning. More teacher–student interactions and student–student interactions are possible. With regular classrooms there is not much interaction unless the teacher initiates it. With a virtual classroom students are "forced" to give opinions and feedback on topics covered in class and lectures. In regular classes the professor lectures and the students take notes (or fall asleep). Overall I am learning more in the virtual class than I would in the regular class. (Spontaneous comment, NJIT student in ALN section of computers and society class, February 2003).

INTRODUCTION

At the core of the concept of an asynchronous learning network is the student as an active—and socially interactive—learner. We begin this chapter with a review of some of the evidence that there is indeed a tendency for ALN courses to elicit more active participation from students than does the typical face-to-face course (at least those conducted on the "lecture" model). Then we review the profile of students who choose to take online courses. This includes quizzes and criteria that can be used to advise students into or out of ALN as a mode for learning. A look at whether any individual characteristics are related to their chances of success in on-line courses (obtaining good grades, high satisfaction, etc.) includes both objective characteristics such as gender, and psychological predictors such as personality type or cognitive styles. The chapter ends with a summary of some multivariate studies that use student characteristics to predict student outcomes.

ALN courses are said to be more learner centered than are traditional courses. That is, in ALN courses the learner takes a more active part in class activities. At Syracuse University, Heckman and Annabi (2003) documented that this is so when the instructor behavior encourages and supports an active role for the student learner in ALN. They conducted a field experiment with four groups of students, each of whom completed two case study discussions, one face to face (FtF) and one via ALN (counterbalanced for order). Heckman and Annabi found significant differences in teacher and student roles in the two modes of learning. The presence of the teacher was much more pervasive in FtF (141 utterances) versus ALN (11 utterances) discussions; the ratio of student to teacher utterances was 5:1 in ALN, compared to 1:1 in the FtF discussions. Moreover, student utterances were longer in ALN (100 words vs. 30 words), whereas teacher utterances were shorter in ALN (50 words vs. 80 words). These results confirm student reports of more active participation in online courses relative to similar FtF courses in the State University of New York (SUNY) Learning Network. Survey respondents ($n =$ 935) were approximately twice as likely to report more active participation in online class discussion when compared to their participation levels in similar FtF courses they had taken (Shea, Swan, Fredericksen, & Pickett 2002).

What is the profile of these students, the "active learners" who choose this mode of instruction and who thrive and succeed in it? How are various characteristics of students, including motivation and learning or cognitive styles, related to success online? Can online learning environments be designed to compensate for some of the individual student differences associated with success or failure in online learning? Finally, what are the fruitful areas for future research into how student characteristics are related to learning in the online setting?

A PROFILE OF ONLINE LEARNERS

Why do students choose online courses? What kinds of advice do college guidance personnel tend to give students about who is suited for this form of learning? How do online learners differ from traditional classroom learners?

Dear Dr. P,

I made it. I'm attaching my first assignment to you in between my contractions. Yes, it looks like this is it, our first baby seems to be ready to face this world. I wanted to send this off to you before I go to the hospital and be out of commission for the next few days. It has been quite an "adventure" finishing this paper while "breaking" for pain, at least it has helped me to stay focused.

Please excuse me for not participating in this week's discussion. I'll make it up when I return.

Please wish me luck.
E_____

The letter in the accompanying box is an actual message received by an instructor in an online course at the New Jersey Institute of Technology (NJIT). Although our brave and motivated student, "E," may not be totally typical, she exemplifies the characteristics of many of the most successful online students. She is mature, motivated, and definitely in need of an "anytime, anyplace" mode of education. In addition, because this is a reading and writing mode of communication, successful online students need to be able to express themselves well in writing, which "E" certainly does, and have the willingness and ability to collaborate/cooperate well with other students.

What Attracts Students to Online Courses?

All online students at the SUNY Learning Network are asked to report their reason for choosing an online course as part of their online registration process. With online enrollments of approximately 40,000 students in the 2001–2002 academic year, this program represents a relatively large sample from which to examine this question. Although it is common to equate "online learning" with "distance learning," results of analyses of students' reasons for choosing to study online indicate that this is a misconception. The most common (and growing) reasons for this choice for SUNY Learning Network students from 2000 to 2002 were related to schedule conflicts stemming from academic, work, family, and other commitments, as shown in Fig. 7.1.

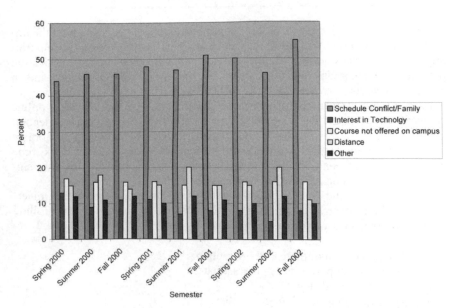

FIG. 7.1.   Reasons for choosing to study online. Source: Data from State University of New York Learning Network

In a much smaller study, students in North Carolina State matched online and traditional classroom courses in introductory computer science (Dutton, Dutton, & Perry, 2002) were asked to rate the importance of various reasons for choosing their mode of instruction, as shown in the accompanying box.

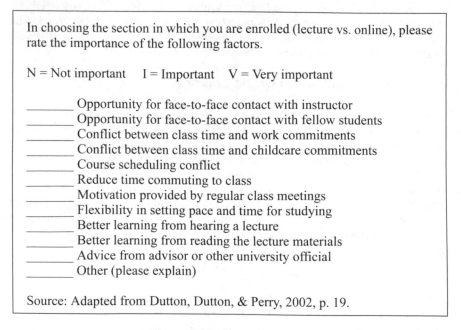

In choosing the section in which you are enrolled (lecture vs. online), please rate the importance of the following factors.

N = Not important   I = Important   V = Very important

_____ Opportunity for face-to-face contact with instructor
_____ Opportunity for face-to-face contact with fellow students
_____ Conflict between class time and work commitments
_____ Conflict between class time and childcare commitments
_____ Course scheduling conflict
_____ Reduce time commuting to class
_____ Motivation provided by regular class meetings
_____ Flexibility in setting pace and time for studying
_____ Better learning from hearing a lecture
_____ Better learning from reading the lecture materials
_____ Advice from advisor or other university official
_____ Other (please explain)

Source: Adapted from Dutton, Dutton, & Perry, 2002, p. 19.

Online and lecture students differed significantly in their assessment of the importance of 8 of the 11 factors. In the lecture students' survey responses, opportunity for face-to-face contact with the instructor and with other students, motivation provided by regular class meetings, better learning from hearing a lecture, and an advice from advisor or other university official were definitely ranked as more important. Dutton et al. noted that because students are less familiar with online courses and may expect these courses to be somehow easier when there is no lecture to attend, it is not surprising that the bulk of official advice cautions against online instruction. Online students deemed conflict between class time and work, time commuting to class, and flexibility in setting pace and time for studying to be significantly more important than did lecture students.

Leasure, Davis, and Thievon's (2000) study of 68 nursing students at the University of Oklahoma uncovered some very similar results. Reasons given for enrolling in the traditional classroom section included:

- The perception of increased interaction.
- Decreased opportunity to procrastinate.
- Immediate feedback.
- More meaningful learning activities.

These are perceptions of students who, for the most part, had never had an online course. Because these perceptions are the basis for choice of mode of delivery of a course (whether or not they accurately reflect the nature of learning online), they are important to recognize.

Reasons given by the nursing students for selecting the Web sections included cost, convenience, and flexibility. These students were also individuals who perceived themselves as being more knowledgeable in how to use a computer. At the end of the semester, both groups of nursing students indicated satisfaction with their choice of either the Internet or in-class section on the course evaluation. Students who were self-directed and had the ability to maintain their own pace and avoid procrastination were most suited to Web-based courses, based on correlations with postcourse information.

From these three studies, we can see that the main reasons for choosing ALN courses—at least for those students taking their first course online—have to do with convenience. It would be interesting to study the reasons for choice among students who have already participated in one or more ALN courses, to see if reasons for delivery medium choice change with experience.

Profiling At-Risk Cyberstudents

That individual differences among students can affect the likelihood of their success in ALN courses is hardly a surprise to any instructor; success in any mode of learning is heavily influenced by what the student brings to the learning situation. There is evidence that students with high motivation to learn, greater self-regulating behavior (or "independence"), and greater confidence in their ability to use computers and to learn online do better than do those who lack these characteristics. Several studies have also found that students with certain learning styles (e.g., visual) perform better in online courses than do learners who are "aural" and passive (Meyer, 2003).

As Wang and Newlin (2002) pointed out:

> The ability of instructors to identify at-risk cyber-students quickly is critical because the usual cues associated with student anxiety, inattentiveness or apathy are not present in the virtual classroom. For instance, cues such as frowning, fidgeting and day-dreaming, which are often readily apparent in the conventional classroom, are not observable by Web-based instructors.

Rather than wait for failure, many distance learning programs take a proactive stance and advise prospective students to take an online quiz to see if they seem to be suited for ALN or other distance modes of learning. NJITs self-scoring quiz for prospective students to take to see if they are suited to ALN is reproduced in Fig. 7.2.

The "quiz" is scored as 3 points for each "a" answer, 2 points for each "b," and 1 point for each "c." Students who score below a certain cutoff point are told to speak to an advisor before selecting an online course, and those who score below a second cutoff point are told that "e-learning does not appear to be right for you."

Wang and Newlin (2002) listed several other psychological characteristics as predictors, although these would be very hard to obtain from students in a precourse selection self-quiz. Several of their predictors also have to do with participation patterns during the course, rather than precourse characteristics of the student. Wang and Newlin noted:

Are eLearning Courses right for YOU?

If you are wondering whether or not to take an online course, why not take a moment or two to complete the following survey? It will help you decide whether this is the right educational format for you.

At the end of this survey, click the Score button to calculate your total and see if you are a good candidate for online courses.

1)	I would rate my computer skills as:
	☐ a) High - I am comfortable with electronic mail, web browsing, and word-processing
	☐ b) Moderate - I can get by if there is not too much typing or special software
	☐ c) Low - I am either a novice computer user or I really don't like using a computer
2)	Considering my academic, work, and personal schedule, the amount of time I have to devote to my online class is:
	☐ a) 9 - 12 hours per week
	☐ b) 4 - 8 hours per week
	☐ c) 0 - 3 hours per week
3)	As a reader, I would classify myself as:
	☐ a) Good - I usually understand text without help
	☐ b) Average - I sometimes need help to understand the text
	☐ c) Slower than average - It takes me much longer to read than my peers
4)	When I am asked to use computers, CD-Roms, vcrs, voice mail or other technologies new to me:
	☐ a) I look forward to learning new skills
	☐ b) I feel a little nervous but try anyway
	☐ c) I feel quite anxious and try to avoid doing it

FIG. 7.2. NJIT's quiz for prospective ALN students course: http://dl1.njit.edu/phpscripts/ (Copyright NJIT, 2001). Reprinted with permission.

(continued on next page)

5)	When I receive feedback from an instructor, I prefer
	☐ a) Written comments so that I can pursue and figure out how to apply them to my work
	☐ b) Written comments with some oral explanation to clarify points I might not understand
	☐ c) I need to talk to the instructor to really understand what I need to do.

6)	When an instructor hands out an assignment, I prefer:
	☐ a) Figuring out the instructions myself
	☐ b) Trying to follow the directions on my own, then asking for help when I need it
	☐ c) Having the instructions explained to me

7)	Classroom discussion is
	☐ a) Important to my learning
	☐ b) Sometimes helpful to me
	☐ c) Rarely helpful to me

8)	I need faculty comments on my work
	☐ a) Within a week so that I can review what I did
	☐ b) Within a day or two or I forget what I did
	☐ c) Right away or I get very frustrated

9)	Who is most responsible for what and how much you learn?
	☐ a) I am ultimately responsible for my own learning
	☐ b) The instructor and I share equal responsibility for what and how much I learn
	☐ c) The instructor is most responsible for what and how much I learn

10)	I would classify myself as someone who:
	☐ a) Often gets things done ahead of time
	☐ b) Needs reminding to get things done on time
	☐ c) Puts off things until the last moment

FIG. 7.2. (*continued*)

In our view, any student who matches four or more of the characteristics on the following list has the potential for low performance in a virtual classroom:

- Does the student have an external locus of control? ...
- Does the student have low self-efficacy regarding [his or her] computer skills? (Bandura, 1997)
- Does the student have low self-efficacy regarding the course content?
- Does the student lack previous experience with online courses?
- Did the student enroll solely because of course availability?
- Does the student have a low [log-in] rate for the course home page?
- Is the student reading and writing few messages on the class forum?
- Is the student quiet or non-responsive in the online chat room?

Wang and Newlin advised that the instructor should check the latter three indicators of early activity, and proactively contact students who show early signs of low participation. This is an area in need of additional investigation. For example, Fredericksen, Pickett, Shea, Pelz, and Swan (2000) found that among SUNY respondents to a survey ($n = 1406$) regarding levels of satisfaction and learning in online courses, students who reported lower levels of incoming computer skills were actually slightly more likely to report high levels of learning and satisfaction in these courses. There may be a mediating factor; computer skills learned in the process of actively engaging in online study contribute to students' overall perceptions of online learning and satisfaction. This assumes, however, that high-quality student support (i.e., a helpdesk) is easily accessible, as was the case for students in this study.

The educational backgrounds of cyberstudents can also serve as early-warning indicators for failure or success in the virtual classroom (Wang & Newlin, 2000). For instance, Osborn's (2001) study showed that the number of previous distance learning courses taken by students reliably discriminates between students who drop out compared to those who complete either Web-based or videoconferencing courses. Students' prior experiences with distance learning courses increase their familiarity with the technological demands of the virtual classroom and their confidence in their ability to take advantage of online learning opportunities available to them. Osborn also found that students who complete distance learning have higher college GPAs compared to those students who drop out of these courses; this is not surprising. Hiltz (1994) noted that, overall, grade point average is the strongest predictor of success in the virtual classroom.

Although withdrawal from a course may be an indicator of low student satisfaction and learning, there may be other, more subtle indicators. Among those who finish online courses, increased familiarity with the format creates higher levels of sophistication and, consequently, higher expectations of quality. Institutions offering courses with poor course design and management may therefore find lower levels of satisfaction and learning among this increasingly discerning population, especially among those who persist. In studies by Shea and colleagues (2002, 2003) the authors asked students to rate their experience with online learning according to criteria for good design and management that reflected high levels of *teaching presence*, a construct developed by Anderson, Rourke, Garrison, and Archer (2001). An analysis of responses among students who completed courses showed a significant correlation between student satisfaction and reported learning and the quality indicators of "teaching presence"—effective instructional design and organization, discourse facilitation, and direct instruction.

Schrum (2002) surveyed 14 experienced ALN educators to validate the list of success factors that they had garnered from the published literature. The six most important of the interrelated factors identified are:

1. *Access to tools:* The more difficulty the student experienced in getting to the equipment, the easier it was to find reasons to drop the course.
2. *Technology experience:* It was not sufficient to have access to the appropriate tools; students needed to have a level of comfort with using the tools—experience in solving simple problems, checking e-mail, and accomplishing basic tasks (e.g., printing or file management)—as well as access to timely assistance from a qualified helpdesk.
3. *Learning preferences:* Individuals must be able to recognize their own abilities and styles, in order to modify the learning styles necessary for online environments.
4. *Study habits and skills:* With greater control over their individual learning also comes substantial responsibility for completing assignments and being prepared; this takes self-discipline to make required postings on time.
5. *Goals and purposes:* Successful students usually have high levels of motivation.
6. *Lifestyle factors:* Students have to be aware of the responsibilities that govern their lives, and need to determine if they will have 10–20 hours a week to devote to studying. The amount of support they have from family, friends, and coworkers as they pursue their studies is important in trying to balance the complexities of their lives, such as work-related travel and childcare.

Often, withdrawal from courses is considered a form of "failure." However, this is not necessarily true for students who take distance courses; usually, the most prevalent reason for course withdrawal is that a family or work emergency occurs that prevents the semester work plan to proceed as intended (Hiltz, 1994). Due to the differences in demographic profiles between distance students and traditional classroom students described in the following section, such role conflicts are much more likely to occur for online students. Diaz (2002) argued that rather than being seen as an indicator of "failure," course withdrawal is often "the right thing to do ... because of the requirements of school, work, and/or family life ... by dropping the class [students] may be making a mature, well-informed decision" that they do not have enough time to devote to the course that semester. Thus, Diaz (2002) concluded, "We should certainly not consider students who drop as 'at-risk' students without further evidence to support such a belief. Further, we should not consider high drop rates as implicit evidence that online education is inferior to traditional education."

Profiles of Online Learners

A handful of studies on specific campuses have described how students who enroll in online classes differ from those who choose traditional on-campus courses. In this section, we look at differences that have been observed in these individual studies, and see if there are generalizations that can be made. It should be noted, of course, that the enrollment policies of universities will affect the composition of online classes. Some universities allow all students to freely enroll in their choice of online versus in-classroom courses, whereas others put barriers in the way of full-time undergraduates, especially those who live on campus, who wish to enroll in online classes. (For example, at NJIT, full-time freshmen are not allowed to enroll in online courses for the first semester.)

Two sections of an introductory computer science course at North Carolina State University were studied by Dutton et al. (2002), using questionnaire responses and student records for 283 students. As would be expected, the online students were slightly older (mean of 27.6 years vs. 22.5 for the classroom). Whereas 85% of the classroom students were enrolled in a traditional 4-year undergraduate degree program, only 48% of the online students were. The online students were more likely to be nonmatriculated students working on a certificate, postgraduate students, and so on. The online students were also more likely to be attending school part time; 43% of them were taking just the one course and only 38% were full-time students (12 credit hours or more), whereas only 9% of the classroom students were enrolled in only one course that semester and 82% were full-time students. Online students at North Carolina State also reported being much more likely to be working that semester (84% vs. 55%); among those who were working, the online students expected to put in about twice the hours per week for the course as did the traditional classroom students. The online students were also more likely to have childcare responsibilities (15% vs. 7%). Finally, the online students were somewhat more likely to have more experience with computers and programming, as would be expected given their age and work experience.

Diaz (2000) looked at 231 students in a health education course at Nova University in Florida. He also found that online students are significantly older, and more likely to have completed more college credit hours, than traditional students. Diaz also noted that the profile of the online learner shows students with more life and academic experience.

STUDENT ATTRIBUTES AND LEARNING EFFECTIVENESS

It may come as a surprise, but demographic characteristics such as age or gender are weak predictors of student success in ALNs. Characteristics having to do with motivation, general academic ability (e.g., grade point average), and making or being able to make regular times for online interaction are much stronger predictors. This section begins with a summary of three studies that looked at a number of predictors of learner success, and then moves on to a more detailed examination of gender and learning style as they may relate to ALN effectiveness.

The SUNY Study

Frederickson et al. (2000) reported on the results of one of the largest studies of ALN learners, based on 1,406 postcourse questionnaires from the 1999 spring semester of the SUNY Learning Network. The findings indicate that pedagogical elements are more important than demographic characteristics in predicting learning outcomes: "Interaction with the teacher is the most significant contributor to perceived learning." Students who do not have adequate access to their instructors feel that they learn less and they are also less satisfied with their courses. However, each of the following hypotheses was also supported at a statistically significant level:

- Student perceived learning and satisfaction in online classes varies with gender. Small but reliable differences exist suggesting that, when compared to their male counterparts, female online learners enjoy several benefits. Details are provided in the expanded section on gender later in this chapter.
- Student perceived learning varies with students' motivation for taking online classes. Students who reported that they were taking the course because it was not offered on campus reported significantly lower levels of learning than did students who were taking the course because of family responsibilities or because of a conflict with their personal schedule. This appears to be a difference between intrinsic and extrinsic motivation. Students who feel that the courses are beneficial because of the flexibility they offer in allowing the completion of goals that are otherwise prohibited may believe that they are learning more than are students who feel they must take the course because there is no other way to do so. Again, documentation regarding successful online learning strategies is useful in helping students decide whether this environment is for them.
- Student perceived learning in online classes varies among age groups. The youngest students (16–25) reported that they learned the least and that they were the least satisfied with online learning. Students in the range of 36–45 years old reported that they learned the most and were the most satisfied with online learning. Unfortunately, there were too few students over 55 to be able to have any confidence in the data for the older age ranges.

The Texas Study: Predicting Course Completion

Osborn's (2001) survey of 396 students enrolled in 19 courses at the University of North Texas included an exploratory factor analysis of responses to Likert-scale items on the course survey. Six of the factors accounted for the majority of the variance:

- Computer confidence.
- External locus of control.
- Study environment.
- Enrollment encouragement.
- Tenacity.
- Motivation.

Study environment, motivation, and computer confidence were the factors most important in predicting completion or noncompletion. Additionally, educational level, GPA, number of credit hours taken, and number of previous distance learning courses were all positively related to course completion. (Note that this study did not take into account the existence or extent of student support, which could overcome problems of students with poor computer skills or low confidence.)

A Wisconsin Study

Arbaugh (2000a) looked at MBA students at the University of Wisconsin who were using Lotus' Learning Space as an ALN system. When looking at bivariate correlations, he found moderate relationships between both age and perceived learning and gender and perceived learning, with females reporting higher levels. However, in the full multivariate regression model, the only variables that were significantly associated with learning were three variables measuring interaction: instructor emphasis on interaction, ease of interaction, and classroom dynamics.

From these three studies, we can conclude that the student's motivation to select the ALN mode is an important factor in success. Confidence in computer skills needed for an online course (computer self-efficacy) is also related. However, the existence of systematic and extensive student support may mediate the effect of low incoming computer skill level on satisfaction and learning online. Age/maturity plays a role, and females may be more satisfied with ALN than are males. However, when multivariate analyses are performed, the amount of interaction between instructor and student, and among the students, is a much stronger predictor of student success in ALN than are individual student characteristics.

Gender Differences in ALN

In two of the three studies previously described, gender was mentioned as perhaps being slightly related to ALN success. What do studies specifically focusing on gender tell us?

Brief Literature Review: Gender Differences in Other Modes.
Studies of gender inequity in traditional face-to-face classes tend to indicate that class participation is male dominated, and that this is caused by gender differences in communication patterns (Spender, 1982; Stalker, 1996). However, with asynchronous computer-mediated communication, the tendency is toward more equal participation. Previous studies of differences in communication patterns between men and women have found that men tend to communicate on the basis of social hierarchy and competition, whereas women tend to be more network oriented and collaborative (Kilbourne & Weeks, 1997; Tannen, 1995). In a study of e-mail, Gefen and Straub (1997) discerned that there was no difference in use associated with gender, but that there were differences in perceptions of the medium: females perceived a higher social presence and usefulness of e-mail, and they wanted to build a cooperative context whereas men focused more on message content. If electronic communication is used merely to disseminate information, as in objectivist or competitive environments, then it might be a better fit for men (Brunner, 1991; Hiltz, Johnson, & Turoff, 1986). But if the medium is used for collaborative efforts, it would be a better fit for women (Herring, 1996; Kilbourne & Weeks, 1997). Electronic communication

also tends to favor women in that the medium lets everyone speak equally instead of one person dominating a conversation (Finley, 1992; Strauss, 1996). This tends to be more favorable to the typical female discourse pattern (Tannen, 1995). The social cues and presence that may favor male participants in classroom discussion are diminished in an electronic format (Rice, 1984; Sproull & Kiesler, 1991). Based on these studies, perhaps the virtual classroom is more welcoming to female students; the online environment may provide a more equitable environment for both male and female students.

Earlier studies noted that women tend to have more negative attitudes toward computers and technology than do men. (Canada & Bruscha, 1991; Dambrot, 1985; Ogletree & Williams, 1990) However, recent studies suggest that these attitudes are changing. Although gender differences toward computer usage may exist among school-age children, they tend to disappear once people are old enough to enter the workspace (Kraut, Sherlis, Mulkhopadhyay, Manning, & Kiesler, 1996; Whitely, 1997). When the experience is supplemented with training, differences in anxiety and performance disappear (Colley, Gale, & Harris, 1994).

The findings about a shrinking U.S. gender gap related to attitudes toward computers are similar to those for a 10-year study of gender differences for entering students at the University of Edinburgh in Scotland, which started in the early 1990s (Gunn, McSporran, Macleod, & French, 2003). Over a decade, the differences in the proportion of males and females believing that they would make substantial use of computing technologies, and that computers would be important for their studies, "have gradually and completely disappeared" (p. 19). Gunn et al. concluded that although males may continue to act more dominant in computer-supported learning environments, this is not necessarily a disadvantage, just a difference—"the conclusion is that women often perform better than men despite the observable differences in interaction style" (p. 14).

Gender and ALN.   In addition to the Frederickson et al. (2000) and Arbaugh (2000a) studies described earlier, eight additional studies of how gender is related to ALN learning outcomes were located and analyzed. Several of these examine communication process differences related to gender in ALN courses.

Ory, Bullock, and Burnaska (1997) studied whether the frequency of ALN use is the same for male and female students, whether male and female students use ALN differently, and whether male and female students differ in their attitudes about using ALN in courses. Ory et al.'s survey results for over 2,000 students at the University of Illinois Urbana–Champaign (UIUC) over two semesters in various courses found that gender was not significantly related to ALN satisfaction or grades. However, Ory et al. found differences in gender use of ALN. Females tended to communicate more with the instructor and other students, whereas males accessed materials on the World Wide Web more often. By contrast, Bourne, McMaster, Rieger, and Campbell (1997), in their study of 84 undergraduate and graduate students in an ALN course, found that there were no observable differences in the way men and women used the course materials.

Arbaugh (2000b) did a case study in an MBA course, testing whether women may find the virtual classroom to be a more welcoming "place" than the traditional classroom, whether an Internet-based course design in a collaborative format favors women, and whether a collaborative environment will further increase women's participation. Arbaugh's argument was that if an ALN is set up to encourage collaboration, the fit between technological medium and preferred learning style should favor the increased participation of women even further. His results showed that women, both individually and collectively, had consistently higher participation patterns than did men. Arbaugh concluded that there is a moderate level of support for the hypothesis of enhanced female participation in class discussion in a collaborative Internet-based course. However, there were no significant differences between men and women in measures of learning and in exam performance.

A study by Gay, Sturgill, Martin, and Huttenlocher (1999) indicated that more female than male students perceived that the use of CMC helped in their course tasks. However, how this may translate into better course outcomes was not addressed.

A study at the University of Central Florida by Moskal and Dziuban (2001) found that females both enroll in and succeed in ALN courses at a rate that is consistently higher than that of male students. However, these differences were not as strong as other predictors, such as the course discipline.

An apparent exception to the pattern of equal or greater participation by females online was reported in a study by Blum (1999), which examined male and female students in relationship to increased reliance on asynchronous-based instruction and to an increased number of female students. The study was a content analysis from an electronic forum open to all students in all courses, rather than being part of course work. Blum studied whether males and females posted an equal number of messages, whether males and females posted an equal number of messages of each type, and whether males responded to more questions than females. The results were that males posted more messages than female students; males still dominated the informal online environment selected, but with different methods. Females asked most of the questions, whereas male students answered most of the questions. Males sent 76.7% of all messages that had a tone of certainty, whereas females sent 66% of all messages of an empathetic nature. Female students sent 83% of all messages containing personal references. All the messages expressing fear of failure were posted by females. It is important to reemphasize that Blum's results were based on an informal, nonclass-related discussion space, rather than on a moderated class discussion.

There have been only a few studies reporting gender differences in outcomes of ALN courses. One of these (Shea, Fredericksen, Pickett, Pelz, & Swan, 2001) discussed results for 1,974 students answering course questionnaires in spring 2000 in a wide variety of courses at SUNY. Shea et al. found small but significant differences indicating that women ALN students, compared to male ALN students, reported that:

- They participated at higher levels than in the classroom.
- They learned more.
- Technical difficulties were less likely to impede their learning.
- They were more likely to want to continue taking online courses.
- They were more satisfied with their specific courses at SLN and more satisfied with online learning in general.

Benbunan-Fich and Hiltz (2002) used postcourse questionnaire data for approximately 2,000 students in sections of traditional and ALN courses at NJIT, on both undergraduate and graduate levels. They compared both objective (grades) and subjective (perceived learning) outcomes by mode and gender, using analysis of variance (ANOVA). Female students obtained higher grades than did their male counterparts, and students in ALN sections earned significantly higher grades, but there was no interaction between condition and gender. In terms of learning perceptions, all conditions reported similar levels, and these perceptions are not affected by gender.

In sum, for the studies summarized, we see that four showed advantages for females in ALN courses (in that they participated more than did males or achieved greater success) and three found no difference by gender. One study indicated male dominance, but this was based on content analysis of an open forum available to all students, rather than on a transcript of a specific course. Among the specific findings were that females are more emotional and self-referenced in posted messages. Females tend to be more satisfied with online learning and find it to be more helpful to course tasks. According to several of these studies' results, male and female students tend to have different learning styles because their communication patterns are different. This suggests that perhaps distance course design should create a learning environment that promotes and encourages collaborative learning for the female "connected" learner, yet allows the male "separate" learner the freedom of learning in a more abstract, autonomous manner.

There are no replications of specific findings. We need future studies that replicate some of the earlier studies of gender differences in ALN in such a way as to determine the conditions under which gender differences do or do not emerge, and which connect a content analysis of actual online interaction patterns associated with gender, with course outcomes for males and females.

Psychological Predictors: Personality Type, Cognitive Style

Studies of whether learners' psychological characteristics are correlated with performance in online courses have included such "global" traits as learning style, sensory preference, hemisphericity/brain dominance, and locus of control (Ehrman, 1990). Global traits refer to characteristics of the individual (e.g., "personality") that are relatively enduring and stable across time and various learning environments. However, as far as predicting cyberstudent success, research on these global characteristics has yielded very little in the way of definitive, statistically significant, and consistent results.

Wang and Newlin's (2002) review of these studies concluded that only one global trait, locus of control, is correlated with performance in the virtual classroom. Specifically, students with an internal locus of control (e.g., "The success I have is largely a matter of my own doing") are more likely to succeed in an online class than are students with an external locus of control (e.g., "The success I have is largely a matter of chance"). Wang and Newlin speculated that this is because learners with an internal locus of control leave little to chance or fate, but instead attempt to manage their activities in a thoughtful manner.

Mielke (1999) described the successful online student as one who exhibits persistence, shows self-direction, and takes individual responsibility for achievement; these traits are very similar to the qualities defined as having an "internal locus of control." Similarly, Wang, Kanfer, Hinn, and Arvan (2001) asserted that self-discipline is the most important characteristic for online learners to possess. However, Hiltz (1994), in a study of several hundred NJIT students in Virtual Classroom® and traditional classroom sections of courses, found that sphere of control was not a very good predictor. The "personal efficacy sphere of control" measure was significantly related to overall course outcomes, and a measure of interpersonal sphere of control was significantly related to the preference for taking another online course, but neither measure was significantly related to the overall rating of the ALN experience.

In contrast to the research on global traits, investigations of situation-specific (i.e., course-specific) learner characteristics have yielded much stronger predictors of cyberstudent performance, according to Wang and Newlin's (2002) review. Situation-specific characteristics are behaviors and beliefs that are associated with a particular activity or environment. One such concept is self-efficacy, which is an individual's belief that he or she can perform a specific behavior to attain a desired goal (Bandura, 1997). It is situation specific because one can have high self-efficacy about accomplishing one task, but low self-efficacy about accomplishing another. When applied to online learning, two types of self-efficacy seem to predict student performance: self-efficacy for understanding course content, and self-efficacy for meeting the technological demands of an online course (e.g., computer self-efficacy or confidence). For example, students who have strong confidence in their computer skills and less computer anxiety were less likely to withdraw from a distance learning class than were students with lower levels of computer confidence (Osborn, 2001). However, consistent access to high-quality assistance with technical problems may ameliorate these differences.

Learning Styles and ALN.   Students tend to prefer to process information in different ways; this is referred to as "learning style" or "cognitive style." The learning style construct assumes that a student's preferred mode for obtaining knowledge affects how well he or she interacts and learns via different media. There are many different classification schemes for learning style and cognitive style, and a lack of agreement on measures. There is also a great deal of controversy about whether aspects of cognitive style significantly predict learner success. This section reviews a few of the studies that have explored this issue in relation to student success in ALNs.

Diaz (2000) used a simple unidimensional classification of the degree to which learners prefer "independent" learning versus "dependent" learning (tied to desire to receive guidance from their teacher). He found that successful online students (defined as those who received a grade of C or better) were more strongly independent learners than were those who were not successful.

Another learning style classification is verbal versus nonverbal learners: The former feel more comfortable with text-based information whereas the latter prefer nonverbal materials, such as images (Monaghan & Stenning, 1998). The text-based communication that is predominant in ALN currently may place nonverbal learners at a disadvantage.

Ally and Fahy (2002) used the Kolb Learning Styles Inventory, which classifies students into divergers, convergers, assimilators, and accommodators. They concluded that convergers demonstrated the highest level of activity in online classes, divergers and accommodators required the least support from the instructor, and assimilators were most dependent on the instructor and needed the most support.

Leuthold (1999) reported a very interesting exploratory study of the impact of learning styles on satisfaction with computer use in ALN, frequency of use, and interaction and motivation. The study is described as exploratory because of the very small sample on which it was based: 40 freshmen economics students in the microeconomics principles class at UIUC, taught in two sections; 19 students completed both a learning-style assessment based on the Gregorc model, and computer preference questionnaires. The Gregorc model is a cognitive model designed to reveal two types of abilities, perception and ordering. Perceptual abilities, the means through which information is grasped, translate into two qualities: abstractness and concreteness. Ordering abilities are the ways in which the learner organizes information: either sequentially (linearly) or randomly (nonlinearly). These qualities combine to form four learning categories: concrete/sequential (CS), abstract/sequential (AS), abstract/random (AR), and concrete/random (CR).

The results of Leuthold's (1999) study were that students with high abstract sequential (AS) scores most frequently used the computer-based features of the course, and students with high concrete random (CR) scores least frequently used these features. Students with high sequential scores had a positive correlation with frequency of class computer use, whereas students with high random scores had a negative correlation. In addition, it was found that sequential learners preferred computer-based instruction, whereas random learners tended to prefer traditional instructional techniques. Random learners seem to have had more problems navigating and using the web site and were bothered more by access problems than were the sequential learners. Sequential learners reported feeling strongly that interaction, particularly with the instructor, was improved with computer-based learning. Sequential learners also experienced increased motivation to learn, and their familiarity with and knowledge of computers increased with computer-based instruction.

Another measure of learning style is LASSI, designed at the University of Texas at Austin, as a means to measure students' study and learning strategies and methods (Loomis, 2000). The tool consists of 10 scales, each measuring a different learning component. Among the 10 scales, 5 predicted at least one type of course outcome assessment:

- *Attitude:* the student's interest and motivation to succeed in college; willingness to perform the tasks necessary for academic success.
- *Time management:* the extent to which the student creates and uses schedules to effectively manage his or her responsibilities.
- *Concentration:* the ability of the student to focus his or her attention, and avoid distractions, while working on school-related tasks (e.g., studying).

- *Selecting main ideas:* the magnitude of the student's ability to ferret out the important information in a learning situation.
- *Study aids:* the student's ability to use or develop study aids that help the learning process.

Attitude predicted course withdrawal. The strongest correlation was found between time management skills and the final grade. Many students with good time management and study aids skills found that the flexibility of ALN actually improved the learning experience, but ALN did not work well for those with a tendency toward procrastination. In addition, the ability to effectively use study aids was significant in the students' performance on the final grade, the final exam, and all activities outside exams (e.g., journal reports, chapter assignments; Loomis, 2000).

Cultural Differences

Although U.S. universities have an international and multicultural student body, and although ALN is spreading around the world, there have been very few studies of cultural differences among students that may affect ALN learning. By "cultural" differences, we mean ethnicity that is often related to nationality and encompasses a shared language, history, traditions, and values. An exploratory study of one graduate-level course in New Zealand suggested that this is a variable that should be studied much more. Morse (2003) used the cultural dimension of "low context" versus "high context" cultures, which was related to Hofstede's (1980) classic distinction between "individualism" versus "collectivism." In "low context" cultures (e.g., the United States and United Kingdom), there are low levels of "programmed, mutually understood" information to provide context; everything needs to be made explicit, and written contracts are often used. In "high context" or collectivistic cultures, there are high levels of mutually understood context that provides meaning; examples are Pakistan and China. Morse found that the cultural background predicted what students were likely to perceive as most valuable about the ALN experience. Low-context culture students most valued personal convenience, whereas high-context culture students most valued the increased ability to articulate what they believed. Both groups of students valued ALN, but for different reasons.

Multivariate Models: Predicting Student Satisfaction From Student Characteristics

We have seen that when examined individually, many student characteristics appear to have some influence on ALN outcomes, but they are often so weak that they disappear when other factors are taken into account. We end this chapter with one final study that used multivariate analysis based on a set of student characteristics.

Lim (2001) reported a study of 235 adult learners who were taking a web-based distance education course at five institutions—Florida Atlantic University, Johns

Hopkins University, Florida International University, the University of Houston, and Rio Salado College—in the spring and summer semester of 1999. The participants were undergraduate, graduate, and continuing education students. Personal and experiential variables were used as predictor variables. Personal variables were age, gender, computer self-efficacy, academic self-concept, and academic status. Experiential variables were years of computer use, frequency of computer use, computer training, Internet experience in a class, and participation in a workshop to prepare for a web-based course. The criterion variables for this study were satisfaction levels with the web-based distance education courses and intent to participate in future web-based courses.

Lim (2001) found a significant relationship between computer self-efficacy and satisfaction. Years of computer use, Internet experience in a class, and academic self-concept had positive relationships with satisfaction. Computer self-efficacy was significantly related to years of computer use ($r = .452, p < .001$), frequency of computer use ($r = .305, p < .001$), academic self-concept ($r = .224, p < .001$), age ($r = -.187, p = .002$), and academic status ($r = -.139, p = .017$). The combination of all these predictor variables produced a predictive model for satisfaction of adult learners in their web-based distance education course. The results of the multiple regression analysis revealed that 15% of the variability in the dependent variable (satisfaction) was explained by the predictor variables. Entering all predictor variables, the percentage of observed variability in intent to take future web-based courses explained was 12%.

We can see from these results that individual student characteristics can predict outcomes in ALN, but, even in combination, only a small proportion of the variance in outcomes can be explained. This brings us back full circle to the SUNY study mentioned near the beginning of this chapter. Some students are more likely to thrive in ALN environments than are others, but the major determinants of outcomes are systematic student and faculty support as well as faculty training that focuses on pedagogy—the course design and instructor behavior that largely determines what goes on inside virtual classrooms.

SUMMARY

What We Know

On the individual level, students who are motivated, self-directed, and confident about having the computer skills necessary to use the technology are those who are most likely to thrive in the ALN environment. Often, these are students who are older than traditional on-campus undergraduates. Females seem on the average to be somewhat more comfortable in ALN courses than are males, perhaps because of their generally higher verbal skills and their greater tendency to enjoy collaborative learning styles.

Based on the empirical studies reviewed in this chapter, the "input box" for student characteristics in the online learning interaction model can be modified slightly, as shown in the accompanying box.

Student Characteristics

Having (small to moderate) relationships with ALN effectiveness (as measured by completion, grades, or subjective satisfaction):

Attitudes
    Motivation
    Personality: independence/self-discipline/internal sphere of control
    Attitudes: Computer self-efficacy
    Time management skills
    Learning style: Visual/convergers/sequential

Experiential/Demographic Characteristics
    Prior online course
    Higher GPA
    Good access to computer/Internet
    Support of family/employer
    Gender (female)
    Age (25+)

What We Need To Know

In looking at gender, most studies examine either interaction modes or course outcomes. We need more studies that look at the relationship among characteristics that may be associated with gender (e.g., verbal skills, learning styles, independence, family responsibilities), interaction patterns online, and course outcomes.

We could use more longitudinal and multivariate studies, across a variety of disciplines and institutions and cultural/national backgrounds of students, that look at how characteristics of the students interact with pedagogy and interaction patterns online to produce course outcomes. Most studies are of a small number of students at one institution (and often in one class), are based only on a cross-sectional questionnaire, and look at only a few variables.

Although examinations of student characteristics may allow us to understand a little about who is likely to succeed in online learning environments, the larger and more important issues may be about how we can help most or all students seeking online education to succeed (e.g., Williams, Wahlstrom, & Shea, 2002). Motivated, self-directed, self-disciplined students are likely to succeed in any learning environment, but we need to know more about how to support weaker students—online environments pose additional challenges and opportunities in this regard. We need additional inquiry in at least three areas: student support, faculty support, and institutional alignment for online learning.

Additional studies of approaches to online learning environments need to focus on student outcomes relative to the existence of support services. Student support services such as the technology helpdesk, academic advisement, orientation, tutoring, and library services are all considered essential in FtF learning environments (see WCET, *Beyond the Administrative Core: Creating Web-Based Student Services for Online Learners*, 2003). Such supports are clearly needed for online learners to succeed as well. Additional study of how best to provide these to online learners may prove fruitful in reducing failure for students with less than ideal levels of motivation, self-direction, and self-discipline.

We also need additional studies on the impact of faculty support. Focusing solely on student traits without also examining faculty behaviors is unlikely to provide a complete analysis of how best to facilitate success. Clearly, systematic approaches to faculty development and support have positive consequence on effective online course design and management (Fredericksen, Pickett, Shea, Pelz, & Swan, 1999; Hartman, Dziuban, & Moskal, 1999; Shea et al., 2002), which, in turn, are likely to result in higher rates of student success. More work is needed in this area.

Finally, additional study on how best to design, develop, and scale online learning at the institutional level is also needed. Identifying, understanding, and confronting common institutional barriers that inhibit the overall growth of online learning environments will result in higher-quality and more sustainable models for online learning—ultimately, a key beneficiary will be the online student.

QUESTIONS FOR DISCUSSION AND RESEARCH

1. We know that convenience is the main reason when students first choose an online course. How do the reasons for choosing between online and traditional delivery change with experience in the online mode? How would you design a study to answer this question?
2. Given the research findings reported in this chapter, design the questions, scoring, and feedback for an online quiz to assess and advise students' suitability for ALN courses. For students who lack one or more crucial characteristics (e.g., computer self-efficacy), what training or support could be provided to better prepare them for success?
3. What can an online instructor do to improve success rates of ALN students who are not motivated and self-directed?
4. Provide examples of institutional barriers that may impede the development of successful online learning environments. What research methods would be most successful in identifying the existence of such barriers at a particular institution?

ACKNOWLEDGMENTS

This work was partially supported by grants from the Alfred P. Sloan Foundation, the New Jersey Center for Multimedia Research, and the New Jersey Center for Pervasive Information Systems. Eunhee Kim and Yi Zhang assisted in compiling studies of learning styles and gender differences in ALN.

REFERENCES

Ally, M., & Fahy, P. (2002). Using students' learning styles to provide support in distance education. In *Proceedings, 18th Annual Conference on Distance Teaching and Learning* (pp. 3–7). Madison: University of Wisconsin Press.

Anderson, T., Rourke, L., Garrison, R. L., & Archer, W. (2001). Assessing teaching presence in a computer conferencing context. *Journal of Asynchronous Learning Networks, 5,* 2. Retrieved March 8, 2004, from http://www.sloan-c.org/publications/jaln/v5n2/pdf/v5n2_anderson.pdf

Arbaugh, J. B. (2000a). How classroom environment and student engagement affect learning in internet-based MBA courses. *Business Communication Quarterly, 63*(4), 9–26.

Arbaugh, J. B. (2000b). Virtual classroom versus physical classroom: An exploratory study of class discussion patterns and student learning in an asynchronous Internet-based MBA course. *Journal of Management Education, 26*(2), 213–233.

Bandura, A. (1997). *Self-efficacy: The exercise of control.* New York: W. H. Freeman.

Benbunan-Fich, R., & Hiltz, S. R. (2002). The effects of course level, course type, and gender on course outcomes in the "virtual university." In *Proceedings of the 35th Hawaii International Conference on System Sciences* [CD-Rom]. Washington, DC: IEEE Computer Society Press.

Blum, K. D. (1999). Gender differences in asynchronous learning in higher education: Learning styles, participation barriers and communication patterns. *Journal of Asynchronous Learning Networks, 3*(1), 24. Retrieved March 8, 2004, from http://www.alnresearch.org/jsp/empirical_research

Bourne, J. R., McMaster, E., Rieger, J., & Campbell, J. O. (1997). Paradigms for on-line learning: A case study in the design and implementation of an asynchronous learning networks (ALN) course. *Journal of Asynchronous Learning Networks, 1*(2), 38–56.

Brunner, C. (1991). Gender and distance learning. In *Annuals of the American Academy of Political and Social Science* (pp. 133–145). Beverly Hills, CA: Sage.

Canada, K., & Bruscha, F. (1991). The technological gender gap: Evidence and recommendations for educators and computer-based instruction designers. *Education Technology Research and Development, 39*(2), 43–51.

Colley, A. M., Gale, M. T., & Harris, T. A. (1994). Effects of gender role identity and experience on computer attitude components. *Journal of Educational Computing Research, 10*(2), 129–137.

Dambrot, F. H. (1985). The correlates of sex differences in attitudes toward and involvement with computers. *Journal of Vocational Behavior, 27*(1), 71–86.

Diaz, D. P. (2000). *Comparison of student characteristics, and evaluation of student success, in an online health education course.* Unpublished doctoral dissertation, Nova Southeastern University, Fort Lauderdale, FL.

Diaz, D. P. (2002, May/June). Online drop rates revisited. *The Technology Source.* Retrieved March 8, 2004, from http://www.ts.mivu.org/archives

Dutton, J., Dutton, M., & Perry, J. (2002). How do online students differ from lecture students? *Journal of Asynchronous Learning Networks, 6*(1). Retrieved March 8, 2004, from http://www.sloan-c.org/publications/jaln

Ehrman, M. (1990). Psychological factors and distance education. *American Journal of Distance Education, 4,* 10–24.

Finley, M. (1992). Belling the bully. *HR Magazine, 37,* 82–86.

Frederickson, E., Pickett, A., Shea, P., Pelz, W., & Swan, K. (1999). Factors influencing faculty satisfaction with asynchronous teaching and learning in the SUNY Learning Network. In J. Bourne & J. C. Moore (Eds.), *Online education* (Vol. 1, pp. 239–267). Needham, MA: Sloan Center for Online Education.

Frederickson, E., Pickett, A., Shea, P., Pelz, W., & Swan, K. (2000). Student satisfaction and perceived learning with on-line courses: Principles and examples from the SUNY Learning Network. *Journal of Asynchronous Learning Networks,, 4*(2). Retrieved March 8, 2004, from http://www.sloan-c.org/publications/jaln

Gay, G., Sturgill, A., Martin, W., & Huttenlocher, D. (1999). Document-centered peer collaborations: An exploration of the educational uses of networked communication technologies. *Journal of Computer-Mediated Communication, 4*(3). Retrieved March 8, 2004, from http://www.ascusc.org/jcmc/vol4/issue3/gay.html

Gefen, D., & Straub, D. W. (1997). Gender differences in the perception and use of e-mail: An extension to the technology acceptance model. *MIS Quarterly, 21*(4), 359–388.

Gunn, C., McSporran, M., Macleod, H., & French, S. (2003). Dominant or different? Gender issues in computer supported learning. *Journal of Asynchronous Learning Networks, 7*(1). Retrieved March 8, 2004, from http://www.sloan-c.org/publications/jaln/v7n1

Hartman, J., Dziuban, C., & Moskal, P. (1999). Faculty satisfaction in ALNs: A dependent of independent variable. In J. Bourne & J. C. Moore (Eds.), *Online education* (Vol. 1, pp. 151–172). Needham, MA: Sloan Center for Online Education.

Heckman, R., & Annabi, H. (2003). A content analytic comparison of FtF and ALN case-study discussion. In *Proceedings of 36th Hawaii International Conference on Systems Science* [CD-Rom]. Washington, DC: IEEE Computer Society Press.

Herring, S. (1996). Bringing familiar baggage to the new frontier: Gender differences in computer-mediated communication. In V. J. Vitanza (Ed.), *Cyberreader* (pp. 144–154). Needham Heights, MA: Allyn & Bacon.

Hiltz, S. R. (1994). *The virtual classroom: Learning without limits via computer networks.* Norwood, NJ: Ablex.

Hiltz, S. R., Johnson, K. D., & Turoff, M. (1986). Experiments in group decision making: Communication process and outcome in face-to-face versus computerized conferences. *Human Communication Research, 13*(2), 225–252.

Hofstede, G. (1980). *Culture's consequence; international differences in work-related values.* Newbury Park: CA: Sage.

Kilbourne, W., & Weeks, S. (1997). A socio-economic perspective on gender bias in technology. *Journal of Socio-Economics, 26*(1), 243–260.

Kraut, R., Sherlis, W., Mukhopadhyay, T., Manning, J., & Kiesler, S. (1996). The HomeNet field trial of residential Internet services. *Communications of the ACM, 39*(12), 55–63.

Leasure, A., Davis, L., & Thievon, S. L. (2000). Comparison of student outcomes and preferences in a traditional vs. world wide web-based baccalaureate nursing research course. *Journal of Nursing Education*, 149–154.

Leuthold, J. H. (1999). Is computer-based learning right for everyone? In *Proceedings of 32nd Hawaii International Conference on Systems Sciences* [CD-Rom]. Washington, DC: IEEE Computer Society Press.

Lim, C. K. (2001). Computer self-efficacy, academic self-concept, and other predictors of satisfaction and future participation of adult distance learners. *The American Journal of Distance Education, 15*(2), 41–51.

Loomis, K. D. (2000). Learning styles and asynchronous learning: Comparing the LASSI model to class performance. *Journal of Asynchronous Learning Networks, 4*(1), 23–32.

Meyer, K. A. (2003). The Web's impact on student learning. *T.H.E. Journal, 30*(10). Retrieved March 8, 2004, from http://www.thejournal.com/magazine/vault1a440.cfm

Mielke, D. (1999). *Effective teaching in distance education* (No. ED436528). Washington, DC: Office of Educational Research and Improvement.

Monaghan, P., & Stenning, K. (1998, August). *Effects of representation modality and thinking style on learning to solve reasoning problems.* Paper presented at the 20th Annual Meeting of the Cognitive Science Society, Madison, WI.

Morse, K. (2003). Does one size fit all? Exploring asynchronous learning in a multicultural environment. *Journal of Asynchronous Learning Networks, 7*(1), 37–55.

Moskal, P. D., & Dziuban, C. D. (2001). Present and future directions for assessing cybereducation: The changing research paradigm. In L. R. Vandervert, L. V. Shavinina,

& R. A. Cornell (Eds.), *Cybereducation: The future of long distance learning* (pp. 157–184). Larchmont, NY: Mary Ann Liebert.

Ogletree, S. M., & Williams, S. W. (1990). Sex and stereotyping effects on computer attitudes and aptitude. *Sex Roles, 23*, 703–712.

Ory, J., Bullock, C. D., and Burnaska, K. K. (1997). Gender similarity in the use of and attitudes about ALN in a university setting. *Journal of Asynchronous Learning Networks, 1*(1). Retrieved March 8, 2004, from http://www.sloan-c.org/publications/jaln/v1n1/v1n1_org.asp

Osborn, V. (2001). Identifying at-risk students in videoconferencing and Web-based distance education. *The American Journal of Distance Education, 15*, 41–54.

Rice, R. E. (1984). *The new media: Communication, research, and technology.* Beverly Hills, CA: Sage.

Schrum, L. (2002). Dimensions and strategies for online success: Voices from experienced educators. *Journal of Asynchronous Learning Networks, 6*(1), 57–67.

Shea, P., Fredericksen, E., Pickett, A., Pelz, W., & Swan, K. (2001). Measures of learning effectiveness in the SUNY Learning Network. In J. Bourne & J. C. Moore (Eds.), *Online education* (Vol. 2, pp. 31–54). Needham, MA: Sloan Center for Online Education.

Shea, P., Swan, K., Fredericksen, E., & Pickett, A. (2002). Student satisfaction and reported learning in the SUNY Learning Network. In J. Bourne & J. C. Moore (Eds.), *Quality online education* (Vol. 3, pp. 145–155). Needham, MA: Sloan Center for Online Education.

Shea, P., Swan, K., Fredericksen, E., & Pickett, A. (2003). A preliminary investigation of "teaching presence" in the SUNY Learning Network. In J. Bourne & J. C. Moore (Eds.), *Quality online education* (Vol. 4, pp. 279–312). Needham, MA: Sloan Center for Online Education.

Spender, D. (1982). *Invisible women.* London: Women's Press.

Sproull, L., & Kiesler, S. (1991). *Connections: New ways of working in the networked organization.* Cambridge, MA: MIT Press.

Stalker, J. (1996, Winter). Women and adult education: Rethinking androcentric research. *Adult Education Quarterly, 46*(2), 98–113.

Strauss, S. G. (1996). Getting a clue: Communication media and information distribution effects on group process and performance. *Small Group Research, 27*(1), 115–142.

Tannen, D. (1995). The power of talk: Who gets heard and why. *Harvard Business Review Studies Journal, 21*, 19–38.

Wang, X. C., Kanfer, A., Hinn, D. M., & Arvan, L. (2001). Stretching the boundaries: Using ALN to reach on-campus students during an off-campus summer session. *Journal of Asynchronous Learning Networks, 5*(1), 1–20.

Wang, A. Y., & Newlin, M. H. (2000). characteristics of students who enroll and succeed in web-based psychology classes. *Journal of Educational Psychology* (92), 137143.

Wang, A. Y., & Newlin, M. H. (2002, May). Predictors of performance in the virtual classroom. *T.H.E. Journal, 29*(10). Retrieved March 8, 2004, from http://www.thejournal.com/magazine/vault/a4023.cfm

WCET (Western Cooperative for Educational Telecommunication). (2003). Beyond the administrative core: Creating web-based student services for online learners. Retrieved May 22, 2003, from http://www.wcet.info/projects/laapl

Whitely, B. E., Jr. (1997). Gender differences in computer-related attitudes and behavior: A meta-analysis. *Computers in Human Behavior, 13*, 1–22.

Williams, B., Wahlstrom, C., & Shea, P. J. (2002). *The successful distance learning student.* Belmont, CA: Wadsworth.

8

Faculty Roles and Satisfaction in Asynchronous Learning Networks

Charles Dziuban
University of Central Florida

Peter Shea
SUNY, State University of New York

J. B. Arbaugh
University of Wisconsin–Oshkosh

> *I think it has added some excitement to teaching, some new challenges. ... Because you are an effective teacher in the classroom does not mean you are an effective teacher in this mode. There are new issues, new challenges, new tools to bring to this.*
>
> *It takes time. An ALN professor is not born; they evolve ... and it takes a long time.*
>
> *(Interviews with ALN faculty members, reported in Coppola, Hiltz, & Rotter, 2002, pp. 183, 185)*

INTRODUCTION

The trend toward web-based learning is altering the role of instructors in colleges and universities (Moskal & Dziuban, 2001) as they experience multiple role expectations that change quickly and dramatically. Although several initial conceptual models of faculty roles and satisfaction have been developed, and much of the emerging empirical research in ALNs has focused on both student and instructor behavioral aspects, the assessment of faculty roles and characteristics that influence their satisfaction with ALNs has received limited empirical attention. In this chapter, we review the literature addressing the ALNs, general education, and social systems to identify characteristics that appear to significantly influence faculty roles and satisfaction. At the individual faculty level, some of these characteristics include changes in role expectations, pedagogical approaches, and uses of technology. We then describe the role of educational institutions in this transformative process and how they might help faculty transition to greater and more effective participation in ALNs. Having laid the theoretical foundation, we then discuss initial results from some large-scale online learning adoption efforts with the SUNY Learning Network and the University of Central Florida, and address some potential implications that these activities may have on future ALN development efforts. We conclude the chapter by using these findings to develop a research agenda for faculty roles in and satisfaction with ALNs.

Multiple Role Expectations

An understanding of the faculty role in ALNs helps to address emerging issues and challenges in the online environment. Jaffee (1998) stated that an institution must recognize and address the faculty development process in web-based learning before it can realize genuine pedagogical and institutional transformation. Social systems theory (Getzels, Lipham, & Campbell, 1968) states that any number of expectations placed on an individual in an organization defines that individual's role. These expectations comprise the cognitive, affective, and behavioral dimensions of what one is supposed to know, believe, and do in order to perform one's job well.

Getzels et al. (1968) also argued that most people experience multiple role expectations, many of which conflict with each other. An instructor, for example, may face various organizational demands as a teacher, counselor, and researcher that conflict with his or her personal demands as a husband or wife, parent, or community member. As instructors make the transition to the online environment, their roles change quickly and dramatically. The new demands can conflict with the customary demands typically encountered in face-to-face teaching, specifically in course organization and presentation, interaction with students, student assessment, maintaining office hours, and organizing course materials. The instructor must resolve these conflicts and deal with an increasing workload as the online instructional environment expands with the use of technology in the university classroom (Wolcott, 1997).

Emerging evidence indicates that instructors who resolve such conflict issues value experience and challenge as their reward and incentive. Schifter (2000) indicated that faculty may be more inclined to favor intrinsic factors when participating in ALNs than most administrators perceive. He reasoned that not all inhibiting factors can be resolved, but conflicts may be overcome when all parties address and recognize the issues and conflicts. Furthermore, the administration's understanding of what motivates participants provides decision makers with information to develop faculty incentives and minimize barriers, thereby facilitating transition to the asynchronous classroom.

Berge (1998) noted that most faculty who choose to teach asynchronously value the development of students as lifelong learners, and value learning as an active, constructive process that depends on cooperation and teamwork. Heberling (2002) maintained that the ability to teach effectively in online courses relates to the nurturing of internal incentives, and an institution should strongly consider both elements when developing policies about online technology and faculty roles. Gold (2001) claimed that if faculty experience a rewarding online instructional experience, they will be more likely to view online teaching as a part of their job and have a decreased need for external incentives.

Pedagogical Transformation

Various perspectives consider strategies for developing pedagogical transformation. Hitt (2001) stated, "advances in information technology are forcing us to reexamine all of the familiar objects that occupy our academic landscape while presenting a daunting landscape of new and unfamiliar technologies and applications that must be incorporated as well. This incorporation goes well beyond what we do already; it changes the very nature of what we do" (p. xi).

Graves (2001) appraised transformed faculty roles, addressing instructorless learning, e-learning materials, and instructors in the e-learning process. Graves concluded that these considerations will bring unprecedented instructional innovation by engaging and supporting faculty to strike the right balance between virtual and traditional models of instruction. Lewis, Massey, and Smith (2001) examined the impact of ALN on the traditional academy, finding the need to reconceptualize many established tenets. Additional issues discussed in the literature regarding asynchronous instruction include engagement (Hagner & Schneebeck, 2001), intellectual property (Hilton & Neal, 2001), generic structures (Hewson & Huges, 2001), campus reengineering (Brown, 2001), and facilitation as a teaching model (Mason, 2001). Sonwalker (2002) proposed an assessment model for web-based teaching that encompasses several instructional factors that greatly expand the transitional framework for moving face-to-face instruction to the online format: content, learning, delivery support, usability, and technological considerations.

Lewis et al. (2001) examined the various issues and also raised several questions regarding transformed faculty expectations for asynchronous learning:

- Is there room for a liberal education in a technological thought world?
- Are the distinctions between education and training becoming less salient?
- Are there important differences between students who receive their degrees online and those who graduate on campus?
- How does a university's mandate for basic research fit into the dialogue over ALN?

Muilenberg and Berge (2001) identified several challenges for prospective faculty when they examined the barriers that instructors encounter when they transition from face-to-face to asynchronous teaching. A large sample of responding instructors cited organizational change and administrative support structures as their main concerns, and additionally mentioned technical expertise and social interaction difficulties. Other issues in the study included faculty compensation, technology threats, legal issues, faculty evaluation, student and faculty access to technology, and student support services. These findings were further supported in a more recent study by Alavi and Gallupe (2003), who also found that institutions often underestimate the need for faculty training and support structures when transitioning to online instruction.

There is no checklist of key issues from these discussions, but one overriding theme emerged: the entire institution must participate in and own the transition (Barone & Hagner, 2001), and the transformation must be a collaborative one (Brown, 2001). Technology may be the focus (Lewis et al., 2001), but it is just one expression of the process. Barone and Hagner (2001) stated that, over time, new faculty roles and behaviors will evolve from the institution's commitment to transformation.

Clark's (1999) paradigm of necessary motivational factors provides a useful model for transition to web-based teaching and learning, even though Clark did not address technological issues. Expanding on Ford (1992), Clark (1999) presented his CANE model (commitment and necessary effort)—a theory based on the multiplicative interactions among personal agency and emotion and task value that lead to some degree of goal commitment. He defined personal agency as two constructs, self-efficacy and social support; defined emotion in a positive to negative continuum; and defined task value nominally by interest, utility, and importance.

Extrapolating Clark's (1999) model, when an instructor attempts to move from face-to-face teaching into technology-mediated instruction, certain conditions are necessary for high goal commitment with likelihood of success: positive motivation, a sense of self-efficacy and task value, and organizational social support. Clark (1999) hypothesized that goal commitment and self-efficacy will interact, producing the necessary effort. Diamond (1999), however, provided insights that augmented Clark's model, and argued that if the condition of even one component is not met, the transition will fail. Clark's (1999) CANE model, therefore, does present an effective way to conceptualize ALN faculty role transformations, but his model ultimately shows that efforts to operationally define those elements present substantial measurement challenges, because no single standardized measure of self-efficacy (Vispoel & Chen, 1990) applies to all studies.

Effective Organizational Transformation

If faculty role changes are to contribute to improvements in higher education, then broader, effective institutional change must occur simultaneously. As Alavi and Gallupe (2003), Brown (2001), Lewis et al. (2001), and Barone and Hagner (2001) indicated, institutional transformation must also be effective.

Latchem and Lockwood (1998) and Hartman and Truman-Davis (2001b) addressed faculty development issues encountered when transforming to online teaching, and focused the process in the context of institutional role change. Hartman and Truman-Davis (2001b) described the need for support resources and the necessary systems and processes when dealing with rapidly increasing support needs, and developed a "systemic environment"—an institutional model characterized by five elements: faculty interest, administrative direction, institutional facilitation of instructional technology adoption, institutional capacity, and advocacy. They concluded that individual interests alone cannot drive an innovation such as technology-enhanced learning throughout an institution.

Although not directly addressing Clark's work, Hartman and Truman-Davis (2001b) determined that faculty interest and administration direction enhance the necessary effort to commitment that Clark's (1999) CANE model described as efficacious, but then asserted that these two elements are insufficient to move an innovation through an institution. Facilitation is required, and the three elements together provide the necessary effort described in the CANE model.

Hartman and Truman-Davis (2001b) determined process scalability to be the most important issue for institutional capacity. Accessible support technology that is as easy to use as possible enhances self-efficacy. Advocacy—the final element in the "systemic environment" model—provides the emotional energy and direction that champions technology-assisted learning and facilitates institutional communication. Clark's (1999) CANE model and Hartman and Truman-Davis's (2001b) conceptualization exhibit many parallel features of motivational constructs and context, enforcing the necessity that faculty role change must be concomitant with institutional change.

Read and Raghunandan's (2001) study suggested that the type of institution (community college, research oriented, metropolitan, etc.) mediates role expectations for faculty teaching initiatives. They found that the university that placed a higher premium on research activities tended to show a corresponding deemphasis on teaching, suggesting that innovation in ALN may come from institutions that give teaching a high priority in their strategic planning. Howell and Symbaluk (2001) discerned that students and teachers encountered role conflict differently, and their results suggested that a fundamental disagreement about effective teaching elements exists between faculty and students, which may have consequences for online teaching. Students and faculty disagreed on the criteria that students use to select a course, the role of instructor accountability, the criteria for instructor effectiveness, and communication between students and faculty. Kolitch and Dean (1999), after evaluating a typical student rating of instruction instrument, pointed out the tendency of colleges and universities to constrict the range of activities and approaches that define effective teaching.

Clearly, faculty must contend with changing role expectations and the fact that their institutions are undergoing parallel shifts as the use of online classes and programs expands on college campuses. Therefore, a holistic approach as suggested by Hartman and Truman-Davis (2001) must adhere to system-level standards, values, and goals.

Emerging Issues

New issues emerge when considering faculty roles in teaching environments in which asynchronous learning networks play a prominent role: teaching strategies, technology relationships, and faculty perceptions and role expectations.

Instructors—even faculty members who are expert teachers in their face-to-face classrooms—must, to some degree, develop new strategies and techniques to become successful in online teaching. Berliner (1988), who addressed expertise in pedagogy, provided insights that transition is not smooth. Many teachers experienced in face-to-face classes operate in a seamless fashion without cognitively negotiating every aspect of their classroom environment. Their expertise—usually gained through years of experience—permits them to function in an almost "a-rational" manner. When these expert instructors consider ALN teaching, however, they revert to novice status in their relationship with technology. According to Berliner (1988), these newfound novices consider each aspect of their online environment, seeking context-free rules for every situation they encounter, and are most fragile in the transformation process—probably scoring lower on Clark's (1999) personal agency dimension.

Laing, Phillipson, and Lee (1966) dealt with the phenomena of perceived role expectations that can be extended to the ALN teaching environment. From their work, we may hypothesize that an online instructor's accurate perception of multiple expectations for the ALN teaching environment is of critical importance. When instructors are unable to perceive expectations, they will invariably attempt to put their face-to-face course verbatim on the web, with the customary unsuccessful results. Laing et al. further define a metaperspective: Faculty must accurately perceive how they are viewed by their students who are at a distance. This appears to be an important enabling component for the ALN teaching environment.

Hanley (2001) also suggested that faculty will need to change their view of teaching in technology-enhanced environments. The traditional conceptualization of teaching as the instructor, the instructor's assignments, and the students will gradually need to shift to a team approach in which learning is the "product of an integrated group of individuals, many of whom are never seen by the students" (Hanley, 2001, p. 59). Hanley identified content specialists—experts in particular tools or programming languages, systems integration and engineering, instructional and graphical design, usability, and project management—as potential "team members" in technology-enhanced teaching and learning environments.

Influencing faculty to change their views of teaching may prove difficult however. Cahn (1986) noted that "few institutions other than colleges and universities permit their members the latitude so much a part of the professor's life" (p. 3). Hagner and Schneebeck (2001) pointed out that "as faculty progress up the tenure and promotion ladder it becomes increasingly difficult to influence almost any aspect of their job performance" (p. 2). In spite of their traditional autonomy, faculty will continue to experience pressure from both students (already familiar with technology) and administrators eager to accommodate the raised expectations of new learners. Hagner and Schneebeck suggested that the needs of different faculty types—including "entrepreneurs," "risk aversives," "reward seekers," and "reluctants"—must all be accommodated to facilitate transformation in technology imbued environments.

Hagner and Schneebeck (2001) provided a general description of each of these groups. Faculty "entrepreneurs" are highly committed to quality teaching and learning, and have an informed competency with new teaching and learning technologies (Brown, 2000). Although they do not seek rewards or recognition for assuming the risk of being educational innovators, they do desire positive feedback from others. Because their work tends to be somewhat idiosyncratic, disseminating their knowledge and expertise to other faculty tends to be somewhat problematic. As a result, they tend to use their own expertise to solve their own instructional problems. Therefore, as long as their work with ALNs lies within predefined institutional parameters, they will be positive contributors to the technological transformation effort.

Faculty "risk aversives" often share the entrepreneurs' commitment to quality teaching, but are more hesitant to adopt new technologies (Geoghegan, 1998). This hesitancy may be driven by issues such as a relative lack of technical expertise, concerns over the transferability of their expertise to the ALN environment, or the need for significant self-examination and/or instructional support. Institutions can help this group assimilate into ALNs by providing examples of success stories with online teaching from people whom they consider to be their peers, and creating support environments that allow them to focus on the teaching and learning rather than the technology.

Faculty "reward seekers" emerge once organizational reward structures have been modified to account for the transition to ALN environments. They tend to see the adoption of technology-based teaching as a way to advance their careers. It is critical for educational institutions to realize that these people will not adopt the technology until the revised reward systems are in place. Therefore, if the institutions view ALNs as a strategic priority, they must modify their reward structures to maximize faculty support.

Faculty "reluctants" are those who lack technological expertise or feel that classroom-based instruction is universally superior to other modes of learning. Although incorporating them in institutional transformation may not be time or cost effective, these faculty need to be made aware that their nonparticipation may have consequences for the perception of their teaching relative to those who adopt the technology. When students expect new technologies and instructors avoid adopting these technologies, the issue becomes a faculty–student concern rather than an administrative concern. Hagner and Schneebeck (2001) suggest that the faculty senate address the issue.

Another aspect of applying technology in ALNs is determining the appropriate level of media variety for these courses. It has been assumed that as bandwidth increases, the incorporation of media such as links to other web sites, audio, and video should become commonplace in ALNs (LaRose & Whitten, 2000). However, initial research on media variety in ALNs shows that the presence of multiple media sources has limited significance in predicting student learning or satisfaction (Arbaugh, 2002a), and that participant behaviors appear to be a more significant predictor to date (Arbaugh, 2002b). Considering the time intensiveness often associated with developing and conducting ALNs (Berger, 1999; Dumont, 1996), these findings suggest that faculty time may be better spent by limiting the variety of media used in their courses in order to focus the course activities on dialogue and information exchange. However, much more research is required to determine the appropriate mix of media used in ALN settings.

An instructor's acknowledgment that asynchronous learning networks constitute a value-added component for their teaching is another important consideration for online teaching success. Hitt (2001) argued that the initiatives like ALN have impact far beyond augmenting the traditional academy because new technologies fundamentally change the nature of higher education. He suggested that the basic building blocks of the academy—students, learning, campus semesters, and the instructor's role—have been modified far differently than anything we have previously experienced. If instructors do not value this transition, they are likely to experience debilitating role conflicts.

ROLE EXPECTATIONS FOR EFFECTIVE INSTRUCTION

The issue—what constitutes effective teaching in higher education—continues to be the subject of intense national conversation. ALN enhancements regarding the learner perspective and teaching models have certainly added to the debate. Chickering and Ehrmann (1996), for example, defined role expectations for instructors based on the seven principles of good practice in undergraduate education and technology-based instructional design. Developed from Chickering and Gamson's (1987) earlier research on effective undergraduate classroom instruction, these principles are presented in Table 8.1.

They asserted that the effective instructor encourages contact between students and faculty while developing reciprocity and cooperation among students. According to Chickering and Erhmann (1996), superior instructors use active learning techniques, give prompt feedback, respect diverse talents and thought, regularly emphasize time on task, and communicate high expectations. In their study of Chickering and Gamson's (1987) seven principles as applied to perceived learning and satisfaction in web-based MBA courses, Arbaugh and Hornik (2002) found that greater student–faculty contact, higher course expectations, feedback, student collaboration, and time on task were at least moderately significant predictors of student learning and satisfaction. Shea and colleagues (Shea, Fredericksen, Pickett, Pelz, & Swan, 2001; Shea, Swan, Fredericksen, & Pickett, 2002) looked at these same variables with similar results. Therefore, we suggest that interpersonal and behavioral aspects of online courses may be more important than technology skills, and they encourage new online instructors to focus initially on generating and maintaining class discussion, knowing that they can cultivate technological skills in future course offerings.

In another national initiative, Kuh (2001) described the basic tenets of the National Study of Student Engagement. According to this initiative, effective professors emphasize student interaction with faculty, student collaboration, and active learning. In addition, Kuh asserted that good instructors provide support systems exemplified by student interaction with faculty, collaborative learning, active learning, a supportive environment, and an academic challenge.

TABLE 8.1
Chickering and Gamson's (1987) Seven Principles of Effective Education.

1. Good practice encourages contacts between students and faculty.

2. Good practice develops reciprocity and cooperation among students.

3. Good practice uses active learning techniques.

4. Good practice gives prompt feedback.

5. Good practice emphasizes time on task.

6. Good practice communicates high expectations.

7. Good practice respects diverse talents and ways of learning.

The Learner Perspective: Models of the Effective Instructor

A substantial body of research centers on the role expectations of effective instructors from the student perspective, or the metaperspective of Laing et al. (1967). Feldman (1976) suggested 20 elements for effective instruction organized according to three constructs: presentation, facilitation, and regulation. Marsh and Roache (1997) proposed a nine-component model for instructional assessment: instructor enthusiasm, organization and clarity, group interaction, individual rapport, breadth of coverage, evaluation and grading, assignments and readings, workload, and difficulty. Kin, Damewood, and Hodge (2000) proposed a multidimensional construct of teaching effectiveness in the affective domain: An effective instructor demonstrates enthusiasm, motivates students to learn, encourages student discussion, is open to constructive criticism, helps students outside the classroom, respects students, and exhibits a positive attitude toward students.

Commonalities

These teaching models share many common elements that have implications for the role of the instructor. All paradigms declare that the effective teacher facilitates interaction between faculty and students. Each investigator asserts that effective instructors create organized and supportive learning environments that foster high academic expectations for students and keep them on their learning tasks. Effective instructors are able to communicate ideas and information effectively, and design equitable and rigorous assessment procedures. Generally, all of the models reviewed here portray the effective instructor as a facilitator of learning rather than as one who dispenses information.

A number of studies suggest that ALN can enhance interaction and that it is a significant predictor of learning and satisfaction. Shea, Fredericksen, Pickett, Pelz, and Swan (2001) found that learners in online courses adapt text-based communications to bond and bridge psychological distance, thereby refuting the often-cited lack of immediacy as a significant drawback. Arbaugh (2001) implied that, given reasonable technical support, instructors with strong classroom skills may be more effective online than may technically proficient faculty who do not possess strong classroom skills. Jiang and Ting's (2000) study indicated that students' perceptions of learning in web-based courses seemed congruent with the constructivist view that students learn better in a constructive environment in which the instructor serves as a facilitator rather than an authoritative figure.

ROLE EXPECTATIONS FOR ONLINE INSTRUCTORS

The review of literature that identified the changing landscape of asynchronous learning networks noted additional role expectations for instructors. Hartman, Dziuban, and Moskal (2000) examined teaching and learning in the web-based environment, and their data analysis indicated that faculty members report a high satisfaction level and confirmed that teaching online courses requires more time than do face-to-face courses. Instructors, however, are reexamining their pedagogical approaches and personal instructional theories, and noted that despite the work involved, online courses are invigorating. Instructors reported further that they needed to reduce ambiguity in teaching online, and paid considerably more attention to instructional design components. Faculty do express concerns, such as decline in student ratings in online courses, tenure and promotion issues, less research time, a role shift to process facilitators, and technology challenges. Again, these concerns have not dissuaded significant numbers of instructors from continuing online teaching.

In other studies, Sonwalker (2002) suggested at least three additional areas for consideration—delivery support, usability, and technology considerations—and Coppola et al. (2002) reported that professors who help their students also become more analytical in their own thinking. Coppola et al. (2002) found that when professors engage in a deeper level of mental processing in the ALN environment, they learn from their students. At the affective level, most ALN faculty perceived greater academic intimacy with students in the ALN environment, even though they tend to develop a more formal "persona" when teaching online.

Spector and de la Teja (2001) claimed that effective online teachers should encourage student reflection, organize active discussions, and be sensitive to cultural differences. Towler, Miller, and Kumari (2000) argued that ALN approaches must be underpinned on the ability of students to engage in independent learning activities. Gillette (1999) contended that online instructors must reexamine their assumptions about student–teacher interactions, and he used the notion of builder first and teacher second in pointing out the altered roles for instructional design and student access. Brower (2003) provided three practical insights for conducting online student–teacher interactions. Her first suggestion—"silence is golden"—means that instructors should resist the temptation to immediately jump into discussions so as to avoid the perception that they have the "correct answer." Her second suggestion—"don't answer, but promote discovery"—encourages instructors to use probing and reflective questioning in their interactions with students, rather than providing direct answers. Her third suggestion—"encourage, inspire, create incentives, PUSH!"—exhorts instructors to strongly encourage student participation through the use of tactics such as personal encouragement and grading class participation.

Faculty in the online environment reported increased planning requirements and substantially more organizational support requirements as inhibiting factors, yet Schifter (2000) asserted that instructors' willingness to incorporate technology into their instructional roles was the motivating factor for instructors in ALN. Based on their work using compressed video, Webster and Hackley (1997) also suggested that the appropriate roles for instructors in the ALN environment include positive affect toward technology and interactive teaching styles.

Challenges and Modified Expectations

A review of literature in asynchronous learning networks also identified challenges and asserted that ALN instructors modify their expectations. Inman, Kerwin, and Mayes (1999) expressed that the role of the web-based teacher shifts to that of a moderator who may have to deal with initial negative attitudes. Rockwell, Schauer, Fritz, and Marx (1999) reported results that online instructors must change their role by enhancing interaction, developing instructional materials, and applying selected technologies. Arbaugh (2001) implied that successful ALN instructors need to develop increased immediacy by reducing the social space in their classes, and argued that if instructors increased immediacy in the web-based environment, learning will be active and students engaged. Beaudin (1999) claimed that distance education teachers will have to modify their role and become more active in keeping online discussions on topic, and Berg (2000) suggested that faculty in distributed learning will have to consider modified policies for compensation.

Anderson, Rourke, Garrison, and Archer (2001) claimed that web-based instructors must reassess their roles in terms of a series of constructs—including "social presence," "teaching presence," and resultant "cognitive presence"—in a community of inquiry. Bonk, Kirkley, Hara, and Dennen (2001) recommended that pedagogical, social, managerial, and technology components be considered when defining role changes for online instructors. Reynolds and Teddlie (1999) identified five factors transcending cultures that might also transcend course modalities of varying web presence: controlled environment, commitment to academic goals, high time on task, good teacher relationships, and a highly interactive classroom. Mason (2001) suggested that the modified role of an ALN instructor must be considered in terms of context, course design, tutor role, and extended resources, whereas Arbaugh (2002b) noted that instructors in the web-based situations should be viewed as facilitators, not performers. Frayer (1999) stated that prospective online instructors will become students as they learn new technologies. Gold (2001) reported that potential web-based instructors who attended a 2-week pedagogical course changed their expectations for online courses; they reported that online instruction was more interactive and participative than was face-to-face instruction. Heberling (2002) cautioned that the role of monitor of student integrity and cheating may also be an emerging role of ALN faculty, raising the issue about the relationship between technology and student character.

RESULTS OF LARGE-SCALE ALN INITIATIVES AND FACULTY SATISFACTION ASSESSMENTS

In a study conducted by the Institute of Higher Education Policy, Phipps and Merisotis (1999) criticized distance education research in general, and web-based courses by extension, for being much too reliant on single-course studies. Partially in response to this criticism, there have been an increasing number of multicourse studies since Phipps and Merisotis's report. These multicourse studies provide methodological benefits such as external validity, increased statistical power, and the ability to control for instructor-specific characteristics. In fact, one of the primary contributions of multicourse research to date is that it has identified the importance of the instructor in web-based learning. Arbaugh and Duray (2001) found that the amount of prior experience an instructor had with web-based learning was a significant predictor of student learning.

Other instructor-related characteristics identified through multicourse studies are the shift from a lecture-based to a more Socratic approach to course conduct (Coppola et al., 2002), the ability to integrate online materials seamlessly into the course, and a broader pool of potential online guests from which to draw. These results occurred in spite of a perceived loss of spontaneity and increased difficulty for instructors in getting their point across (Smith, Ferguson, & Caris, 2001). Hartman et al. (2000) also found that instructors reported increased course interaction, and that in spite of the fact that they thought web-based courses required more work, they were excited about teaching more of them in the future. These studies have also found that faculty can often develop stronger one-to-one relationships with students in online courses than in face-to-face ones (Coppola et al., 2002; Hiltz & Wellman, 1997; Smith, 2002; Swan et al., 2000).

An increasing number of researchers examining larger asynchronous learning networks have begun to characterize online teaching and learning as rewarding and satisfying (Hartman & Truman-Davis, 2001a; NEA, 2000; Shea et. al., 2001, 2002b; Shea, Pelz, Fredericksen, & Pickett, 2002; Thompson, 2001). Some of the commonly noted positive results in this line of inquiry reported by faculty who actually have taught online can be found in Table 8.2. That these results are reported by research on multicourse and even multi-institution implementations of online learning adds weight to the findings. It also provides some of the evidence initially missing, according to critics of online teaching and learning such as Phipps and Merisotis (1999).

Thompson (2003) pointed out that a recent survey of distance education faculty conducted by the NEA revealed that by far the most frequently mentioned positive factor that adds to faculty satisfaction is increasing students' access to higher education opportunities. Of course, increased opportunities for high-quality interaction with students and perceived positive student outcomes are also important determi-

TABLE 8.2
Positive Results from Teaching Online, as Reported by Faculty

1. More and higher-quality interaction with students (Hartman, Dziuban, & Moskal, 2000; Kashy, Thoennessen, Albertelli, & Tsai, 2000; NEA, 2001; Shea, Fredericksen, Pickett, Pelz, & Swan, 2000; Smith, 2001).

2. Convenience and flexibility for their teaching and students' learning (Arbaugh, 2000; Hartman & Truman-Davis, 2001a; NEA, 2001).

3. Increased access to untapped student populations and increased access for students to higher education (NEA, 2001).

4. Better understanding of educational technology (Alavi & Gallupe, 2003; Fredericksen, Pickett, Shea, Pelz, & Swan, 1999; Rockwell, Schauer, Fritz, & Marx, 1999; Thompson, 2001).

5. Enhanced opportunities for professional recognition and research (Hartman & Truman-Davis, 2001; Hislop & Atwood, 2000; Smith, 2001).

6. High levels of student learning (Hartman, Dziuban, & Moskal, 2000; NEA, 2000; Shea et al., 200; Thompson, 2001).

7. Greater necessity/opportunity for more systematic design of online instruction and a corollary positive impact on student learning and classroom teaching. (Shea et al., 2002a).

nants of faculty satisfaction with ALN. However, there are several key factors that are "necessary conditions" for satisfaction with the online experience (Thompson, 2003). These are adequate institutional support (including a "robust and reliable infrastructure"), and support in designing, developing, and delivering courses.

IMPLICATIONS FOR BUILDING ALNS

Hershfield (1980) commented, "Thus, the decision to use a particular method of instruction is an individual one reserved to each faculty member, and getting a new method of that instruction adopted widely requires thousands of faculty members to make *individual* decisions to use the new method" (p. 48). This quote reminds us that issues of faculty engagement in the use of new instructional technologies are not new. Hershfield's advice on garnering faculty adoption of new teaching approaches is as relevant today as it was more than 20 years ago. Yet, it may be easy to forget that others have already struggled with issues we now confront. To promote faculty adoption, Hershfield made several policy recommendations that should resonate with individuals attempting to build asynchronous learning networks. These include the creation of a regular funding mechanism to provide the capital necessary to develop and deliver technology-based instruction. He also recommended a team approach (not unlike Hanley, 2001, did 2 decades later), citing the need for faculty, instructional designers, and "technologists" to develop high-tech course materials. Additionally, he touched on the issue of scalability, citing the need to consider which courses to develop. Hershfield noted that courses with relatively stable curricula may be better candidates for technology-enhanced delivery in light of the potentially high cost and faculty efforts associated with frequent course revision.

Hershfield's (1980) comments on the thousands of individual faculty choices necessary to affect broad-scale change are familiar to practitioners involved in the creation of large-scale ALNs. There is a considerable amount of "heavy lifting" required to sway faculty to make such choices. Fredericksen (2000) explained that the relatively high levels of participation in the State University of New York (SUNY) Learning Network required years to achieve. With more than 1,500 faculty teaching from 55 colleges, 2,500 annual online course offerings in 52 complete online degree and certificate programs, the SUNY Learning Network represents one of the large-scale ALNs mentioned earlier. Fredericksen, Shea, Pelz, and Swan (2000) suggested a comprehensive approach to faculty engagement. This strategy emphasizes the importance of simultaneous and ongoing dialogue with all stakeholders including faculty, academic vice presidents, campus-based registrars, information technology professionals, librarians, representatives from student services, and others who will need to participate to make the project successful. Bringing all the stakeholders to the table helps each to see the bigger picture and understand the scale of the project, and provides a perspective on the importance of their contributions as well as the benefit of participation.

In addition to providing faculty with a broader perspective on their role in online learning, great attention must be paid to issues of faculty development and support. Shea et al. (2001) outlined a comprehensive system including the hardware, software, resources, people, and processes necessary to allow faculty to focus on their roles as well-supported developers and autonomous teachers of their online courses. This system includes the physical network of servers and information technology (IT) professionals to ensure that the online course is functional; the well-staffed and operational helpdesk to answer faculty and student questions; a team of instructional designers to assist with course design and technological implementation; and administration and an advisory board for policy and planning. Another component of the system is a four-stage faculty development program that combines 20 hours of sequenced, face-to-face training with ongoing support from an assigned instructional designer. Under this model, faculty are "taught to fish" rather than "given a fish" (i.e., the instructors' ownership of materials and instructional processes are encouraged through faculty-developed courses). Research on faculty satisfaction in this system (Shea et al., 2001, 2002b) indicates high levels of faculty satisfaction directly attributable to the existence of adequate levels of support.

In designing faculty training and support programs, administrators can read about and share "best practices" on the Sloan Consortium web site (http://www. aln.org/effective/SortByFacultySat.asp). However, in addition, they will need to create supportive policies at the university level. This includes instituting positive consideration for online teaching in promotion and tenure decisions, as well as policies providing release time for preparation of new ALN courses (Giannoni & Tesone, 2003).

IMPLICATIONS FOR FURTHER RESEARCH

One of the challenges of conducting research on faculty and ALNs is that until relatively recently it was rather difficult to find significant numbers of faculty with substantial ALN experience. Nearly all of the studies of faculty to date have focused on novice ALN instructors (Coppola et al., 2002; Gosen, 2001; Hartman et al., 2000). However, with the rapid increase of ALN offerings, the numbers of experienced ALN faculty are increasing dramatically as well. This expansion of the population should prove rather fruitful for those who research faculty-related ALN topics for the foreseeable future. Based on our review, we see several research streams that particularly merit attention. We describe these streams and some potential directions for each next.

As we have already discussed, most of the research on faculty and ALNs to date have focused on behavioral characteristics. Perhaps it is time to begin to take a step back and address the question: Are there characteristics that allow some faculty to be more effective in the ALN environment than other faculty? Some of the characteristics that might be studied are dispositional, attitudinal, experiential, and/or skill related in nature. Focusing on such characteristics would complement recent calls for further research into psychological processes and ALNs (Alavi & Leidner, 2001). Initial research suggests that introverted students are more likely to be attracted to ALNs (Fornaciari & Matthews, 2000). Could this also be true of faculty? Are these characteristics "prewired," or can they be taught? Also, is faculty satisfaction with ALNs based primarily on experiential characteristics, or is this level of satisfaction better explained by or in conjunction with other factors? Future research on faculty characteristics would almost certainly carry practical implications. For instance, if a certain "preferred ALN faculty type" was identified, institutions choosing to offer both ALN and traditional courses could more readily select or encourage faculty with those characteristics to become further involved in ALN instruction. Carried to an extreme, colleges and universities could also use this information to help them in faculty recruitment and selection decisions.

Another characteristic that is intertwined with cognitive and dispositional characteristics of the faculty member is the relative importance of the academic discipline and/or course content in ALNs. Recent research suggests that subject matter effects explain significant but a relatively small amount of ALN course outcomes (Arbaugh, 2003). Without further study of the instructor–content relationship, one could develop a probably faulty interpretation of research to date that as long as instructors cultivate participant interaction, establish a clear course structure, and engage in conduct to reduce the social distance between them and their students, those instructors would be qualified to teach anything from engineering to the liberal arts to the sciences to business in an ALN setting. An even more dire implication of this interpretation is that this approach would call into question the need for faculty that is doctorally qualified in ALNs for colleges and universities. Therefore, if for nothing other than self-preservation purposes, university ALN researchers need to gain a better understanding of the relationship between the instructor and the academic discipline and/or subject matter in ALN environments.

As we see an increase in the number of experienced ALN instructors, the effects of time in relation to faculty and ALNs should be much easier to study. There are a number of time-related questions that merit additional attention. For instance, research to date suggests that instructors' ALN experience may influence their effectiveness in teaching subsequent ALN courses (Arbaugh & Duray, 2001). How do the behaviors and/or characteristics that influence this effectiveness evolve over time? Is extensive experience in delivering one or a few courses online or in delivering a variety of courses online the better way to develop online faculty? Future researchers can also examine whether and how faculty roles in ALNs change over time and/or by course material. Is there an evolution to or from a constructivist approach over time? Do faculty play differing roles depending on the subject matter or student population?

Finally, researchers can give further attention to faculty time requirements relative to traditional instruction for developing and conducting ALNs. Historically, ALN research has suggested that courses delivered via the Internet are much more time intensive than are those delivered via traditional classrooms (Berger, 1999; Dumont, 1996; Hartman et al., 2000; Shedletsky & Aitken, 2001). However, this concern is increasingly coming into question. DiBiase (2000) found that when factors such as commuting from office to classroom, precourse setup, and fielding questions after class was over were considered, ALNs were actually less time intensive than were classroom courses. Also, one could make the argument that the first offering of any course is much more time intensive, whether it is online or in traditional classrooms. We are probably finally now in the position to ask whether there are faculty learning curves from offering ALNs, and, if so, just how steep are these curves? What factors might moderate those learning effects?

Another area critical for both faculty and program satisfaction is the need for effective knowledge transfer for ALN effectiveness between and among faculty and support teams. Initial research shows a strong relationship between the prior ALN experience of faculty and student learning (Arbaugh & Duray, 2001), but the knowledge gained from this experience is often not efficiently transferred to other faculty members. This uneven level of faculty expertise is likely to result in student frustration, especially as the novelty of ALNs disappears (Arbaugh, 2001; Gibson & Gibson, 1995). Because the transparent nature of ALNs imply that student-switching costs to other providers may be lower than for traditional education providers, ensuring a minimum quality threshold will become particularly important for colleges and universities seeking to market their ALNs beyond their traditional student populations. Although instructional designers and other support personnel have been helpful (Gallini, 2001; Kang, 2001; Shea et al., 2001), for the sake of a program's or college's reputation faculty must also work together to establish a minimum threshold for ALN expertise. Research that develops models or frameworks for such collaboration is much needed (Alavi & Gallupe, 2003).

One particularly interesting research stream emerging from these collaborative relationships is the issue of conflict. As we mentioned earlier in this chapter, faculty have historically held control over development and presentation of course content and are rather reluctant to relinquish that control. However, this insistence on complete control could diminish the effectiveness of the ALN experience for students. Therefore, empirically tested models of conflict generation and resolution could greatly enhance these new collaborative relationships. These faculty–support staff relationships provide other opportunities for empirical research as well. Although there are several conceptual models of these relationships, empirical support for any of the models is rather limited. Studies such as these would also help answer calls from other chapters of this book for further examination of institutional effects on ALNs (see chap. 6) and the use of multi-institutional research samples (see chap. 4).

SUMMARY

Among the findings for which these and multiple empirical studies provide support is the applicability of Chickering and Gamson's (1987) general principles of effective learning to the ALN environment. The greater the student–faculty contact online, and the higher the student collaboration, course expectations, time on task, and the more prompt the feedback given for student postings, the higher the student learning and satisfaction (Arbaugh & Hornik, 2002; Shea et al., 2001, 2002b) will be. However, although the "principles of good teaching" remain the same, there are several fundamental shifts in the nature of faculty roles. Discussion facilitation rather than presentation skills becomes most key for online faculty in an ALN. The most frequently reported change in studies of ALN faculty is more and higher-quality interaction with students.

In this chapter, we have reviewed several of these emerging faculty roles and sources of satisfaction with ALNs. After this review, we can say that there are abundant opportunities for additional research in this area. However, unlike many of the topics in the chapters of this book, this area has the advantage of readily available conceptual frameworks from several well-established research streams that could be used or modified to build on existing research on faculty roles and satisfaction in ALNs. Literatures such as social and cognitive psychology, education, and organizational behavior should be quite informative for shaping our research agenda. When these established bodies of literatures are applied to a context in which experience in delivering ALNs is increasing rapidly, there should be abundant opportunity to question historical assumptions on the role of faculty and support staff in the ALN. Therefore, we anticipate that there will be great strides made in our knowledge of these new intraorganizational relationships and their effectiveness during the next decade.

QUESTIONS FOR DISCUSSION AND RESEARCH

1. What are the reasons why many faculty are "doubters" or "resistors" in regard to teaching online? Explore this issue by designing a short semistructured interview guide and interviewing three faculty members who have never taught online.
2. What faculty training, support, and extrinsic rewards (e.g., release time) are available to support new ALN faculty at your university? How do these compare to the "best practices" at leading ALN institutions, such as SUNY?
3. What are some of the factors that influence faculty success with ALNs? Describe a process by which ALN faculty expertise might increase over time.

REFERENCES

Alavi, M., & Gallupe, R. B. (2003). Using information technology in learning: Case studies in business and management education programs. *Academy of Management Learning and Education, 2*(2), 139–153.

Alavi, M., & Leidner, D. E. (2001). Research commentary: Technology-mediated learning—a call for greater depth and breadth of research. *Information Systems Research, 12*(1), 1–10.

Anderson, T., Rourke, L., Garrison, D. R., & Archer, W. (2001). Assessing teacher presence in a computer conferencing context. *Journal of Asynchronous Learning Networks, 5*(2).

Arbaugh, J. B. (2000). Virtual classroom characteristics and student satisfaction in Internet-based MBA courses. *Journal of Management Education, 24*, 32–54.

Arbaugh, J. B. (2001). How instructor immediacy behaviors affect student satisfaction and learning in web-based courses. *Business Communication Quarterly, 64*(4), 42–54.

Arbaugh, J. B. (2002a). A longitudinal study of technological and pedagogical characteristics of web-based MBA courses. *Proceedings of the 62nd Annual Meeting of the Academy of Management* (CD), MED A1–A6. ISSN1543-8643.

Arbaugh, J. B. (2002). Managing the on-line classroom: A study of technological and behavioral characteristics of web-based MBA courses. *Journal of High Technology Management Research, 13*, 203–223.

Arbaugh, J. B., & Duray, R. (2001). Class section size, perceived classroom characteristics, instructor experience, and student learning and satisfaction with web-based courses: A study and comparison of two on-line MBA programs. In D. Nagao (Ed.), *Academy of Management Best Papers Proceedings* [CD-Rom]. Retrieved March 7, 2004, from http://www.google.com/search?q=cache:13mz_wpbdimj:widw.aomonline.org/aom-asp%3fid%3d101+academy+of+management+best+papers+proceedings&hl=em&ie=utf-8

Arbaugh, J. B. (2003, August). *How much does "subject matter" matter? A study of disciplinary effects in web-based MBA courses.* Paper presented at the 2003 meetings of the Academy of Management, Seattle, WA.

Arbaugh, J. B., & Hornik, S. C. (2002, November). *Predictors of perceived learning and satisfaction in web-based MBA courses: A test and extension of Chickering and Gamson's (1987) seven principles of good practice in education.* Paper presented at the 33rd annual meeting of the Decision Sciences Institute, San Diego, CA. Retrieved March 7, 2004, from http://www.decisionsciences.org/meet_02/call2002frame.html

Barone, C. A., & Hagner, P. R. (Eds.). (2001). *Technology-enhanced teaching and learning: Leading and supporting the transformation on your campus* (Vol. 5). San Francisco: Jossey-Bass.

Beaudin, B. P. (1999). Keeping online asynchronous discussions on topic. *Journal of Asynchronous Learning Networks, 3*(2), 41–53.

Berg, G. A. (2000). Early patterns of faculty compensation for developing and teaching distance learning courses. *Journal of Asynchronous Learning Networks, 4*(1). Retrieved March 29, 2004, from http://www.aln.org/publications/jaln/v4n1/v4n1_berg.asp

Berge, Z. L. (1998). Barriers to online teaching in post-secondary institutions: Can policy changes fix it? *Online Journal of Distance Learning Administration, 1*(2).

Berger, N. S. (1999). Pioneering experiences in distance learning: Lessons learned. *Journal of Management Education, 23,* 684–690.

Berliner, D. C. (1988). *The development of expertise in pedagogy.* New Orleans, LA: American Association of Colleges for Teacher Education.

Bonk, C. J., Kirkley, J., Hara, N., & Dennen, V. P. (2001). Finding the instructor in post-secondary online learning: Pedagogical, social, managerial and technological locations. In J. Stephenson (Ed.), *teaching and learning online: Pedagogies for new technologies* (pp. 76–97).). Sterling, VA: Stylus.

Brower, H. H. (2003). On emulating classroom discussion in a distance-delivered OBHR course: Creating an on-line community. *Academy of Management Learning and Education, 2*(1), 22–36.

Brown, D. G. (2000). *Interactive learning: Vignettes from America's most wired campuses.* Bolton, MA: Anker.

Brown, S. (2001). Campus re-engineering. In F. Lockwood & A. Gooley (Eds.), *Innovation in open and distance learning* (pp. 122–132). Sterling, VA: Stylus.

Cahn, S. (1986). *Saints and scamps: Ethics in academia.* Totowa, NJ: Rowman & Littlefield.

Chickering, A. W., & Ehrmann, S. C. (1996, October). Implementing the seven principles: Technology as lever. *American Association for Higher Education Bulletin, 3*–6.

Chickering, A. W., & Gamson, Z. (1987). Seven principles of good practice in undergraduate education. *AAHE Bulletin, 39,* 3–7.

Clark, R. E. (1999). The CANE model of motivation to learn and to work: A two-stage process of goal commitment and effort. In J. Lowyck (Ed.), *Trends in corporate training.* Leuven, Belgium: University of Belgium Press.

Coppola, N. W., Hiltz, S. R., & Rotter, N. G. (2002). Becoming a virtual professor: Pedagogical roles and asynchronous learning networks. *Journal of Management Information Systems, 18*(4), 169–189.

Diamond, J. (1999). *Guns, germs, and steel: The fates of human societies.* New York: Norton.

DiBiase, D. (2000). Is distance teaching more work or less work? *American Journal of Distance Education, 14*(3), 6–20.

Dumont, R. A. (1996). Teaching and learning in cyberspace. *IEEE Transactions on Professional Communication, 39*(4), 192–204.

Feldman, K. A. (1976). The superior college teacher from the student's view. *Research in Higher Education, 5,* 243–288.

Ford, M. E. (1992). *Motivating humans: Goals, emotions, and personal agency beliefs.* Newbury Park, CA: Sage.

Fornaciari, C. J., & Matthews, C. S. (2000). Student personality types and predispositions toward distance education. In S. J. Havlovic (Ed.), *Proceedings of the Sixtieth Annual Meeting of the Academy of Management* (CD), MED A1–A6). ISSN 1543-8643.

Frayer, D. A. (1999). Creating a campus culture to support a teaching and learning revolution. *CAUSE/EFFECT*, *22*(2), 10–18. Also available online at www.educause.edu/ir/library/html/cem9923.html

Fredericksen, E., Pickett, A., Swan, K., Pelz, W., & Shea, P. (1999). Factors influencing faculty satisfaction with asynchronous teaching and learning in SUNY Learning Network. Albany State University of New York.

Fredericksen, E., Pickett, A., Shea, P., Pelz, W., & Swan, K. (2000). Student satisfaction and perceived learning with online courses: Principles and examples from the SUNY Learning Network. *Journal of Asynchronous Learning Networks*, *4*(2), 7–36.

Gallini, J. K. (2001). A framework for the design of research in technology-mediated learning environments: A sociocultural perspective. *Educational Technology*, *41*(2), 15–21.

Geoghegan, W. H. (1998). Instructional technology and the mainstream: The risks of success. In D. Oblinger & S. Rush (Eds.), *The future compatible campus: Planning, designing, and implementing innovation technology in the academy*. Bolton: Anker.

Getzels, J., Liphan, J., & Campbell, R. (1968). *Educational administration as a social process: Theory, research, practice*. New York: Harper & Row.

Giannoni, D. L., & Tesone, D. V. (2003). What academic administrators should know to attract senior level faculty members to online learning environments. *Online Journal of Distance Learning Administration*, *6*(1). Retrieved March 7, 2004, from http://www.westga.edu/%7edistance/ojdla/springul.htm

Gibson, C., & Gibson, T. (1995). Lessons learned from 100+ years of distance learning. *Adults Learning*, *7*(1), 15.

Gillette, D. (1999). Pedagogy, architecture, and the virtual classroom. *Technical Communication Quarterly*, *8*(1), 21–37.

Gold, S. (2001). A constructivist approach to online training for online teachers. *Journal of Asynchronous Learning Networks*, *5*(1). Retrieved March 7, 2004, from http://www.aln.org/publications/jaln/v5n1/v5n1_gold.asp

Gosen, J. (2001, November). *The effectiveness of the Internet for MBA course delivery: The instructor's perspective*. Paper presented at the First International Conference on Electronic Business, Hong Kong.

Graves, W. H. (2001). Transforming traditional faculty roles. In C. A. Barone & P. R. Hagner (Eds.), *Technology-enhanced teaching and learning: Leading and supporting the transformation on your campus* (pp. 35–43). San Francisco: Jossey-Bass.

Hagner, P. R., & Schneebeck, C. A. (2001). Engaging the faculty. In C. Barone & P. Hagner (Eds.), *Technology-enhanced teaching and learning, educause leadership strategies* (Vol. 5, pp. 1–12). San Francisco: Jossey-Bass.

Hanley, G. (2001). Designing and delivering instructional technology—a team approach. In C. Barone & P. Hagner (Eds.), *Technology-enhanced teaching and learning, educause leadership strategies* (Vol. 5, pp. 57–64). San Francisco: Jossey-Bass.

Hartman, J., Dziuban, C., & Moskal, P. (2000). Faculty satisfaction in ALNs: A dependent or independent variable. *Journal of Asynchronous Learning Networks*, *4*(3). Retrieved March 7, 2004, from http://www.aln.org/alnweb/journal/jaln-vol4issue3.htm

Hartman, J. L., & Truman-Davis, B. (2001a). Factors relating to the satisfaction of faculty teaching online courses at the University of Central Florida. In J. Bourne & J. Moose (Eds.), *Online education: Proceedings of the 2000 Sloan Summer Workshop on Asynchronous Learning Networks* (Vol. 2 in the Sloan-C series). Needham, MA: Sloan-C Press.

Hartman, J. L., & Truman-Davis, B. (2001b). The holy grail: Developing scalable and sustainable support solutions. In C. A. Barone & P. R. Hagner (Eds.), *Technology-enhanced teaching and learning: Leading and supporting the transformation on your campus* (pp. 45–56). San Francisco: Jossey-Bass.

Heberling, M. (2002). Maintaining academic integrity in online education. *Online Journal of Distance Learning Administration*, *5*(1).

Hershfield, A. (1980). Education's technological revolution: An event in search of leaders. *Change, 12*(8), 48–52.

Hewson, L., & Hughes, C. (2001). Generic structures for online teaching and learning. In F. Lockwood & A. Gooley (Eds.), *Innovation in open and distance learning* (pp. 76–87). Sterling, VA: Stylus.

Hilton, J. L., & Neal, J. G. (2001). Responding to intellectual property and legal issues. In C. A. Barone & P. R. Hagner (Eds.), *Technology-enhanced teaching and learning: Leading and supporting the transformation on your campus* (pp. 65–78). San Francisco: Jossey-Bass.

Hiltz, S. R., & Wellman, B. (1997, September). Asynchronous learning networks as a virtual classroom. *Communications of the ACM* , 40(9), 44–49).

Hislop, G., & Atwood, M. (2000, September). ALN teaching as routine faculty workload. *Journal of Asynchronous Learning Networks, 4*(3). Retrieved March 7, 2004, from http://www.sloan-c.org/publications/jaln/v4n3/v4n3_hislop.asp

Hitt, J. C. (2001). Foreword. In C. A. Barone & P. R. Hagner (Eds.), *Technology-enhanced teaching and learning: Leading and supporting the transformation on your campus* (pp. xi–xii). San Francisco: Jossey-Bass.

Howell, D. P., & Symbaluk, D. G. (2001). Published student ratings of instruction: Revealing and reconciling the views of students and faculty. *Journal of Educational Psychology, 93*(4), 790–796.

Inman, E., Kerwin, M., & Mayes, L. (1999). Instructor and student attitudes toward distance learning. *Community College Journal of Research and Practice, 23*, 581–591.

Jaffee, D. (1998, September). Institutionalized resistance to asynchronous learning networks. *Journal of Asynchronous Learning Networks, 2*(2). Retrieved March 7, 2004, from http://www.aln.org/publications/jaln/v2n2/v2n2_jaffee.asp

Jiang, M., & Ting, E. (2000). A study of factors influencing students' perceived learning in a web-based course environment. *International Journal of Educational Telecommunications, 6*(4), 317–338.

Kang, S. (2001). Toward a collaborative model for the design of web-based courses. *Educational Technology, 41*(2), 22–30.

Kashy, E., Thoennessen, M., Albertelli, G., & Tsai, Y. (2000, September). Implementing a large on-campus ALN: Faculty perspective. *Journal of Asynchronous Learning Networks, 4*(3). Retrieved March 7, 2004, from http://www.aln.org/publications/jaln/v4n3/v4n3_kashy.asp

Kim, C., Damewood, E., & Hodge, N. (2000). Professor attitude: Its effect on teaching evaluations. *Journal of Management Education, 24*(4), 458–473.

Kolitch, E., & Dean, A. V. (1999). Student ratings of instruction in the USA: Hidden assumptions and missing conceptions about "good" teaching. *Studies in Higher Education, 24*(1), 27–43.

Kuh, G. D. (2001). Assessing what really matters to student learning. *Change, 10*, 12–15, 17, 66.

Laing, R. D., Phillipson, H., & Lee, A. R. (1966). *Interpersonal perception: A theory and a method of research*. New York: Springer.

LaRose, R., & Whitten, P. (2000). Re-thinking instructional immediacy for web courses: A social cognitive exploration. *Communication Education, 49*, 320–338.

Latchem, C., & Lockwood, F. (1998). *Staff development in open and flexible learning*. New York: Routledge.

Lewis, B., Massey, C., & Smith, R. (2001). *The tower under siege: Technology, power, and education*. London: McGill-Queen's University Press.

Marsh, H. W., & Roache, L. A. (1997). Making students' evaluations of teaching effectiveness effective: The critical issues of validity, bias, and utility. *American Psychologist, 52*(11), 1187–1225.

Mason, R. (2001). Effective facilitation of online learning: The open university experience. In J. Stephenson (Ed.), *Teaching and learning online: Pedagogies for new technologies* (pp. 67–75). Sterling, VA: Stylus.

Moskal, P. D., & Dziuban, C. D. (2001). Present and future directions for assessing cybereducation: The changing research paradigm. In L. R. Vandervert, L. V. Shavinina, & R. A. Cornell (Eds.), *Cybereducation: The future of long-distance learning* (pp. 157–184). New York: Mary Ann Liebert.

Muilenburg, L. Y., & Berge, Z. L. (2001). Barriers to distance education: A factor-analytic study. *The American Journal of Distance Education, 15*(2), 7–22.

National Education Association. (2000). *A survey of traditional and distance learning higher education members*. Washington, DC: Author.

National Educational Association. (2001). *Focus on distance education, update 7*(2). Washington, DC: Author.

Phipps, R., & Merisotis, J. (1999). *What's the difference? A review of contemporary research on the effectiveness of distance learning in higher education*. Washington, DC: The Institute for Higher Education Policy. (http://www.isep.com/pub.ht.m#diff)

Read, W. J., & Raghunandan, K. (2001). The relationship between student evaluations of teaching and faculty evaluations. *Journal of Education for Business, 76*(4), 189–192.

Reynolds, D., & Teddlie, C. (1999). *Worldclass school: A preliminary analysis of data from the international school effectiveness research project*. Newcastle, UK: University of Newcastle upon Tyne Department of Education, ISERP Team.

Rockwell, K., Schauer, J., Fritz, S. M., & Marx, D. B. (1999, Winter). Incentives and obstacles influencing higher education faculty and administrators to teach. *Online Journal of Distance Learning Administration, 3*(4). Retrieved March 7, 2004, from http://www.westga.edu/~distance/rockwell24.html

Rockwell, K., Schauer, J., Fritz, S. M., & Marx, D. B. (2000). Faculty education, assistance and support needed to deliver education via distance. *Online Journal of Distance Learning Administration, 3*(2).

Schifter, C. C. (2000, Spring). Faculty participation in asynchronous learning networks: A case study of motivating and inhibiting factors. *Journal of Asynchronous Learning Networks, 4*(1). Retrieved March 7, 2004, from http://www.westga.edu/~distance/schifter31.html

Shea, P., Fredericksen, E., Pickett, A., Pelz, W., & Swan, K. (2001). Measures of learning effectiveness in the SUNY Learning Network. In *Online education: Learning effectiveness, faculty satisfaction, and cost effectiveness*. Needham, MA: Sloan Consortium of Online Education, Vol. 4, Issue 2, September 2000. Retrieved March 7, 2004, from http://www.google.com/search:q=cache:kereg199ensj.

Shea, P., Pelz, W., Fredericksen, E., & Pickett, A. (2002). Online teaching as a catalyst for classroom-based instructional transformation. In *Elements of quality online education* (pp. 000–000). Needham, MA: Sloan Center for Online Education.

Shea, P., Swan, K., Fredericksen, E., & Pickett, A. (2002). Student satisfaction and perceived learning with online courses: Principles and examples from the SUNY Learning Network. In *Online education* (pp. 000–000). Needham, MA: Sloan Center for Online Education. Retrieved March 7, 2004, from http://www.aln.org/alnweb/journal/jaln-volume4issue3.htm

Shedletsky, L. J., & Aitken, J. E. (2001). The paradoxes of online academic work. *Communication Education, 50*, 206–217.

Smith, L. (2001).). Faculty satisfaction in LEEP. A web-based graduate degree program in library and information science. In *Online education volume 2: Learning effectiveness, faculty satisfaction, and cost effectiveness* (pp. 87–108). Needham, MA: Sloan Center for Online Education.

Smith, G. G., Ferguson, D., & Caris, M. (2001). Online vs face-to-face. *THE Journal, 28*(9), 18–25.

Sonwalker, N. (2002, March). A new methodology for evaluation: The pedagogical rating of online courses. *Syllabus*. Retrieved March 29, 2004, from htp://www.sylla-bus.com/syllabusmagazine/article.asp?id=6134

Spector, J. M., & de la Teja, I. (2001). *Competencies for online teaching* (No. EDO-IR-2001-09). East Lansing, MI: National Center for Research on Teacher Learning.

Swan, K., Shea, P., Fredericksen, E., Pickett, A., Pelz, W., & Maher, G. (2000). Building knowledge building communities: Consistency, contact and communication in the virtual classroom. *Journal of Educational Computing Research, 23*(4), 389–413.

Thompson, M. (2001). Faculty satisfaction in Penn State's world campus. In *Online education volume 2: Learning effectiveness, faculty satisfaction, and cost effectiveness* (pp. 129–144). Needham, MA: Sloan Center for Online Education.

Thompson, M. (2003). Faculty satisfaction in the on-line teaching–learning environment. In J. Bourne & J. C. Moore (Eds.), *Quality studies: Online education practice and direction* (Vol. 4, p. 189). Needham MA: Sloan Center for Online Education.

Towler, A. J., Miller, L. M., & Kumari, D. S. (2000). A case study of Project OWLink: Teachers' reflections. *Teacher Education Quarterly, 27*(1), 29–38.

Vispoel, W. P., & Chen, P. (1990, April). *Measuring self-efficacy: The state of the art*. Paper presented at the American Educational Research Association, Boston.

Webster, J., & Hackley, P. (1997). Teaching effectiveness in technology-mediated distance learning. *Academy of Management Journal, 40*, 1282–1309.

Wolcott, L. L. (1997). Tenure, promotion, and distance education: Examining the culture of faculty rewards. *The American Journal of Distance Education, 11*(2), 3–18.

9

Technology-Mediated Collaborative Learning: A Research Perspective

Maryam Alavi
Emory University

Donna Dufner
University of Nebraska at Omaha

> *I give them things to think about. So, for leadership, I'll ask them to think about what a transformational leader is, is there a moral dimension to leadership, if there is what is it, or is it just about making money and looking good in Forbes? I give them four or five questions. ... Sometimes they bring up other issues, ... I get a lot of stuff from their personal experiences, their worklives. (School of management faculty member, NJIT, as quoted in Coppola, Hiltz, & Rotter, 2002, p. 177)*
>
> *Despite the fact that students' participation in asynchronous discussion is vital to maintaining interest, motivation and engagement in active learning, participation remains problematic. Consequently, promoting discourse has become a major role of the e-moderator. (Oliver & Shaw, 2003)*

INTRODUCTION

Some learning theories emphasize the social genesis of learning and view it as a process involving interpersonal interactions in a cooperative (vs. a competitive) context. Over the past 2 decades, one such theory, collaborative (group or team based) learning, has gained in popularity. Several studies have demonstrated the positive motivational and learning outcomes of collaborative learning in higher education. The Internet and World Wide Web offer platforms and new opportunities supporting new approaches to collaborative learning. These new approaches augment or replace face-to-face interactions among the student team members with interactions that take place via information technologies. Although research regarding the role of information technologies in support of collaborative learning has gained some momentum over the last decade, much remains to be learned about this topic. The objective of this chapter is to motivate future research and dialogue about technology-mediated collaborative learning by pointing out some potentially productive research venues in this field. The chapter opens with an overview and a description of various perspectives on collaborative learning in general. Second, current and emerging technology environments for the support of collaborative learning are discussed. Next, the literature on technology-mediated collaborative learning is reviewed and summarized. The literature review provides a basis for the development of a framework that integrates findings of the previous work. The chapter concludes with some specific suggestions for future research in the area of technology-mediated collaborative learning.

COLLABORATIVE LEARNING: DEFINITION AND OVERVIEW

Collaborative learning is a learner-centered and team-based approach based on the constructivist and social learning theories. The constructivist learning theory contends that learning is a proactive and goal-oriented process in which individuals acquire knowledge and meaning by processing information through their cognitive structures and then placing it in their long-term memory for retrieval or further processing at later times (Alavi, 1994; Hiltz, Coppola, Rotter, Turoff, & Benbunan-Fich, 2000; Shuell, 1986; Wittrock, 1978). The constructivist theory primarily focuses on the creation of understanding in an individual's mind and calls for learning-centered instructions. That is, it assumes that individuals learn better when they develop meaning through direct interaction with information rather than when they are told the information (Leidner & Jarvenpaa, 1995).

The constructivist theory assumes that learning emerges from interactions between an individual and the information (material) to be learned, the social learning theory assumes that learning emerges as an individual interacts with other individuals. Thus, the social learning theory advocates learning as a social process that occurs through interpersonal interactions. According to this theory, knowledge is created and shared most effectively when learners interact with each other while performing a task. The social learning theory is complementary (rather that contradictory) to the constructivist perspective in that it postulates that individual cognition and thinking are socially rooted and are initially shared between people, although they are gradually internalized by individuals (Brown & Palincsar, 1989; Vygotsky, 1978). Furthermore, learning in groups can exercise high-order thinking processes such as elaboration of ideas, analysis, and problem solving.

Several studies have established the superiority of face-to-face collaborative learning approaches relative to competitive and individualistic approaches (see Brown & Polincsar, 1989, for an extensive review of relevant studies). These studies have shown that collaborative learning is more effective than individualistic instructional strategies in terms of student achievement, attitudes toward their learning experience, and motivation to learn (Flynn, 1992; Leidner & Jarvenpaa, 1995). The relative superiority of collaborative learning has been primarily attributed to the processes of co-elaboration and co-construction, which in turn result from the social settings that support the development, elaboration, and justification of various perspectives on and solutions to the group learning task (Bryant, 1982; Russell, 1982). The social settings are also thought to model roles that further enhance learning outcomes and provide context for support of group members. Collaborative learning has also been shown to lead to higher levels of student satisfaction with the learning process and classroom experience. Studies of college courses have found that, relative to traditional lecture methods, students participating in collaborative learning classrooms were more satisfied with their learning experience and evaluated their courses more favorably (Alavi, 1994; Bligh, 1972). Although the major goal of collaborative learning is the acquisition and construction of knowledge through social processes, it has also been shown to result in enhanced student communication and listening skills.

Until recently, the application of collaborative learning strategies has been restricted to the face-to-face modes of learning and interactions. The advent of communication and information technologies, particularly the Internet and the World Wide Web, has extended the application of collaborative learning across time and/or geographic distance. This is possible because interactions among the learners take place through the technology. This technology-mediated form of collaborative learning (vs. the more traditional face-to-face form) is the focus of this chapter. Collaborative learning has been successfully employed in a variety of disciplines, including education, mathematics, languages, and the law. In this chapter, we focus primarily on technology-mediated collaborative learning applications in the domains of business and management, as well as computer information systems. These are the areas for which empirical studies exist.

Collaborative Versus Cooperative Learning

Sometimes, the terms *collaborative* and *cooperative* learning are used interchangeably. In this chapter, we consider these two as related but distinct learning strategies. Both learning processes rely on cooperative team interactions (vs. competition) among students in order to achieve learning objectives. Both learning approaches draw on the constructivist and social learning theories. The differences between the two approaches, however, stem in part from their different origins (Bruffee, 1999). According to Bruffee, cooperative and collaborative learning were developed originally for educating students of different ages, experience, and prior knowledge. Thus, each approach makes different assumptions about a student's background, knowledge, and motivation to learn.

The locus of control of the learning activities and interactions in the cooperative learning process is assumed to reside in the instructor, and is therefore external to the student teams. For example, in cooperative learning, the teacher assigns specific roles to student team members in terms of their learning responsibilities and their focus on the content. As such, cooperative learning teams have a relatively high degree of task interdependency built into the group process and often follow relatively structured processes in their learning interactions. This is to increase student accountability, reduce competition among the students, and avoid chronic dependence on team members. According to Bruffee (1999), in cooperative learning, teachers establish carefully defined and operationalized principles and structures for the students to cooperate in completing a learning task, and each team member is accountable for the completion of the task. Considering the relatively high levels of structure, student accountability, and teacher monitoring, cooperative learning is frequently used in the education of children and early adolescents (Bruffee, 1999).

Collaborative learning, on the other hand, is more learner centered and less structured. It assumes a relatively high level of prior knowledge, autonomy, and intrinsic motivation to learn on the part of the students. As such, this learning approach is typically used in adult, college, and university education. In a classroom conducted according to the tenets of collaborative learning, the teacher assumes the role of a learning peer or resource, rather than that of a learning monitor or authority. The group process and interactions are defined and developed by the team members and are not structured by the teacher. Thus, in contrast to cooperative learning, the group governance (e.g., issues regarding cooperation and student accountability) and locus of control in a collaborative learning environment reside within the student teams and not with the instructor.

In summary, collaborative learning provides the students with higher levels of autonomy, and more flexibility in terms of both group interaction processes and the development of the task completion approach.

Technology-Mediated Collaborative Learning

Two primary modes of technology-mediated collaborative learning can be identified: synchronous and asynchronous. The synchronous mode involves real-time technology-mediated interactions among the members of the learning team during the learning process. Asynchronous mode, the predominant mode of communication used for asynchronous learning networks (ALNs), involves technology-mediated interactions among team members that are distributed across time and, typically, over geographical distances.

Research has indicated the relative learning effectiveness of both synchronous and asynchronous distributed learning processes. For example, the findings of a study (Alavi, 1994) involving 127 MBA students showed that student teams that used information technologies in support of their synchronous collaborative learning process had a higher perception of their learning and were more satisfied with their classroom experience relative to the student teams that did not use any technology in their collaborative learning process. Furthermore, the final test grades of the student teams that used technology were significantly higher than those of the nontechnology-supported student teams. In another study (Alavi, Wheeler, & Valacich, 1995), two types of synchronous collaborative learning environments using desktop videoconferencing were investigated in a longitudinal study: one involving local student groups (i.e., nonproximate student teams on the same campus), and the other involving nonproximate students on two separate university campuses. The findings indicated that both of the learning environments were equally effective in terms of student learning and satisfaction with the learning process. However, the students in nonproximate teams using the desktop videoconferencing were more committed and more attracted to their groups.

By freeing learners from time and geographic constraints, ALNs make collaborative learning a viable learning strategy in distance education. A number of studies (described later in this chap.) have shown the effectiveness of asynchronous collaborative learning and have established no significant difference between these and the face-to-face learning environments. A noteworthy research objective is drawing now on information and communication technology capabilities to design technology-mediated collaborative learning environments that may be pedagogically superior to alternative forms of learning environments. Information technology tools that might be used for this purpose are described as follows.

TECHNOLOGIES FOR SUPPORT
OF COLLABORATIVE LEARNING

In this section, we provide an overview of three categories of collaborative learning technologies: group support systems, collaboratories, and integrated learning environments. We focus on information technology capabilities that extend collaborative learning beyond face-to-face environments and into distance education. The Internet and the World Wide Web as ubiquitous communication and information platforms have played a key role in the development and growth of collaborative distance learning technologies. Their impact on two areas has been particularly significant: the provision of globally scalable connectivity among the members of collaborative learning groups, and the establishment of the browser as a ubiquitous user interface for various collaborative learning software applications.

Group Support Systems

Group support systems (GSS)[1] refers to software and hardware capabilities designed to support communication, coordination, and interactions among group members. Dominant GSS capabilities for the support of communication among group members include e-mail and computer conferencing (Alavi, 1999).[2] These two GSS capabilities are the most cost-effective and prevalent forms of GSS applications for technology-mediated collaborative learning. E-mail is used for the support of one-to-one and one-to-many exchanges of messages among the members of the collaborative learning team, whereas computer conferencing can provide both synchronous and asynchronous modes of interactions among the team members. The synchronous mode of computer conferencing (also referred to as *instant messaging* or *online chat*) involves interactive and real-time exchanges of text messages among the participants in a computer conference. A user can join a chat session in progress by accessing an existing "channel" and then communicating

---

[1] Other terms, including *groupware, group decision support systems,* and *computer-supported cooperative work* have been used to refer to this capability.

[2] Only advanced software- and hardware-based technologies are of interest here. More traditional forms of communication tools, such as telephone and fax, are not described here, although they can effectively support communication among the members of a group.

interactively with all the other users already on the channel. An identifier (a user's name) is attached to all of the individual's messages. The messages typed by an individual can be seen by all of the others on the channel, and vice versa. More advanced synchronous conferencing systems can provide an expanded set of capabilities consisting of screen and application sharing, group annotation, and collaborative brainstorming. These expanded features can effectively support real-time task collaboration in small, geographically dispersed learning teams.

Asynchronous computer conferencing resembles an electronic bulletin board for posting and responding to messages and provides data management capabilities to structure and organize conference transactions. A useful feature of these GSS tools is the provision of discussion "threads." A *thread* refers to a series of related messages. A conference may contain multiple discussion threads. By providing threading capability, conference discussions remain relatively structured and coherent, and users can easily track the evolution of group discussions around specific topics. The Internet has become a popular public messaging system used as the backbone of cost-effective and flexible e-mail and computer conferencing services.

Communication and interactions among the collaborative learning team members may also be supported by videoconferencing, another type of synchronous group support system. Videoconferencing provides two-way, full-motion video and audio communication between two or more geographic locations. For example, the executive MBA program at the School of Business of the Queen's University in Canada uses real-time multipoint videoconferencing technology to interconnect professors to students in several remote sites in several time zones across Canada. In some distributed collaborative learning applications, videoconferencing may be used in combination with advanced synchronous conferencing systems. For example, the Alavi et al. (1995) study described earlier employed point-to-point desktop videoconferencing and software application sharing to support collaborative learning by MBA student teams. However, due to its relatively high cost and the necessity of a relatively high-capacity bandwidth infrastructure, videoconferencing has not been frequently used to support small-team collaborative learning.

Some key capabilities for the support of collaborative learning teams involve the coordination of the team members' activities around the learning task, as well as structuring and organizing the task processes. Examples include group project management software and tools for systematically directing the pattern, timing, or content of group activities. For example, a GSS consisting of a computerized voting and tabulation tool can be used by the collaborative team members to choose a course of action from a set of alternatives, or a computerized Delphi Technique can be employed to efficiently generate and rank a number of solutions to the group's task. By coordinating and structuring group activities, a GSS can enhance group effectiveness and efficiency by reducing group process losses (e.g., production blocking and evaluation apprehension) and enhancing group synergy.

In summary, group support systems can enhance collaborative learning in several ways. They perform a number of functions, including:

- Transcending time and space barriers that constrain face-to-face collaborative learning interactions.

- Improving learning and group performance and effectiveness by reducing group process losses through more efficient, coordinated, and streamlined group interactions.
- Enhancing the timeliness, range, depth, and format of information available to collaborative learning group members.

Web-based collaboratories offer a software environment that transcends the traditional boundaries of GSS and virtual workspaces by reaching outside the system for data, information, and resources. Collaboratories are discussed next.

Collaboratories

Envisioned for scientific collaboration, the term *collaboratory* was first used by William Wulf in 1989, who defined it as a "center without walls, in which the nation's researchers can perform their research without regard to geographical location—interacting with colleagues, accessing instrumentation, sharing data and computational resources, and accessing information in digital libraries" (Wulf, 1989, Appendix A; see also Kouzes, Meyers, & Wulf, 1996). Even though collaboratories have their roots in the sciences (Barua, Chellappa, & Whinston, 1995; Kouzes et al., 1996; Wulf, 1989), they can also be integrated into asynchronous learning networks to provide collaborative learning experiences for geographically and temporally dispersed students. However, collaboratory use in the learning mode requires technical and social coordination. The delays between questions or comments and responses can be a week or more, making "conversation" difficult and confusing. For example, once a group has begun moving through a decision process, members who have lagged behind may suddenly enter the "conversation." Unexpected or inappropriate input generates process losses or inefficiencies due to the extraneous comments from members trying to make sense of comments or questions as the lagging member performs his or her assignment (McGrath & Hollingshead, 1994).

Tools embedded in the collaboratory software can provide mechanisms, constraints, or structures for team member coordination. Agendas, computer-supported facilitation tools, group support system tools, or automated facilitation (which uses timing and software to open and close access to activities such as voting) can prevent group members from lagging behind, speeding ahead of the group, or entering the group process at a point when confusion will result.

Collaboratories are designed for science, teaching and learning, and conducting business or health care at a distance. A combination of basic and domain-specific functionality is required. The following basic components are considered essential for simply sharing data (Cerf et al., 1993):

- Electronic libraries.
- Archives of data.
- Systems to support retrieval of data from any or all sources.

Web-based learning collaboratories require tools for use by students and educators, such as collaborative writing and editing tools, and methods for organizing the work of the group (Dufner, Kwon, & Hadidi, 1999; Dufner, Kwon, & Rogers, 2001).

Collaborative learning opportunities can be provided for distributed students by incorporating collaboratories and group learning spaces within the ALN design (Barua et al., 1995; Dufner et al., 2001). Team projects can help reduce the feeling of social isolation reported by some distributed students and can provide successful learning experiences for students in general. Web-based collaboratories provide geographically and temporally distributed students with the opportunity for team learning, drawing on resources both within and outside of the team environment. A collaboratory is a virtual workplace in which tools and structures can be used to control and to coordinate group processes, making team projects into feasible and enjoyable learning experiences.

In contrast to collaboratories, which draw on external resources, an emerging trend in the application of GSS in support of collaborative learning is development of technology environments that combine several GSS tools in a self-contained and seamless software environment. These integrated learning management systems are discussed next.

Integrated Learning Management Systems

Current and emerging learning management systems draw on the Internet and the World Wide Web infrastructure to combine a set of information management, productivity tools, and GSS features for support and management of individual and collaborative learning. These features include multimedia information and document management (for storing, retrieving, and organizing the learning content and discussions), advanced e-mail (with spell check, multiple views for sorting messages, and extensive message editing capabilities), threaded discussions for asynchronous interactions, as well as instant messaging for support of synchronous exchanges among the learning team members. These systems also provide capabilities, including student registration, testing, grading, and management of question-and-answer sessions, for managing the learning process.

The objectives of integrated learning management systems are twofold. First, they provide a single and easy-to-use learner interface to the various facilities of the system, thereby simplifying the shift from one to another and reducing the need for learning new styles of interface and commands. Second, they provide instructors with high-level and easy-to-use software support to develop instructions. More advanced systems may include components for modeling and interactive simulations, as well as point-to-point and multipoint videoconferencing capabilities. Some of these systems are developed and distributed commercially. Others may be developed in-house for support of specific technology-mediated collaborative learning programs. Key examples in the first category consist of Blackboard™ (blackboard.net), Lotus LearningSpace (Lotus.com), and WebCT (webct.com). The Virtual Classroom® System (developed at the New Jersey Institute of Technology, or NJIT) and Web-Tyco (developed by the University of Maryland) represent examples of in-house systems. The commercial systems may be licensed for in-house installation and use, or they can be "leased" from vendors.

We believe that the trend toward seamless integration of various GSS and other technology tools in forming collaborative learning applications will continue in the foreseeable future. These applications will increasingly draw on the ubiquity and capabilities of the Internet and the World Wide Web to enhance the richness, scalability, and cost-effectiveness of collaborative learning environments. For example, Looi and Ang (2000) described a prototype of a collaborative learning environment called *space*ALIVE!, which integrates multi-user environments such as multi-user dimensions (MUDs) and object-oriented MUDs (MOOs) with the World Wide Web capabilities, enabling users to create and manipulate objects in multimedia forms. The augmentation of MUDs and MOOs by synchronous messaging capabilities further enables the users to collaborate by simultaneously controlling and manipulating shared documents and objects.

Bieber et al. (2002) presented a vision of how technology could further evolve to support collaborative knowledge creation and learning. The vision involves the development of an integrated set of several tools and support techniques for their application and use by group members. The authors advocated a tool set including a multimedia library, group communication and decision support, community process support, advanced hypermedia features, and conceptual knowledge structures.

LITERATURE REVIEW

An impressive theoretical body of knowledge for collaborative learning has been accumulated over the years (Ansari & Simon, 1979; Bok, 1986; Bouton & Garth, 1983; Boyer, 1987; Brown & Palincsar, 1989; Bruffee, 1984; Cross, 1981; Cyrs, 1977; Daloz, 1987; Darkenwald & Merriam, 1982; Glasser & Bassok, 1989; Johnson, 1981; Johnson, Maruyama, Johnson, Nelson, & Skon, 1981;Kolb, 1984). However, most of this theory is based on traditional models of collaborative learning developed using face-to-face pedagogy (Bonk & Dennen, 2003). The dimensions of technology, mode of communication, and pedagogy appropriate for technology-mediated collaborative learning are not considered. To confirm existing theoretical constructs or to develop new theory for distributed collaborative learning using ALNs, the roles of technology, mode of communication and coordination, and pedagogy must be considered.

The following sections present and discuss studies that incorporate these factors. These studies have their historical foundations in computer-mediated communication (CMC), and the first forays into online collaborative learning (Hiltz, 1988; Hiltz & Turoff, 1978, 1981, 1992; Turoff, 1982, 1985; Turoff & Hiltz, 1982, 1986).

Theoretical Foundations for Technology-Mediated Collaborative Learning

Hiltz (1988) was the first theoretician to develop a research model—the Systems Contingency Model depicted in Fig. 9.1—within which to conduct and understand her research findings in the area of technology-mediated collaborative learning. Her research emphasis, at that time, was CMC. Collaborative learning, an intervening variable, played a smaller role. According to the Systems Contingency Model, systems or technologies are embedded within an environment. A system is

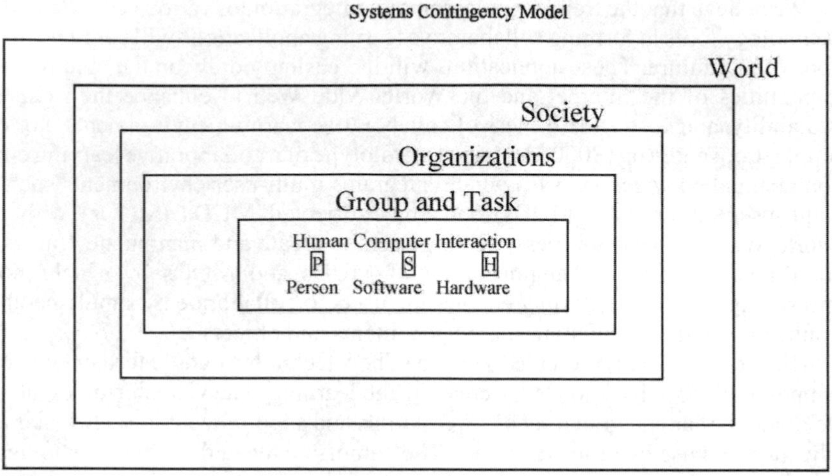

Systems Contingency Model

FIG. 9.1.   Systems Contingency Model (adapted from Hiltz, 1988, p. 1440).

defined and shaped by that environment, which consists of an organization with a culture; a society with beliefs, mores, and values; and the world. User perception and usage of the system or technology (human-computer-interaction) as well as the technological implementation (hardware and software) also shape the manner in which a system is used and understood. All of these actors or forces are parts of the overall system and must be considered.

Much later, Bruckman (2002) reinforced Hiltz's early insight into the nature of information systems and contingency by stating, "Internet is just one component of a new socio-technical system with great learning potential. Just as it matters which books students read, it matters which Internet software they use. And it matters what activities and social practices surround the process of Internet use in schools and at home" (p. 1).

The causal model for the Virtual Classroom® presented by Hiltz et al. (2000; see also chap. 3 of this vol.) is a modification of the contingency model presented in Fig. 9.1. Using the Systems Contingency Model, causal relationships between learning outcomes and such intervening variables as social presence (Rice et al., 1984) and media richness (Daft & Lengel, 1984) can be inferred. There has been little other new theory developed for technology-mediated learning, particularly in the areas of pedagogical strategies (Bonk & Dennen, 2003; Bonk, Ehman, Hixon, & Yamagata-Lynch, 2002) and the integration of technology and team learning (Johnson & Johnson, 1996).

In the face-to-face mode of communication, technology and task must be integrated with team processes (discussions, role playing, debate, group projects, etc.) in order for collaborative learning to occur. In the case of ALN, we are concerned with the nature of collaborative learning whereby technology, teamwork, task, and time are intertwined with learning. This interplay is made even more complex because the element of conversation is lost. Communication replaces conversation and becomes defined by the content, media, and the delays between comments and feedback.

Even though research is hampered by the lack of robust theory, the difficulty of measuring collaborative learning, and the complex interplay of the variables, key factors as enhancers and detractors of collaborative learning emerge. These key factors are an excellent starting point from which to further develop and refine existing theory.

Key Factors in Technology-Mediated Collaborative Learning

In 1993, Hiltz examined the impact of technology, the Virtual Classroom® system, on educational processes and outcomes. She evaluated use, subjective satisfaction, and benefits as dependent variables. Collaborative learning was studied as an intervening variable. Hiltz hypothesized that students who experienced collaborative learning when using the Virtual Classroom® were more likely to judge the outcomes of an online course to be superior to those of traditional courses.

Hiltz found the research subjects' satisfaction with the Virtual Classroom® favorable when compared to traditional classrooms. Fifty-five percent of Virtual Classroom® students reported that motivation increased because other students and the instructor were able to read their work, thus supporting the conclusion that collaborative learning was encouraged by the technological delivery system.

In this study, Hiltz also found CMC to be well suited to group or collaborative learning. Knowledge is a result of "active dialogue," the interaction among students and teachers. CMC facilitates that communication. Hiltz addressed the question "Is the Virtual Classroom® a viable option for educational delivery?" The answer was yes, as long as the student brings emotional maturity and ability to class.

Using case-based learning Bonk, Malinowski, Angeli, and East (1998) studied the effects of different levels of mentor support or intervention on learning. The first half of the subjects were provided with heavy scaffolding for 3 weeks and weak scaffolding for the following 3-week period. The other half of the subjects were supported first with weak then with heavy scaffolding. The subjects (student teachers) were tasked with generating case studies using their own personal experience in teaching. It was found that 60% of all responses to student-generated cases (mentor to student and peer to peer) occurred during the weeks of support with heavy scaffolding (HS), which involved mentors. In the HS condition, 80% more cases were produced, the amount of messaging was 52% greater, and subjects received approximately 30% more feedback.

On the other hand, expert judges rated student case structures generated in the weak scaffolding condition more positively than those generated in the HS condition. The level of scaffolding did not affect learning outcomes.

For both conditions, a 20% drop in the number of posted messages occurred during the second 3-week period of the study, perhaps indicating a decline in the subjects' level of interest. On the positive side, Bonk and his colleagues found conferencing with peers and mentors did reduce the social isolation of student teachers in the field.

Intervening variables such as member participation (group members lagging behind or free riding; Dufner, Hiltz, Johnson, & Czech, 1995; Graham, Scarborough,

& Goodwin, 1999; Hiltz et al., 1999; Hiltz, Dufner, Holmes, & Poole, 1991) and messages without real content (the equivalent of nodding or agreeing in face-to-face meetings) may have obscured the impact of scaffolding in this study. Independent variables such as the subjects' level of maturity and individual abilities (Hiltz, 1993) may also have contributed to the findings. Whether the degree of scaffolding affects learning outcomes remains an unanswered question and a fruitful area for further investigation.

Dufner, Park, Kwon, and Peng (2002) and Dufner and her colleagues (2001), used ALN (a CyberCollaboratory) for the performance of collaborative learning projects. Students from each of three different geographically and temporally distributed universities were quasirandomly assigned to each research group. Baseline (face-to-face) groups were comprised of students from the same university because travel for meetings would not have been feasible otherwise. The students performed the collaborative tasks as assignments within the context of a traditional course at their own university. In the first experiment, six student groups were studied, each learning to conduct systems analysis and design (SAD) projects. The subjects reported a high degree of satisfaction using the CyberCollaboratory; and student projects were found to be equivalent in quality or better than the SAD face-to-face projects from the previous semester. The task was of high value to the students and they were given a semester to complete the task (a normal time frame).

A second study of 33 student groups (Dufner et al., 2002) found lower levels of satisfaction, low task completion rates, and high dropout rates. The research tasks were viewed by subjects as having low value and were of short duration. The researchers concluded that task significance to the subject and time for task completion are important factors for collaborative learning success.

Alavi et al. (1995) found that face-to-face, distant, and local collaborative learning are equally effective methods for the acquisition of declarative learning, thus demonstrating the transparency of technology in the learning process studied. On the other hand, they also found distance collaborative subjects "demonstrated the highest level of critical thinking" (p. 305). The researchers suggested that novelty may have played a role in this unexpected outcome and therefore recommended future research.

Gallini and Helman (1995) also found a positive link between distance and educational outcomes. They studied technology-mediated peer-to-peer and teacher-to-student communication. The writing scores for *more effective* and *interesting* communication were significantly higher for students who had communicated with peers located at a distance than were those of students closer in proximity. The authors speculated that students had the need to communicate more information to a peer located at a distance because of the lack of a shared frame of reference. Peers at a distance need more effectively communicated information. The positive relationship between geographical distance and writing scores opens an interesting area for future research in technology-mediated collaborative learning.

Graham et al. (1999) assigned students to tutorial groups (six per group). Students were encouraged to solve economics problems collaboratively without face-to-face interactions. The researchers found that composition and size of the groups played a significant role in the group dynamics. Groups need to be small enough to discourage free riding or withdrawal, yet large enough to maintain group movement and progress through the group process. The researchers also found that clear guidelines and expectations of participation for staff and students need to be developed, spelled out, and made readily available.

The Sener and Stover (2000) distance education program is of interest because of the duration of the study (spring 1995 through summer 1999), the diversity of courses, and the number of students studied. The program was initially developed as a self-paced, independent study based on continuous enrollment. Students could follow a single thread through courses unfettered by registration deadlines. According to the authors, the continuous enrollment policy was later rescinded for most courses in order to facilitate face-to-face activities and other types of cohort formation to foster collaborative learning. The authors described face-to-face lab sessions as collaborative learning activities. The reader is left to guess what actual "collaborative learning activities" were performed in the lab sessions.

Continuous enrollment was reinstated for the mathematics courses, in which teacher–student relationships were deemed to be more important to students than was collaborative learning. However, a review of the data would suggest that continuous enrollment could have been reinstated for all courses except Chemistry 111/112 (Sener and Stover, 2000). Faculty teaching the Chemistry 111/112 listed "Collaborative Learning w/appropriate preparation" as important, whereas, faculty teaching the other courses (Engineering 120, Math 277/291, and Information Science and Technology 128) did not.

Moreover, the authors made no attempt to assess collaborative learning. The authors provided the subjective opinion of one teacher who thought that face-to-face sessions fostered collaboration, camaraderie, and more productive online interactions. Collaborative learning as a research variable was never defined or explored. No evaluation method was listed for the assessment of collaborative learning, and no students were asked about collaborative learning. Thus, although the authors suspended continuous enrollment to foster collaborative learning, they neglected to describe the collaborative learning activities for which they did this suspension, and to measure the outcomes of those activities. In this study, continuous enrollment was not the factor that prohibited collaborative learning. Faculty attitudes concerning collaborative learning seemed to be a more important factor in fostering collaborative learning.

Another key factor in all learning is assessment. Kwok and Ma (1999) studied *collaborative* assessment using GSS-supported project teams and teams without GSS support (face-to-face teams). Students in both conditions and teachers collaboratively developed evaluation criteria for team projects. The subjects were given a list of "suggested" assessment criteria to begin the discussions. Then, using the Delphi method and GSS tools (brainstorming, voting, and weighting), assessment criteria and an evaluation scheme were developed in collaboration with team members and educators. Throughout the semester, students assessed their own work and that of other students. Educators assessed all student work based on the agreed-on criteria and scheme.

The Study Process Questionnaire (SPQ; Biggs, 1991) was used to assess *student approach to learning*. Kwok and Ma (1999) hypothesized that the GSS-supported teams would take a deeper approach to learning (e.g., studying gives the student a deep sense of satisfaction) than would the students in the unsupported control groups. SPQ responses confirmed the GSS-supported students did take a deeper approach to learning than did the unsupported teams. The GSS-supported teams also received better project grades than did the unsupported teams, even though both groups were involved in developing the assessment criteria and strategy.

The studies presented here demonstrate that, contrary to what may be commonly held beliefs, technology is not the only important factor in ALN environments. Other key factors did emerge from the studies presented here, including student level of maturity, importance of the task to the subject, length of time given to complete the task, structure of the collaborative process (e.g., level of scaffolding), clarity of guidelines and expectations, regularity of staff and student participation, assessment of collaborative work, and geographical distance. Pedagogy emerged as an important factor in many of these studies as well. The role of pedagogy is presented and discussed in the next section.

The Role of Pedagogy

Interaction between peers, facilitators, group members, instructors, and students, as well as task and time all play important roles in the effectiveness of collaborative learning. However, one of the results we see in many of the studies presented above is the importance of pedagogy. Hiltz et al. (2000) found that pedagogy and instructor differences played a greater role in research outcomes than did media. The pedagogy or differences between facilitators, even in what seem to be small ways, can dramatically change outcomes.

The State University of New York Learning Network (SLN) course template (pedagogy) includes a section encouraging the use of online and small group discussions (Fredericksen, Pickett, Shea, Pelz, & Swan, 2000a). Fredericksen et al. stated that effective online teaching strategies or pedagogy include discussion and small-group activities (Fredericksen, Pickett, Shea, Pelz, & Swan, 2000b, p.13). Among SLN template best practices, Fredericksen et al. (2000b) included creating a sense of community and providing community-building opportunities and interactions. A sense of community, coupled with student interactions, provides the foundation for effective collaborative learning.

Jiang and Ting (2000) studied 19 Internet-based courses delivered through SLN in 1997. Eighteen of the courses incorporated an online discussion element. Jiang and Ting (2000) found that even though the grade weight for participation varied, the grade for discussion and requirements for discussion were significantly positively correlated with students' perceptions of learning. In general, students reported higher perceptions of learning in online courses.

The Carr-Chellman and Dyer (2000) study asked, "Are teachers ready for technology-mediated teaching designed to support free learning?". Even though both teachers and students reported some level of concern over the minimized role of the teacher of the future portrayed in the research scenarios, teachers were more concerned (67%) with the lack of structure in free learning than with the technology. Could free learning become "free riding"? Teachers' responses clearly show a greater concern about the underlying educational processes than about the technology. The importance of pedagogy to these teachers is clear. Yes, teachers are ready for technology in which learning processes are supported and the teacher interacts with the student and plays a major role in the learning process.

We have seen the importance of pedagogy in these and other studies. However "there is a dearth of knowledge about pedagogical tools and strategies for the Web" (Bonk & Dennen, 2003, p. 336). In other words, we now need to focus our attention on developing pedagogical tools and strategies specifically for the Web and ALN in order to glean the educational benefits the Web surely has to offer.

In summary, research has examined the outcomes of technology-mediated learning in a variety of contexts, and has established the relative learning effectiveness of this approach. One of the major areas where further research is needed is highlighted in the next section.

Making Online Discussions Effective

One of the most frequently used forms of collaborative learning is the discussion, in which the students are invited to contribute information, experiences, and opinions about a specific course topic. These tend to be considered valuable by both students and instructors. For example, Dziuban and Moskal (2001) reported results based on survey data from over 50,000 University of Central Florida students that showed a very high correlation between interaction in online courses and student satisfaction. However, not all online discussions are equally effective. Some recent research has begun to explore what the instructor can do to improve the quality of online discussions and students' learning from them.

An exploratory study was conducted in spring 2002 at NJIT via a postcourse questionnaire designed to explore this issue. Respondents included 116 students in two undergraduate courses and one graduate course (Wu & Hiltz, 2003). Over half of the students felt that they learned a great deal from their peers through online discussion, and 69% of the students thought online discussion increased their learning quality. These and several other items were formed into an index measuring perceived learning from online class discussions. Following is a list of some of the hypotheses supported:

- Students who perceive more motivation and enjoyability from online discussion will report higher perceptions of learning from online discussion.
- The instructor plays an essential role in promoting students' motivation, enjoyability, and perceptions of learning online.

In describing the main problems perceived with their online discussions, most students pointed to steps that can be taken by the instructor, such as providing a clear structure and timely feedback. One student noted, "The motivation put forth by the professor is very important" (Wu & Hiltz, 2003, p. 694).

One strategy that is used to motivate regular participation is assigning a grade to it. However, as Oliver and Shaw (2003) pointed out, this can sometimes backfire. A content analysis of discussions in medical sciences courses indicated that contributions were frequently not very "interactive" (i.e., students post but do not respond well to one another). Some students "were simply playing the game of assessment, making postings that earned marks but rarely contributing otherwise ... it seems likely that giving credit for postings changes behavior without necessarily improving learning" (p. 1). Nevertheless, if participation in discussion and other online collaborative activities is not graded, then many students will not participate at all. The key is to grade for quality of participation and for responding to others as well as for making new postings. Oliver and Shaw (2003) reached a conclusion similar to that of the NJIT study: "The major factors for stimulating student participation in asynchronous discussion are tutor enthusiasm and expertise. It appears that the tutor may be the root cause of engagement in discussions" (p. 2).

Literature Review Summary

A modified version of Hiltz's (1988, p. 1440) contingency model is depicted in Fig. 9.2 and provides a good foundation to accommodate what we have studied and learned over the past 2 decades about the use of ALNs. Today, organizations lack the rigid boundaries of the past. Instead, shifting, permeable boundaries meet the needs of stakeholders such as students, educators, or employees. Consequently, the solid line that represented organizational boundaries in the original contingency model has been changed to a dotted line in Fig. 9.2. The dotted line symbolizes the use of pervasive computing and telecommunications to enable the distribution of students and educators in space and time. The dotted line also symbolizes the permeable nature of today's organizational boundaries. Using the technological support developed over the last decade, students may no longer need to come to campus. Time has been added as a strong constraint, using a heavy line to

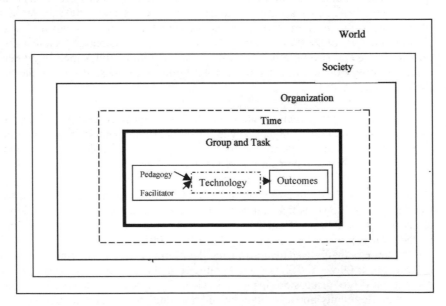

FIG. 9.2.   Modified contingency model for ALN-supported collaborative learning in a "boundaryless" organization. (Adapted from Hiltz, 1988.)

show the importance of the loss of "conversation" in the asynchronous mode of communication. Human and computer interaction remains an important part of the model; however, we now know that the technology does not necessarily play a more important role than does the pedagogy or facilitator/instructor in affecting group process and educational outcomes. The model has been altered to reflect the importance of the instructor or facilitator. Because organizations still exist within a society and the world, those elements are retained.

Many studies report positive benefits of using technology for collaborative learning (Alavi, 1994; Alavi et al., 1995; Alavi, Yoo, & Vogel, 1997; Benbunan-Fich & Hiltz, 1999; Dufner et al., 2001; Hiltz, 1994). On the other hand, some of these same researchers find mixed results, up to and including drawbacks when using collaborative learning (Bruffee, 1999; Dufner et al., 2002). Even when confronted with occasional drawbacks, researchers continue to look for ways to use ALN-supported collaborative learning effectively, and remain optimistic about its value for students as a rich and enjoyable learning experience (Alavi, 1994; Alavi et al., 1995; Benbunan-Fich & Hiltz, 1999; Bruffee, 1999; Dufner et al., 2001, 2002; Hiltz et al., 2000).

Suggestions for Future Research

The improved performance–price ratios of computing equipment and the increase in prevalence of the Internet and the World Wide Web have provided opportunities for the development and deployment of technology-mediated collaborative learning environments. However, in most cases these environments have been developed without explicit consideration of the underlying group learning process and other contextual factors. In some cases, this approach has resulted in the development of technically state-of-the-art environments without clear guidelines on how they may be deployed to achieve favorable learning outcomes. Under these circumstances, despite the expenditure of resources, the opportunity is lost to create collaborative learning environments that are pedagogically effective. Thus, it is important to continue inquiry and investigation into the design of effective technology-mediated collaborative learning approaches. Several important research questions need to be addressed.

The previous research in this area, despite some inconsistencies, has established the overall effectiveness of the outcomes of these environments by establishing that there is "no significant difference" between ALNs and the traditional learning environments. We suggest that future research should extend beyond simple comparisons between ALNs and traditional learning, and instead should aim at the design of ALN environments that lead to improved and enhanced learning outcomes. Furthermore, as displayed in Fig. 9.2, past research reveals a number of contextual variables that impact the outcomes of ALNs, including pedagogy, facilitator, technology, task, and group interaction processes. Studies that investigate the relationships among the contextual factors and the ALN outcomes are needed. For example, the selection and application of technology in previous ALN studies has been primarily based on the availability and/or cost effectiveness of specific technology environments, instead of being guided by relevant theories or empirical findings regarding the fit between technology, task processes, the group, and learning task processes.

As discussed in this chapter, a growing set of technologies offering various capabilities is available for the design of ALN environments. The choice of technology for the design of collaborative ALN environments can be enhanced through the conduct of systemic studies of effectiveness of various technologies. For example, it would be useful to map out the relationship between different GSS capabilities (e.g., computer conferencing, information management, etc.) and the ALN outcomes. Also of interest would be studies combining different GSS technologies and the sequence of their application on the outcomes of distributed collaborative learning. This line of inquiry would be important for the development of technology environments conducive to and supportive of distributed learning.

Missing from most studies of ALNs is the consideration of the collaborative processes and dynamics through which learning occurs. As postulated by social learning theories, knowledge is cocreated through the collaborative processes as group members variously raise issues, respond to questions and requests for clarification, and seek to perform the assigned team task. Future research can investigate the dynamics of knowledge creation and learning in the ALN environments by analyzing the content and flow of the exchanges among learners. This analysis will facilitate the interpretation of the meaning of the exchanges among team members and will enhance our understanding of the way learners interact and learn collaboratively. Furthermore, research needs to be extended to investigate the way in which technology features can engage group processes that contribute to the learning outcomes. To design effective environments for ALNs, it is important to conceptualize technology features in a manner directly relevant to pedagogical approaches and group dynamics.

Several studies cited in this chapter show the importance of pedagogy and instructor or facilitator differences and their effect on learning outcomes (Bonk & Dennen, 2003; Hiltz, et al., 2000); however, the impact of the technology cannot be separated from asynchronous collaborative learning. ALN would not exist without some sort of technological infrastructure to ensure delivery. Pedagogy is filtered through the technology to the student and back to the instructor.

Two questions come to mind:

- Can we adjust the technology to compensate for pedagogical differences and the differences in instructors and facilitators that we see?
- How do we accurately assess collaborative learning when ALNs are used?

Today's subjective measures of student interaction and self-reported learning levels may not provide an accurate picture of collaborative learning outcomes. The impact of instructor or facilitator differences, as well as differences in pedagogy as these variables are filtered through the technology, remain fruitful areas for future research.

Past work has established that it is not the technology features alone that impact ALN outcomes in a given context, but instead the mutual influence of technology features, pedagogy, and group processes. This makes ALN research a complex and challenging endeavor involving both the design and construction of innovative learning environments and the simultaneous assessment of their effectiveness.

SUMMARY

In conclusion, many studies report positive benefits of using technology for collaborative learning (Alavi, 1994; Alavi, Wheeler, & Valacich, 1995; Alavi, Yoo, & Vogel, 1997; Benbunan-Fich & Hiltz, 1999; Dufner, Kwon, & Rogers, 2001; Hiltz, 1994). On the other hand, some of these same researchers find mixed results, up to and including drawbacks, when using collaborative learning (Bruffee, 1999; Dufner et al., 2002). Even when confronted with occasional drawbacks, researchers continue to look for ways to use ALN-supported collaborative learning effectively and remain optimistic about its value for students as a rich and enjoyable learning experience (Alavi, 1994; Alavi, Wheeler, & Valacich, 1995; Benbunan-Fich & Hiltz, 1999; Bruffee, 1999; Dufner et al., 2002; Dufner, Kwon, & Rogers, 2001; Hiltz et al., 2000).

QUESTIONS FOR DISCUSSION AND RESEARCH

1. Instructors may use "heavy scaffolding" (detailed instructions) or "light scaffolding" (give students a task and a deadline, and let them decide how to do it) for collaborative ALN assignments. Which do you think is more effective at the university level, and why? Might it depend on how well developed the teams are at the time the assignment is given?

2. Most popular ALN platforms seem to focus their design on delivery of material, rather than on supporting collaboration. Think about the software you are currently or have most recently used. What do you think are the one or two features that would be most important to add to provide better support for collaborative learning?

3. What is the ideal group size for different types of ALN collaborative assignments, and why?

4. The authors wrote: "How do we accurately assess collaborative learning when ALNs are used? Today's subjective measures of student interaction and self-reported learning levels may not provide an accurate picture of collaborative learning outcomes." Can you design a field experiment in which collaborative learning would be measured by something other than self-reports?

REFERENCES

Alavi, M. (1994). Computer-mediated collaborative learning: An empirical evaluation. *MIS Quarterly, 18*(2), 159–174.

Alavi, M. (1999). Group support systems: Tools and applications. In *Encyclopedia of Microcomputers* (pp. 159–173). New York: Dekker.

Alavi, M., Wheeler, B. C., & Valacich, J. S. (1995). Using IT to reengineer business education: An exploratory investigation of collaborative telelearning. *MIS Quarterly, 19*(3), 293–312.

Alavi, M., Yoo, Y., & Vogel, D. R. (1997). Using information technology to add value to management education. *Academy of Management Journal, 40*(5), 1310–1333.

Ansari, Y., & Simon, H. A. (1979). The theory of learning by doing. *Psychological Review, 86*(2), 124–140.

Barua, A., Chellappa, R., & Whinston, A. B. (1995). Creating a collaboratory in cyberspace: Theoretical foundation and implementation. *Journal of Organizational Computing, 5*(4), 417–442.

Benbunan-Fich, R., & Hiltz, S. R. (1999). Impacts of asynchronous learning networks on individual and group problem solving: A field experiment. *Journal of Group Decision and Negotiations, 8*(5), 409–426.

Bieber, M., Engelbart, D., Furuta, R., & Hiltz, S. R. (2002, Spring). Name of article. *Journal of Management Information Systems, 18*(4), 11.

Biggs, J. B. (1991). Assessing learning quality: Reconciling institutional, staff and educational demands. *Assessment and Evaluation in Higher Education, 21*(1), 5–15.

Bligh, D. A. (1972). *What's the use of lectures*. Harmondsworth, UK: Penguin.

Bok, D. (1986). *Higher learning*. Cambridge, MA: Harvard University Press.

Bonk, C. J., & Dennen, N. (2003). Frameworks for research, design, benchmarks, training, and pedagogy in Web-based distance education. In M. G. Moore & B. Anderson (Eds.), *Handbook of distance education* (pp. 329–346). Mahwah, NJ: Lawrence Erlbaum Associates.

Bonk, C. J., Ehman, L., Hixon, E., & Yamagata-Lynch, E. (2002). The pedagogical TICKIT: Teacher institute for curriculum knowledge about the integration of technology. *Journal of Technology and Teacher Education, 10*(2), 205–233.

Bonk, C. J., Malinowski, S., Angeli, C., & East, J. (1998). Web-based case conferencing for pre-service teacher education: Electronic discourse from the field. *Journal of Educational Computing Research, 19*(3), 269–306.

Bouton, C., & Garth, R. Y. (1983). *Learning in groups*. San Francisco: Jossey-Bass.

Boyer, E. (1987). Toward school-college collaboration. *Thought and Action, 3*(2), 7–18.

Brown, A. L., & Palincsar, A. S. (1989). Guided, cooperative learning and individual knowledge acquisition. In L. B. Resnick (Ed.), *Knowing, learning, and instruction: Essays in honor of Robert Glaser* (pp. 393–451). Hillsdale, NJ: Lawrence Erlbaum Associates.

Bruckman, A. (2002). The future of e-learning communities. *Communications of the ACM, 45*(4), 60–63.

Bruffee, K. A. (1984). Collaborative learning and the "Conversation of Mankind." *College English, 46*(7), 635–652.

Bruffee, K. A. (1999). *Collaborative learning: Higher education, interdependence, and the authority of knowledge* (2nd ed.). Baltimore: Johns Hopkins University Press.

Bryant, P. (1982). The role of conflict and of agreement between intellectual strategies in children's idea about measurement. *British Journal of Psychology, 73*, 243–251.

Carr-Chellman, & Dyer, D. (2000). The pain and ecstasy: Pre-service teacher perceptions on changing teacher roles and technology. *Educational Technology & Society, 3*(2), 96–105.

Cerf, V. G., et al. (Eds.). (1993). *National collaboratories: Applying information technologies for scientific research*. Washington, DC: National Academy Press. Available: http://books.nap.edu/books/0309048486/html/R1.html#pagetop

Coppola, N. W., Hiltz, S. R., & Rotter, N. G. (2002). Becoming a virtual professor: Pedagogical roles and asynchronous learning networks. *Journal of Management Information Systems, 18*(4), 169–189.

Cross, K. P. (1981). *Adults as learners*. London: Jossey-Bass.

Cyrs, T. E. (Ed.). (1977). *New directions in teaching and learning, teaching and learning at a distance: What it takes to effectively design, deliver, and evaluate programs*. San Francisco: Jossey-Bass.

Daft, R. L., & Lengel, R. H. (1984). Information richness: A new approach to managerial behavior and organization design. *Research In Organizational Behavior, 6*, 191–233.

Daloz, L. A. (1987). *Effective teaching and mentoring: Realizing the transformational strategies for adult learning experiences*. San Francisco: Jossey-Bass.

Darkenwald, G. G., & Merriam, S. B. (1982). *Adult education: Foundations of practice*. New York: Harper & Row.

Dufner, D. K., Hiltz, S. R., Johnson, K., & Czech, R. M. (1995). Distributed group support: The effects of voting tools on group perceptions of media richness. In L. Chidambaram (Ed.), *Group decision and negotiation, 4,* 235–250. [Special issue on distributed communication systems]

Dufner, D., Kwon, O., & Hadidi, R. (1999). Web-CCAT: A collaborative learning environment for geographically distributed information technology students and working professionals. *Communications of the Association of Information Systems, 1*(12), 1–32.

Dufner, D., Kwon, O., & Rogers, B. (2001). Enriching asynchronous learning networks through the provision of virtual collaborative learning spaces: A research pilot. In *Proceedings of the 34th Annual Hawaii International Conference on Systems Sciences* (pp. 1004–1014). Los Alamitos, CA: IEEE Computer Society Press.

Dufner, D., Park, Y-T., Kwon, O., & Peng, Q. (2002). Asynchronous team support: Perceptions of the group problem solving process when using a cyber collaboratory. In *Proceedings of the 35th Annual International Conference on System Sciences.* Los Alamitos, CA: IEEE Computer Society Press.

Dziuban, C., & Moskal, P. (2001). *Emerging research issues in distributed learning.* Paper presented at the 7th Sloan-C International Conference on Asynchronous Learning Networks, Orlando, FL, November 16–18.

Flynn, J. L. (1992, October). Cooperative learning and Gagne's events of instruction: A syncretic view. *Educational Technology,* pp. 53–60.

Fredericksen, E., Pickett, A., Shea, P., Pelz, W., & Swan, K. (2000a). Factors influencing faculty satisfaction with asynchronous teaching and learning in the SUNY Learning Network. *Journal of Asynchronous Learning Networks, 3*(2). Retrieved May 2, 2002, from

Fredericksen, E., Pickett, A., Shea, P., Pelz, W., & Swan, K. (2000b). Student satisfaction and perceived learning with on-line courses: Principles and examples from the SUNY Learning Network. *Journal of Asynchronous Learning Networks, 4*(2). Retrieved May 2, 2002, from

Gallini, J. K., & Helman, N. (1995). Audience awareness in technology-mediated environments. *Journal of Educational Computing Research, 13*(3) 245–261.

Glasser, R., & Bassok, M. (1989). Learning theory and the study of instruction. *Annual Review of Psychology, 40,* 631–666.

Graham, M., Scarborough, H., & Goodwin, C. (1999). Implementing computer mediated communication in an undergraduate course—A practical experience. *Journal of Asynchronous Learning Networks, 3*(1).

Hiltz, S. R. (1986). The virtual classroom: Using computer-mediated communication for university teaching. *Journal of Communication, 36*(2), 95–104.

Hiltz, S. R. (1988). Productivity enhancement from computer-mediated communication: A systems contingency approach. *Communications of the ACM, 31,* 1438–1454.

Hiltz, S. R. (1993). Correlates of learning in a virtual classroom. *International Journal of Man–Machine Studies, 39,* 71–98.

Hiltz, S. R. (1994). *The virtual classroom: Learning without limits via computer networks.* Norwood, NJ: Ablex.

Hiltz, S. R., Coppola, N., Rotter, N., Turoff, M., & Benbunan-Fich, R. (2000). Measuring the importance of collaborative learning for the effectiveness of ALN: A multi-measure, multi-method approach. *Journal of Asynchronous Learning Networks, 4*(2). Retrieved May 2, 2002.

Hiltz, S. R., Dufner, D. K., Fjeremestad, J., Kim, Y., Rana, A., Ocher, R., & Turoff, M. (1999). Distributed group decision support systems: Tools and processes for coordination. In G. Olsen, T. Malone, & J. Smith (Eds.), *Coordination theory and collaborative technology.* Hillsdale, NJ: Lawrence Erlbaum Associates.

Hiltz, S. R., Dufner, D. K., Holmes, M. E., & Poole, M. S. (1991). Distributed group support systems: Social dynamics and design dilemmas. *Journal of Organizational Computing, 2*(1), 135–159.

212   ALAVI AND DUFNER

Hiltz, S. R., & Turoff, M. (1978). *The network nation: Human communication via computer.* New York: Addison-Wesley.

Hiltz, S. R., & Turoff, M. (1981). The evolution of user behavior in a computerized conferencing system. *Communications of the ACM, 24*(11), 739–751.

Hiltz, S. R., & Turoff, M. (1992). Structuring computer-mediated communication to avoid information overload. In D. Marca & G. Bock (Eds.), *Groupware: Software for computer-supported cooperative work* (pp. 384–393). Washington, DC: IEEE Computer Society Press.

Jiang, M., & Ting, E. (2000). A study of factors influencing students' perceived learning in a web-based course environment. *International Journal of Educational Telecommunications, 6*(4), 317–338.

Johnson, D. W. (1981). Student–student interaction: The neglected variable in education. *Educational Research, 10*(1), 5–10.

Johnson, D. W., & Johnson, R. T. (1996). Cooperation and the use of technology. In D. H. Jonassen (Ed.), *Handbook of research for educational communications and technology* (pp. 1017–1044). New York: Macmillan.

Johnson, D. W., Maruyama, G., Johnson, R., Nelson, D., & Skon, N. L. (1981). Effects of cooperative, competitive, and individualistic goal structures on achievement: A meta-analysis. *Psychological Bulletin 89*, 1, 47–62.

Kolb, D. A. (1984). *Experiential learning.* Englewood Cliffs, NJ: Prentice-Hall.

Kouzes, R. T., Meyers, J. D., & Wulf, W. A. (1996). Collaboratories: Doing science on the Internet. *Computer, 29*(8), 40–46.

Kwok, R. C. W., & Ma, J. (1999). Use of a group support system for collaborative assessment. *Computers & Education, 32*, 109–125.

Leidner, D., & Jarvenpaa, S. (1995). The use of information technology to enhance management school education: A theoretical view. *MIS Quarterly, 9*, 265–291.

Looi, C.-K., & Ang, D. (2000). A multimedia-enhanced collaborative learning environment. *Journal of Computer Assisted Learning, 16*(1), 2–15.

McGrath, J. E., & Hollingshead, A. B. (1994). *Groups interacting with technology.* Thousand Oaks, CA: Sage.

Oliver, M., & Shaw, G. P. (2003). Asynchronous discussion in support of medical education. *Journal of Asynchronous Learning Networks, 7*(1). Retrieved February 2003 from http://www.aln.org/publications/jaln/v7n1/index.asp

Rice, R., et al. (1984). *The new media: Communication, research and technology.* Beverly Hills, CA: Sage.

Russell, J. (1982). Cognitive conflict, transmission, and justification: Conservation attainment through dyadic interaction. *Journal of Genetic Psychology, 140*, 283–297.

Sener, J., & Stover, M. L. (2000). Integrating ALN into an independent study distance education program: NVCC case studies. *Journal of Asynchronous Learning Networks, 4*(2). Retrieved from http://www.aln.org/publications/jaln/v4n2/index.asp

Shuell, T. J. (1986). Cognitive conceptions of learning. *Review of Educational Research, 56*(4), 411–436.

Turoff, M. (1982, April). *On the design of an electronic university.* Paper presented at the Proceeding of the Conference on Telecommunications and Higher Education, New Jersey Institute of Technology, Newark.

Turoff, M. (1985). Information and value: The internal information marketplace. *Journal of Technological Forecasting and Social Change, 27*(4), 357–373.

Turoff, M., & Hiltz, S. R. (1982). Computer support for group versus individual decisions. *IEEE Transactions on Communications, 30*(1), 82–91.

Turoff, M., & Hiltz, S. R. (1986). Remote learning: Technologies and opportunities. In *Proceedings, World Conference on Continuing Engineering Education,* Vol. 11, 754–764. New York: IEEE.

Turoff, M., & Hiltz, S. R. (1995). Designing and evaluating a virtual classroom. *Journal of Information Technology for Teacher Education, 4*(2), 197–215.

Vygotsky, L. S. (1978). *Mind in society: The development of higher psychological processes.* Cambridge, MA: Harvard University Press.

Wittrock, M. C. (1978). The cognitive movement in instruction. *Educational Psychologist, 13,* 15–29

Wu, D., & Hiltz, S. R. (2003). Online discussions and perceived learning. In *Proceedings of the America's Conference on Information Systems* (CD-Rom Ed.). Tampa, FL: Association for Information Systems.

Wulf, W. A. (1989, March). *The national collaboratory—a white paper.* Paper presented at a workshop at Rockefeller University, New York.

10

Media Mixes and Learning Networks[1]

Ronald E. Rice, Starr Roxanne Hiltz, and David H. Spencer

> *The effectiveness of employing a symbol system for instructional pruposes depends on the extent to which the specifically selected coding elements activate in the learners mental skills that are sufficiently mastered by them and are relevant to the requirements of the learning task. (Salomon, 1979, p. 110)*
>
> *Media do not influence learning any more than the truck that delivers groceries influences the nutrition of a community. (Clark, 2001b, p. 5)*
>
> *All methods required for learning can be delivered by a variety of media and media attributes.... Therefore, aside from the identification of necessary methods for learners and tasks, it is important to derive media that are capable of delivering the method at the least expensive rate and in the speediest fashion. (Clark, 2001c, p. 313)*

INTRODUCTION

There has been little research on the effect of different media mixes and sequencing on the process and outcomes of asynchronous learning networks (ALNs). The past decade of research on distance education has primarily emphasized design issues, interactivity, active learning, and learner characteristics, mostly through descriptive research (Berge & Mrozowski, 2001). This chapter reviews some of the theories and findings about media characteristics in general that seem most applicable to conceptualizing the pros and cons of incorporating multimedia into online courses, and selected studies that included medium as a variable. The following sections introduce the diversity of ALNs, and summarize some relevant media

---

[1]Portions of this chapter were adapted from Rice (1992) and Spencer (2002). Eunhee Kim contributed to the review of multimedia studies.

typologies, media characteristics theories, and educational media theories. Then extant studies using multiple new media for educational settings are reviewed to try to identify both particular lessons learned and implications for new media implementation in ALNs.

THE MEDIA CORNUCOPIA

Rumble (2001) identified a variety of changes in the concept and application of distance education from 1971 to 2001. Relevant among these are a shift from a transmission model of education toward a more constructivist model, facilitated by computer-mediated communication, and a related shift from a bureaucratic, assembly-line approach toward a greater focus on the student, flexibility, and global reach. Note the paradoxical shift to more communicative and interactive learning associated with the use of technology, often critiqued as a depersonalizing factor.

"Text-only" computer-mediated communication (CMC) through threaded conferences or e-mail lists dominated the first decade of asynchronous learning networks (e.g., Harasim, 1990; Hiltz, 1986, 1994). Recently, however, the hardware, software, and high-speed network connections have become available to allow the integration of many other forms of digitized, networked, and interactive computer-mediated communication. Chief among these are synchronous chats; asynchronous, digital audio via freely available software, such as Real Audio® or Powerpoint® slide shows with digital audio accompaniment; real-time classwide data analysis; posting of digital photos or diagrams or graphics (including animated graphics); synchronous "net meetings" via video or audio; group decision support systems; and interaction via "virtual reality" types of mechanisms, such as avatars. Current developments include extremely mobile or pervasive devices such as hand-held computers, wireless-enabled tablet PCs, and asynchronous digital voice message boards accessible from mobile phones.

These developments mean that courses may now combine face-to-face, traditional media, text-based CMC media, and new audiovisual media to deliver materials, coordinate group projects, provide access to processible information and discussions from local as well as international institutions, and foster interaction among students and external participants. Printed textbooks, articles, and chapters may be replaced with CD-Roms or online libraries, which can add audio, video, graphics, databases, and interactive exercises. Of course, traditional classes have used a variety of media, including chalkboards, music players, videocassette recorders and TV monitors, maps, and so on.

ALNs can be seen as a way of freeing the individual learner from time and space barriers to two-way communication, which, in supportive situations, can foster self-learning (Keegan, 1986). Learning networks can also be thought of as a way to increase the efficiency of educational delivery, applying industrial production methods of division of labor (Peters, 1988). A third approach emphasizes both the learner's independence and freedom of choice as well as the communication process of learning, because ALNs can provide access and guided conversation to diverse learners (Holmberg, 1989).

Many mediated courses use a mix of face-to-face meetings, online discussions (synchronous or asynchronous), and lectures delivered by television, videotape,

CD-Roms, or online multimedia. One pattern for a mixed media or "blended" or "hybrid" course is an intensive weeklong session on campus at the beginning of a year followed by online reading, discussion, and testing, such as for the University of Illinois online master's program in library science. Another pattern is face-to-face meetings at the beginning and end of a semester, as in Rutgers University's undergraduate communication internship program, during which students discuss and evaluate each other's experiences through a web-based structured discourse space. A third and probably the most common pattern for hybrid courses is regularly scheduled face-to-face sessions that are combined with online discussions and group work; an example of this is at the University of Central Florida, where many courses meet face to face only 1.5 hours a week instead of 3, and do the other half of the course online.

What do we know about the effects of using multiple media in online courses, or about the appropriate sequencing of such media? What theories can help to frame research questions about the effect of media mixes on the process and outcomes of online classes?

DO MEDIA DIRECTLY AFFECT LEARNING?

Whether media by themselves actually have measurable impacts on the process and outcomes of education is controversial. Clark (2001a) argued that results consistently show no significant learning benefits from any specific medium per se. Meta-analytic studies show (when controlling for differences in content or instructional method across media, for novelty effects for new media, for variations across instructors, curricular reform, or effort) little or no remaining independent effect of the medium (Clark & Craig, 2001; Russell, 1999; Schramm, 1977). The counter point of view says that, of course, pedagogy and content are the important variables, but certain media may be better suited than others to support specific types of content and/or specific pedagogies (e.g., collaborative learning strategies), thus representing independent effects of the medium (Kozma, 2001b; Orr, 1997).

As pointed out in Hiltz's (1994) study of a Virtual Classroom®, computer-mediated communication is especially well suited to collaborative or cooperative learning strategies. For example, most courses in the original 3-year Virtual Classroom® study included one or more "seminar"-type segments in which the students became the teachers. Individual or small groups of students were responsible for reading material not assigned to the rest of the class, preparing a written summary for the class of the most important ideas in the material, and leading a discussion on the topic or material for which they were responsible.

The online seminar format had several advantages compared to the face-to-face seminar. First of all, in the face-to-face situation the seminar format is generally restricted to small classes of very advanced students, because it is too time consuming to have more than about 15 students doing major presentations. Second, less advanced students may feel very embarrassed and do not present material well in oral reports to their peers, and are even worse at trying to play the role of teacher in conducting a discussion. In the written mode, students can take as long as they need to polish their presentations, and the emphasis is placed on the quality of their work and ideas, not their public speaking skills. Other students can read material in a much shorter time than it would take to sit through oral presentations. If the material is poorly presented, members of the class may press the "break" key, whereas etiquette dictates that they must sit and suffer through a poor student presentation in the face-to-face situation. Finally, in an online course it is easier for students to interact directly with each other, and provide class content, than in face-to-face classes (Quinn, Mehan, Levin, & Black,1983).

Another example of how collaborative learning is facilitated by ALN is the group project. At NJIT, most students do not live on campus, and are also working either part time or full time. Thus, it is almost impossible for a team of students to find a convenient time and place outside of class hours to work on a project together. The online asynchronous team conference not only allows them to work together "anytime, anywhere," but also motivates more equal participation, because the instructor can observe the group work and determine if all members have contributed to the project. Just knowing that the instructor can and will do this tends to discourage "free riding" or "social loafing" among group members.

Dede (1996), among others, emphasized the importance of "learning through doing," which involves individualized presentational and constructivist experiences in problem-solving, case-based contexts, available to students on demand. Dede maintained that new forms of distributed learning, especially those offering multimedia and hypermedia, have the potential to provide this kind of learning process. Multimedia educational applications supply information in multiple formats, allowing those with different learning styles to use material in preferred presentational modes (Alavi & Leidner, 2001). Hyperlinking capabilities allow the development of knowledge webs that provide distributed access to experts, archival resources, experiential environments, and collaborative learning. Other computer-based capabilities help to facilitate communication among participants while structuring group dialogue and decision making. Examples include using a group support system (GSS) in anonymous mode, fostering brainstorming to generate ideas for discussion, or providing a simulation of a newsroom for a journalism class.

RELEVANT MEDIA THEORIES

Research is a constant interplay between theory and evidence. There are several theories about the dimensions and characteristics of different media on the process and outcomes of group communication that can help to frame investigations of media-mix effects in online classrooms. Rice and Gattiker (2000; see also Culnan & Markus, 1987; Rice, 1993a) offered three propositions about the role of media characteristics in general.

First, media may be compared in many ways, and comparisons must take into account the communicative context and how the medium is implemented, so that no medium is absolutely preferable or inherently better or worse. The characteristics typically associated with specific media (discussed later) are not completely fixed or inherent but can result from intentional design, moderator roles, participation patterns, implementation, and user choices and involvement (Eastmond, 1993; Rice, 1987, 1999), although of course some features or capabilities are constrained or enabled by technology.

Second, CMC has many more capabilities than just the by-now familiar "overcoming constraints of time and space." Because content is processed through computers in digital form, the ability to reprocess, combine, and analyze information in many forms from multiple sources has profound implications (Rice & Gattiker, 2000).

Third, much of what we feel is "natural" about traditional media is largely an artifact resulting from the confounding of particular characteristics (e.g., material production, forms of access, oral or print mode, social conventions, etc.) with a particular communication medium in the context of familiar or habitual use (e.g., the traditional telephone in the home; Rice, 1993a, 1999; Smith & Dillon, 1999).

Bretz's Media Typology

In 1970, Bretz published a foundational analysis of media characteristics for instructional purposes. He first clarified that communication media are systems as well as subsystems of larger user systems such as instruction, advertising, and so on. The larger user system includes the sender and receiver, both of whom use the communication system (which includes people in the programming, etc.) Bretz noted, "Each medium requires the message to be encoded into a different format, using a different set of techniques, and resulting in a different kind of program" (p. 37) and each medium allows many kinds of programs (i.e., formatting). Thus, it is misleading to posit that a particular medium has one specific effect or single best application. Furthermore, a particular media system cannot be fully evaluated within its own system—it must be evaluated within the larger user system(s) and coordinated by the "user" with many other functions.

Bretz's typology argued that there were two primary dimensions of instructional media: telecommunication (transmission) versus recording/storing; and combinations of sound, visual (picture, line graphics, print), and motion (and semi-motion). Icons (pictures and line graphics) are more appropriate for representing people, places, and things, because they represent something; symbols (line graphics and print) are more appropriate for generalities and abstract concepts. Combinations of these two dimensions result in seven classes of media: audio-motion-visual, audio-still-visual, audio-semimotion, motion-visual, still-visual, audio, and print.

These seven types can be combined into multimedia, in sequential or simultaneous conditions. Thus, for instance, a still-visual (not time based; e.g., a photograph) can be synchronized with a time-based medium (e.g., videotaped panning and zooming over photographs). To serve for self-instruction and as an object of study, such a single or multiple medium needs playback, freeze, and other features under the control of the learner, while maintaining synchronization across all displays.

Social Presence and Media Richness

Social presence (Short, Williams, & Christie, 1976) and media richness (Daft & Lengel, 1986) theories both emphasize how communication media differ in the extent to which (a) they can overcome various communication constraints of time, location, permanence, distribution, participation, and distance; (b) transmit the social, symbolic, and nonverbal cues of human communication; and (c) convey equivocal information. The essential underlying principle is contingency theory.

A good match between the characteristics of a new medium (e.g., relatively high social presence or media richness in multimedia conferencing) and one's communication activities (e.g., equivocal tasks like strategic decision making) will lead to "better" (more effective, less time consuming, more satisfying, etc.) communication performance. Thus, a medium may not only be "too lean" for particular tasks, but also "too rich" for others.

Social presence theory argues that different media foster different levels of perceived intimacy and immediacy. Face-to-face contact yields the highest level of social presence, and asynchronous written communication provides the lowest level of social presence (Rice, 1993b; Short et al., 1976). Presence in general is thought to have an intensifying effect on media users, increasing or enhancing enjoyment, involvement, task performance and training, desensitization, persuasion, memory/socioemotion, and parasocial interaction (Lombard, Ditton, & Reich, 1997). Short et al. (1976) reviewed and conducted social psychological surveys and experiments that suggested a set of activities as likely to be affected by differences in a medium's social presence: less personal tasks (exchanging information, problem solving and making decisions, exchanging opinions, generating ideas), and more socioemotional tasks (persuasion, getting the other on one's side of an argument, resolving disagreements or conflicts, maintaining friendly relations/staying in touch, bargaining, and getting to know someone; Rice, 1993b).

Greater perceived social presence predicted greater student satisfaction in an interactive television class (Hackman & Walker, 1990). Bretz (1983) summarized a study of two audio conferencing systems and two video conferencing systems by Hough and Panko (1977). The video systems were rated on average as 20% more satisfactory for six personal (the socioemotional ones listed previously) activities than were the audio systems (48% vs. 40%), whereas only 3% more so for six impersonal (the more task-oriented ones listed previously) activities. Rice and Case (1983) found that upper-level university administrators rated e-mail as less appropriate for tasks requiring greater social presence—bargaining, negotiating, managing conflict. However, technical managers rated e-mail as somewhat more appropriate for those tasks, indicating that familiarity and social context can affect perceptions and effects of social presence. In another study, Gunawardena and Zittle (1997) analyzed a graduate course in distance education involving 50 students from five universities. They found that student satisfaction with the conference was primarily (58%) explained by social presence, followed by perception of equal opportunity to participate (12%), and somewhat by technical skills and experience with CMC, and attitude toward CMC.

Similarly, media richness theory proposes that the relation between media use and performance is influenced by task equivocality, media richness, and users' "media awareness" of the suitability of new media to these tasks. Media richness is the extent to which a medium can support language variety, feedback, nonverbal cues, and learning. Proposed rankings of media on social presence or richness scales are generally consistent across studies, although proposed associations of those perceptions with outcomes of usage of new organizational media for high or low task equivocality are weakly supported and inconsistent across studies (Rice, 1993b; Rice, D'Ambra, & More, 1998; Rice et al., 1992; Rice, Hughes, & Love, 1989). For example, managers in many studies use e-mail contrary to media richness predictions, CMC can support considerable socioemotional content, and media use does not have to be nor is necessarily intentional (Lea, 1991; Rice, 1987, 1993b; Rice et al., 1992; Rice & Love, 1987; Trevino, Lengel, & Daft, 1987). The negative effects associated with using media low in information richness or social presence for equivocal contexts may be limited to a narrow set of situations including laboratory experiments, zero-history groups, and short initial usage periods (Walther, 1992).

A text-based ALN would theoretically be classified as low on social presence. However, studies have shown that a sense of both personality and community can be generated in such a communication environment, often using a variety of communication conventions (e.g., keywords, shorthand, nonverbal cues in text, playfulness and humor, emoticons, and smilies), to increase social presence (Murphy & Collins, 1997; Rovai, 2002). Rice and Love (1987) found that one third of messages in a CMC forum contained socioemotional content, indicating that a medium with supposed low social presence can support quite social communication. Participants in the Gunawardena and Zittle (1997) study who perceived a high level of social presence wanted to enhance their experience (and satisfaction) by utilizing alternative forms of social-emotional expression, such as emoticons (e.g., the "smiley" or "winky" ;=)—i.e., punctuation and alphanumeric characters used to represent emotions).

Paradoxically, precisely because cues that ordinarily regulate speaking, turn taking, and attention are reduced or absent (e.g., physical appearance, voice, dress, gender, status, etc.; Rice, 1984), CMC may foster greater participation from and among students, especially those who are shy or anxious, are minorities or have speech or sight disabilities, or are not typically dominant in face-to-face settings. Discussion via CMC may include more diversity of viewpoints, egalitarian participation, interpretative risk taking, and challenges to textual authority than in traditional face-to-face settings. Furthermore, the relative lack of social presence in online settings can foster relationships with people who have more diverse social characteristics than might normally be encountered in person. CMC's very lack of forced immediate feedback (as in face-to-face interaction) gives participants more control over the timing and content of their self-disclosures.

Swan (2002) reported one of the most comprehensive comparisons of online media, assessing 22 course design factors and student perceptions across 73 online courses offered by the State University of New York (SUNY) Learning Network in spring 1999. The three most important influences on student perceptions were course design consistency and clarity, feedback and contact from course instructors, and valued and active discussion. Other studies have also discerned that computer-mediated communication can be conceptualized as a way to increase individual and dyadic interaction in the traditional large lecture course, thus taking a computer-assisted personalized approach (Thoennessen, Kashy, Tsai, & Davis, 1999). For example, students can identify with and work in groups via listservs, and poorly performing students can be individually contacted by personalized e-mail from the instructor to encourage better performance. Additionally, chat can be used as part of an examination support medium (Witfelt, Philipsen, & Kaiser, 2002).

The potential for more equal participation, however, does not necessarily mean equal attention from others (especially in noncooperative social contexts), because it is far easier to be selectively attentive in CMC than in face-to-face communication. For example, some argue that the use of CMC in traditional ways may just reinforce existing gender and power inequities (Brail, 1996; Collins-Jarvis, 1996; Ebben, 1993; Frissen, 1992; Selfe & Meyer, 1991; Sparks & van Zoonen, 1992). Precisely because context may be depersonalized due to anonymity and weak social feedback, online communication may be more disinhibited and critical, and lessen public awareness of social sanctions.

The general argument would be that for educational goals that involve more socioemotional or equivocal aspects, media with greater social presence or richness are more appropriate. Thus, an initial synchronous online meeting of class members, arriving with different backgrounds, might generate equivocality-reducing information in the minds of the students. Conversely, a print and/or online medium would be appropriate for reducing uncertainty by providing easy access to the syllabus and course schedule. The completely asynchronous online class and the completely face-to-face class *both* leave the students and teacher with only one communication medium.

OTHER CHARACTERISTICS AND INFLUENCES

Other theoretical approaches extend both the range of media characteristics as well as the influences on perceptions and use of media, including:

*   *Social contexts and influences:* Usage contexts (Moore & Jovanis, 1988), social influences (Fulk, 1993; Rice & Aydin, 1991; Rice, Grant, Schmitz, & Torobin, 1990), and symbolic aspects (Bozeman, 1993; Sitkin, Sutcliffe, & Barrios-Choplin, 1992; Trevino et al., 1987).
*   *Differences in users' status or role:* Status differences across lines of authority and organizational boundaries (D'Ambra & Rice, 1994), and distinctions between initiator and responder (Zmud, Lind, & Young, 1990).
*   *Changes in usage and understanding of a medium over time:* The ability to process social information in CMC content (in order to convey socioemotional content and to develop personal relationships with others) increases over time (Walther, 1992), experience with the medium and communication partners (Carlson & Zmud, 1994), the extent to which problem solving becomes routinized over time (Dawson, 1995; McKenney, Zack, & Doherty, 1992), and timeliness and sequential patterns in using different media (Valacich, Paranka, George, & Nunamaker, 1993).

Media synchronicity theory (MST) extends media richness theory to give a dynamic time-changing value to the richness of the media (Valacich, Paranka, George, & Nunamaker, 1993). MST proposes five significant media characteristics: *immediacy of feedback, symbol variety* (use more than one representation of the information or to match the symbol to the type of information), *parallelism* (number of channels that can simultaneously be in use in the medium), *rehearsability* (ability to read and edit messages before transmission or after reception), and *reprocessibility* (receiver may read, watch, or listen to the message more than once). Rich, synchronous media at one period may not be optimal at another period. When information *conveyance* is the task, media providing low synchronicity (low feedback and high parallelism) will be of benefit, whereas when information *convergence* is the goal (or task) of the users, media providing high synchronicity (high feedback and low parallelism) will be most appropriate. One can presume that the need of newly formed online classes to resolve ambiguity in group well-being and individual support can be served by high media synchronicity. The class needs for information such as what is provided by the syllabus (that can resolve uncertainty about the schedule and assignments) may be best communicated with low synchronicity media that allow reprocessibility.

Another extension of the media characteristics approach is Smith and Dillon's (1999) classification based on research related to *learning and motivation*. The authors proposed that the essential distinction in media attributes is the extent of support for learners' *cognitive* or *social* processing (to some extent related to conveyance and convergence). For example, text-based databases or organizers can support cognitive processing, whereas real-time video can help distant groups improve their social interactions. Smith and Dillon suggested three primary attributes of media that should differentially support these learning processes: *realism/bandwidth, feedback/interactivity,* and *branching/interface.* Greater bandwidth supports greater realism (images, motion) but may also make it more difficult to identify and ignore irrelevant information, swamping the abstract concepts communicated through word or sound. Feedback and interaction (via video, audio, and text) improve cognitive processing and learner motivation. Branching (or contingent response) provides instruction based on prior responses, thus tailoring the content to the user. Branching can also be simultaneous, as part of an interface providing contingent access to multiple resources.

Computer-based media have intrinsic advantages over traditional mass media for instruction, because interactive media can provide channels for interpersonal communication to reinforce and extend the learning. According to Lieberman (2001), particular characteristics possible through interactive media include: *network interconnectivity* (to diverse and updateable content), *interactivity, personalized content* (and format based on users' characteristics and choices), *user control* (over timing, format, and content), *communication* (asynchronous and synchronous, private or public), *multiple input and presentation modes* (providing greater entertainment and motivation), and *portability* (smaller, wireless, continuous access, in diverse environments). Kozma (2001a) identified five other media attributes that could facilitate learning: *present moving objects* onscreen, allow user to *manipulate objects,* present *complex contexts that in turn stimulate dynamic mental images, search and display information,* and provide *visual and social context.* Thus, for example, a multimedia computer-based approach may be better at conveying rich and complex social situations than may a face-to-face class, so that students can better understand and act in those environments.

Another significant technical and social factor is *critical mass,* which means enough initial users to stimulate rapid later adoption by others (Markus, 1990; Rice, 1982, 1990; Rice et al., 1990). The value of a communication network rises, and the relative cost of each person's potential adoption of the network decreases, more and more users engage through the system, as the number of possible interactions rises much faster than the number of additional participants. Eventually a critical mass develops, where there are sufficient users and interactions to sustain the social system and generate additional value to each participant. A critical mass of users also fosters initial and adaptive uses of the new medium to become shared with and accepted by subsequent users. Local critical masses (e.g., course teams or project groups) are especially crucial to the successful diffusion of a new communication medium, because members are more likely to share similar benefits and costs.

THEORIES OF EDUCATIONAL MEDIA

Some educational theories specifically consider the interaction of media characteristics with students' cognitive processes and abilities (as well as teaching methods, tasks, etc.; Clark & Salomon, 2001). These include:

- *Symbol systems theory* (Goodman, 1968) proposes specific dimensions of symbol systems (e.g., the extent to which a symbol system has explicit notations), so that each symbol system has different biases, or would foster different informational or behavioral aspects of learning.
- Olson's (1976) *theory of instructional means* asserts that media and techniques influence the development of relevant cognitive skills, because they influence how environmental information is perceived, converted, stored, and retrieved. The content of a medium affects the acquisition of knowledge through rules and principles, whereas message codes affect the development of skills and strategies. Hence, for example, text-based instruction may emphasize (be biased toward) analytic, scientific, and philosophical knowledge, whereas oral-based instruction may emphasize negotiation, social relations, and context.
- Salomon's (1979) *media attributes theory* argues that the mind as well as media uses symbols, and these mental symbol systems may be influenced by or acquired from media symbol systems. The more unique a medium's symbol system is, the more distinctive the required mental skills must be. Alternatively, the more the symbol system of the particular medium matches the student's learning style and mental representations, the easier the student can process and understand the message. Some cognitive skills can be improved through experiencing their use in media, whereas others can be inhibited by being dominated by various media symbol systems.
- *Dual coding theory* (Paivio, 1985) claims that recall scores are greater when a learner processes both words and pictures, because visual and verbal information are separately cognitively coded. Visuals can be recalled from various relative positions, but text can only be processed sequentially. Thus, perceiving and storing material in two coding systems improves recall and understanding.

The fundamental assumption of these theories—that the medium per se can influence learning outcomes—is subject to several critiques. Clark (2001a), as did Bretz (1970), argued that any media system can provide most types of symbols, and thus effects are not logically necessarily due to a particular medium. Some symbolic modes may serve no instructional purpose, and many modes may serve the same cognitive processing purpose. Another question Clark raised is whether images or propositions are the more fundamental cognitive representations, thus invoking visual/audio or textual media codes. Or, if most content is processed through propositional rules, then the original image or textual form may not matter much, except in the initial stages of decoding (Clark & Salomon, 2001), which at least would affect learning speed. Hence, different media modes may support different cognitive functions, rather than having specific cognitive effects. That is, sequential logic could be fostered through computer programming but could also be developed through personal tutoring.

Additionally, does a skill developed through use of a particular medium transfer to other situations? Media symbol systems may cultivate particular cognitive skills, but those may well not be especially useful, unique, or transferable. Clark and Salomon (2001) asserted that the active learner affects how any of these stimuli are experienced, anyway—so anticipations, assumptions, or expectations about a particular medium, including expected levels of effort required as well as student self-efficacy, may be the most significant influences, often affecting learning positively, whereas satisfaction and enjoyment are less associated with learning. Subsequent tests of dual coding theory concluded that visual and verbal forms of instruction do not by themselves affect memory activation.

SOME STUDIES OF THE EFFECTS
OF EDUCATIONAL MEDIA MIXES

As should be clear from the previous review, no one medium has all of the characteristics that perfectly match the needs of ALN users through all phases of a course. Furthermore, any medium might be sufficient to accomplish some or even many of the needs of teachers and learners, depending on the pedagogical approach and the social context. In combination, the sufficiency of any medium may be increased by judicious use of complementary media, or even the same medium, in various time periods or phases. The following sections review studies that may provide some evidence related to the supposition that combinations of media with different sets of characteristics will result in better outcomes than relying on text-based ALN alone.

Video and Audio Content

By the late 1960s, there was enough experience with educational uses of radio and video instructional technologies to allow a comprehensive review by Chu and Schramm (1967; see also Schramm, 1977). These instructional media studies showed that, about 75% of the time, there was no significant difference between video/television and face-to-face instruction; the other 25% of the time was about evenly split between improved and decreased learning. However, video had certain advantages: enriches audiovisual content, puts more effort into lessons/program, can raise average lesson quality, permits access by multiple audiences over multiple time periods, and can allow the instructor do other important activities (e.g., "interaction, understanding, encouragement and informal progress appraisal ... group leader ... adult model to emulate"; Bretz, 1970, p. 50).

On the other hand, there were also several sources of communication failure associated with video and radio instruction: transmission or recording, program display subsystem, program production, and message origination. Applying Bretz's (1970) notion of higher-level media constraints, video is not good for a large amount of print, or for high-resolution, print. Also, full motion, although transmittable through both streaming video or full-motion video, is not usually needed for instructional presentations and can be a distraction (Bretz, 1970). The added realism or dynamic quality doesn't seem to have much of an effect on learning outcomes, although it may affect some aspect of the learner's affective domain (or, as noted earlier, even create sensory overload and distraction). Indeed, Matarazzo and Selen (2000) found that students in distributed work groups in a narrowband video condition reported higher satisfaction and lower task completion time compared to those in a broadband video condition.

Kelsey (2000)—who studied 73 students and 5 site facilitators in an animal science course delivered to five locations by interactive compressed video (ICV) technology—also highlighted some of the obstacles to interaction. Very little interaction occurred in any of the types of course communication forms (face-to-face interactions among students and facilitator within each site, question-and-answer sessions at the end of each class, a web-based discussion board, e-mailing of content-related questions, and informal luncheon discussions with guest speakers at the originating site). In general, interactive compressed video did not foster much interaction among participants, especially with participants at other sites. The primary barriers to interactions included social concerns, technology failures, time, content, camera shyness, site facilitator's role, and additional time for processing content. However, knowing that they could be seen through the system did increase students' sensory awareness, their attention, and their modeling of appropriate behavior, compared to students working with delayed videotape.

Machtmes and Asher (2000) analyzed 11 experiments that used video and either one-way or two-way audio compared to traditional instruction. There was little average difference, although there was considerable variation. Of the 10 factors evaluated, the only positive effect was due to the presence of two-way interaction. A study of a two-way audio/two-way video system of delivery (Hilgenberg & Tolone, 2000) found no difference in students' satisfaction levels or ratings of the instructor between main site and remote site participants, nor in opportunities for critical thinking between students in general in the two sites. However, education students in the main site perceived greater critical thinking opportunities than did education students at the remote site, or nursing students in either site. Thus, it's possible that familiarity with pedagogical processes is necessary to take advantage of those complex approaches, regardless of medium.

One of the most rigorous designs testing for effects of educational video media compared three forms of video—videoconference and one-frame webcasting across a LAN, a two-frame webcast across a LAN, and a three-frame webcast across the Internet, while applying the same presenter and teaching material in each condition—on three aspects: presentational, technical, and educational (Reynolds & Mason, 2002). There were no differences in presenter and teaching material across the media conditions. However, videoconferencing was deemed more suitable for major lectures whereas webcasting was better for a one-to-one situation. In terms of technical aspects, webcasting demands, setup time, and audio were better than for videoconferencing, but suffered from bandwidth congestion. The three-frame Internet webcasting benefited from the use of a chat box that allowed students to consider their comments before responding.

Audio combined with (tele)graphics is a less frequently used instructional medium, but does provide the two primary communication modes of sound and text/images. Oliver and McLoughlin (1997) studied the role of interactivity in this mixed medium through analysis of videotapes of six teachers providing audiographics lessons to remote schools in Western Australia. Although various kinds of classroom interactions were possible within the same technological media combination, the teachers tended to use didactic instructional approaches that limited learner-initiated communication and collaborative activity. There was little communication between teacher and students on equal terms, to pursue meaning, or to construct personal ideas, and the teachers tended to use the communication feature to "control" the remote classroom. Partially this was due to an incomplete understanding by the teachers of the possible types and forms of interactivity available through computer conferencing, but such results warn of the more general issue that instructor pedagogy can be the most constraining and limiting influence on student learning, regardless of medium.

When using or assessing video conferencing, one must consider the interaction of video characteristics with the social context. Bretz (1983) used the example of video conferencing to show that different design, image size, perspective, and depth of field characteristics of different video conferencing systems represent different kinds of social distance, which may or may not be appropriate for the kinds of learning situation desired (e.g., group discussion vs. public lecture). As a related example, an exploratory study by Steeples (2002) of a course involving learning technology professionals concluded that both digital video clips (of the "talking head" variety) and audio clips could be rapidly created. The participants were initially uneasy with the video clips, and found that it was much more engaging to have an interviewer–interviewee clip than a single talking head. The participants felt that the use of video or audio clips did help create a sense of social presence, and that the video clips were helpful in enabling the learning community to exchange and explain aspects of their professional practice. Note that the medium is not the crucial factor here: It was the ability of students to adapt the medium (i.e., conceptualizing that there were different formats and display approaches within the larger media system) that allowed a more effective use to emerge.

Adding Additional Media to Text-Based Asynchronous Learning

Text-based communication may not create an optimal learning environment for some learners, given that learners have different learning styles and preferences in terms of type or medium of information (Kim, Hiltz, Scher, & Turoff, 2003). For example, nonverbal learners are likely to learn better with nonverbal materials, such as images (Monaghan & Stenning, 1988). ALN based on text-only communication, by which information is organized sequentially, may not be an optimal communication mode for random learners (Leuthold, 1999). Thus, at least for some students, combining one or more other media with text-based asynchronous text may improve learning.

Incorporating Synchronous Chat

Spencer (2002; Spencer & Hiltz, 2003) studied the effect of mixed-media modes on teachers' and students' satisfaction with the learning process in 29 course sections. Media mode, the independent variable, had four levels derived from the mixture of asynchronous discussion forums with various levels of synchronous media use: ALN only, ALN plus face to face, ALN with one synchronous session, and ALN plus multiple synchronous chats. Instructors reported during interviews that (synchronous) chat sessions were hard to schedule because of students' time commitments, thus making it very difficult to achieve critical mass. The hypothesis that social presence would be higher in courses that included chat than in ALN-only courses was not supported. Nevertheless, many instructors reported some small success in their first chat session and felt that the experience led to better facilitation in subsequent sessions. Significantly, students found chat more "rewarding" and less "complex" in classes that scheduled chat sessions two or more times than did students in ALN-only classes, meaning that student familiarity or experience with a particular (here, computer-based) medium can improve their perceptions of that medium's social presence.

Lantz (2001) similarly found that, over time, ratings for chat meetings rose for four participants who had three meetings using chat, one using a collaborative virtual environment (CVE), and one using face to face. However, although task-oriented work was rated higher in the chat and CVE meetings (indeed, the face-to-face meeting encountered excessive social communication—i.e., it was too rich a medium), the range of topics discussed was narrower. Veerman, Andriessen, and Kanselaar (2000) noted that the kinds of argumentation, focusing, and production of constructive activities among pairs of students using synchronous CMC (NetMeeting) varied according to different discourse facilitation (i.e., the teacher's pedagogical style). Haythornthwaite's (2000) study of four multimedia distance learning classes found that those students who use the system more for communication also communicated more frequently with others in general and had more socially supportive relations. The closer ties helped foster a stronger sense of belonging to the class, and perceptions of greater social interaction among other students. Furthermore, pairs who had strong ties used more media to interact and to maintain their ties, including the development of greater "virtual proximity" by using chat (IRC) during synchronous classes and by exchanging e-mails late at night.

Adding Pictures, Graphics, or Video

Media richness theory and social presence theory predict that having a digital (online) photo of other students available to class members should result in stronger, faster feelings of affection and attraction among the members of a virtual team or class than having text only. However, media synchronicity theory or social information processing (SIP) theory assume that in some ways text-only asynchronous communication may be superior to face-to-face meetings or other supposedly "richer" media, allowing users to construct idealized impressions of the members of the class over time, and thus to form strong feelings of group identity.

Walther, Slovacek, and Tidwell (2001) conducted a study of eight cross-national student teams working together, some with text-only CMC, and some with a digital photo gallery of the team members. In new, unacquainted teams, seeing one's partners' pictures promoted the swift formation of feelings of affection and attraction. In long-term online groups, however, introducing photographs after group members had developed a sense of bonding "dampened affinity." Indeed, participants in groups with no photographs reported the highest levels of intimacy and affection and felt the CMC system was the most helpful in achieving a good impression! Thus, when it comes to media richness, more is not necessarily better, and sequencing or timing can make a difference.

In many disciplines, graphics can be very valuable for representing a complex set of relationships (e.g., flow charts or conceptual/causal diagrams). Suthers, Hundhausen, and Girardeau (2003) reported an exploratory comparison in one course that compared synchronous online communication using a graph that students could build together, with face-to-face communication in which a similar graphing tool was present. Suthers et al. found that the visual knowledge representation played a greater role in supporting discourse among the dispersed learners than among the face-to-face learners, and it seemed to benefit their task communication in such areas as evidential relation and epistemic classification. These researchers plan to focus in the future on using such representational graphics for collaborative interaction in the asynchronous condition.

In one study of adding video to ALN, Matarrazzo and Selen (2000) had participants use two screens, one with shared task-oriented documents displayed and one with either high- or low-bandwidth video of participants' faces; all participants also had an audio channel. Subjects in the narrowband video condition focused more on their task, completed it faster, and were more satisfied than those in a wideband video condition, who seem to have been distracted by the streaming video, especially with larger numbers of participants (4 vs. 2).

On the other hand, Nancy Mundorf, director of the Early Childhood Learning Community distance learning program at the University of Cincinnati, related a case of the successful use of video clips plus conference calls to supplement the use of their Blackboard® ALN system for the student teaching segment of the curriculum. She described their experiences as follows (personal communication, 2002):

We had 13 students from around the country ready to student teach this fall.... We created four "best practice videos" of 30–45 minutes of raw footage focusing on a master teacher that became a part of the student teaching seminar. It was further decided that having student teachers have themselves videotaped and then discussing the videotape on a conference call with the student teacher, mentor teacher, and university supervisor would be acceptable in assessing the student's teaching....

The student was asked to write a journal entry the day of the taping and send it to the mentor and university supervisor as a lead in to the video. Approximately one week later, the student teacher, mentor teacher, and university professor had a conference call while all three watched the video on their own computers. The conferences were quite reflective and not defensive. Student teachers were able to pick up on habits, things they missed, expressions on a child's face, and other subtle things because we were watching them together. They could remember what they were thinking and why they did something and explain their reasoning while we watched. I felt the conferences were more reflective and reached a greater depth than the traditional face-to-face meeting.

Adding Audio

There are now several software packages that allow digitized audio to be posted for playback as part of asynchronous computer-mediated communication. This became of particular interest at the New Jersey Institute of Technology in 2001–2002 when an external accrediting team ruled that students in online programs had to have courses in which they made "oral presentations" to the class, not just written ones. In a class on computers and society, students were told of the new requirement and asked to share their knowledge and tips about how to best and most easily produce a 3- to 5-minute oral presentation to be posted in an online class conference. All the students managed to do it, and expressed some enthusiasm about how this made them feel that they knew one another better. Several suggested that this be made a mandatory addition to the self-introduction that each student must make at the beginning of the online course.

However, in the few studies analyzing adding a digital audio capability to asynchronous communication, the results were mixed. Bargeron et al. (2002) found that when given a choice of text versus audio in threaded discussions, subjects were more likely to choose text and reply to text messages, because they found it faster to read text than to listen to audio, and easier to edit text inputs than to edit audio comments. On the other hand, as summarized previously, Steeples (2000) found some promise for the use of audio annotations for video clips, for researchers presenting to one another about professional practice issues. However, Steeples' subjects reported that it was more difficult to pay attention to content in the video-only condition. The participants did report that adding voice annotations to the video clips was useful for providing background or contextual information.

SUMMARY

One rather broad conclusion to these kinds of studies is that there probably is no necessary (at least not simple or linear) causal relationship between the use of any particular new medium and success in teaching or learning. Thus, teachers and students will have to understand the possible new roles and responsibilities that come with these technological developments (Gibson, 1996). Furthermore, as Alavi and Leidner (2001) state, "It is important to conceptualize technology features and attributes in a manner directly relevant to instructional and learning processes" (p. 5). For example, constructivist approaches to student learning should understand how ALNs can foster greater participation, collaboration, feedback, and involvement by course members. Also needed is extensive and creative professional development, for both instructors and learners, to develop new strategies that emphasize collaboration, critical thinking, and lifelong learning, and how new media (including "simple" text-based ALNs) may help to support these processes.

As part of that development, administrators, teachers, and learners need to become more familiar with the array and implications of the primary media characteristics discussed or identified by this review of theories and research on media in general and newer ALN media in particular. Each of these media has a learning curve and some difficult challenges. It is probable that an instructor would do best to select only one of these supplementary modes of interaction, and foster multiple uses of that medium and the development of a critical mass of contributions and participants, while emphasizing the primary use of text-based asynchronous exchanges, structured in various ways (e.g., conversational threads or topic-based forums). In terms of media choice for online learning, the data tend to support the point of view that many different media can be sufficient to support teaching and learning. Adding the "newest" medium, such as full-motion video, may be distracting and counterproductive. Use of synchronous chat, a picture gallery of class members, or asynchronous audio clips may increase the sense of social presence and help a class to form a virtual learning community more quickly.

It is important to distinguish between the effects of the *delivery (conveyance) technology* versus those of the *instructional (convergence) technology*. Often, instructional approaches are confounded empirically or conceptually with the delivery medium or process (Clark, 2001b). For example, Clark and Craig (2001) pointed out that "interactivity" is really an instructional method (functionality)—feedback and content based on student response—and not a characteristic intrinsic to select media. There may be different evaluation criteria and possibly even data and analysis for each (cost, time, number of students, etc. for the delivery technology; learning, socialization, etc. for the instructional technology). Therefore, Simonson, Schlosser, and Hanson (1999) advocated developing a set of equivalent learning experiences that would be available to both distance and local students. Sometimes, a particular criterion learning goal requires longer or most costly instructional technology, and there may be different evaluations for different stakeholders across delivery and instructional technologies (i.e., teachers, administrators, students). Swan (2002) proposed that the most significant role of technology is to foster opportunities for interaction among the participants, which emphasizes the convergence aspect.

Our own position is that you can do many, if not most, things in face-to-face classrooms that you can do with online media. However, CMC can also support new, different class processes, that, if not impossible, would at least be very difficult and require a lot of intentionality to accomplish in face-to-face settings. This includes in-process interactivity and cross-student and even out-of-class communication.

Of course, the most important variables are still how the instructor applies these various media characteristics in combination with a pedagogical strategy to lead the students to engage in fruitful discussion and collaboration, student learning styles, and desired course outcomes (ranging from cognitive to affective to behavioral; Alavi & Leidner, 2001). Media, teachers, administrators, learners, and their family and friends may all interact to foster or impede different kinds of cognitive and social understandings. The best implementation strategy is to identify what instructional technologies (methods) are suitable for what goals, and find the media functionalities (available in a variety of communication media) that best support those methods, in order to lower cost and time while increasing access (Clark & Craig, 2001). Much remains to be understood about various media characteristics in ALNs, and their relative advantages and disadvantages.

QUESTIONS FOR DISCUSSION AND RESEARCH

1. Clark's famous "delivery truck" statement at the beginning of this chapter was originally made before the Internet and online education existed. Do you think it is true that ALN no more shapes the content of a course than a delivery truck changes the contents of the packages inside it? What theories or evidence can you cite to support your position?

2. How do you think that the spread of handhelds, tablet PCs, and high-bandwidth wireless Internet connections will affect the practicality of combining various other digital media with text-based asynchronous communication in courses? What kinds of studies should be conducted to identify problems and possibilities for online learning that have been introduced by such new technologies?

3. Can you provide an example from your own experience in which a medium that was supposedly low in social presence or media richness, or otherwise supposedly insufficient for the education purpose, was used in such a way as to foster significant learning or innovation? Alternatively, can you provide an example in which one or more media with high social presence or media richness were used in such a way as to limit learning and creativity?

4. Select five of the media characteristics provided in the section on "Other Characteristics and Influences" to analyze and compare a very traditional learning context—a large lecture class scheduled twice a week—and a new learning context—an ALN with links to multimedia Internet pages and dyadic "chat."

5. Which courses or departments in your college or university use multiple media to enhance student learning? Which seems to be the most successful? Using the theories and research in this chapter, suggest why this is the case.

REFERENCES

Alavi, M., & Leidner, D. E. (2001). Research commentary: Technology-mediated learning—a call for greater depth and breadth of research. *Information Systems Research, 12*(1), 1–10.

Bargeron, D., Grudin, J., Gupta, A., Sanocki, E., Li, F., & Leetiernan, S. (2002). Asynchronous collaboration around multimedia applied to on-demand education. *Journal of Management Information Systems, 18*(4), 117–145.

Berge, Z., & Mrozowski, S. (2001). Review of research in distance education, 1990 to 1999. *American Journal of Distance Education, 15*(3), 5–19.

Bozeman, D. (1993). Toward a limited rationality perspective of managerial media selection in organizations. In D. Moore (Ed.), *Academy of Management best papers proceedings* (pp. 278–282). Madison, WI: Omni.

Brail, S. (1996). The price of admission: Harassment and free speech in the wild, wild west. In I. L. Cherny & E. Weise (Eds.), *Wired-women: Gender and new realities in cyberspace* (pp. 157–182). Seattle, WA: Seal.

Bretz, R. (1970). *A taxonomy of communication media.* Englewood Cliffs, NJ: Educational Technology Publications.

Bretz, R. (1983). *Media for interactive communication.* Beverly Hills, CA: Sage.

Carlson, J., & Zmud, R. (1994). Channel expansion theory: A dynamic view of media and information richness perceptions. In D. Moore (Ed.), *Best papers Proceedings of the Academy of Management* (pp. 280–284). Madison, WI: Omni.

Chu, G., & Schramm, W. (1967). *Learning from television: What the research says.* Washington, DC: National Association of Educational Broadcasters.

Clark, R. E. (2000). Evaluating distance education: Strategies and cautions. *Quarterly Review of Distance Education, 1*(3), 16.

Clark, R. E. (Ed.). (2001a). *Learning from media: Arguments, analysis, and evidence.* Greenwich, CT: Information Age Publishing.

Clark, R. E. (2001b). Media are "mere vehicles": The opening argument. In R. E. Clark (Ed.), *Learning from media: Arguments, analysis, and evidence* (pp. 1–12). Greenwich, CT: Information Age Publishing.

Clark, R. (2001c). New directions: Evaluating distance education technologies. In R. E. Clark (Ed.), *Learning from media: Arguments, analysis, and evidence* (pp. 299–317). Greenwich, CT: Information Age Publishing.

Clark, R., & Craig, T. (2001). What about multimedia effects on learning? In R. E. Clark (Ed.), *Learning from media: Arguments, analysis, and evidence* (pp. 89–101). Greenwich, CT: Information Age Publishing.

Clark, R. E., & Salomon, G. (2001). Why should we expect media to teach anyone anything? In R. E. Clark (Ed.), *Learning from media: Arguments, analysis, and evidence* (pp. 37–70). Greenwich, CT: Information Age Publishing.

Collins-Jarvis, L. (1996, May). *Discriminatory messages in on-line discussion groups: The role of gender identity and social context.* Paper presented at the International Communication Association, Chicago, IL.

Culnan, M. J., & Markus, M. L. (1987). Information technologies. In F. Jablin, L. Putnam, K. Roberts, & L. Porter (Eds.), *Handbook of organizational communication* (pp. 420–443). Newbury Hills, CA: Sage.

Daft, R. L., & Lengel, R. H. (1986). Organizational information requirements, media richness and structural design. *Management Science, 32*(5), 554–571.

D'Ambra, J., & Rice, R. E. (1994). The equivocality of media richness: A multi-method approach to analyzing selection of voice mail for equivocal tasks. *IEEE Transactions on Professional Communication, 37*(4), 231–239.

Dawson, K. (1995). Comments on "Read me what it says on your screen...." *Technology Studies, 2*, 80–85.

Dede, C. (1996). The evolution of distance education: Emerging technologies and distributed learning. *American Journal of Distance Education, 10*(2), 4–36.

Eastmond, D. (1993). Adult distance study through computer conferencing. *Distance Education, 15*(1), 129–151.

Ebben, M. (1993, October). *Women on the net: An exploratory study of gender dynamics on the Soc.women computer network.* Paper presented at the Organization for the Study of Communication, Language and Gender 16th Annual Conference, Tempe, AZ.

Frissen, V. (1992). Trapped in electronic cages? Gender and new information technologies in the public and private domain: An overview of research. *Media, Culture & Society, 14*, 31–39.

Fulk, J. (1993). Social construction of communication technology. *Academy of Management Journal, 36*(5), 921–950.

Gibson, C. (1996). Toward emerging technologies and distributed learning: Challenges and change. *American Journal of Distance Education, 10*(2), 47–49.

Goodman, N. (1968). *Language of art.* Indianapolis, IN: Hackett.

Gunawardena, C., & Zittle, F. (1997). Social presence as a predictor of satisfaction within a computer-mediated conferencing environment. *American Journal of Distance Education, 11*(3), 8–26.

Hackman, M., & Walker, K. (1990). Instructional communication in the televised classroom: The effects of system design and teacher immediacy on student learning and satisfaction. *Communication Education, 39*(3), 196–209.

Harasim, L. (Ed.). (1990). *Online education: Perspectives on a new environment.* New York: Praeger.

Haythornthwaite, C. (2000). Online personal networks: Size, composition and media use among distance learners. *New Media & Society, 2*(2), 195–226.

Hilgenberg, C., & Tolone, N. (2000). Student perceptions of satisfaction and opportunities for critical thinking in distance education by interactive video. *American Journal of Distance Education, 14*(3), 59–74.

Hiltz, S. R. (1986). The "vitrual classroom": Using comptuer-mediated communication for university teaching. *Journal of Communication, 36*(2), 95–104.

Hiltz, S. R. (1994). *The virtual classroom: Learning without limits via computer networks.* Norwood, NJ: Ablex.

Holmberg, B. (1989). *Theory and practice of distance education.* London: Routledge.

Hough, R., & Panko, R. (1977). *Teleconferencing systems: A state of the art survey and preliminary analysis.* Menlo Park, CA: Stanford Research Institute.

Keegan, D. (1986). *The foundations of distance education.* London: Croom Helm.

Kelsey, K. D. (2000). Participant interaction in a course delivered by interactive compressed video technology. *American Journal of Distance Education, 14*(1), 63–74.

Kim, E., Hiltz, S. R., Scher, J., & Turoff, M. (2003, August). *Multimedia diversification of the ALN learning environment.* Paper presented at the Americas Conference on Information Systems, Tampa, FL.

Kozma, R. (2001a). Kozma reframes and extends his counter argument. In R. E. Clark (Ed.), *Learning from media: Arguments, analysis, and evidence* (pp. 179–198). Greenwich, CT: Information Age Publishing.

Kozma, R. (2001b). Learning with media. In R. E. Clark (Ed.), *Learning from media: Arguments, analysis, and evidence.* Greenwich, CT: Information Age Publishing.

Lantz, A. (2001). Meetings in a distributed group of experts: Comparing face-to-face, chat and collaborative virtual environments. *Behaviour & Information Technology, 20*(2), 111–117.

Lea, M. (1991). Rationalist assumptions in cross-media comparisons of computer-mediated communication. *Behaviour and Information Technology, 10*(1), 153–172.

Leuthold, J. H. (1999). Is computer-based learning right for everyone? In *Proceedings of 32nd Hawaii International Conference on Systems Sciences* (CD-Rom ed.). Washington, DC: IEEE Computer Society.

Lieberman, D. (2001). Using interactive media in communication campaigns for children and adolescents. In R. E. Rice & C. K. Atkin (Eds.), *Public communication campaigns* (3rd ed., pp. 373–388). Thousand Oaks, CA: Sage.

Lombard, M., Ditton, T., & Reich, R. (1997). The role of screen size in viewer responses to television fare. *Communication Reports, 10*(1), 95–106.

Machtmes, K., & Asher, J. (2000). A meta-analysis of the effectiveness of telecourses in distance education. *American Journal of Distance Education, 14*(1), 27–46.

Markus, M. L. (1990). Toward a critical mass theory of interactive media: Universal access, interdependence and diffusion. In J. Fulk & C. Steinfield (Eds.), *Organizations and communication technology* (pp. 194–218). Newbury Park, CA: Sage.

Matarazzo, G., & Selen, G. (2000). The value of video in work at a distance: Addition or distraction? *Behavior & Information Technology, 19*(5), 339–348.

McKenney, J., Zack, M., & Doherty, V. (1992). Complementary communication media: A comparison of electronic mail and face-to-face communication in a programming team. In N. N. R. Eccles (Ed.), *Networks and organizations: Structure, form and action* (pp. 262–287). Boston, MA: Harvard Business School Press.

Monaghan, P., & Stenning, K. (1998, August). *Effects of representation modality and thinking style on learning to solve reasoning problems.* Paper presented at the 20th Annual Meeting of the Cognitive Science Society, Madison, WI.

Moore, A., & Jovanis, P. (1988). Modeling media choices in business organizations: Implications for analyzing telecommunications-transportation interactions. *Transportation Research, 22A*, 257–273.

Murphy, K. L., & Collins, M. P. (1997). Development of communication conventions in instructional electronic chats. *FirstMonday, 2*(11). Retrieved October 15, 2003, from http://www.firstmonday.dk/issues/issue2_11/murphy

Oliver, R., & McLoughlin, C. (1997). Interactions in audiographics teaching and learning environments. *American Journal of Distance Education, 11*(1), 34–54.

Olson, D. (1976). Towards a theory of instructional means. *Educational Psychologist, 12*, 14–35.

Orr, B. (1997). *A Significant Difference.* Retrieved October 15, 2003, from http://teleeducation.nb.ca/english/article.cfm

Paivio, A. (1985). *Mental representations: A dual approach*: New York: Oxford University Press.

Peters, O. (1988). Distance teaching and industrial production: A comparative interpretation in outline. In D. Sewart, D. Keegan, & B. Holmberg (Eds.), *Distance education: International perspectives* (pp. 95–113). New York: Routledge.

Quinn, C., Mehan, H., Levin, J., & Black, S. (1983). Real education in non-real time: The use of electronic message systems for instruction. *Instructional Science, 11*, 313–327.

Reynolds, P. A., & Mason, R. (2002). On-line video media for continuing professional development in dentistry. *Computers and Education, 39*(1), 65–98.

Rice, R. E. (1982). Communication networking in computer conferencing systems: A longitudinal study of group roles and system structure. In M. Burgoon (Ed.), *Communication yearbook* (Vol. 6, pp. 925–944). Newbury Park, CA: Sage.

Rice, R. E. (1984). Mediated group communication. In R. E. Rice et al. (Eds.), *The new media: Communication, research and technology* (pp. 129–154). Newbury Park, CA: Sage.

Rice, R. E. (1987). Computer-mediated communication and organizational innovation. *Journal of Communication, 37*(4), 65–94.

Rice, R. E. (1990). Computer-mediated communication system network data. Theoretical concerns and empirical examples. *International Journal of Man–Machine Studies, 32*(6), 627–647.

Rice, R. E. (1992). Contexts of research on organizational computer-mediated communication: A recursive review. In M. Lea (Ed.), *Contexts of computer-mediated communication* (pp. 113–144). London: Harvester-Wheatsheaf.

Rice, R. E. (1993a). Artifacts, freedoms, paradoxes and inquiries: Some ways new media challenge traditional mass media and interpersonal effects paradigms. *MultiMedia Review/Virtual Reality World, 4*(2), 30–35.

Rice, R. E. (1993b). Media appropriateness: Using social presence theory to compare traditional and new organizational media. *Human Communication Research, 19*(4), 451–484.

Rice, R. E. (1999). What's new about new media? Artifacts and paradoxes. *New Media and Society, 1*(1), 24–32.

Rice, R. E., & Aydin, C. (1991). Attitudes towards new organizational technology: Network proximity as a mechanism for social information processing. *Administrative Science Quarterly, 36*, 219–244.

Rice, R. E., & Case, D. (1983). Computer-based messaging in the university: A description of use and utility. *Journal of Communication, 33*(1), 131–152.

Rice, R. E., D'Ambra, J., & More, E. (1998). Cross-cultural comparison of organizational media evaluation and choice. *Journal of Communication, 48*(3), 3–26.

Rice, R. E., & Gattiker, U. (2000). New media and organizational structuring. In F. Jablin & L. Putnam (Eds.), *New handbook of organizational communication* (pp. 544–581). Newbury Park, CA: Sage.

Rice, R. E., Grant, A., Schmitz, J., & Torobin, J. (1990). Individual and network influences on the adoption and perceived outcomes of electronic messaging. *Social Networks, 12*(1), 27–55.

Rice, R. E., Hart, P., Torobin, J., Shook, D., Tyler, J., Svenning, L., et al. (1992). Task analyzability, use of new media, and effectiveness: A multi-site exploration of media richness. *Organization Science, 3*(4), 475–500.

Rice, R. E., Hughes, D., & Love, G. (1989). Usage and outcomes of electronic messaging at an R&D organization: Situational constraints, job level, and media awareness. *Office: Technology and People, 5*(2), 141–161.

Rice, R. E., & Love, G. (1987). Electronic emotion: Socio-emotional content in a computer-mediated communication network. *Communication Research, 14*(1), 85–105.

Rovai, A. A. P. (2002). A preliminary look at the structural differences of higher education classroom communities in traditional and ALN courses. *Journal of Asynchronous Learning Networks, 6*(1). Retrieved October 15, 2003, from www.aln.org/publications/jaln/v6n1_rovai.asp

Rumble, G. (2001). Re-inventing distance education, 1971–2001. *International Journal of Lifelong Education, 20*(½), 31–43.

Russell, T. (1999). *The no significance difference phenomenon.* Chapel Hill: North Carolina State University Office of Instructional Telecommunications.

Salomon, G. (1979). *Interaction of media, cognition and learning.* San Francisco: Jossey-Bass.

Salomon, G. (1981). *Communication and education.* Beverly Hills, CA: Sage.

Schramm, W. (1977). *Big media, little media.* Beverly Hills, CA: Sage.

Selfe, C., & Meyer, P. (1991). Testing claims for on-line conferences. *Written Communication, 8*(2), 163–192.

Short, J., Williams, E., & Christie, B. (1976). *The social psychology of telecommunications.* London: Wiley.

Simonson, M., Schlosser, C., & Hanson, D. (1999). Theory and distance education: A new discussion. *American Journal of Distance Education, 13*(1), 60–75.

Sitkin, S., Sutcliffe, K., & Barrios-Choplin, J. (1992). A dual-capacity model of communication media choice in organizations. *Human Communication Research, 18*(4), 563–598.

Smith, P. L., & Dillon, C. L. (1999). Comparing distance learning and classroom learning: Conceptual considerations. *American Journal of Distance Education, 13*(2), 6–23.

Sparks, C., & van Zoonen, L. (1992). Gender and technology. *Media, Culture and Society, 14*, 5–7.

Spencer, D. (2002). *A field study of the use of synchronous computer-mediated communication in asynchronous learning networks.* Unpublished doctoral dissertation, Rutgers University, Newark, NJ.

Spencer, D., & Hiltz, S. R. (2003). A field study of use of synchronous chat in online courses. In *35th Annual Hawaii International Conference on System Sciences* (CD-Rom ed.). Washington DC: : IEEE Computer Society.

Steeples, C. (2002). Voice annotation of multimedia artifacts: Reflective learning in distributed professional communities. In *Proceedings of the 35th Annual Hawaii International Conference on System Sciences* (CD Rom-ed.). Washington, DC: IEEE Computer Society.

Suthers, D., Hundhausen, C., & Giradeau, L. (2003). Comparing the roles of representations in face-to-face and online computer supported collaborative learning. *Computers and Education, 41*(4), 335–351.

Swan, K. (2002). Building communities in online courses: the importance of interaction. *Education, Communication and Information, 2*(1), 23–49

Thoennessen, M., Kashy, E., Tsai, Y., & Davis, N. E. (1999). Impact of asynchronous learning networks in large lecture classes. *Group Decision and Negotiation, 8*(5), 371–384.

Trevino, L. K., Lengel, R. H., & Daft, R. L. (1987). Media symbolism, media richness and media choice in organizations: A symbolic interactionist perspective. *Communication Research, 14*(5), 553–575.

Valacich, J., Paranka, D., George, J., & Nunamaker, J. (1993). Communication concurrency and the new media. *Communication Research, 20*(2), 249–276.

Veerman, A. L., Andriessen, J. E. B., & Kanselaar, G. (2000). Learning through synchronous electronic discussion. *Computers & Education, 34*, 269–290.

Walther, J. (1992). Interpersonal effects in computer-mediated interaction: A relational perspective. *Communication Research, 19*(1), 52–90.

Walther, J. B., Slovacek, C. L., & Tidwell, L. C. (2001). Is a picture worth a thousand words? Photographic images in long-term and short-term computer-mediated communication. *Communication Research, 28*(1), 105–134.

Witfelt, C., Philipsen, P. E., & Kaiser, B. (2002). Chat as media in exams. *Education and Information Technologies, 7*(4), 343–349.

Zmud, R., Lind, M., & Young, F. (1990). An attribute space for organizational communication channels. *Information Systems Research, 1*(4), 440–457.

11

The Development
of Virtual Learning Communities

Karen Swan
Kent State University

Peter Shea
State University of New York

> *Successful online instructors realize that building a sense of "community" in the online classroom is necessary for successful learning outcomes. ... The development of community becomes a parallel stream to the content being explored in online courses. (Woods & Ebersole, 2003)*
>
> *An intimate community of learners: Strange as it may sound, one instructor after another notes the surprisingly close relationships that they have developed with their online students. They say that it is common for participants in online courses to develop a strong sense of community that enhances the learning process. (Kassop, 2003)*

INTRODUCTION

Becoming a learning community can be thought of as both a means and a goal for online classes; not all classes are able to achieve full development of this potential. This chapter explores research and theory concerned with social support for learning and the development of virtual learning communities in online educational environments. This is an important topic both because of the continuing emphasis on social learning in general, and because of historical questions concerning the ability of online learning environments to support affective communication and the development of social relationships. In addition, research on online learning has consistently identified asynchronous course discussion as one of its more unique and promising features. This has led to considerable investigation into the phenomenon; in particular, into social interaction among discussion participants and its relationship to the development of learning communities.

The chapter opens with a review of the major theoretical constructs in this area, including social theories of learning, what has come to be known as "social presence" research, and the notion of virtual learning communities. The remainder of the chapter focuses on what we know and what we need to know, such as operationalizing the concept of learning communities, investigating the relationship between teaching presence and the development of a sense of community, and exploring the potential technological affordances of online environments for supporting the social construction of knowledge.

SOCIAL LEARNING THEORIES

The notion that learning is, in some fundamental sense, social is generally accepted by most contemporary educational researchers and theorists (Bransford, Brown, & Cocking; 1999). Social learning theory therefore must be addressed in any discussion of learning online. In social learning theories, "fundamentally social in nature" means that learning always involves interactions among people on some level, whether these be direct or mediated, or perhaps even remembered. Such theories are not new. Indeed, Plato maintained that the invention of writing was a bad thing because it usurped essential social interactions between teachers and learners. John Dewey (1963) argued strongly for a social view of learning, as did Lev Vygotsky (1962), whose rediscovered theories underlie much of the current increasing emphasis on the social dimensions of learning in virtually all areas of educational research. Many learning theories that are distinctively social have been advanced. Although there is great variety in these, three common themes can be identified: cognition is situated in particular social contexts, knowing is distributed across groups, and learning takes place in communities.

Situated Learning

Situated learning (Brown, Collins, & Duguid, 1989; Lave & Wenger; 1990; McLellan, 1996) refers to the belief that all learning is situated in the particular physical and social contexts in which it takes place. Situative approaches contend that the activities in which knowledge is developed and deployed are neither separable from nor ancillary to learning and cognition, that neither are they neutral, but rather that the physical and social situations of learning are an integral part of what is learned. Situative theorists thus recommend pedagogical approaches that embed learning in meaningful activities that make deliberate use of their social and physical contexts. They contrast such authentic learning with the decontextualized presentation and manipulation of concepts common in traditional classrooms; indeed, they argue that the reason students so often fail to learn is precisely because traditional classroom activities are so far removed from actual practice (Bruner, 1986; Collins, Brown, & Newman; 1989; Cognition and Technology Group at

Vanderbilt, 1990). In particular, situative theorists point out that traditional classwork is rarely social.

Distributed Cognition

Whereas situated learning focuses on learning activities and contexts, *distributed learning* focuses on learning interactions and cognitive tools. Theories of distributed cognition contend that knowing is distributed across the individual, others, and artifacts. Distributed cognition theorists argue that our understandings develop not in isolation but rather through our interactions with other people and the cognitive tools that support such interactions, and that knowing, therefore, resides in these interactions and not only in the individual. Strong theories of distributed cognition insist that all cognition is distributed (Cole, 1991); weak theories maintain that cognition is shared across individuals, others, and cognitive tools in differing combinations at different times (Perkins, 1993; Salomon, 1993). Regardless of how it is conceptualized, distributed cognition suggests distributed learning; that is, if knowing is distributed across individuals, others, and tools, then learning must be as well. Distributed cognition thus views learning as situated in these interactions and accordingly champions pedagogies that support them.

Learning Communities

The notion of *learning communities* is rooted in the observation that knowledge and learning are a natural part of the life of communities that share values, beliefs, languages, and ways of doing things (Bransford et al., 1999). Knowledge, in this view, is inseparable from practice, and practice is inseparable from the communities in which it occurs. Etienne Wenger (1997), for example, wrote of learning communities in terms of communities of practice. He based his ideas on extensive study of various workplaces as well as classroom communities. He maintained that authentic communities of practice are characterized by mutual engagement, joint enterprise, shared repertoire, and negotiated meaning; that authentic learning environments share such characteristics; and that all learning environments should work to develop them. An important part of Wenger's notion of communities of practice is the idea that all learning is situated in practice, and that all practice is essentially social in nature.

Whereas Wenger focused on the general concept of practice, of which he viewed knowledge construction a part, Marlene Scardamalia and Carl Bereiter (1996) were particularly concerned with knowledge construction in K–12 classrooms. They thus applied the notion of community directly to classroom learning and the development of what they termed *knowledge-building communities* within them, taking as their model knowledge creation in scholarly communities. Scardamalia and Berieter designed methodologies, most notably methodologies centered on the use of a computer-based resource formerly called formerly CSILE (now called Knowledge Forum), for supporting the growth of similar learning communities in classrooms and schools. They reported that their approaches are particularly supportive of higher-order learning when compared with traditional approaches. As in distributed approaches, an important notion in the CSILE environment is that of shared tools and artifacts around which the co-construction of knowledge takes place.

In summary, social theories of learning, although variously focusing on cognition and learning as situated in activities, interactions, practice, and knowledge construction, commonly recognize all these as both essential to learning and fundamentally social in nature. What makes such recognition particularly troubling for online educators are questions concerning the capacity of online environments to support social activities and interactions, and/or the development of learning communities. These kinds of questions have typically been explored in what has come to be called *social presence* research.

IMMEDIACY AND SOCIAL PRESENCE

Research on social presence in online learning environments is directly related to research on immediacy in traditional classrooms. Indeed, there is a considerable body of research on face-to-face teaching and learning that suggests that teacher immediacy behaviors can significantly affect student learning (Christophel, 1990; Gorham, 1988; Richmond, 1990; Rodriguez, Plax, & Kearney, 1996). *Immediacy refers to behaviors that lessen* the psychological distance between communicators (Weiner & Mehrabian, 1968). Immediacy behaviors can be verbal (i.e., giving praise, soliciting viewpoints, using humor, offering self-disclosure), or nonverbal (i.e., physical proximity, touch, eye contact, facial expressions, gestures).

Educational researchers have found that teachers' verbal and nonverbal immediacy behaviors lead, directly or indirectly (depending on the study), to greater learning. Although early research on immediacy posited a direct relationship between teachers' immediacy behaviors and both cognitive (Gorham, 1988; Kelly & Gorham, 1988) and affective learning (Kearney, Plax, & Wendt-Wasco, 1985; Richmond, Gorham, & McCrosky, 1987), more recent immediacy research has held that intervening variables mediate the relationship. In motivation models (Christophel, 1990; Frymier, 1994; Richmond, 1990), the intervening variable is hypothesized to be state motivation; teachers' immediacy behaviors are conceptualized as increasing students' motivation to learn, resulting in greater affective and cognitive learning. In Rodriguez et al.'s (1996) affective learning model, affective learning itself is seen as the intervening variable. Teacher immediacy behaviors are viewed as increasing students' affective learning, which in turn affects their cognitive learning.

Whatever the proposed model of the relationship between teacher immediacy and learning, a positive relationship between the two has been clearly documented in the research literature. This research has important implications for online learning. Work on social presence theory (Short, Williams, & Chrisite, 1976), media richness theory (see Rice, 1992, and chap. 10 in this vol. on media mixes), has argued that differing media have differing capacities to transmit the nonverbal and vocal cues that produce feelings of immediacy in face-to-face communications, and thus have questioned the capacity of some media to promote learning.

In part, what is at issue here is social learning theorists' notion that learning is socially supported (e.g., Vygotsky's concept of the zone of proximal development). These communications scholars assert that low-bandwidth media have low social presence (Short et al., 1976), and thus cannot convey the social support necessary to sustain learning. Researchers experienced with online teaching and learning, however, contest the view that ALN is lacking in richness or social presence. They argue that participants in computer-mediated communications create social presence through their communications. What is important, these researchers contend, is not media capabilities, but rather personal perceptions of presence (Gunawardena & Zittle, 1997; Richardson & Swan, 2003; Rourke, Anderson, Garrison, & Archer, 2001). Of course, online discussions are quite different from discussion in face-to-face classrooms. In particular, in online discussions the role of instructors often shifts from discussion leaders to discussion facilitators, and students commonly assume more responsibility (Coppola, Hiltz, & Rotter, 2001; Poole, 2000). Research on immediacy in face-to-face classrooms has focused on teacher immediacy behaviors. Research on social presence in online environments, however, has accordingly concerned itself with the immediacy behaviors of all discussion participants.

Gunawardena and Zittle (1997), for example, developed a survey to explore student perceptions of social presence in computer-mediated course discussions. In two separate studies, they found that students rated course discussions as being highly interactive and social. The researchers concluded that course participants created social presence by projecting their identities through the use of affective textual devices (see Swan, 2003) to build a discourse community among themselves. Richardson and Swan's (2003) research, using a survey adapted from Gunawardena and Zittle, replicated and extended these findings. They determined that students' overall perception of social presence was a predictor of their perceived learning in seventeen different online courses. Picciano (2002) reported similar findings.

Indeed, several investigators have noted that online education is particularly well constructed to support social learning because of the unique nature of asynchronous course discussions (Chickering & Ehrmann, 1996; Wells, 1992). To begin with, all students have a voice and no student can dominate the conversation. The asynchronous nature of the discussion makes it impossible for even an instructor to control the proceedings. Whereas discussion in traditional classrooms is, for the most part, transacted through and mediated by the instructor, online discussion evolves among participants. Accordingly, many researchers have noted that students perceive online discussion as being more equitable and more democratic than traditional classroom discourse (Harasim, 1990; Levin, Kim, & Riel, 1990). In addition, because it is asynchronous, online discussion affords participants the opportunity to reflect on their classmates' contributions while creating their own, and on their own writing before posting it. This tends to create a certain mindfulness and a culture of reflection in online courses (Hawkes & Romiszowski, 2001; Hiltz, 1994; Poole, 2000).

However, as Eastmond (1995) reminded us, computer-mediated communication is not inherently interactive, but depends instead on the frequency, timeliness, and nature of the messages posted. Ruberg, Moore, and Taylor (1996) found that computer-mediated communication encouraged experimentation, sharing of ideas, increased and more distributed participation, and collaborative thinking. However, Ruberg et al. also discerned that for online discussion to be successful, it required a social environment that encouraged peer interaction facilitated by instructor structuring and support. Hawisher and Pemberton (1997) related the success of the online courses they reviewed to the amount of discussion those courses required. Picciano (1998) likewise found that students' perceived learning from online courses was related to the amount of discussion actually taking place in them. Similarly, Swan, Guerrero, Mitrani, and Shoener (2000) study of 268 online courses determined that students who rated their level of interaction with classmates as high also reported significantly higher levels of learning. In addition, this study discovered a strong correlation between students' perceptions of their interactions with peers and the actual frequency of interactions, the required frequency of student participation, and the average length of discussion responses.

To account for such findings, Danchak, Walther, and Swan (2001) argued for an equilibrium model of the development of social presence in mediated environments. Equilibrium, in this sense, refers to an expected level of interaction in communications (Argyle & Cook, 1976). When communicative equilibrium is disrupted, research shows that communication participants work to restore it. In this case, when fewer affective communication channels are available to transmit immediacy via conventional vocal and nonverbal cues, participants in mediated communications increase their verbal immediacy behaviors to the extent needed to preserve a sense of presence. Indeed, content analyses of online discourse support such an equilibrium model (Rourke et al., 2001; Swan, 2001; Swan, Polhemus, Shih, & Rogers, 2001).

To further explore the function of verbal immediacy behaviors in the development of social presence in online discussions, Rourke et al. (2001) distinguished among three kinds of immediacy responses: affective responses (personal expressions of emotion, feelings, beliefs, and values), cohesive responses (behaviors that build and sustain a sense of group commitment), and interactive responses (behaviors that provide evidence that the other is attending). They tested these categories in a pilot content analysis of online discussion and found them quite reliable. Their pilot analysis also determined significant differences between courses in what the researchers termed *social presence density*.

Swan et al. (2001) used the categories devised by Rourke et al. to develop similar protocols for the content analysis of online discussion, and applied these to the analysis of discussions in a graduate education course (Swan, 2001). The analyses revealed that although the use of affective indicators mirrored the general flow of the course discussions across time, cohesive indicators declined in frequency as the course progressed whereas the use of interactive indicators increased. These findings suggest that different kinds of immediacy indicators perform different functions in the development and maintenance of social presence, and that the importance of these functions varies across time and context.

Most studies of social presence in online discourse are premised on the assumption that social presence enhances learning. Such a premise, of course, derives from research on immediacy in face-to-face classrooms. As we have seen, however, online discussion is significantly different from traditional classroom discussion. In addition, immediacy research in traditional classrooms has focused exclusively on teacher behaviors, whereas the social presence research in online courses examines the behaviors of all discussion participants. Thus, a relationship between social presence and learning through online discussion needs to be empirically identified and described.

An important and interesting step in this direction was undertaken by Picciano (2002), who related student perceptions of social presence to actual and perceived interactions and learning in an online graduate course in education. Picciano analyzed the relationships among student perceptions of social presence, learning, and interactions in the course; students' actual interactions in the course discussions; and students' scores on a multiple-choice exam and a written assignment. He discovered that perceptions of social presence were correlated with perceptions of learning and interaction, that perceived learning and perceived interactions were also correlated, but that perceived social presence was correlated with neither actual interactions nor actual performance. He did discern, however, that when students were grouped by their perceptions of social presence, those experiencing the highest levels of social presence scored significantly higher on the written assignment than did other students. There were no such differences in exam scores. The findings at least hint at a relationship between social presence and learning online, but also suggest that such a relationship is considerably more complex than the relationship between immediacy and learning found in traditional classrooms. The study should be replicated for different types of courses, with a large-enough number of students to provide more adequate statistical power for testing the relationships that Picciano explored.

VIRTUAL LEARNING COMMUNITIES

The notion of virtual learning communities grows out of the research on social presence and Wenger's (1997) studies of communities of practice. The research on social presence tells us that students perceive themselves as interacting socially in online courses and that they relate such perceptions to learning. These findings suggest that online courses might well be understood and investigated as communities of practice; indeed, most such courses can be shown to exhibit mutual engagement, joint enterprise, a shared repertoire, and negotiated meanings. Studies of online communities, moreover, have shown that members have a strong commitment to their communities (Rheingold, 1993), that they recognize boundary conditions relating to such membership (Marvin, 1995), and that they socially construct behavioral rules concerning the same (Bruckman, 1998). Wegerif (1998) specifically likened success in online courses to induction into a community of practice. He found that the individual success or failure of students enrolled in an online course at the Open University depended on their ability to cross a threshold from feeling like outsiders to feeling like insiders in that community.

Many researchers, in fact, assume a link between social presence or social interaction and the development of learning communities (Caverly & MacDonald, 2002; Poole, 2000; Rheingold, 1993; Russell & Daugherty, 2001; Swan, 2001; Walther & Boyd, 2002); that is, they use evidence of social interaction and support to demonstrate the development of community. Walther and Boyd (2002), for example, showed that the five forms of social support identified in the communications literature—informational support, emotional support, esteem support, tangible aid, and social network support—can be found in virtual communities, but that the nature of this support is substantially altered by changes in the communication process engendered by the mediation of online environments.

Other researchers directly explore the development of virtual communities and identify conditions or factors supporting that process. Coppola, Hiltz, and Rotter (2002), for example, found that the development of successful online collaborative teams was related to their ability to instill "swift trust" in the initial weeks of a course on information systems. Geoffrey Liu (1999) similarly argued that "virtual settlement" was a necessary condition for the development of virtual community. Norris, Bronack, and Heaton (2000) identified several factors contributing to the development of learning communities in online education courses utilizing the University of Virginia's CONNECT website to support online discussion. First, they maintained, the intended consequences of the discussion must be made explicit and agreed on. Second, online discourse must be convenient, familiar, accessible, meaningful, and focused. Third, sufficient regard must be given to environmental, social, and motivational factors that sustain online discussion and move it forward.

Ruth Brown (2001), via repeated interviews with a theoretical sampling of students from three online courses, studied the processes through which community was formed in graduate courses in educational administration. Participants' descriptions of learning community focused on mutuality—mutual interests, experiences, goals, or values—and joint responsibility for learning. Interestingly, 5 of the 21 study participants reported feeling no sense of community in the online classes, and 4 were ambiguous on the question. Explanations for this lack of response were found to include: a participant did not even think about community or defined community in a way that could not include online learning, a participant did not prioritize the class at a level that would allow the development of community or was for some reason "out of synch" with it, or a participant did not want to be part of the community.

Among the participants who did experience a sense of community, Brown identified three levels or stages in the development of feelings of belonging to a class community. The first level involved making online acquaintances, usually through discovered similarities. The second level, community conferment, reportedly resulted from engagement in a long threaded discussion, after which participating students felt a kinship with each other. The third level of community, camaraderie, was only achieved after long-term and intense association with others through personal communication. Camaraderie was generally found only among students who had been through multiple classes together. Brown also delineated preconditions necessary to the development of community. These begin with students' online behaviors being modified by the instructor and/or veteran students and proceed through students becoming comfortable with using the communication technologies, asynchronous communication itself, the course pedagogy and content, and the scheduling demands of online learning. After these conditions are met, other preconditions to developing community are negotiated, including finding similarities with other students about which to communicate, engaging in that communication, and discovering personal and/or academic needs to become part of the community before the beginning stages of community development are reached.

Brown (2001) argued that her findings suggest ways in which the development of community can be supported by online course developers and facilitators. Such argument is echoed in the work of Alfred Rovai (2002), who developed a sense of classroom community index (SCCI) to measure students' sense of community in both traditional and online classes. Comparing the two, Rovai found much greater variability among online classes. This finding suggests that although a sense of community in some sense grows naturally out of the common experience of being in face-to-face classes, it must be consciously supported in online environments.

WHAT WE KNOW/WHAT WE NEED TO KNOW

To recap, we know that learning is in some fundamental sense social (Bransford et al., 1999). Many of us also believe that thinking, and thus learning, take place in communities (Scardamalia & Bereiter, 1996; Wenger, 1998), are situated in particular social and physical contexts (Brown et al., 1989; Wenger, 1998), and are distributed across individuals, tools, and artifacts (Salomon, 1993). We don't know whether and how these ideas, developed from research on face-to-face teaching and learning, translate to virtual environments. For example, what are the "physical" contexts of virtual learning? Do the online documents form web-based courses, or instead do the differing physical spaces in which individual students work form these contexts? How do these contexts, both very different from traditional classroom contexts, affect learning, both singly and perhaps in concert? Very little research has explored these contexts; and what research exists, for the most part, centers on technology and interface issues (Hillman, Willis, & Gunawardena, 1994).

Another area clearly deserving investigation is the notion of distributed cognition. Many online courses are, in an important sense, jointly created by their participants—instructors and students—through online discussions, collaborative projects, and shared products. The digital record created by these activities might yield important insights concerning knowledge creation and distributed learning online (and perhaps distributed cognition in general), but it is difficult to know how to approach it. For example, one aspect of online learning that seems quite different from face-to-face learning involves class discussions. If we want to explore the creation of knowledge through online discussions, do we examine the discussion transcript simply as a text, or do we consider its evolution over time?

Online discussion does not evolve linearly through time, as classroom discussion does, but rather seems to grow like crystals from multiple conceptual seeds in many dimensions at once. Thus, examining the straight text does not necessarily capture the evolution of ideas. In addition, if we examine the whole discussion as text, what should be the unit of analysis—individual messages, discussion threads, idea units? Each provides unique insights but is also difficult to compare with the others. What should we look for in the discussion, whatever the units we choose to analyze? What might be evidence of distributed learning or knowledge creation? If we examine the evolution of a discussion over time, how might we conceptualize time—absolutely, in hours, days, or weeks, or relatively, by the growth of discussion threads or particular themes? The latter approach might be particularly useful for exploring the ways in which knowledge creation and learning are distributed across discussion participants. Of course, transcript analysis cannot tell us what those participants read and internalize (Sutton, 2001), but we can look to see how particular ideas and/or uses of language might be introduced, adopted, and transformed by discussion participants over time. These notions deserve further investigation.

We know quite a bit about the development of social relationships among participants in online courses through course discussions in particular. We know that discussion participants, in the absence of vocal and nonverbal affective cues, utilize verbal immediacy indicators to lesson the psychological distance between them (Rourke et al., 2001; Swan, 2001), and that, as a result, students often perceive online discussion as highly interactive and social (Gunawardena & Zittle, 1997; Walther, 1994). We also know that students who experience a greater "social presence" from their classmates believe they learn more in online classes (Picciano, 1998; Richardson & Swan, 2003; Swan et. al., 2000).

What is less clear is the relationship between perceived social presence and actual learning online (Picciano, 2002). There are indications of a link between social presence and certain kinds of learning, namely conceptual learning and the taking of multiple perspectives (Parker & Gemino, 2001; Picciano, 2002), but these are tentative and clearly need further investigation. In particular (and unlike the face-to-face immediacy research), general analyses tend to show no significant differences in learning relative to social presence; it is only when different kinds of learning and/or different groupings of course participants have been considered that these relationships appear, suggesting potential negative correlations as well. Indeed, there is some suggestion that online discussion in particular is less supportive of convergent thinking and the development of particular skills (Parker & Gemino, 2001; Twigg, 2000). In addition, the conditions and mechanisms surrounding such relationships are essentially unknown and should be explored. Anecdotal reports suggest that social supports for learning online are more or less important to different students in different content area courses at differing times. Who, for example, benefits from online discussion, and how do they benefit? Who doesn't, and why don't they? When does discussion support learning? When might it hinder learning? When is it irrelevant? Whether and how social interaction might (or might not) affect learning online is clearly an important area for future research.

Virtual Learning Communities

Many researchers report that online learning takes place in and is supported by online learning communities (Coppola et al., 2002; Goldman-Segall, 1992; Swan, 2001; Walther & Boyd, 2002). We know that success in online programs can be linked to induction into learning communities (Wegerif, 1998), and some researchers have developed descriptive and/or prescriptive overviews of online community development (Brown, 2001; Norris, et al., 2000; Walther & Boyd, 2002).

An important issue that needs to be addressed, however, is development of a common, working definition of *virtual learning community*. Indeed, virtual learning communities have been variously defined by differing authors, and variations on the term, such as *virtual classrooms* (Hiltz, 1994), *computer-supported knowledge-building communities* (Scardamalia & Bereiter, 1996), or *communities of inquiry* (Rourke et al., 2001) confuse the issue even further. Definitions, for example, range from Bruckman and Jenson's (2002) "a group of people interacting with one another in some fashion" (p. 22) through Cuthbert, Clark, and Linn's

(2002) "supporting networks of personal relationships that enable the exchange of resources and the development of a common framework for analysis of these resources" (p. 212) to Levin and Cervantes' (2002) notion of virtual learning communities as systems that, like biological organisms, are "born, undergo growth, reach a level of mature functioning, and then undergo decline and cease to function" (p. 269). Burrows and Nettleton (2002) saw the development of virtual learning communities as a symptom of "reflexive modernization." Each of these various conceptualizations suggests very different measures for identifying and studying virtual learning communities.

Most conceptualizations, however, seem to center on one of two focuses relating to the more general work on learning communities. Some researchers focus on learning, more specifically, on Scardamalia and Bereiter's (1996) notion of learning as knowledge building. Beverly Hunter (2002), for example, asserted that a defining characteristic of a virtual community is that "a person or institution must be a contributor to the evolving knowledge base of the group.... That there is a mutual knowledge-building process taking place" (p. 96). Hoadley and Pea (2002) concurred. Such definitions are operationalized in terms of evidence of knowledge building and support for knowledge building processes. Other researchers focus on communities and on the social relationships that support them (Wenger, 1997). Caroline Haythornthwaite (2002), for example, contended that the best way to understand virtual learning communities is to focus on the underlying social networks developing in those communities. Her conceptualization mirrored that of computer-mediated communication (CMC) pioneer Herbert Rheingold, who wrote in 1993 that "*virtual communities* are social aggregations that emerge from the Net when enough people carry on ... discussions long enough, with sufficient human feeling, to form webs of personal relationships in cyberspace" (p. 5). Haythornthwaite (2002) also suggested studying virtual learning communities by mapping the "social support" and "task support" relationships within them. Much of the survey research on social presence (Gunawardena & Zittle, 1997; Swan, 2001) also falls into this category.

Separating "learning" from "community," however, doesn't tell us much about what is really important in the notion of "virtual learning communities," namely, the relationship between the two. The most promising definitional approaches, therefore, may be those that combine concepts of learning and community. Nolan and Weiss (2002), for example, located virtual learning communities at "the intersection of the social organization of an environment and the activities expected and conducted by participants in a particular setting" (p. 294). Likewise, Renninger and Shumar (2002) saw virtual learning communities as lodged in the particular interactions of participants in those communities. Garrison, Anderson, and Archer's (2000) community of inquiry model (Fig. 11.1) views virtual learning communities as developing out of the interactions of three sorts of "presence": "Cognitive presence" is related to knowledge building through inquiry; "social presence," as previously described, involves the development of relationships between community members; and "teaching presence," a third element these researchers identified as being critical, links the other two through the design and facilitation of learning activities (Anderson, Rourke, Garrison, & Archer, 2001). These researchers have developed protocols for analyzing online discourse to assess all three types of

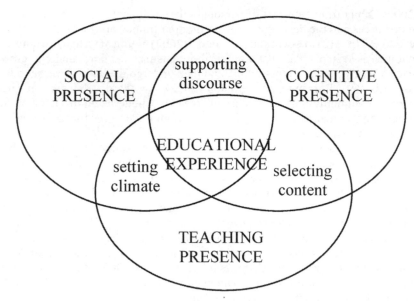

FIG. 11.1.   Community of inquiry model (Garrison et al., 2000). Reprinted with permission.

presence. They have not, however, linked any of these in their research, nor have they related them to the development of a sense of community.

An overall measure of learning community, the sense of classroom community index (SCCI), was developed by Alfred Rovai (2002) to explore the development of learning communities in both traditional and online environments. Rovai identified four essential elements in such communities: spirit (the recognition of community membership), trust, interaction, and learning. The SCCI measures students' sense of each of these elements, such that comparisons between learning communities can be made both in terms of overall sense of community and/or on each of the subscales.

Using the SCCI, Rovai compared classroom communities among adult learners enrolled in a mix of 14 traditional and asynchronous online undergraduate and graduate courses at two urban universities. Although Rovai found no differences in overall sense of community between the two media formats, he discerned greater variability in overall SCCI scores among the online courses. Indeed, the five (of seven) online courses with the highest SCCI scores had significantly higher sense-of-community ratings than did the seven traditional courses. Similar dropping of low-scoring traditional classes did not result in significant differences between these and the entire group of online classes. Rovai suggested that this indicates that the development of community in online courses is more sensitive to course design and pedagogical factors than is its development in traditional environments. In this vein, he also found a moderate positive correlation between classroom community ratings and interactivity (as measured by the number of discussion postings) in the online courses and a corresponding emphasis on spirit in face-to-face classes. Such findings support both the social presence literature and Anderson et al.'s (2001) contentions concerning the importance of teaching presence. They also point to important areas for further investigation.

Teaching Presence

As previously noted, there appears to be a significant link between instructor activity and the development of virtual learning communities in online courses (Rovai, 2002). Some research seems to support such a view. Shea, Swan, Fredericksen, and Pickett (2001), for example, noted significant differences in perceived learning between students reporting differing levels of interaction with their instructors. Students who reported high levels of interaction with their instructors also reported higher levels of learning from them. Jiang and Ting (2000) similarly discovered a strong correlation between student perceptions of learning and their perceived interactions with instructors, as did Swan et al. (2000). Richardson and Swan (2003) reported a significant correlation between student satisfaction with their instructors and their perceived learning online. There is, moreover, some indication that students' perceptions are accurate, at least concerning instructor activity. Jiang and Ting (2000) found that both perceived learning and perceived interaction with instructors were linked to the actual average numbers of responses per student that instructors made. Swan et al. (2000) also noted a correlation between students' perceived interaction with their instructors and the actual frequency of instructor participation in online course discussions, and Picciano (1998) reported that instructors' actual activity in online education courses was related to students' perceived learning from them.

These findings indicate the importance to students of interactions with their instructors, and allude to the importance of instructors in the development of a sense of virtual community. However, connections between specific instructor activities and/or between student interactions with their instructors and the development of community have yet to be documented. What sorts of instructor behaviors support the development of learning communities, and how do these relate to learning itself? It is possible, for example, that too much instructor participation stifles online discourse? Also of interest are the ways in which instructors facilitate the development of social presence among students in online course discussions and how these relate to learning. All of these topics are promising areas for further investigation.

Research focusing on the roles instructors play in online discussions and their relationship to community, knowledge creation, and learning is clearly needed. Also of interest are other sorts of interactions between online instructors and students such as instructor feedback on assignments, journaling between instructors and students, and instructors' presence in online lectures. In this vein, several researchers have attempted to categorize the roles that online instructors perform to reflect the ways in which they project their presence. Berge (1995), for example, maintained that moderators of online discussions must fulfill four major functions—managerial, social, pedagogical, and technical. Paulsen (1995) reduced these to three—organizational, social, and intellectual—perhaps in recognition of the fact that technical obstacles to online learning are, for whatever reason, disappearing. Rossman (1999) provided empirical support for similar categories through the analysis of over 3,000 student course evaluations. He found that student comments and complaints concerning their online instructors clustered into three major categories—teacher responsibility, facilitating discussions, and course requirements.

Anderson et al. (2001) termed instructors' ability to project themselves in online courses "teaching presence," which they defined as "the design, facilitation and direction of cognitive and social processes for the purpose of realizing personally meaningful and educationally worthwhile outcomes" (p. 4). They conceived of teaching presence as being composed of three categories of activities roughly analogous to those defined by Berge, Paulsen, and Rossman—instructional design and organization, facilitating discourse, and direct instruction—and created protocols to measure teaching presence in terms of these categories through the content analysis of thematic units in online discussions. The protocols have been tested in the analysis of the complete transcripts of two online courses, and proved both reasonably reliable and useful in identifying differences in both the quantity and quality of the teaching presence projected by differing online instructors. How these differences might relate to community have not yet been hypothesized, let alone investigated, but, as previously noted, these protocols and their cognitive and social presence counterparts (Garrison et al., 2000; Rourke et al., 2001) might provide a starting point for such investigations.

Shea, Fredericksen, Pickett, and Pelz (2002) developed a survey instrument, the Teaching Presence Survey, based on the categories developed by Anderson et al. (2001) that they piloted with students enrolled in State University of New York (SUNY) Learning Network summer courses. Preliminary results from their study indicated that more than three quarters of the students responding to the survey agreed with statements describing the three categories of teaching presence in terms of the indicators proposed by Anderson et al.

Moreover, Shea et al. found correlations between student satisfaction with and perceived learning from the courses and all five indicators of instructional design and organization, the six facilitating discourse indicators, and the five direct instruction indicators. It is interesting to note in this regard that in the facilitating discourse and direct instruction categories, the Teaching Presence Survey included indicators relating to both instructor activity and student behaviors, to acknowledge the new and important roles that students are beginning to play in these categories in online learning environments. Although correlations with satisfaction and perceived learning were found for all indicators for both instructors and course participants, the correlations were a good deal stronger for instructor indicators than they were for the same indicators applied to course participants. Although the low response rate for the study makes it difficult to generalize the findings, they provide support for Anderson et al.'s notion of teaching presence and intriguing indications of the critical role that instructors may play in developing social presence and a sense of community in online courses. That role clearly deserves further investigation.

In this vein, Coppola et al. (2001) investigated the changing roles of instructors online through semistructured interviews with 20 faculty members who had prepared and delivered at least one online course at the New Jersey Institute of Technology (NJIT). Coppola et al. asserted that, in any environment, teachers have three roles—cognitive, affective, and managerial. The instructors they interviewed believed that in online environments their cognitive role shifted to one of deeper complexity, their affective role required finding new tools to express emotion, and their managerial role necessitated greater attention to detail, more structure, and additional student monitoring. Anderson et al. (2001) reported similar shifts in instructor responsibilities.

Both studies also noted that instructors spend considerably more time on online courses than they do on traditional ones; thus, research designed to explore the effect of particular instructor activities on the development of social learning communities might be particularly useful. Many instructors, for example, report being especially active in course discussions at the beginning of a course but then gradually scaling back their participation as the course progresses. Others make students responsible for different strands of online discussion and/or other course activities. Are these strategies useful? What is their effect on the development of virtual learning communities? Indeed, Anderson et al. (2001) conceived of teaching presence not as belonging exclusively to online instructors, but rather as being distributed across instructors and students. Although Shea et al.'s (2002) research suggests that instructors' activities in this regard have more effect on the development of community than do students', it nonetheless suggests that student activities are also linked to such development. Investigations into the effect on social learning of particular instructor and student activities and/or specific combinations of the two could be especially helpful.

Technological Affordances

All media are selective. Each medium of communication emphasizes, amplifies, and enhances particular kinds of experience. Each medium privileges certain ways of knowing. At the very same time, each medium of communication also inhibits, restricts, and diminishes other kinds of experience, and hence marginalizes other ways of knowing. All media both afford and constrain learning in their own particular ways (Gibson, 1966). Thus, Gavriel Salomon (1981) asserted that all media have unique attributes that matter or that can be made to matter in teaching and learning. One promising area of investigation into virtual learning communities, then, might center on an exploration of the unique affordances that asynchronous online environments hold for social learning.

Carol Twigg (2000) contended that the biggest obstacle to innovation in online learning is thinking that things can or should be done in traditional ways. Trying to make online education "as good" as traditional education, she maintained, often encourages us to make it the same as traditional education. Trying to make online education "the same" as traditional education most likely will lead to less than optimal learning, when, in fact, online education has the potential to support significant paradigm changes in teaching and learning. Twigg focused on the potential of online environments to support individualized instruction; conversely, other researchers have focused on the potential of online environments to support social learning. Randy Garrison (2002), for example, argued for the unique ability of asynchronous online discussion to support both reflection and collaboration, and related these to Dewey's notion of the inquiry cycle and the higher-order learning that can result from it. He wrote, "asynchronous online learning is more than a means to access information. It has the potential to significantly enhance the intellectual quality of learning environments and outcomes" (p. 48). There is some research support for his position (Garrison et al., 2000; Parker & Gemino, 2001; Picciano, 2002).

Robbie McClintock (1999) contended, "Digital technologies are for education as iron and steel girders, reinforced concrete, plate glass, elevators, central heating and air conditioning were for architecture. Digital technologies set in abeyance significant, long-lasting limits on educational activity". First, he argued, the contents of the world's cultures are being converted to digital form and made available to any person at any place and any time. Digital technologies thus have the potential to replace an educational paradigm based on scarcity and isolation with one based on abundance. Second, digital multimedia enlarge the repertoire of resources available to serve inquiry, thought, and the creation of knowledge, and hence, potentially, education. Third, powerful digital tools have the potential to make the practical mastery of diverse basic skills—calculation, computation, spelling, drafting, remembering, comparing, selecting, visualizing, and testing hypotheses—once considered an outcome of education, a given at its outset. With digital information technologies, McClintock maintained, what is pedagogically possible changes; digital technologies could change our instructionist, factory model of education into a constructivist model focused on the creation of knowledge. He contended that how this can be accomplished is through the creation of virtual learning communities that "engage a diversity of people with challenging learning activities, providing each with appropriate resources and useful intellectual tools".

As Twigg (2000) and McClintock (1999) asserted, capitalizing on the technological affordances of online environments has the potential to significantly change education as we know it. At the very least, it seems the most promising path to explore if all we seek is to increase the efficacy of online learning. Twigg's focus on individualized instruction, although certainly supported by considerable research on computer-assisted instruction (Kulik, Kulik, & Bangert-Drowns, 1985; Swan, Guerrero, Mitrani, & Schoener, 1990) as well as her own work, seems in some sense tied to the old paradigm. The potential of online environments to support the social construction of knowledge, on the other hand, although perhaps yet to be fully realized, suggests real paradigm change and clearly deserves serious investigation.

SUMMARY

The initial online interaction model focused on learning processes in terms of individual versus collaborative learning activities, the amount and type of online (discussion) activities, and perceived media sufficiency. The research theories and results reviewed in the previous three chapters suggest (a) the extent that the emergence of a learning community is dependent on such processes, and (b) the emergence of a virtual learning community improves student satisfaction and learning in ALNs. The revised portion of the model is shown in Fig. 11.2.

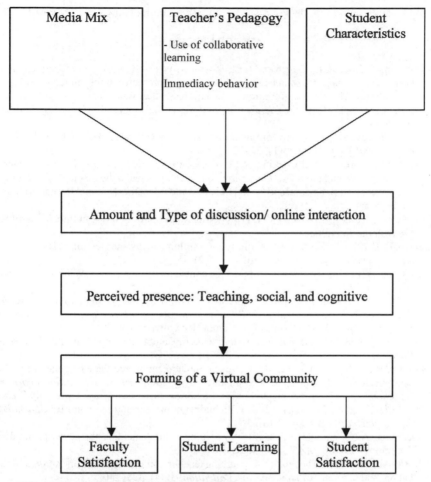

FIG. 11.2.   Emergence of a learning community.

QUESTIONS FOR DISCUSSION AND RESEARCH

1.   With what definition of a *virtual learning community* do you agree? How would you measure the extent to which an online class forms a community?
2.   Do you believe that the formation of a learning community is essential to the effectiveness of ALN, or that at least some students might learn as well as do isolated individuals interacting only with online resources such as tutorials? What evidence supports your point of view?
3.   In order to encourage the development of a learning community, what one or two things is it most important for an instructor to do?

4.   How could you design a study to test the model shown in Fig. 11.2?

REFERENCES

Anderson, T., Rourke, L., Garrison, D. R., & Archer, W. (2001, April). *Assessing teaching presence in a computer conferencing context.* Paper presented at the annual meeting of the American Educational Research Association, Seattle, WA.

Argyle, M., & Cook, M. (1976). *Gaze and mutual gaze.* Cambridge, UK: Cambridge University Press.

Berge, S. L. (1995). Facilitating computer conferencing: Recommendations from the field. *Educational Technology, 15*(1), 22-30.

Bransford, D., Brown, A., & Cocking, R. (1999). *How people learn: Brain, mind, experience and school.* Washington, DC: Committee on Developments in the Science of Learning, Commission on Behavioral and Social Sciences and Education National Research Council, National Academy Press.

Brown, J. S., Collins, A., & Duguid, P. (1989). Situated cognition and the culture of learning. *Educational Researcher, 18*, 32–42.

Brown, R. E. (2001). The process of community-building in distance learning classes. *Journal of Asynchronous Learning Networks, 5*(2), 18–35.

Bruckman, A. (1998). Community support for constuctionist learning. *CSCW: The Journal of Collaborative Computing, 7*, 47–86.

Bruckman, A., & Jenson, C. (2002). The mystery of the death of MediaMOO. In K. A. Renninger & W. Shumar (Eds.), *Building virtual communities: Learning and change in cyberspace* (pp. 21–34). Cambridge: Cambridge University Press.

Bruner, J. S. (1986). *Actual minds, possible worlds.* Cambridge, MA: Harvard University Press.

Burrows, R., & Nettleton, S. (2002). Reflexive modernization and the emergence of wired self-help. In K. A. Renninger & W. Shumar (Eds.), *Building Virtual communities: Learning and change in cyberspace* (pp. 249–268). Cambridge, UK: Cambridge University Press.

Caverly, D. C., & MacDonald, L. (2002). Techtalk: Online learning communities. *Journal of Developmental Education, 23*(3), 36–37.

Chickering, A., & Ehrmann, S. C. (1996, October). Implementing the seven principles: Technology as lever. *AAHE Bulletin,* pp. 3–6.

Christophel, D. (1990). The relationship among teacher immediacy behaviors, student motivation, and learning. *Communication Education, 39*(4), 323–240.

Cognition and Technology Group at Vanderbilt. (1990). Anchored instruction and its relationship to situated cognition. *Educational Researcher, 20*(4), 9–13.

Cole, M. (1991). On socially shared cognitions. In L. Resnick, J. Levine, & S. Behrend (Eds.), *Socially shared cognitions* (pp. 398–417). Hillsdale, NJ: Lawrence Erlbaum Associates.

Collins, A., Brown, J. S., & Newman, S. E. (1989). Cognitive apprenticeship: Teaching the crafts of reading, writing, and mathematics. In L. B. Resnick (Ed.), *Knowing, learning, and instruction: Essays in honor of Robert Glaser* (pp. 453–494). Hillsdale, NJ: Lawrence Erlbaum Associates.

Coppola, N. W., Hiltz, S. R., & Rotter, N. (2001). Becoming a virtual professor: Pedagogical roles and ALN. In *Proceedings of the 34th Hawaii International Conference on Systems Sciences.* Honolulu: IEEE Press.

Coppola, N. W., Hiltz, S. R., & Rotter, N. (2002). Building trust in virtual teams. *Communications of the ACM, 45*(4), 56–59.

Cuthbert, A. J., Clark, D. B., & Linn, M. C. (2002). WISE learning communities: Design considerations. In K. A. Renninger & W. Shumar (Eds.), *Building virtual communities:*

Learning and change in cyberspace (pp. 215–246). Cambridge, UK: Cambridge University Press.

Danchak, M. M., Walther, J. B., & Swan, K. (2001, November). *Presence in mediated instruction: Bandwidth, behavior, and expectancy violations.* Paper presented at the Seventh Annual Sloan-C International Conference on Online Learning, Orlando, FL.

Dewey, J. (1963). *Experience and education.* New York: Macmillan.

Eastmond, D. V. (1995). *Alone but together: Adult distance study through computer conferencing.* Creskill, NJ: Hampton.

Frymier, A. B. (1994). A model of immediacy in the classroom. *Communication Quarterly, 42*(2), 133–144.

Garrison, D. R. (2002, September). *Cognitive presence for effective asynchronous online learning: The role of reflective inquiry, self-direction and metacognition.* Paper presented at the Fourth Annual Sloan ALN Workshop, Boltons Landing, NY.

Garrison, D. R., Anderson, T., & Archer, W. (2000). *Critical inquiry in a text-based environment: computer conferencing in higher education.* Unpublished manuscript.

Gibson, J. J. (1966). *The senses considered as perceptual systems.* Boston: Houghton Mifflin.

Goldman-Segall, R. (1992). Collaborative virtual communities: Using Learning Constellations, a multimedia ethnographic research tool. In E. Barrett (Ed.), *Sociomedia: Multimedia, hypermedia, and the social construction of knowledge* (pp. 257–296). Cambridge, MA: MIT Press.

Gorham, J. (1988). The relationship between verbal teacher immediacy behaviors and student learning. *Communication Education, 37*(1), 40–53.

Gunawardena, C., & Zittle, F. (1997). Social presence as a predictor of satisfaction within a computer mediated conferencing environment. *American Journal of Distance Education, 11*(3), 8–26.

Harasim, L. (1990). *On-line education: Perspectives on a new environment.* New York: Praeger.

Hawisher, G. E., & Pemberton, M. A. (1997). Writing across the curriculum encounters asynchronous learning networks or WAC meets up with ALN. *Journal of Asynchronous Learning Networks, 1*(1). Retrieved December 2, 2002, from http://www.aln.org/publications/v1n1/v1n1_hawisher.asp

Hawkes, M., & Romiszowski, A. (2001). Examining the reflective outcomes of asynchronous computer-mediated communication on inservice teacher development. *Journal of Technology and Teacher Education, 9*(2), 285–308.

Haythornthwaite, C. (2002). Building social networks via computer networks: Creating and sustaining distributed learning communities. In K. A. Renninger & W. Shumar (Eds.), *Building virtual communities: Learning and change in cyberspace* (pp. 159–190). Cambridge, UK: Cambridge University Press.

Hillman, D. C., Willis, D. J., & Gunawardena, C. N. (1994). Learner interface interaction in distance education: An extension of contemporary models and strategies for practitioners. *American Journal of Distance Education, 8*(2), 30–42.

Hiltz, S. R. (1994). *The virtual classroom: Learning without limits via computer networks.* Norwood, NJ: Ablex.

Hoadley, C., & Pea, R. D. (2002). Finding the ties that bind: Tools in support of a knowledge-building community. In K. A. Renninger & W. Shumar (Eds.), *Building virtual communities: Learning and change in cyberspace* (pp. 321–354). Cambridge, UK: Cambridge University Press.

Hunter, B. (2002). Learning in the virtual community depends upon changes in local communities. In K. A. Renninger & W. Shumar (Eds.), *Building virtual communities: Learning and change in cyberspace* (pp. 96–126). Cambridge, UK: Cambridge University Press.

Jiang, M., & Ting, E. (2000). A study of factors influencing students' perceived learning in a web-based course environment. *International Journal of Educational Telecommunications, 6*(4), 317–338.

Kassop, M. (2003, May/June). Ten ways online education matches, or surpasses, face-to-face learning. *The Technology Source.* Available through http://www.alnresearch.org/jsp/other_research

Kearney, P., Plax, T. G., & Wendt-Wasco, N. J. (1985). Teacher immediacy for affective learning in divergent college classes. *Communication Quarterly, 33*(1), 61–74.

Kelly, D., & Gorham, J. (1988). Effects of immediacy on recall of information. *Communication Education, 37*(2), 198–207.

Kulik, J. A., Kulik, C. C., & Bangert-Drowns, R. L. (1985). Effectiveness of computer-based education in elementary schools. *Computers in Human Behavior, 1*(1), 59–74.

Lave, J., & Wenger, E. (1990). *Situated learning: Legitimate peripheral participation.* Cambridge, UK: Cambridge University Press.

Levin, J., & Cervantes, R. (2002). Understanding the life cycles of network-based learning communities. In K. A. Renninger & W. Shumar (Eds.), *Building virtual communities: Learning and change in cyberspace* (pp. 269–292). Cambridge, UK: Cambridge University Press.

Levin, J. A., Kim, H., & Riel, M. M. (1990). Analyzing instructional interactions on electronic message networks. In L. Harasim (Ed.), *On-line education: Perspectives on a new environment* (pp. 185–213). New York: Praeger.

Liu, G. Z. (1999). Virtual community presence in Internet relay chatting. *Journal of Computer-Mediated Communications, 5*(1). Retrieved January 7, 2002, from http://www.ascusc.org/jcmc/vol5/issue1

Marvin, L. (1995). Spoof, spam, lurk and lag: The aesthetics of text-based virtual realities. *Journal of Computer-Mediated Communication, 1*(2). Retrieved December 15, 2002, from http://www.ascusc.org/jcmc/vol1/issue1

McClintock, R. O. (1999). *The educator's manifesto: Renewing the progressive bond with posterity through the social construction of digital learning communities.* New York: Institute for Learning Technologies, Teachers College, Columbia University.

McLellan, H. (1996). *Situated learning perspectives.* Englewood Cliffs, NJ: Educational Technology Publications.

Nolan, D. J., & Weiss, J. (2002). Learning in cyberspace: An educational view of the virtual community. In K. A. Renninger & W. Shumar (Eds.), *Building virtual communities: Learning and change in cyberspace* (pp. 293–320). Cambridge, UK: Cambridge University Press.

Norris, A. S., Bronack, S. C., & Heaton, L. (2000). Web-based discussions: Building effective electronic communities for preservice technology education. *Journal of Technology and Teacher Education, 8*(1), 3–11.

Parker, D., & Gemino, A. (2001). Inside online learning: Comparing conceptual and technique learning performance in place-based and ALN formats. *Journal of Asynchronous Learning Networks, 5*(2). Retrieved December 14, 2002, from http://www.sloan-c.org/publications/jaln/v5n2_parkergemino.asp

Paulsen, M. P. (1995). Moderating educational computer conferences. In A. L. Berge & M. P. Ollins (Eds.), *Computer-mediated communication and the on-line classroom in distance education. Cresskill, NJ: Hampton.*

Perkins, D. N. (1993). Person-plus: A distributed view of thinking and learning. In G. Salomon (Ed.), *Distributed cognitions: Psychological and educational considerations* (pp. 88–110). New York: Cambridge University Press.

Picciano, A. G. (1998). Developing an asynchronous course model at a large, urban university. *Journal of Asynchronous Learning Networks, 2*(1). Retrieved September 10, 2002, from http://www.aln.org/publications/jaln/v2n1/v2n1_picciano.asp

Picciano, A. G. (2002). Beyond student perceptions: Issues of interaction, presence, and performance in an online course. *Journal of Asynchronous Learning Networks, 6*(1), 21–40.

Poole, D. M. (2000). Student participation in a discussion-oriented online course: A case study. *Journal of Research on Computing in Education, 33*(2), 162–177.

Renninger, K. A., & Shumar, W. (2002). Community building with and for teachers at the Math Forum. In K. A. Renninger & W. Shumar (Eds.), *Building virtual communities: Learning and change in cyberspace* (pp. 60–95). Cambridge, UK: Cambridge University Press.

Rheingold, H. (1993). *The virtual community: Homesteading on the electronic frontier.* Reading, MA: Harper Perennial.

Rice, R. E. (1992). Contexts of research in organizational computer-mediated communication. In M. Lea (Ed.), *Contexts of computer-mediated communication* (pp. 113–144). New York: Harvester Wheatsheaf.

Richardson, J., & Swan, K. (2003). An examination of social presence in online learning: Students' perceived learning and satisfaction. *Journal of Asynchronous Learning Networks, 7*(1). Retrieved September 12, 2003, from http://www.aln.org/publications/jaln/v7n1/v7n1_richardson.asp

Richmond, V. P. (1990). Communication in the classroom: Power and motivation. *Communication Education, 39*(3), 181–195.

Richmond, V. P., Gorham, J. S., & McCrosky, J. (1987). The relationship between selected immediacy behaviors and cognitive learning. In M. McLaughlin (Ed.), *Communication yearbook* (Vol. 10, pp. 574–590). Beverly Hills, CA: Sage.

Rodriguez, J. L., Plax, T. G., & Kearney, P. (1996). Clarifying the relationship between teacher nonverbal immediacy and student cognitive learning: Affective learning as the central causal mediator. *Communication Education, 45*, 293–305.

Rossman, M. (1999). Successful online teaching using an asynchronous learner discussion forum. *Journal of Asynchronous Learning Networks, 3*(2). Retrieved March 7, 2002, from http://www.sloan-c.org/publications/aln/v3n2/index.asp

Rourke, L., Anderson, T., Garrison, D. R., & Archer, W. (1999). Assessing social presence in asynchronous text-based computer conferencing. *Journal of Distance Education, 14*(2), 50–71.

Rourke, L., Anderson, T., Garrison, D. R., and Archer, W. (2001). Assessing Social Presence in Asynchronous Text-based Computer Conferencing. *Journal of Distance Education,* 2001. http://cade.athabascau.ca/vol114.2/rourke_et_al.html

Rovai, A. P. (2002). A preliminary look at the structural differences of higher education classroom communities in traditional and ALN courses. *Journal of Asynchnronous Learning Networks, 6*(1), 41–56.

Ruberg, L. F., Moore, D. M., & Taylor, C. D. (1996). Student participation, interaction, and regulation in a computer-mediated communication environment: A qualitative study. *Journal of Educational Computing Research, 14*(3), 243–268.

Russell, D., & Daugherty, M. (2001). Web crossing: A context for mentoring. *Journal of Technology and Teacher Education, 9*(3), 433–446.

Salomon, G. (1981). *The interaction of media, cognition, and learning.* San Francisco: Jossey-Bass.

Salomon, G. (1993). No distribution without individuals' cognition: A dynamic interactional view. In G. Salomon (Ed.), *Distributed cognitions: Psychological and educational considerations* (pp. 111–138). New York: Cambridge University Press.

Scardamalia, M., & Bereiter, C. (1996). Computer support for knowledge-building communities. In T. Koschmann (Ed.), *CSCL: Theory and practice of an emerging paradigm.* Mahwah, NJ: Lawrence Erlbaum Associates.

Shea, P. J., Fredericksen, E. E., Pickett, A. M., & Pelz, W. E. (2002, September). *A preliminary investigation of "teaching presence" in the SUNY Learning Network.* Paper presented at the Fourth Annual Sloan ALN Workshop, Boltons Landing, NY.

Shea, P. J., Swan, K., Fredericksen, E. E., & Pickett, A. M. (2001). Student satisfaction and reported learning in the SUNY Learning Network. In J. Bourne & J. C. Moore (Eds.), *Elements of quality online education* (Vol. 3, pp. 145–156). Olin and Babson Colleges, Sloan Center for Online Education.

Short, J., Williams, E., & Christie, B. (1976). *The social psychology of telecommunications.* Toronto: Wiley.

Sutton, L. A. (2001). The principle of vicarious interaction in computer-mediated communications. *International Journal of Educational Telecommunications, 7*(3), 223–242.

Swan, K. (2001). Building learning communities in online courses: The importance of interaction. *Distance Education, 22*(2), 306–331.

Swan, K. (2003). Developing social presence in online discussions. In S. Naidu (Ed.), *Learning and teaching with technology: Principles and practice* (pp. 147–164). London: Kogan.

Swan, K., Guerrero, F., Mitrani, M., & Schoener, J. (1990). Honing in on the target: Who among the educationally disadvantaged benefits most from what CBI? *Journal of Research on Computing in Education, 22*(4), 381–403.

Swan, K., Polhemus, L., Shih, L.-F., & Rogers, D. (2001, April). *Building knowledge building communities through asynchronous online course discussion.* Paper presented at the Annual Meeting of the American Educational Research Association, Seattle, WA.

Swan, K., Shea, P., Fredericksen, E., Pickett, A., Pelz, W., & Maher, G. (2000). Building knowledge building communities: Consistency, contact and communication in the virtual classroom. *Journal of Educational Computing Research, 23*(4), 389–413.

Twigg, C. (2000). *Innovations in online learning: Moving beyond no significant difference.* Retrieved January 7, 2003, from http://www.center.rpi.edu/ResMono.html

Vygotsky, L. S. (1962). *Thought and language.* Cambridge, MA: MIT Press.

Walther, J. B. (1994). Interpersonal effects in computer mediated interaction. *Communication Research, 21*(4), 460–487.

Walther, J. B., & Boyd, S. (2002). Attraction to computer-mediated social support. In C. A. Lin & D. Atkin (Eds.), *Communication technology and society: Audience adoption and uses of the new media* (pp. 153–188). Cresskill, NJ: Hampton Press.

Wegerif, R. (1998). The social dimension of asynchronous learning. *Journal of Asynchronous Learning Networks, 2*(1), 34–49.

Weiner, M., & Mehrabian, A. (1968). *Language within language: Immediacy, a channel in verbal communication.* New York: Appleton-Century-Crofts.

Wells, R. (1992). *Computer-mediated communication for distance education: An international review of design, teaching, and institutional issues* (Vol. Monograph No. 6). University Park, PA: American Center for the Study of Distance Education.

Wenger, E. (1998). *Communities of practice: Learning, meaning, and identity.* New York: Cambridge University Press.

Woods, R., & Ebersole, S. (2003). Becoming a "communal architect" in the online classroom—integrating cognitive and affective learning for maximum effect in web-based learning. *The Online Journal of Distance Education Administration, 6*(1). http://www.westga.edu/~distance/jmain11.html

12

Asynchronous Learning Networks: Looking Back and Looking Forward

Ricki Goldman and Starr Roxanne Hiltz
New Jersey Institute of Technology

> *Sloan-C Listserv Message*
>
> *May 20, 2003*
>
> *Boria Sax*
>
> *Perhaps one might compare the switch to online learning to the use of the vernacular instead of Latin as the language of scholarship and instruction. That change opened education to a far wider range of people, thereby undermining many elite claims of learned communities. The switch from Latin encountered resistance from those who, perhaps with some justification, claimed that the language of the masses was not subtle enough for learned discourse. In a similar way, the use of online courses is resisted on the grounds that it is incapable of matching the subtleties of face-to-face communication. ...*
>
> *One could even compare the switch to online education to that from oral to written tradition, which was often resisted by priestly elites.... The use of books in the ancient world, like the use of the Internet today, undermined face-to-face communication. In Plato's Phaedrus, Socrates makes objections to the written word that sound uncannily like the objections raised against online learning today. He says, for example, that writing is only a counterfeit of speech, much the same way that people now say that the online classroom is only an imitation of the geographic one.*

INTRODUCTION

Throughout this book, descriptions of theories and empirical studies have been provided that highlighted the state of the art in asynchronous learning network (ALN) research. Our focus in this chapter is to review the most salient elements of the current research and theories. Now that we know more what has been learned from research studies in our recent past, we can predict how learning as collaborative communities of inquiry will emerge as we look forward. We also return to two broader questions: What is the nature of learning using emerging learning networks, and, more important, what is the nature of cultural change as opposed to top-down (commercially driven) systemic reform? In closing, we highlight views of educational theorists, futurists, cybergurus, and skeptics to engage you, our readers, in the controversial debates taking place in the academy today.

THE PRESENT: WHY AND HOW WE LEARN

In the future, how, what, and where we learn will be affected by—but not totally dependent on—technological advances in the emerging social ecologies within which we participate. Nevertheless, changes will occur swiftly as technologies advance. What remains a bit less transitory and somewhat elusive is *why we learn* and *what the nature of learning is* in ALN settings. In other words, learning is both an internally motivated action and a culturally driven action, continually interacting in the present moment. Learning is a necessity of our organism to survive the challenges of feeding and taking care of the embodied identity, to connect with diverse communities in order to communicate what we know, to love and care for others, and to understand the ecological footprint of our actions on the environment within which we are members. Learning is also an activity we share and communicate with others so that knowledge gleaned from experience and reflection can be adapted under diverse contexts.

Learning is a complex interaction between the living world and the virtual one of technologies. It is most powerful when engagement occurs with what we want and need to learn. In his landmark book, *Deschooling Society* (1972), Ivan Illich reminded us that we should not concern ourselves as much with the content of *what someone should learn*; instead we ask, "What kinds of things and people might learners want to be in contact with in order to learn?" (p. 111).

Most people are taught within disciplinary boundaries such as astronomy, anthropology, or physics, because those subjects are a source of curiosity, passion, or delight. Others learn to create a balance among family activities, work, play, service to one's community, and participation in civic affairs. Others learn to receive credentials in order to practice a profession or get a job. Why do people continue to learn? Learning, especially lifelong learning, occurs because people want to find ways to live and love, to connect with and take care of each other, and to search for the relevance of experiences and thoughts. People want not only to adjust and rectify their misconceptions, but also their *missed conceptions*.

Linking *learning* with the formal institution called *schooling* is a rather recent development, in spite of the fact that its roots are embedded in many centuries of biblical and mystical tradition. Only with the advent of the Gutenberg printing press did reading and writing enter the public sphere. Scholars from a variety of academic circles have compared advances made by the printing press to the use of computer technologies. This comparison is used to demonstrate the expanded democratization that computer tools and the Internet are having on society. For example, in *ABC: The Alphabetization of the Popular Mind,* Illich with his colleague, Barry Sanders (1988), referred to earlier times when the education a person received was affected by continual interpretation as the oral story took on new renderings.

Not only have learning and schooling been inextricably linked, but a nation has the power to set standards and specific guidelines according to the ideology of its governing body. Citizens may disagree with the political agenda of these guidelines, but there are often too few methods of protest available to make a considerable difference. Ruling parties aim to perpetuate their own ideology in educating young people—future voters. Young learners can be unaware that they are being initiated into a highly particular mindset. Parents also want their children to partake in the education ritual that comes closest to what they experienced when they were growing up. And, indeed, as centuries of evidence has shown us, children typically are inducted into the professions of their parents or are encouraged to break into professions that were coveted by the earlier generation. Alumni of Ivy League universities provide opportunities for their children to walk the halls of their alma mater. Religious parents seek charter schools to ensure that their children learn the basic tenets of the core religious beliefs. Marxists raise their children to see the world as a continual struggle of power. In other words, learning is can be perceived by society as a means to replicate in others what is already known, or believed to be known, rather than as a means to elicit in others the freedom of creating new ways to challenge and change the past. As Illich (1971) reminded us, "schools are fundamentally alike in all countries, be they fascist, democratic, or socialist, big or small, rich or poor" (p. 106). They are used as indoctrination tools.

What did Illich offer as an alternative to indoctrination by formal schooling? Why do we believe that these ideas are relevant in the beginning of the 21st century when alternative online forms of learning are now practiced by millions of people in dispersed locations? More important, how could asynchronous learning networks be designed to connect with Illich's original vision of "the learner [creating] new links to the world instead of continuing to funnel all educational programs through the teacher?" (1972, p. 104)

In 1971, Illich coined the terms *learning webs, opportunity webs, education webs,* and *networks* long before any educator discussed learning in this systemic way. He noted, "What are needed are new networks, readily available to the public and designed to spread equal opportunity for learning and teaching" (p. 110). Illich continued, "We must conceive of new relational structures which are deliberately set up to facilitate access to these resources for the use of anybody who is motivated to seek them for his education. Administrative, technological, and especially legal arrangements are required to set up such web-like structures" (p. 112).

In a chapter he titled *Learning Webs,* Illich (1972) proposed four approaches for learners to have access to educational resources and fulfill her or his own goals:

- Reference services to educational objects.
- Skill exchanges.

- Peer matching.
- Reference services to educators at large.

Reference services are available at any time, whether the learner is in a factory, on a farm, or in a more formal learning setting such as a library, laboratory, museum, or showroom. Skill settings, the most advanced of Illich's webs, are settings in which people with skills of all kinds can list their skills. These people would use their skills to enable others to learn. In later conversations with peers, Illich recommended a system in which each person would be given a set of learning "tickets" that every citizen could freely use to fulfill a learning need. Additional tickets would be issued for teaching to others the skills that one has learned. The process of exchanges also creates models for others who are interested in learning a given set of skills. Peer matching is a more personal exchange in which partnerships are formed in the process of the inquiry. Peer matching creates a deeper level of engagement with a given topic to be investigated. Reference services are listed in a directory of experts, professionals, and freelancers who can post their particular expertise. Educators would be selected by either polling or consulting with those who received the services.

Although the learning web sounds remarkably similar to many of the characteristics of asynchronous learning networks, there is a significant difference. Illich's idea was to break the institutional monopoly, the tyranny of conformity, and to recommend free exchange of ideas *outside* academic hierarchy. Conviviality is the cornerstone of his theoretical perspective—the tools needed to create this new society must be easy to use, accessible to everyone, and beneficial. Seymour Papert (1990), inspired by Illich's call for convivial tools, responded to the *technocentrism* of computer use in instruction by reminding us that technologies will neither promise a perfect world with all problems solved, nor will they create a society of desensitized automatons:

> We are entering this computer future; but what will it be like? What sort of a world will it be? There is no shortage of experts, futurists, and prophets who are ready to tell us, but they don't agree. The Utopians promise us a new millennium, a wonderful world in which the computer will solve all our problems. The computer critics warn us of the dehumanizing effect of too much exposure to machinery, and of disruption of employment in the workplace and the economy.
>
> Who is right? Well, both are wrong—because they are asking the wrong question. The question is not "What will the computer do to us?" The question is *"What will we make of the computer?" The point is not to predict the computer future. The point is to make it.*

Learners, in ALN settings or in face-to-face classrooms, need to create and invent knowledge in their own way. Online teachers should guide students to construct their diverse points of viewing about a complex learning topic as means of advancing the creative and inventive processes (Goldman-Segall, 1998). The most constructive way of combatting indoctrination and dehumanization is to engage learners to interact with both each other and existing knowledge in order to build new representations. The responsibility of learners—in any content domain or interdisciplinary endeavor—is to advance creative thoughtful interaction, not only with each other, but also with a world that requires care and acts of kindness. For this to occur, once we have learned from our past *missed conceptions*, we need to find ways to communicate openly, freely, and internationally to solve problems. ALN is one of the important tools that could be used to promote convivial learning, both locally and globally.

THE PAST: WHAT WE HAVE LEARNED

Context, Culture, and Comparisons

What stands out in the literature that has been discussed is that there is no one best scenario for learning. ALN is not better than classroom instruction for all students or teachers. Nor is it worse. *ALN learning is different.* That difference needs to be understood in the coming decades.

Learning takes place in a social and political context. There are conditions under which it is obvious that ALN is better suited for learning, just as there are conditions for which meeting at the same time in one place is best. The key is to offer choices for a new generation of learners who cannot always meet in the same place at the same time. And, as more students seek higher education and the need for universities subsequently increases, it is only reasonable that alternatives to the location-based university will evolve. What is needed is continued rigorous investigation of how to create cultures that address the learning needs of all learners.

For example, when students enter a synchroous learning environment called Tapped In (Schlager & Schank, 1997), they are immediately connected synchronously with their peers in a virtual classroom. Working with peers in Tapped In, a participant senses immediacy, engagement, interesting confusion, and contact. One student gets a cup of coffee. There is chat about the weather. Another student says her child has a cold and she will have to leave class early. Others send their wishes for a speedy recovery. The more serious discourse on the subject being discussed is fast and furious—short comments, conversational chunks, IM (instant messaging) writing, all kinds of abbreviations (e.g., I C U instead of "I see you")—all employed to keep the flow. Conversational flow is essential.

The ALN critique of SLN (synchronous learning networks) is that students whose language skills are not very good may not become equal participants, or as reflective. For example, the more "vocal" outgoing students participate more than the ESL student. In other words, some of the same problems in face-to-face classes can be replicated in SLN. On the other hand, SLN attracts students who need instant feedback on their ideas—the kind of comments that a student receives in face-to-face classrooms. Although one can reduce the face-to-face classroom to being merely a dynamic performance experience presented by the teacher, one has to remember that people are drawn to the performance of narrative structures for inspiration. Jerome Bruner, in *Acts of Meaning* (1990), characterized narrative as an interaction of narrator perspective, agentivity, sequencing, and breech of sequence as factors contributing to meaning making. In other words, there is no one best way to learn or teach. Although comparisons among face-to-face learning, synchronous learning networks, and asynchronous learning networks need to be made to understand the diverse natures of each category, we know that the best learning occurs when various methods are available to engage learners in constructing and reflecting on new knowledge. In fact, the greater range of diverse methods exist not among the categories of face-to-face classrooms, ALNs, and SLNs, but rather *within* each category.

Teaching in ALNs

Reflecting on the empirical studies cited in this book, we conclude that the most important factor in the success of an online course is not the technology being used, but instead the effort, skill, and pedagogy of the instructor. This brings several questions to mind, including how will universities attract and reward good teachers to develop courses and teach online (Giannoni & Tesone, 2003) if that is what some students will need to promote their learning? There are intrinsic rewards that will attract and retain the innovators. For example, the innovative and challenging environment of ALNs tends to attract a disproportionate share of motivated, verbally adept students, the very type that faculty members most like to teach (Stake & Hoffman, 2001). However, intrinsic rewards will not be sufficient by themselves to attract good teachers if the balance of effort to reward is not favorable.

One issue not yet addressed is the issue of teaching via ALN if you are *not* an ALN researcher. For ALN researchers, their teaching is their research. Extra time required to become an ALN teacher or to find the right blend among ALN, SLN, and face-to-face teaching is time consuming. For example, let us suppose that a child psychologist offers an ALN course. She also has a research project in her laboratory on how children blink when they reflect on what they are building. The course she teaches is about child development, but not about blinking. Her research and her teaching have no neatly dovetailing connections. For the ALN researcher, time spent designing courses, teaching courses, or even marking assignments can be part of the collection of research data. There is an internal incentive not only to gather the data but also to write about it, and write about it with a favorable view because, after all, that is one's field of study. Ideally, we propose, research teams should include skeptics and non-ALN researchers who are fully prepared to recognize the weaknesses of ALNs as well as their strengths. Moreover, we recommend that faculty members at a university should not be coerced into teaching online.

A study by Beverly Bower (2001) reported concerns and deterrents to faculty considering teaching via any type of distance education. These also apply to ALN, and include concerns about intellectual property rights, monetary rewards for developing and updating instructional materials and for teaching online, fears about having the necessary technological skills and proper technical support for themselves and their students; and worries about online teaching taking much more time than traditional courses. To allay these concerns, administrations need to give load reductions for initial course development, and institute adequate training and support programs for both faculty and students in the use of the software systems adopted by the institution (Giannoni & Tesone, 2003). Promotion and tenure policies need to be examined to make sure that faculty who spend considerable time on course development rather than publishing research will not be penalized.

However, as far as the common perception that teaching online takes more time, there are indications that once a course has been developed, teaching time required is not remarkably different in terms of total time expended. However, this teaching time is spread out over the whole week, rather than being concentrated in 1 or 2 days, and thus it can "feel" like it takes more time. For example, Hislop (2001) paid instructors to record detailed time logs for matched face-to-face and online sections of courses. Although the instructors at Drexel University perceived teaching online as taking substantially more time, in fact the differences were small and not consistent.

Differences in the type, amount, and distribution of efforts throughout the week and the course are a topic that needs much further research, but in the meantime, faculty and administrators need to talk about this issue openly to avoid serious legal consequences. Often, those who have chosen a career in which teaching is an important component of the profession have preferred methods of interacting with learners. Although one learns new methods about teaching throughout one's career, personal preferences, experience, knowledge, and incentives empower teachers to experiment with new approaches to learning.

Learning in ALNs

Learners face additional complications in an ALN's discussion board. As noted in chapter 7, the more technologically inclined the student is, the easier it is for this student to be successful. ALNs do not seem like a highly difficult environment to master (not technically, at least): One person posts a comment to start. Others add their comments. The threads grow as more comments are added. However, students find that comments can be repetitive, no matter how much the instructor guides the conversation to more focused discussions. Moreover, not everyone is interested in the subtleties of online discussion boards. Many students, especially those in technical and science classes, are quite task-oriented and find the process too slow and much too chatty. However, students who enjoy the embellishment of a discussion about a complex subject find the process liberating. They have as much time and space as they want to fill up the text waves.

One also expects that some students will lurk rather than participate in the online environment. Is this a new form of being shy? Does lurking have any ramifications for students who do all the "talking"? Are the more active students contributing their ideas without knowing how other students may use them later? In a perfect world, one would not have to worry about intellectual theft, and yet students complain that they are reluctant to place their best ideas in a public forum. Ideas have become part of the currency of academia. Will the text-based online environment breed more intellectual property theft? Could students assert that once an idea, like an invention, is put out in the public domain, it is free for everyone to use? How does one argue with this retort? How do teachers using ALNs help students participate with each other? How do we explain to students the importance of attributing ideas of their peers and professors in the texts that they write?

Cheating is a word that educators at most universities do not want to address. Educators tend to think favorably of their students. With the introduction of digital technologies and the pervasive use of Kazaa and other tools that have enabled *X-treme sharing,* the lines become a bit fuzzier. How do ALN students (and others for that matter) who use electronic media as their source of information learn that attribution of what they have read or heard increases the scholarly respect they receive from their instructors? How can we convince them that they don't need to worry about handing in drafts that will lead them to a tighter last version? Most faculty members are looking for serious engagement with ideas that are always co-constructions with other people's ideas—whether these ideas are co-constructed in conversations or in texts produced for the purpose of communication. How do both students and their teachers negotiate this new reality?

Tools and Methods for Conducting ALN research

Asynchronous learning networks have been studied with traditional quantitative methods, mostly using surveys of both teachers and learners. As ALN environments integrate various media forms, so will the methods used for understanding what we know in the ALN environment. For example, with easy access to digital video, learners will have the ability to view video chunks of lecturers demonstrating a procedure, such as a medical procedure that may be hard or even impossible to describe. Video technologies will also be used to capture the distributed learning events of students. Imagine the scenario in which a snapshot of each member of the ALN class is posted. If a video thread is available, the image is brighter or in focus, signaling to other learners that there is a new video thread of the conversation available. Clicking on it starts the video. While a user views the video, a camera in the student's wireless computer records the gestural response as a thread and then adds another comment. In this way, the asynchronous environment begins to feel immediate. Learners and teachers understand what was communicated to others better.

Quisitive research, a term coined by Goldman and discussed more fully in chapter 5, is a blend of quantitative and qualitative methods using new media analysis tools. Quisitive research takes full advantage of video-based discourse forms by enabling users to blend media forms together to create the full spectrum of inquiry into the nature of a learning community. Using rich video cases, researchers now have opportunities to layer their views as a collaborative team, building robust and valid interpretations of the learning and teaching experience.

For example, they could use an online video ethnographic tool such as ORION (2000)—a tool developed by Goldman—to cluster the ALN video chunks into what Goldman called a *constellation* (see <http://orion.njit.edu>). A research team can access the video chunks and constellations, adding their views, comments, and links, and then rate the descriptors that act as keyword attributes. The rating scheme is numerical and provides a method for researchers to rate the data independently or collaboratively as a team. ORION is an example of a type of tool that will be used by researchers to code rich media ALN data of student performance and activity. The coming years will bring about a range of tools and methods that blend research paradigms and use the full array of media forms. The purpose of this form of research is to create research communities that include those who are the subjects of the research intervention. Learners and teachers will join the research endeavor, changing the nature of how we have known research. Moreover, large databases of video and text data will require new kinds of networked tools that are robust enough to support large-scale studies as well as smaller ethnographic investigations. As Kozma and Quellmalz (2002) pointed out:

As the electronic data become pervasive, network-based tools will be developed for searching large databases for specific types or patterns of data. These tools will need to be sensitive to a range of data that include numbers, text, and multimedia information. And they will need to assist evaluators in annotating, coding, and sorting data in ways that will support logical analysis, as well as statistical analysis. (http://www.ed. gov/Technology/Futures/kozma.html)

THE FUTURE: PREDICTING AND PLANNING CHANGES

There is no crystal ball, but there are some trends and problem areas that are strong enough so that one can predict with considerable confidence that we will see extensive changes in the next decade. This includes improvements in software, and related changes in hardware (moving toward more mobile devices). We will also see more multi-institution consortia developing degree programs in areas that might have previously been considered "impossible" to do via ALNs, such as using ALNs for medical education. Most important, these changes will be accompanied by changes in the students and those who teach them.

ALN Software Must Be Improved

There is a great deal of room for improvement in the software that supports ALNs. Three major forms of software are used today. One is the "course management system," such as WebCT® and Blackboard®, which incorporates functions such as exams, a digital library, and a discussion space into the same system. Most of these systems are provided by outside, commercial vendors, although some universities have constructed their own. A second form is a computer conferencing system or discussion board that is structured to organize the various conversations and activities in which the class engages during the course of a semester. Many educators (and students) find the existing course management systems to be complex and rigid, whereas they find the "plain vanilla" conferencing systems to be missing some key functions. A third type of system is the web-based laboratory simulation or game, including, for example, a simulation of the dissection of virtual frogs or a simulation of a conflict situation. However, none of the systems today seem to be constructed with the primary purpose of supporting collaborative, multimedia, and synchronous and asynchronous communication.

Software functionality to support education should include:

- Support for teacher–student communication (e.g., ability to send a private e-mail from within the system).
- Support for content delivery (including electronic library sources and knowledge databases that may be used in the course, and multimedia lectures or simulations).
- Support for class administration (e.g., assignments, testing, grading). In addition, we need smart routines to supplement and assist the instructor in such tasks as assessing the quality as well as quantity of class participation by each student, and moderating discussions.

- Support for student–student communication and class or small-group discussions that will create self-organizing records or transcripts. One possibility is visualizations to help support collaborative discourse structures (Turoff, Hiltz, Bieber, Fjermestad, & Rana, 1999).
- Support for collaboration, including the ability of the instructor or group leader to turn anonymity on or off, to create structures in which group members must first contribute to a topic before they see what all the others have contributed, and many other possible software options that are useful in specific stages of a group's collaboration.
- Support for sharing artifacts (e.g., shared media spaces, support for design).
- Support for dynamic voting as a means of focusing class discussions and for obtaining feedback on course structure and materials (Wang, Li, Turoff, & Hiltz, 2003).

What we are hopefully moving toward is something that would have more functionality than the current course management systems do—especially in the area of supporting collaborative groups working on projects together—but that would also be easier to learn and to use, so that courses developed on one platform could easily be transferred to another. Any new system should also be affordable. Many universities are currently complaining that when they first contract for a specific course management system, the price is reasonable. However, once they are locked into a platform in the sense that a lot of people have invested a lot of time in organizing courses on that platform, the price of the platform seems to rise, just about every year, to the point at which the charges are no longer affordable.

In terms of usability and related issues for course management systems (CMS), consider some results from a study at the University of Wisconsin that was conducted by Glenda Morgan of EduCause, presented in the accompanying box. Note that it is the students, perhaps even more than the faculty, who reported some problems with using the current systems. Particularly in completely ALN courses for which it is not possible to include a face-to-face training session on software, getting students comfortable with a platform they have not used before can sometimes take weeks. One answer may be better training on software for both faculty and students, delivered via online tutorials that lead users through the features of a system and give feedback on their practice attempts to use each key feature. However, what we really need is software that is transparent and easy enough to use that extensive training is not necessary.

June 10, 2003

Study of Wisconsin Professors Finds Drawbacks to Course-Management Systems

By Dan Carnevale ·

As course-management systems become staples of college instruction, some students and professors find it harder than expected to learn to use the software, a survey of faculty members within the University of Wisconsin System has found.... According to the study (which was based on 730 questionnaires and 130 interviews), faculty members find course-management systems time-consuming and inflexible, and students find them difficult to use. Some faculty members at Wisconsin reported that their students actively discourage the use of course-management systems.

Because of cost, lack of ease of use, and lack of desired functionality, many universities are beginning to talk about developing open-source software that is tailored to their needs but also available to other users, much like the LINUX operating system. These considerations were discussed in a 2003 conversation on the Sloan Consortium listserv, as excerpted in the accompanying box: Notice the words on the surface in the box. There are many problems that will have to be solved before it becomes feasible for universities to assemble and operate their own platforms based on choosing a set of functions from an open-source library of tools. One is the technical problem of making sure that such modules are written according to standards that make them interchangeable. Another is that whereas LINUX is being developed by the main stakeholders—that is, system developers themselves—the main stakeholders in course management systems are faculty and students, who lack the skills and the time to be the main contributors to such systems.

June 6, 2003

Is It Worth Investing in the Development of In-house Courseware Systems?

Michael Thoennesen

We are currently developing an open-source system and are struggling with how to make it sustainable.... We believe that the use of commercial and proprietary systems is not in the best interest of universities. The cost of their licenses is starting to reach the level of other enterprise solutions (namely, expensive), and the mostly closed architecture of these systems is against the grain of academic computing culture. Very quickly, dependencies are created, and over time, switching away from a certain proprietary solution becomes less and less of an option.

As an alternative to spinning-off, and encouraged by the success of the Linux operating system, projects are turning to the open-source software development model in order to address the problem of sustainability; see http://www.xplana. com/whitepapers/archives/Open_Source_Courseware for a review of systems "on the market" today. The reasoning makes sense on the surface: knowledge about the inner workings of the system gets distributed across many academic institutions and personnel, and the project becomes increasingly independent of administrative decisions at one particular institution....

Pervasive/Mobile Computing

Although we have referred to asynchronous as meaning "anywhere, anytime" communication, at present this in practice has meant anywhere and anytime you have a PC (portable or desktop) and an Internet connection. Pervasive computing refers to small (handheld, belt-clipped, wearable, or even embedded devices) that use wireless Internet connections and truly allow people to work with information anywhere, at any time. Just as the PC transformed both business and personal life in the 1990s, a new generation of information appliances will transform the work-place, the home, and education in the next decade. These new systems will be much more powerful than today's systems are.

Within a few years, we anticipate that almost all faculty and students at universities in the more developed parts of the world will routinely be carrying handheld, wireless enabled computers, just as they carry cell phones now. (In fact, cell phone functionality with computer functionality is already available.) For viewing large pieces of text or diagrams, there may be screens that can be attached to the small device.

Students and faculty are likely to incorporate much more synchronous communication into their online courses once these devices become truly pervasive. Although it will be possible, with plug-ins, to use a regular keyboard and a large display, many people will not want to be bothered. This will have enormous implications for what has until now been a largely text-based mode for ALNs. Studies of how groups of students make use of such technology in working together collaboratively and building their learning networks are just being conducted now. We can only guess how this will change online learning, but we can perceive that the change will be substantial.

International, Virtual Universities

By a virtual university, we mean one that is located primarily in cyberspace, rather than having a physical campus. Some of these virtual universities will be for profits, and many, we predict, will be based on consortia of traditional institutions that pool their resources to build and offer one or more online degree programs. Increasingly, by using blended learning that combines ALNs, computer-based tutorials and simulations, and some amount of location-based, face-to-face training, even skills-based professions such as medicine can be offered online. Consider for instance, the announcement reproduced in the accompanying box. Particularly in light of the tremendous need for medical training in areas that lack high-quality medical schools, this is an extremely important development. Students could be based at any of the participating medical schools, in a hospital, or at home. Like those enrolled in traditional programs, students in the virtual medical school will spend their first 2 years taking an intensive set of basic science courses, whereas in the next 2 to 3 years they will focus on applying their knowledge in clinical settings. The clinical work will need to be arranged with local hospitals and clinics, and coordinated or supervised both on site and by a faculty member at the International Virtual Medical School.

October 9, 2002

Colleges in 16 Countries Work to Create Virtual Medical School
http://chronicle.com/free/2002/10/2002100901t.htm

By Katherine S. Mangan

Led by Scotland's University of Dundee, an international group of medical schools is trying to create the world's first online medical school. More than 50 institutions in 16 countries have helped plan the International Virtual Medical School, which its organizers plan to open in the summer of 2004. The institutions include all five of Scotland's medical schools, at the Universities of Aberdeen, Dundee, Edinburgh, Glasgow, and St. Andrews.... The virtual school would allow students around the world to pursue a medical education through a combination of computer-based learning and clinical experience in local health facilities. The goal is to counteract the "brain drain" of students from developing countries who, having left to pursue a medical education, often don't return.

Among the American medical schools participating in the project are those at Brown, Wake Forest, and West Virginia Universities, and the University of Miami. Stephen R. Smith, Associate Dean at Brown University Medical School, has developed a "virtual practice" set of simulations that can be used in the Virtual Medical School, in which students examine fictional patients daily, using computerized medical records similar to those used in real practices. For example, students can "listen" to a patient's heartbeat through vibrations in their computer mouse. They can learn that giving a virtual patient too much medicine can kill the patient, or provoke a panicked call in the middle of the night from the patient's family. Simulated patients, whose responses are programmed into the computer, play out the scenarios. These simulated cases can prepare the students for handling their first real patients in the local clinical setting.

In addition to working with simulated patients, it is possible to use digital video to broadcast from operating rooms, or to have remote students "accompany" teaching physicians on rounds, and to ask and answer questions remotely. In this way, even though their local hospitals might not have the most sophisticated equipment, students from around the world can see how such equipment is used in medical practice.

Although medical education is probably the first arena for such degree programs for professions or occupations that require hands-on types of skills that one cannot learn from a book—or an online lecture or discussion that does not include the ability to use equipment needed for the profession—it is probable that many programs will follow in other areas of professional practice. This is something that is crucial if the world is going to be able to keep up with the need to educate and train all those who will be needed to support its burgeoning population in an era of strained resources.

To attain international virtual universities, however, there is much to be done in solving issues related to cultural and language differences. Most systems assume English as the *lingua franca*, but some systems are designed to offer more choices of interface language. Most important, however, there are many cultural differences, including differences in the pedagogical system to which learners are used, that need to be explored and resolved (Bates, 2001).

The Younger Generation: Gen-Net

Perhaps the generation that is coming of age now will be known as "Gen-Net." Being online is more "real" and engaging to many young people than are the pastimes of previous generations, such as playing softball or hanging out near the corner candy store. As Sherry Turkle (1995) pointed out in *Life on the Screen: Identity in the Age of the Internet:*

> "RL is just one more window, and it's usually not my best one." These are the words of a college student who considers the worlds he inhabits through his computer as real as RL—real life. He's talking about the time he spends "being" four different characters in three different MUDs—multi-user domains—as well as the time he spends doing his homework on the computer. As he sees it, he splits his mind and "turns on one part" and then another as he cycles from window to window on his screen. The computer and the Internet allow him to explore different aspects of himself. As another user puts it, "You are who you pretend to be." (pp. 13–14)

Using instant messaging, computer games and simulations, and multi-tasking with various digital media seems natural to many young people. We can also presume that it seems natural to these students to take their courses online. As a result, we can expect to see increasing use of ALNs at much earlier levels than undergraduate university courses. Rimer (2003) described a recent phenomenon that we are likely to see a lot more of in the next 10 years: the cyberschool. Given the high levels of computer literacy of the current generation of young people, and the increasing pervasiveness and decreasing cost of the devices and services needed to use the Internet, it is safe to assume that in a few years such graduation ceremonies will become commonplace enough that they will no longer be newsworthy.

June 12, 2003

High School Is Virtual, but the Caps and Gowns Are Real

By Sara Rimer

The musicians struck up "Pomp and Circumstance." The parents raised their cameras. It could have been any small town high school graduation. Except for one thing: Almost none of the 56 graduates, marching in procession in

> their royal blue caps and gowns, had ever met before.
>
> It was the third graduation of the Western Pennsylvania Cyber Charter School here, where the age of online learning and virtual classrooms has come to an old steel town. The graduates had emerged from cyberspace—from behind their computers in living rooms, bedrooms, basements and kitchens all over the state—to collect their diplomas....
>
> [The school] seems to be working well. The elementary and secondary students, whose numbers have grown to nearly 2,000 from 500, have performed well on state achievement tests.... In just two years, the number of cyberschools [nationwide] has doubled—to 67 schools with nearly 16,000 students, in Pennsylvania, California, Washington, Ohio, Florida, Arizona and 11 other states, according to the Center for Education Reform, a nonprofit organization that supports charter schools.

CONCLUSION: CHANGE AS EVOLUTION

Technologies do not have one or two good and bad promises locked within them, awaiting their right use or wrong misuse. They have multiple potentials that are structured by the existing social relations guiding their control and application. (Luke, 2001, p. 156)

For more than 2 decades now, educational theorists have been debating whether introducing digital technologies into the learning environment actually *changes* education. A striking example of this debate, as described fully by Goldman-Segall and Maxwell (2002), started with a controversial article appearing in the *Journal for Educational Computing Research*. Kurland and Pea (1985) conducted an evaluation to see if Logo, a programming language used in schools, had an effect on children's thinking skills. Kurkland and Pea came to the conclusion that no significant effects on cognitive development by using Logo could be confirmed, and called for more rigorous research to be conducted. In the 1980s, Logo was the most innovative technology being used in schools; it was certainly the only one claiming that children became epistemologists while programming computers to create and construct innovative representations. Seymour Papert, an inventor and MIT professor, rebuked his critics for looking for cognitive effects by isolating variables as if classrooms were "treatment" studies rather than cultures that evolve. Over the years, he has argued that "change" and "reform" are not the same. Commenting on David Tyack and Larry Cuban's *Tinkering Toward Utopia: A Century of Public School Reform* (1995), Papert advocated incremental evolution rather than a top-down deliberate reform.

"Reform" and "change" are not synonymous. Tyack and Cuban clinched my belief that the prospects really are indeed bleak for deep change coming from deliberate attempts to impose a specific new form on education. However, some changes, arguably the most important ones in social cultural spheres, come about by evolution rather than by deliberate design. (Papert, 1997, p. 417)

Papert recommends creating the conditions for Darwinian evolution: "Allow rich diversity to play itself out" (1997, p. 427).

Pondering the nature of evolutionary changes that occur when new technologies are introduced, one can point out how technologies for learning, including ALNs, enable learners and teachers to participate on a virtual *platform of multiloguing* (Goldman-Segall, 1998). Asynchronous learning networks create many modes of inquiry for multiple learners to add a range of viewpoints. The *points of viewing theory* (Goldman-Segall, 1998) describes how knowledge is cooperatively constructed as multiple learners layer their perspectives on a given subject. ALNs can supply a particularly rich environment for understanding how the points of viewing theory works. Multiple users at various times enter the learning network, adding their viewpoints on the topic they are studying. Eventually, the discussion coalesces around several key themes, and then both teachers and learners participate as members of a community. ALNs can create rich and layered learning webs involving each participant as a builder of knowledge within a discourse community. Technologies that promote these new forms of learning are called *perspectivity technologies* (Goldman-Segall & Maxwell, 2002), enabling learners to share their perspectives on a topic and reflect more deeply as they design artifacts such as term papers, videos, animations, games, or other media objects. Asynchronous learning networks provide opportunities to create knowledge in these threaded discussions and media-rich events by eliciting the views of all the stakeholders, thus bringing about an evolutionary change in understanding.

We now present the views of those who predict that education will become just another big system, like any other big business, to be managed. Although some of these claims may seem alarmist, we argue that they need to be voiced and considered so that commercialization of learning will be challenged before it is too late.

Stakeholder Views

Participating stakeholders hold conflicting points of view about what ALN means to the future of education. Some see it as a basic transformation in the nature of the educational institution. In *The Work of Education in the Age of E-College*, Chris Wherry (2001) reviewed more heated debates. The stakeholders hold many conflicting points of view about what online education means to the future of education. Some see it as a basic transformation in the nature of the educational institution, similar to the changes exhibited in health care by giant pharmaceutical companies and HMOs. In *The Work of Education in the Age of E-College,* Chris Wherry (2001) reviews competing models and heated debates that surround the issue of e-learning. He quotes management guru Peter Drucker as asserting that 30 years from now the big university campuses will be relics; the college won't survive as a residential institution.

Drucker's alarmist view is the kind of hyperbole that researchers reject. However, it does address the fact that universities must change if they are to survive.

Some e-commerce analysts predict that the change will be toward huge for-profit educational systems.

Moreover, educators are compelled to participate in their own form of commercialization of higher education. Some have argued that there is no choice—these changes will occur:

> Too many educators live with the illusion that they have a choice about whether or not these changes will occur.... Whether we like it or not, the restructuring that corporations underwent as they moved from an industrial to a postindustrial or information economy is now occurring in higher education. (Taylor, 2000, p 000)

Note that these comments were all made before the tragic attack on the World Trade Center on September 11, 2001, the stock market meltdown, and the dot-com bust. Nevertheless, it is easy to see why many faculty members, in particular, feel threatened and perhaps frightened by the specter of corporate takeovers of higher education through e-learning. They do not want to see education become a commercial product that is aimed at profit rather than at expanding and transmitting knowledge for its own sake, and they do not want to lose their control over the content and system of transmitting education. David Noble, in his rhetorical rousing *Digital Diploma Mills* (1998), described how teachers at York University in Canada were told that they would be required to put their research and teaching materials online, and to sign ownership rights to the university. The faculty refused, went on strike over this issue, and eventually won. Wherry (2001) critiqued Noble's collection of assertions and summed them up as follows:

> Some of the fears articulated by Noble ... and others may perhaps be overdrawn. To some extent the dreams of corporate planners and educational entrepreneurs remain just that—dreams.... Online education is still in its infancy, and at this stage the term itself perhaps suggests a unity that is belied by the enormous variety of practices that are currently being carried out in its name. (Http://firstmonday.org/issues/issue6_5/werry/index.html).

There are two basic models being used for learning online. One is focused on the automation and mass production of educational materials, turning educational materials into a commodity and converting education into a factory-type system. The second is the approach we advocate in this book, the ALN model, which changes the mode of communication but otherwise builds on the craftsmanship and artistry of the face-to-face classroom, with its focus on communication and social interaction between the instructor and the members of a class. ALNs can greatly increase access to educational opportunities in terms of geographic or time barriers, but they do not necessarily decrease the cost of education, because the optimum number of students in each class cannot be much more than 30 if a learning community is to be built and sustained. On the other hand, one could argue that if it is a choice between automated e-education and no education at all, then there is definitely a niche for online courses in which the interaction is primarily between the learner and a computer program or web page.

We predict that both students and faculty will come to understand that there are many ways of using the Internet for courses, just as there has already been segmentation in the face-to-face university market, with community colleges having a much lower cost than research universities or small, elite residential colleges. However, just as the community college has taken some part of the higher education market from the 4-year residential college, so too will automated e-learning threaten at least some of the market for both residential colleges and ALN-based online learning.

In looking at the evolutionary future of online learning, we share the hope and vision of Timothy Luke (2001), who stressed that faculty and administrators will need to work together to create the pedagogic, administrative, and political conditions by which a successful program of online education should be guided. He wrote that online education must be designed to:

> Change (but not increase) faculty workloads, enhance (but not decrease) student interactions, equalize (and not shortchange) the resources, prestige, and value of all disciplines, balance (and not overemphasize) the transmittal of certain vital skills, concentrate (and not scatter) the investment of institutional resources, and strengthen (and not reduce) the value of all academic services. (p. 156)

What are administrators, teachers, and the learning public to do if they agree with Luke's vision of the technologies and education? What is the role of education? Stephen Downes (1999), echoing Papert's call for incremental and evolutionary change, stated:

> The way to proceed in online learning is—ironically, given the nature of the Internet—slowly and cautiously. *The introduction of new technology must be ... a product of evolution.* Pilot delivery and evaluation should be conducted before the announcements and promises are made. Staff should be acclimatized and trained in new technologies and methodologies. (http://www.atl.ualberta.ca/downes/threads/column041499.htm).

Online education needs to proceed from a pedagogical model that addresses how students learn and how different media can best be used to support learning. Software and policies over such issues as the ownership of courseware should proceed from this learner-centered model that recognizes the primary position played by cognitive and social interaction and community building. Critical to the continuing healthful evolution of these emerging online learning cultures is this issue of intellectual property.

We close with a critical question for future research: How will intellectual contribution be acknowledged and rewarded given the nature of online learning networks that are often not "owned" individually but rather emerge as a result of collaborative experience? As we have underscored throughout this volume, learning online together is most rewarding, ethical, and effective when communication between learners and teachers is rooted in the values of intellectual freedom, open access, respect for privacy and intellectual property, and the construction of new knowledge.

ACKNOWLEDGMENTS

The section in this chapter on software has benefited from contributions by Donna Dufner, Murray Turoff, Gerry Stahl, and John W. Maxwell.

REFERENCES

Bates, T. (2001). Cultural and ethical issues in international distance education. *Presentation for the Open University of Catalonia.* Retrieved April 10, 2003, from http://www.uoc.edu/web/eng/art/uoc/bates1201/bates1201.html

Bower, B. (2001). Distance education: Facing the faculty challenge. *The Online Journal of Distance Learning Administration, IV,* II. Retrieved may 31, 2003, from http://www.westga.edu/~distance/ojdla

Bruner, J. (1990). *Acts of meaning.* Cambridge, MA: Harvard University Press.

Carnevale, D. (2003). Study of Wisconsin professors finds drawbacks to course-management systems. *Chronicle of Higher Education* (online), June 10, 2003. Retrieved June 10, 2003, from http://chronicle.com/daily/2003/06/2003061001t.htm

Downes, S. (1999). *What happened at California Virtual University?* Retrieved may 31, 2003, from http://www.atl.ualberta.ca/downes/threads/column041499.htm

Giannoni, D. L., & Tesone, D. V. (2003). What academic administrators should know to attract senior level faculty members to online learning environments. *The Online Journal of Distance Learning Administration, VI,* I (Spring). Retrieved March 10, 2004, from http://www.westga.edu/~distance/ojdla

Goldman, R. (2000). ORION, an online video analysis tool. Retrieved June 2003 from http://orion.njit.edu

Goldman-Segall, R. (1998). *Points of viewing children's thinking: A digital ethnographer's journey.* Mahwah, NJ: Lawrence Erlbaum Associates.

Goldman-Segall, R., & Maxwell, J. W. (2002). Computers, the Internet, and new media for learning. In W. M. Reynolds & G. E. Miller (Eds.), *Handbook of psychology. Volume 7: Educational psychology* (pp. 393–427). New York: Wiley.

Hislop, G. W. (2001). Does teaching online take more time? *Proceedings of the 31st ASEE/IEEE Frontiers in Education Conference* (CD-Rom Ed.). Washington, DC: IEEE Computer Society.

Illich, I. (1971). *Deschooling society.* New York: Harrow Books.

Illich, I., & Sanders, B. (1988). *ABC: The alphabetization of the popular mind.* New York: Random House.

Kurland, D. M., & Pea, R. D. (1985). Children's mental models of recursive Logo programs. *Journal of Educational Computing Research, 1*(2), 235–243.

Kozma, R., & Quellmalz, E. (2002). Issues and needs in evaluating the educational impact of the National Information Infrastructure (NII). In *The future of networking technologies for learning.* [White Paper, commissioned by the Department of Education]. Retrieved May 5, 2003, from http://www.ed.gov/Technology/Futures/kozma.html

Luke, T. W. (2001). Building a virtual university: Working realities from the Virginia Tech Cyberschool. In C. Werry & M. Mowbray (Eds.), *Online communities: Commerce community action, and the virtual university* (pp. 153–173). Upper Saddle River, NJ: Prentice-Hall.

Mangan, K. S. (2002, October 9). Colleges in 16 countries work to create virtual medical school. *Chronicle of Higher Education.* Retrieved May 9, 2002, from http://chronicle.com/free/2002/10/2002100901t.htm

Noble, D. (1998). Digital diploma mills: The automation of higher education. *First Monday, (3)*1 Retrieved May 20, 2003, from http://firstmonday.org/issues/issue3_1/noble/

Papert, S. (1990). A critique of technocentrism in thinking about the school of the future. *M.I.T. Media Lab Epistemology and Learning Memo No. 2.* Retrieved May 10, 2003, from http://www.papert.org/articles/ACritiqueofTechnocentrism.html

Papert, S. (1997). Why school reform is impossible. *Journal of the Learning Sciences 6*(4), 417–427.

Rimer, S. (2003, June 14). High school is virtual, but the caps and gowns are real. *The New York Times.* Retrieved May 10, 2003, from http://www.nytimes.com/2003/06/14/education/14GRAD.html?th

Schlager, M., & Schank, P. (1997). TAPPED IN: A new on-line community concept for the next generation of Internet technology. In R. Hall, N. Miyake, & N. Enyedy (Eds.), *Proceedings of the Second International Conference on Computer Support for Collaborative Learning* (pp. 231–240). Hillsdale, NJ: Lawrence Erlbaum Associates.

Stake, J., & Hoffman, F. (2001). Changes in student social attitudes, activism, and personal confidence in higher education: The role of women's studies. *American Educational Research Journal, 38*(2), 411–436.

Taylor, M. C. (2000, July/August). Useful Devils. *Educause Review,* pp. 38–46.

Turkle, S. (1995). *Life on the screen: Identity in the age of the Internet.* New York: Simon & Schuster. (As excerpted on Dr. Turkle's website: Retrieved June 10, 2003, from http://web.mit.edu/sturkle/www/Life-on-the-Screen.html)

Turoff, M., Hiltz, S. R., Bieber, M., Fjermestad, J., & Rana, A. (1999). Collaborative discourse structures in computer-mediated group communications. *Journal of Computer-Mediated Communication, 4*(4). Retrieved March 15, 2003, from http://www.ascusc.org/jcmc/

Tyack, D. B., & Cuban, L. (1995). *Tinkering toward Utopia: A century of public school reform.* Cambridge, MA: Harvard University Press.

Wang, Y., Li, Z., Turoff, M., & Hiltz, S. R. (2003, August). *Using a social decision support system toolkit to evaluate achieved course objectives.* Paper presented at the Americas Conference on Information Systems, Tampa, FL.

Wherry, C. (2001). The work of education in the age of e-college. *First Monday, (6)*5. Retrieved April 17, 2003, from http://firstmonday.org/issues/issue6_5/werry/index.html

Author Index

Note: *f* indicates figure, *n* indicates footnote,
t indicates table

A

Achtemeier, S. D., 87, *98*
Ahmad, R., 47, 48, 74, *79,* 91, 94, *101,*
    125, 129, 131, *143*
Airasian, P. W., 22, *35*
Aitken, J. E., 183, *189*
Alavi, M., 22, 23, *35,* 50, 51, *78,* 91, 93,
    94, 96, *98,* 124, 127, 129, 131,
    133, 134, *140,* 172, 180*t,* 182,
    184, *185,* 192, 193, 194, 195,
    196, 202, 207, 209, *209,* 218,
    230, 231, *232*
Albertelli, G., 180*t, 188*
Allen, G., 33, *35,* 43, 52, *78*
Allen, I. E., viii, *xiv,* 13, *16*
Ally, M., 161, *165*
Althaus, S. L., 95, *99,* 128, 130, *140*
Altheide, D. L., 106, *116*
Anderson, T., 28, *36,* 109, 110, 111, *117,*
    119, 123, *142,* 152, *166,* 179,
    185, 243, 244, 248, 249, 250*f,*
    251, 252, 253, 254, *256, 257,*
    259
Andriessen, J. E. B., 228, *237*
Andriole, S. J., 47, 53, *78,* 89, *99,* 129, 131,
    140
Ang, D., 199, *212*
Angeli, C., 201, *210*
Annabi, H., 12, *17,* 43, 65, *78,* 146, *167*
Ansari, Y., 199, *209*

Arbaugh, J. B., 47, *78,* 89, 91, 93, 94, 95,
    99, 108, *116,* 125, 126, 127,
    129, 130, 131, 137, *140,* 155,
    157, *166,* 175, 176, 177, 179,
    180*t,* 183, 184, *185, 186*
Archer, W., 28, *36,* 109, 110, 111, *119,*
    123, *142,* 152, *166,* 179, *185,*
    243, 244, 248, 249, 250*f,* 251,
    252, 253, 254, *256, 257, 259*
Argyle, M., 244, *256*
Arnone, M., 8, *16*
Arvan, L., 47, 48, 54, *78,* 89, *99,* 133, *140,*
    160, *168*
Asher, J., 226, *234*
Ashworth, D., 113, *120*
Atkinson, M., 129, *140*
Atkinson, P., 107, 108, *117*
Atwood, M., 180*t, 188*
Avtgis, T. A., 128, *141*
Aydin, C., 222, *235*

B

Bailey, E. K., 89, 93, *99*
Bandura, A., 160, *166*
Bangert-Drowns, R. L., 254, *258*
Bargeron, D., 230, *232*
Barker, D., 7, *16*
Barker, T., 112, *116*
Barone, C. A., 172, *186*

Richards, M., 94, *99*
Richardson, J. C., 28, *37,* 108, *119,* 243, 248, 251, *259*
Richmond, V. P., 242, *259*
Ricketts, J., 132, *143*
Rieger, J., 157, *166*
Riel, M. M., 109, 110, 115, *118, 119,* 243, *258*
Rimer, S., 274, 276, *280*
Roache, L. A., 177, *188*
Robins, G., 110, 111, *118*
Roblyer, M. D., 22, *37*
Rockwell, K., 178, 180*t, 189*
Rockwell, S. K., 135, *143*
Rodriguez, J. L., 242, *259*
Rogers, B., 198, 202, 207, 209, *211*
Rogers, D., 244, *260*
Romiszowski, A., 109, 111, *118,* 243, *257*
Roschelle, J., 28, 29, *37*
Rossman, M., 252, *259*
Rotter, N., 6, 7, *17,* 27, *36,* 69, *79,* 89, 92, 94, *100,* 108, 110, 111, *116, 118,* 124, 127, 131, 132, *141, 142,* 169, 178, 179, 180, 182, *186,* 191, 192, 200, 204, 207, 208, 209, *210, 211,* 243, 246, 248, 252, *256*
Rotzien, J., 91, *101*
Rourke, L., 109, 110, 111, *119,* 152, *166,* 179, *185,* 243, 244, 248, 249, 251, 252, 253, *256, 259*
Rovai, A. P., 74, *79,* 108, 111, *119,* 221, *236,* 246, 250, 251, *259*
Ruberg, L. F., 243, *259*
Rumble, G., 216, *236*
Russell, D., 111, *119,* 245, *259*
Russell, J., 193, *212*
Russell, T., 217, *236*
Ryder, M., 111, *119*

S

Salmon, G., 131, *143*
Salomon, G., 15, *17,* 215, 224, 225, *233, 236,* 241, 247, 253, *259*
Sandercock, G. R. H., 47, 75, *79,* 91, *101,* 124, 132, *143*
Sanders, B., 263, *279*
Sanocki, E., 230, *232*
Sayeed, L., 91, *102,* 125, 127, *144*

Scarborough, H., 201, 202, *211*
Scardamalia, M., 241, 247, 248, 249, *259*
Schank, P., 265, *280*
Schauer, J., 135, *143,* 178, 180*t, 189*
Scher, J., 227, *234*
Schifter, C. C., 170, 178, *189*
Schlager, M., 265, *280*
Schlosser, C., 231, *236*
Schmitz, J., 222, 223, *236*
Schneebeck, C. A., 171, 174, 175, *187*
Schneider, D., 22, *36*
Schoener, J., 244, 254, *260*
Schön, D. A., 108, *119*
Schramm, W., 217, 225, *233, 236*
Schrum, L., 153, *168*
Schuck, S., 132, *141*
Seaman, J., viii, *xiv,* 13, *16*
Selen, G., 226, 229, *234*
Selfe, C., 222, *236*
Sen, R. J., 108, *118*
Sener, J., 32, *37,* 76, *79,* 203, *212*
Shapira, B., 112, *118*
Shaw, G. P., 47, 74, *79,* 91, *101,* 124, 132, *143,* 191, 205, 206, *212*
Shea, K. A., 28, *37*
Shea, P. J., 8, 15, *17,* 89, 95, *100, 102,* 108, 111, *119, 120,* 124, 127, *141, 144,* 146, 152, 154, 157, 158, 164, 165, *166, 168,* 176, 177, 180, 180*t,* 181, 182, 184, *187, 189, 190,* 204, *211,* 248, 251, 252, 253, *259, 260*
Shedletsky, L. J., 183, *189*
Shen, J., 84, *101*
Sherlis, W., 157, *167*
Shih, L.-F., 244, *260*
Shin, D., 76, *80*
Shoemaker, J., 71, *79*
Shoemaker, S., 110, 111, *117*
Shook, D., 220, 221, *236*
Short, J., 219, 220, *236,* 242, 243, *260*
Shuell, T. J., 192, *212*
Shulman, L., 14, *17*
Shumar, W., 110, *119,* 249, *259*
Simon, H. A., 199, *209*
Simon, S. J., 48, *79*
Simonson, M., 231, *236*
Sitkin, S., 222, *236*
Skon, N. L., 199, *212*
Slater, T. F., 85, *101*
Slovacek, C. L., 229, *237*

Subject Index